The MICHELIN Guide

San Francisco
Bay Area & Wine Country

RESTAURANTS
2016

Michelin Travel Partner

Société par actions simplifiées au capital de 11 288 880 EUR
27 Cours de l'Ile Seguin - 92100 Boulogne Billancourt (France)
R.C.S. Nanterre 433 677 721

© **Michelin, Propriétaires-Éditeurs**

Dépôt légal septembre 2015

Printed in Canada - septembre 2015
Printed on paper from sustainably managed forests

Compogravure : Nord Compo à Villeneuve d'Ascq (France)
Impression et Finition : Transcontinental (Canada)

Dear Reader

*I*t's been an exciting and formative year for the entire team at the MICHELIN guides in North America, and it is with great pride that we present you with our 2016 edition to San Francisco, Bay Area & Wine Country. Over the past year our dynamic inspectors have extended their reach to include a variety of establishments and multiplied their anonymous visits to restaurants in our selection in order to accurately reflect the rich culinary diversity this great city has to offer.

The Michelin Red Guides are an annual publication that recommends an assortment of delicious destinations and awards stars for excellence to a select few restaurants. Our company's founders, Édouard and André Michelin, published the first MICHELIN guide in 1900, to provide motorists with useful information about where they could service and repair their cars as well as find a good quality meal. Later in 1926, the star-rating system was introduced, whereby outstanding establishments are awarded for excellence in cuisine. Over the decades we have made many new enhancements to the Guide, and the local team here in San Francisco eagerly carries on these traditions.
As part of the Guide's historic, highly confidential, and meticulous evaluation process, our inspectors have anonymously and methodically eaten their way through the entire city, Bay Area, and Wine Country with a mission to marshal the finest in each category for your enjoyment. While they are expertly trained professionals in the food industry, the Guides remain consumer-driven and provide comprehensive choices to accommodate your every comfort, taste, and budget. By dining and drinking as "everyday" customers, our inspectors are able to experience and evaluate the same level of service and cuisine as any other guest. This past year has seen some unique advancements in San Francisco's dining scene. Some of these can be found in each neighborhood introduction, complete with photography depicting our favored choices.

For more information and to get our inside scoop, you may follow the Inspectors on Twitter (@MichelinGuideSF) and Instagram (@michelininspectors) as they chow their way around town and talk about unusual dining experiences, tell entertaining food stories, and detail other personal encounters. We thank you for your patronage and truly hope that the MICHELIN guide will remain your preferred reference to San Francisco's restaurants.

Contents

The MICHELIN Guide

"This volume was created at the turn of the century and will last at least as long".

This foreword to the very first edition of the MICHELIN guide, written in 1900, has become famous over the years and the Guide has lived up to the prediction. It is read across the world and the key to its popularity is the consistency in its commitment to its readers, which is based on the following promises.

→ Anonymous Inspections

Our inspectors make anonymous visits to restaurants to gauge the quality of cuisine offered to the everyday customer. They pay their own bill and make no indication of their presence. These visits are supplemented by comprehensive monitoring of information—our readers' comments are one valuable source, and are always taken into consideration.

→ Independence

Our choice of establishments is a completely independent one, made for the benefit of our readers alone. Decisions are discussed by the inspectors and editor, with the most important considered at the global level. Inclusion in the guide is always free of charge.

→ The Selection

The Guide offers a selection of the best restaurants in each category of comfort and price. A recommendation in the Guides is an honor in itself, and defines the establishment among the "best of the best."

How the MICHELIN Guide Works

➜ Annual Updates

All practical information, the classifications, and awards, are revised and updated every year to ensure the most reliable information possible.

➜ Consistency & Classifications

The standards and criteria for the classifications are the same in all countries covered by the Michelin Guides. Our system is used worldwide and is easy to apply when selecting a restaurant.

➜ The Classifications

We classify our restaurants using XxXxX-X to indicate the level of comfort. A symbol in red suggests a particularly charming spot with unique décor or ambience. The ✿✿✿-✿ specifically designates an award for cuisine. They do not relate to a chef or establishment and are unique from the classification.

➜ Our Aim

As part of Michelin's ongoing commitment to improving travel and mobility, we do everything possible to make vacations and eating out a pleasure.

How to Use This Guide

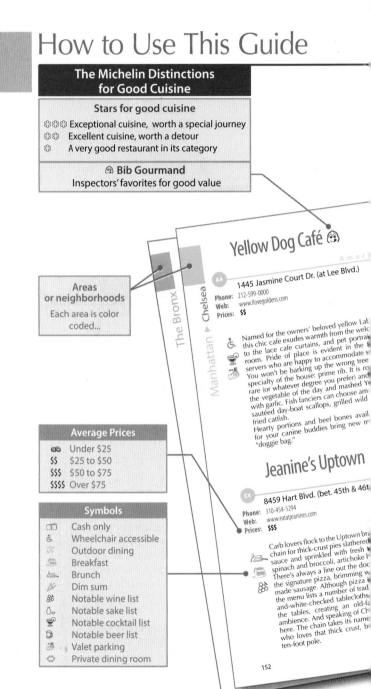

The Michelin Distinctions for Good Cuisine

Stars for good cuisine

❀❀❀ Exceptional cuisine, worth a special journey
❀❀ Excellent cuisine, worth a detour
❀ A very good restaurant in its category

❀ Bib Gourmand
Inspectors' favorites for good value

Areas or neighborhoods
Each area is color coded...

The Bronx ▸ Chelsea ▸ Manhattan

Yellow Dog Café ❀

Ameri

A4 1445 Jasmine Court Dr. (at Lee Blvd.)

Phone: 212-599-0000
Web: www.Ilovegoldens.com
Prices: $$

Named for the owners' beloved yellow Lab
this chic cafe exudes warmth from the welc
to the lace cafe curtains, and pet portrai
room. Pride of place is evident in the
servers who are happy to accommodate s
You won't be barking up the wrong tree
specialty of the house: prime rib. It is ro
rare (or whatever degree you prefer) and
the vegetable of the day and mashed Y
with garlic. Fish fanciers can choose am
sautéed day-boat scallops, grilled wild
fried catfish.
Hearty portions and beef bones avail
for your canine buddies bring new m
"doggie bag."

Jeanine's Uptown

C4 8459 Hart Blvd. (bet. 45th & 46t

Phone: 310-454-5294
Web: www.eatatjeanines.com
Prices: $$$

Carb lovers flock to the Uptown bra
chain for thick-crust pies slathered
sauce and sprinkled with fresh
spinach and broccoli, artichoke h
There's always a line out the doc
the signature pizza, brimming w
made sausage. Although pizza i
the menu lists a number of trad
and-white-checked tablecloths
the tables, creating an old-fa
ambience. And speaking of Ch
here. The chain takes its name
who loves that thick crust, b
ten-foot pole.

152

Average Prices

⊜	Under $25
$$	$25 to $50
$$$	$50 to $75
$$$$	Over $75

Symbols

💵	Cash only
♿	Wheelchair accessible
🌳	Outdoor dining
🍽	Breakfast
🥐	Brunch
🥢	Dim sum
🍷	Notable wine list
🍶	Notable sake list
🍸	Notable cocktail list
🍺	Notable beer list
🚗	Valet parking
⟳	Private dining room

8

Restaurant Classifications by Comfort

More pleasant if in red	
X	Comfortable
XX	Quite comfortable
XxX	Very comfortable
XxrX	Top class comfortable
XxXxX	Luxury in the traditional style
▣	Small plates

Map Coordinates

Sonya's Palace ✿ ✿

Italian XXXX

Manhattan ▶ Chelsea

A4 100 Reuther Pl. (at 30th Street)

Dinner daily

Phone: 415-867-5309
Subway: 14th St - 8 Av
Web: www.sonyasfabulouspalace.com
Prices: $$$

Home cooked Italian never tasted so good than at this unpretentious little place. The simple décor claims no big-name designers, and while the Murano glass light fixtures are chic and the velveteen-covered chairs are comfortable, this isn't a restaurant where millions of dollars were spent on the interior.

Instead, food is the focus here. The restaurant's name may not be Italian, but it nonetheless serves some of the best pasta in the city, made fresh in-house. Dishes follow the seasons, thus ravioli may be stuffed with fresh ricotta and herbs in summer, and pumpkin in fall. Most everything is liberally dusted with Parmigiano Reggiano, a favorite ingredient of the chef.

For dessert, you'll have to deliberate between the likes of creamy tiramisu, ricotta cheesecake, and homemade gelato. One thing's for sure: you'll never miss your nonna's cooking when you eat at Sonya's.

153

San Francisco ▶ Nob Hill

...s.)

Lunch daily

retriever,
waitstaff
e dining
friendly
guests.
der the
edium
ied by
inged
ch as
pan-

ome
rm

meat with a

107

X

nly

eria
nara
ganic

about
ouse-
here,
. Red-
adorn
aurant
choice
ughter,
with a

Where to Eat

San Francisco

Castro

The Castro, once a cluster of farmland, is today a pulsating community punctuated by chic boutiques, hopping bars, and handsomely restored Victorians. In fact, it's a perpetual party here, with everybody waiting to sample the area's range of shabby to sleek bars and dance clubs that spin tunes from multi-platinum pop icons. To feed its buzzing population of gym bunnies, leather daddies, and out-of-towners on tour to this mecca, the Castro teems with cool cafeterias. Start your day right at **Kitchen Story**, where the mascarpone-stuffed, deep-fried French toast has a following as large as the district's diversity. Then, stop in at **Thorough Bread & Pastry** if only

to watch their bakers craft the best almond croissant in town. Linger at **Café Flore**, whose quaint patio is more evocative of its Parisian namesake than the simple continental fare. Primo for a quick lunch, the original **Rosamunde Sausage Grill** serves a variety of sandwiches like those stuffed with links of wild boar, cheddar brat, and chicken habanero. Counter seats are limited, so grab your sausage and head next door to enjoy it with a pint at **Toronado**. While gourmands may prefer **La Mediterranee**, one of many establishments for worthwhile cuisine, word on the street is that the best flavors here are served on the run. Look no further than the kitschy kiosk **Hot Cookie**, perfect for that hint of sweet.

COLE VALLEY

Neighboring Cole Valley may be small in size, but flaunts huge personality. Cradling a mix of yuppies and families, this snoot-free quarter also embraces global flavors as seen in purveyors like **Say Cheese**, filled with quality international varieties. On Monday nights, dog-lovers treat the whole family to dinner at **Zazie**. Equally fun is a visit to **Val de Cole**, a wine shop offering value table wines to go with a delish dinner. The back garden patio at quaint **Cafe Reverie** is a stroller-friendly

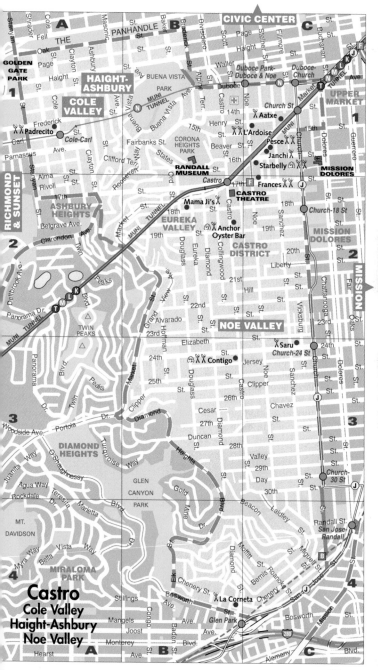

Castro
Cole Valley
Haight-Ashbury
Noe Valley

spot for a snack, whereas the 1930's throwback **Ice Cream Bar** with a soda fountain and lunch counter is mobbed by hipsters. Counter-culturalists have long sought haven in the hippiefied Haight-Ashbury, where despite the onslaught of retail chains, smoke shops and record stores dominate the landscape. **Second Act** is an alluring marketplace for artisan food vendors including **Crêpe La Vie**, which serves sweet and savory versions of this tradtional French staple. The Valley's aversion to fine dining and adoration for laid-back spots is further evident in lines that snake out the door of Puerto Rican favorite, **Parada 22** for

authentic *pernil asado*; or **Cha Cha Cha**, a groovy tapas bar flowing with fresh-fruit sangria. Nurse that hangover with greasy hash browns and hotcakes at **Pork Store Cafe**, or head to **Haight Street Market** for a ready-made gourmet feast. On game night, kick back with a pint and plate of wings at old-school **Kezar Pub**.

NOE VALLEY

Noe Valley is known for its specialty shops, and Italian emporium **Pasta Gina** sells everything you might need for a night in with *nonna*. **Noe Valley Bakery** bakes the best bread, after which a pour of coffee from **Castro Coffee Company** is in order. Meats are front and center at **E & J Fine Meats**, and **Marcello's** is mecca for for fast, fresh, and fab pizza. Keeping pace with this sense of "spirit," **Swirl on Castro** is a sleek space that is big on boutique wines. However, if booze doesn't fit the mood, then head for a soothing brew at **Samovar Tea Lounge**, specializing in artisan loose-leaf teas.

Aatxe

Spanish ✗

C1

2174 Market St. (bet. 14th & 15th Sts.)

Phone: 415-471-2977   Dinner nightly
Web: www.aatxesf.com
Prices: $$

The name is pronounced "ahh-chay" and the food is pronounced "delicious" at this Spanish charmer, where *pintxos* like *boquerones* with green olive, smoked salmon deviled eggs, and chanterelle *croquetas* taste straight out of San Sebastián. Keep it classic with shrimp *al ajillo*, bathed in sizzling garlic-chili oil, or try the adventurous "Spanish fried rice," a take on paella packed with smoky chorizo, tender cuttlefish, and nuggets of tortilla Española.

Set in the historic Swedish-American Hall, the small, modern art-packed space has an open kitchen and a thumping, clubby vibe—it's not the place for quiet conversation. But thanks to the well-curated menu of gin and tonics (a Spanish favorite), it's ideal for letting loose and having fun.

Anchor Oyster Bar 😊

Seafood ✗

B2

579 Castro St. (bet. 18th & 19th Sts.)

Phone: 415-431-3990   Lunch Mon – Sat
Web: www.anchoroysterbar.com   Dinner nightly
Prices: $$

Landlubbers seeking a taste of the sea can be found pulling up a stool at this Castro institution, where waves of waiting diners spill out the doors. This tiny, minimally adorned space filled with old-fashioned charm is better for twosomes than groups.

While the menu may be petite, it's full of fresh fare like a light and flavorful Dungeness crab "burger" on a sesame bun; Caesar salad combining sweet prawns and tangy anchovy dressing; or a cup of creamy Boston clam chowder loaded with fresh clams and potatoes. As the name portends, raw oysters are a specialty, so fresh and briny that the accompanying mignonette may not be necessary. And while the cioppino is only an occasional special, it's worth ordering if available, as it's a signature.

Contigo 🐨

B3

Spanish 🍴🍴

1320 Castro St. (bet. 24th & Jersey Sts.)

Phone: 415-285-0250   Dinner Tue – Sun
Web: www.contigosf.com
Prices: $$

Contigo is Spanish for "with you," and you'll certainly want to bring some of your favorite people along to linger at this Iberian charmer's warm dining room and pretty back patio. Sustainability is a watchword here: the design incorporates re-used and recycled materials, and each dish reflects the season's best ingredients.

Tempting small plates include smoky caramelized *coca* (flatbread) with garlicky house-made *txistorra* pork sausage, Manchego, and sliced summer squash. Simple yet delicious offerings go on to feature slices of crusty levain topped with smashed fresh peas, roasted porcini, trumpet mushrooms, and more Manchego shavings. Their outstanding pork-lamb-jamón meatballs in a tangy tomato-sherry sauce are among the best *albondigas* you'll find.

Frances

C2

Californian 🍴🍴

3870 17th St. (at Pond St.)

Phone: 415-621-3870   Dinner nightly
Web: www.frances-sf.com
Prices: $$

This tiny, intensely personal restaurant from Chef/owner Melissa Perello has been a neighborhood hit from the get-go. Chic, cozy, and perpetually packed, it's as perfect for a low-key date night as it is for dinner with the kids. And while reservations are a nigh-impossible score, the gracious staff saves ten counter seats for walk-ins—and serves every diner with equal aplomb.

Perello eschews trendy powders and foams for hearty, seasonal fare, like bacon beignets with maple-chive crème fraîche, vibrant spinach and green garlic soup with black pepper cookies, and pan-seared wild trout with sunchokes and spiced yogurt. An array of exquisite desserts, like buttermilk panna cotta with strawberries, offers a fresh, light conclusion.

Janchi

Korean   ✗

C1

2251 Market St. (bet. Sanchez & 16th Sts.)

Phone: 415-558-8567

Web: N/A

Prices: $$

Lunch Sat – Sun
Dinner nightly

Koreans know their drinking snacks, and this Seoul-inspired "gastropub" boasts some great ones, including KFC (the K is for "Korean"—no colonels involved) coated in peppery, crunchy, garlicky breading and gleaming with an optional sweet and spicy chili glaze. Or try the fried pancakes, loaded with kimchi and onion. On the lighter side, there's a great salad with large cubes of tofu and crisp greens topped with tangy vinaigrette and dollops of chili sauce. With this booze-friendly menu, great drinks are paramount, and Janchi's list brims with Korean beers, *soju*, sake, and cocktails to prime your palate for the next bite.

The simple space outfitted with dark wood furnishings and red accents is no-frills, but for an easygoing night out it's just right.

La Corneta

Mexican   ✗

B4

2834 Diamond St. (bet. Bosworth & Chenery Sts.)

Phone: 415-469-8757

Web: www.lacorneta.com

Prices:

Lunch & dinner daily

Make sure you've got cash, plenty of patience to wait in line, and a huge appetite before arriving at this massively popular spot. Inside, vivid murals and walls painted in bright hues of orange and yellow create a cheery yet very clean atmosphere. Tasty favorites like burritos (beware of anything with the word "super"—they mean it); made-to-order salmon tacos; nachos smothered in black beans, cheese, and guac; or shrimp and steak-stuffed quesadillas are all freshly made, utterly satisfying, and seriously filling. Place your order at the counter and stroll down the line to pick your protein (chicken, steak, prawns, or tofu), beans (black, pinto, or refried), and *pico de gallo* (hot or mild). If you still have room, go for a warm, sugary churro...bliss.

L'Ardoise

French ✗✗

C1

151 Noe St. (at Henry St.)

Phone:	415-437-2600	Dinner Tue – Sat
Web:	www.ardoisesf.com	
Prices:	**$$**	

Local couples do date night in high Parisian style at this long-running Duboce Triangle bistro, where a largely French staff serves up classics like coq au vin and steak frites. The seafood *cassolette* brings together plump prawns, huge mussels, and flaky fish over a bed of mashed potatoes, then swaths them in a velvety lobster bisque reduction. A floating island of caramelized meringue is especially indulgent, when served in a pool of crème anglaise with strawberries and caramel sauce.

Set on a charming, tree-lined block, L'Ardoise's secret weapon is its softly lit back area, whose rich burgundy walls draw in diners. Given their compact space and subdued ambience, save this one for a tête-à-tête, not a big group.

Mama Ji's

Chinese ✗

B2

4416 18th St. (bet. Douglass & Eureka Sts.)

Phone:	415-626-4416	Lunch & dinner daily
Web:	www.mamajissf.com	
Prices:	🅢🅢	

Dim sum options outside of Chinatown and the Avenues are rare, which explains why this cute little Cantonese spot has become a Castro favorite in its first year. While the crowd is more local than Chinese, the bilingual menu is nonetheless full of authentic preparations, from the tender and flavorful *xiao long bao* to meltingly soft tofu topped with steaming shrimp in a soy-ginger broth.

Service is basic but very friendly, and the simple, mini space is full of natural light from the quiet tree-lined street outside. Large groups should head elsewhere; but smaller ones will delight in sharing chewy, spicy cold noodles loaded with vegetables and chili paste, or roasted eggplant stuffed with gingery shrimp—especially at these prices.

Padrecito

Mexican ✖✖

901 Cole St. (at Carl St.)

Phone: 415-742-5505
Web: www.padrecitosf.com
Prices: $$

Lunch Fri – Sun
Dinner nightly

Like its baby sib Mamacita, this easygoing cantina serves modern Cal-Mex food crafted with excellent, locally sourced ingredients. Padrecito bears a bohemian, south-of-the-border spirit with a buzzy cocktail bar that pours a remarkable list of tequilas. Its dining room is rife with reclaimed wood, but climb a few colorful steps to arrive in the lovely mezzanine decked in chandeliers glinting over the main room.

Adept, smiling servers whirl around diners cradling such specials as *sopa Azteca*, a purée of ancho chilies and tomato bobbing with tender *queso* Oaxaca and avocado; or grilled Arctic char tacos sauced with crimson-red achiote and crowned with mango-jicama slaw. Warm, sugary churros with mascarpone-coffee *crema* offer mucho fulfillment.

Pesce

Italian ✖✖

2223 Market St. (bet. 15th & 16th Sts.)

Phone: 415-928-8025
Web: www.pescebarsf.com
Prices: $$

Dinner nightly

Like any good SF renter, when Pesce saw an opportunity for more space, it made the move and uprooted from Polk Street to the Castro. Its commodious new home is minimalist yet warm, with wood tables, bistro chairs, and a pressed-tin ceiling. But some things stay the same, namely, the Venetian-inspired, seafood-heavy cuisine and wonderfully warm service for which it's known.

As the Market Street crowds pass by, groups of friends sip wine and share small plates like *fritto misto*; or caramelized potato gnocchi with shreds of milk-braised pork, sage, and crispy pancetta. The silky hamachi crudo is a must-order, accented with citrus-infused olive oil and a tangle of micro greens. Creamy, none-too-sweet panna cotta is a comforting conclusion.

Saru

Japanese ✗

C3

3856 24th St. (bet. Sanchez & Vicksburg Sts.)

Phone: 415-400-4510
Web: www.akaisarusf.com
Prices: $$

Lunch & dinner Tue – Sun

Hilly, idyllic Noe Valley is the perfect setting for this little jewel of a sushi restaurant, whose L-shaped counter and handful of tables are always full. The menu is thoroughly Japanese, with a few quirky California touches—think grilled shishito peppers tossed with ribbons of crunchy daikon in a ponzu dressing.

Be sure to start with the perfectly sized tasting spoons, two tiny helpings of rotating specials like tuna tartare with *yuzu kosho* or monkfish liver with grated radish and scallions. Though rolls are available, regulars opt for the excellent nigiri, which might include marinated wild sardines, soy-kissed *madai*, and creamy uni. If you'd like the chefs to choose, several omakase (including an all-salmon variation) are also on offer.

Starbelly ⓐ

Californian ✗✗

C1

3583 16th St. (at Market St.)

Phone: 415-252-7500
Web: www.starbellysf.com
Prices: $$

Lunch & dinner daily

The simplest things are often the best, as a meal at Starbelly deliciously proves. Whether you're twirling a forkful of garlicky tomato spaghetti with jalapeños and house-made bacon, or squeezing a lime wedge over exquisite cornmeal-crusted fish tacos with spicy cabbage slaw, you're sure to savor something beautifully made, seasonal, and unfussy. Even an old-school sticky toffee cake is elevated with fresh Medjool dates and tangy mascarpone.

A nexus of the Castro social scene, the cheerful, wood-paneled space is always full of locals hopping from table to table to greet their friends, and the back patio (heated and sheltered when it's foggy) is an appealing refuge. Be sure to make reservations: this is a local favorite, and for good reason.

Civic Center

Anchoring this old, new, and now fashionable district is the gilded beaux arts-style dome of City Hall, whose architectural splendor gleams along the main artery of the Civic Center. Following in these footsteps, refined details grace the neighborhood's prized cultural institutions like the War Memorial & Performing Arts Center, as well as the Asian Art Museum. On Wednesdays and Sundays, SF's oldest market, **Heart of the City**,

Asian ingredients like young ginger and Buddha's hand. Ground zero for California's marriage equality movement and countless political protests, City Hall's plaza is also home to galas like LovEvolution; the SF Symphony's biennial Black & White Ball; as well as the annual St. Patrick's Day parade and festival.

Neighboring Tenderloin successfully alleviates this region's now-defunct repute

erupts in full form on the vast promenade outside City Hall. This independent and farmer-operated arcade is a hit among locals thanks to an extensive offering of high-quality, locally sourced, and attractively priced produce—not to mention rare

as a "food desert." Similar, in some ways, to Manhattan's Meatpacking District and home to a vast Asian—particularly Vietnamese—population, this once tough but now trendy "underbelly" boasts an incredible array of authentic ethnic eateries. Gone are those gangs of organized crime, and in place Larkin Street (also known as "**Little Saigon**") is crowded with mom-and-pop shops like **Saigon Sandwich**—leading the way with spicy *bánh mì* made from fresh, crusty baguettes for only $3.75 a pop. Nearby, **Turtle Tower** has amassed quite a patronage (celebrity chefs included) for fragrant *pho ga*; while romantic little **Bodega Bistro** is best known for bold aromas, French flavors, and more *pho*. Score points among family and friends by treating them to an authentic and elaborate Vietnamese spread at the **Four Seasons Restaurant**. After indulging in a shining plate of their garlicky noodles, savor an equally excellent selection of classic cocktails reinterpreted at **Bourbon & Branch**—a sultry hideaway and former speakeasy. For a more sober and substantial

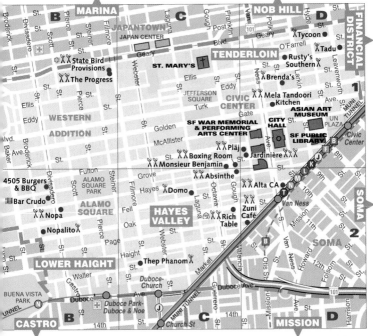

in **Fatted Calf Charcuterie** where fresh, smoked, and cured meats abound in loaded display cases. Here the cheese selection is solid too, so do all your stocking up, pre-picnic. Then, sate all these salty eats with a quenching sip from **True Sake**, a super-cool and all-sake business, whereas caffeine junkies can get their daily dose of **Blue Bottle** straight from the kiosk on Linden Street. Finish with a tour of Europe at **Miette**, an impossibly charming confiserie jammed with rare chocolates, salted licorice, taffy, and gelées; or **Christopher Elbow Artisanal Chocolate** for a smidge of bliss.

LOWER HAIGHT

Steps to the west, the Lower Haight attracts sporty troupes and hipster groups for sake-infused cocktails at **Noc Noc**, followed by fantastic live tunes at The Independent, a standing room-only music venue. Some dress to impress the über-cool scene at **Maven**, where inventive cocktails, tasty bites, and groovy tunes guarantee a great night out. Speaking of beats, the Fillmore Jazz District continues to seduce (and save) music lovers today. Settled by African-American GI's at the end of World War II, the Lower Haight hummed with jazz greats like Billie Holiday and Miles Davis. With the attempted resurgence of the jazz district, the Fillmore today goes on to resound with tunes from rock icons like Jimi Hendrix and The Dead. Of course, the annual Fillmore Jazz Festival is a must-see celebration of musical magnificence.

meal, local suits head to **Elmira Rosticceria** for a range of Italian-inspired eats—take advantage of their flourishing take-out business during the lunch rush. Come nightfall, the Tenderloin's muddle of strip clubs and bars becomes a hot hub for a decadent nightlife. Boasting an impressive craft beer selection with over 350 bottle offerings, **Amsterdam Café** is a laid-back but forever loved watering hole featuring knowledgeable bartenders who can't wait to steer guests to their next favorite brew.

West of the Civic Center, Hayes Valley is undeniably polished, with a coterie of designer boutiques set amid a medley of sleek retreats. Some residents find themselves smitten by **Chantal Guillon**, which spotlights exquisitely flavored macarons served in a French-style setting. Carnivores delight

Absinthe

Mediterranean XX

C2

398 Hayes St. (at Gough St.)

Phone: 415-551-1590

Lunch & dinner daily

Web: www.absinthe.com

Prices: $$$

The original colonist of Hayes Valley's now-bustling restaurant row, this "green fairy" still has plenty of sparkle, thanks to its timeless brasserie atmosphere and classic French- and Mediterranean-inspired menu. Even a lowly chicken breast gets the magic treatment here, with crunchy skin, perfectly wilted lacinato kale, and swirls of luscious Bourbon-yam purée. The same goes for a little gem lettuce salad with fine herbs dressed in a red wine-shallot vinaigrette.

Perched between formal and casual, the restaurant draws relaxed alfresco lunchers with dogs by day and stylish symphony or opera patrons by night. In either incarnation, it's a lovely place for a cocktail—a few may earn you a wink from those fairies, flitting across the dining room mural.

Alta CA

Californian XX

D2

1420 Market St. (bet. Fell St. & Van Ness Ave.)

Phone: 415-590-2585

Lunch Mon – Fri

Web: www.altaca.co

Dinner nightly

Prices: $$

Though this hip techie gathering place is relaxed at lunch—it wouldn't be uncommon to see diners pecking away at their laptops—it's the place to be after work. There, in the shadow of the Twitter building across the street and beneath a massive floor-to-ceiling shelf loaded with bottles, sharply attired CEOs and hoodied engineers congregate for cocktails at the triangular bar.

The Eastern European-influenced menu kicks off with drinking snacks like wispy, savory beef tendon puffs, then moves into hearty plates like pierogies, beef stroganoff, and house-cured pastrami stuffed inside soft, chewy bialys. And when it comes to dessert, even the most plugged-in programmers will put away their iPhones for a bite of the creamy lemon and poppy seed sundae.

Bar Crudo

Seafood

B2

655 Divisadero St. (bet. Grove & Hayes Sts.)

Phone: 415-409-0679
Web: www.barcrudo.com
Prices: $$

Dinner Tue – Sun

Seafood, and plenty of it, is the specialty at this Divisadero hot spot. As the name suggests, their crudo is supreme: whether it's Arctic char with horseradish crème fraîche, wasabi tobiko, and dill; or perhaps raw scallop with sweet corn purée, tarragon oil, and popped sorghum, the combinations are fresh and delicious. Platters of shellfish are available, and there are a few hot dishes like head-on Louisiana prawns in a lobster broth, served beside a baby fennel-pea shoot salad. This small and popular restaurant is often standing-room-only, with only a handful of tables; most guests pack in at or around the bar. Grab a glass of wine or a beer, peek into the open kitchen, and be sure to check out the futuristic mermaid art on the walls.

Boxing Room

Southern XX

C1

399 Grove St. (at Gough St.)

Phone: 415-430-6590
Web: www.boxingroom.com
Prices: $$

Lunch & dinner daily

A trip to the real-life Big Easy may be short on veggies (unless fried okra counts), but northern California balances the Cajun and Creole indulgences on offer at this lively restaurant, leading to dishes like a spicy-sweet fig and arugula salad with spiced pecans and pan-seared goat cheese. Casual and sleek, it draws business types for lunch and happy hour, when they cluster around the oyster bar with beers and boiled peanuts. All the classics can be found here including gumbo, fried alligator, and a perfect jambalaya studded with spicy andouille and tender roasted duck. The simple and high-ceilinged dining room encourages lingering—as does the airy angel-food "strawberry shortcake" with lemon verbena ice cream and tangy whipped yogurt.

Brenda's

D1

Southern ✗

652 Polk St. (at Eddy St.)

Phone:	415-345-8100	Lunch daily
Web:	www.frenchsoulfood.com	Dinner Wed – Sun
Prices:	**$$**	

Big portions and even bigger flavors are the draw at this taste of New Orleans, helmed by Louisiana-bred Chef/owner Brenda Buenviaje. Chicken étouffée offers a smoky, dark roux packed with vegetables, while a flawless *muffuletta* is packed with savory meat, provolone, and spicy olive salad (it's great with an ice-cold Abita beer). Sweet and salty golden beignets, filled with cheesy crawfish or molten Ghirardelli chocolate, could be a meal on their own.

The Tenderloin address is rough around the edges, but Brenda's interior is quite lovely, with a light-filled dining room, bright murals, and high ceilings. Count on a wait here now that the secret is out, particularly at lunch and brunch. Or, check out the equally delicious sequel, Brenda's Meat & Three.

Domo

C2

Japanese ✗

511 Laguna St. (bet. Fell & Linden Sts.)

Phone:	415-861-8887	Lunch Mon – Fri
Web:	www.domosf.com	Dinner nightly
Prices:	**$$**	

This Hayes Valley sushi joint is roughly the size of a shoebox, with only a dozen stools and a pair of sidewalk tables to choose from. Reservations aren't accepted, which means there's almost always a wait (make the most of it by perusing the daily specials on the mirror). Once seated, you'll likely have a few hungry diners eyeing your spot, so don't bring a group or plan to linger.

For your trouble, you'll be rewarded with straightforward, high-quality sushi, whether you opt for simply prepared salmon and albacore nigiri (with well-seasoned rice) or the elaborate Domo roll, a baked California version with salmon, scallops, mayo, unagi glaze, tobiko, and scallions. To spice things up, try the lemon juice- and jalapeño-spiked hamachi maki.

4505 Burgers & BBQ

Barbecue ✗

B2

705 Divisadero St. (bet. Fulton & Grove Sts.)

Phone: 415-231-6993
Web: www.4505meats.com
Prices: 🍪🍪

Lunch & dinner daily

With lines out the door and the scent of wood smoke heavy in the air, one thing is clear: this Civic Center barbecue spot is smokin' hot. And with no service or ambience to speak of (diners order at the counter, claim a spot at one of the picnic tables arranged in the parking lot, and then dig in), the focus is firmly on the food.

Chef and butcher Ryan Farr offers succulent bites by the plate or pound. Select a trio and revel in a meaty heap of pork ribs, super moist pulled chicken, and the Bay Area's best brisket accompanied by a Parker House roll, pickles, and sliced onion. Sides like the *frankaroni* (a mac and cheese fritter studded with hot dog) are average, but follow the crowd and pair your platter with 4505's "best damn grass-fed cheeseburger."

Jannah

Middle Eastern ✗✗

A2

1775 Fulton St. (bet. Central & Masonic Aves.)

Phone: 415-567-4400
Web: www.yayacuisine.com
Prices: $$

Lunch & dinner Tue – Sun

The name of Yahya Salih's lovely Middle Eastern restaurant translates to "heaven," a concept echoed by its blue walls and ceiling, adorned with puffy white cloud paintings and glowing chandeliers. From the large front bar to the back patio, it's an airy and inviting choice for groups or families.

Paradise extends to the plate, where seasonal California ingredients are highlighted in Kurdish and Iraqi specialties like grilled, mint-marinated lamb kabobs with outstanding accompaniments including creamy hummus, ultra-fresh tabbouleh, and crisp *lavash*. But diners veer towards more unique dishes like the *perdaplow*, a richly flavorful, *basteeya*-like phyllo pastry enclosing tender shredded chicken, fragrant cardamom, and sweet golden raisins.

Jardinière

Californian XxX

D1

300 Grove St. (at Franklin St.)

Phone: 415-861-5555
Web: www.jardiniere.com
Prices: $$$

Dinner nightly

For a memorable night on the town, don your best dress, find a hand to hold, and head to this longtime favorite—tinged with a sense of bygone romance. Stop off at the circular bar and join the well-heeled couples sipping cocktails pre- or post-opera. Prime seats on the upstairs balcony overlook the bustling lower level, and stunning arched windows show off views of the street. Approachable, seasonal dishes abound on Jardinière's menu, from tender *tajarin* pasta with morel mushrooms and butter to a Mediterranean-inspired duo of lamb belly and shoulder with fresh fava beans and smoked yogurt sauce.

Indecisive sweet tooths will thrill to the *bonne bouche*, an array of candies, cookies, small cakes, and profiteroles that makes a striking conclusion.

Mela Tandoori Kitchen

Indian XX

D1

536 Golden Gate Ave. (bet. Polk St. & Van Ness Ave.)

Phone: 415-447-4041
Web: N/A
Prices: $$

Lunch Mon – Fri
Dinner Mon – Sat

If "*mela*" means "fair" in Hindi, then Tandoori Kitchen is aptly named. As fun and lively as a carnival, this welcoming spot sports brightly striped walls and colorful splashes of paint set aglow by stylish pendant lights. Its menu displays a vast litany of eats, and obliging servers are happy to lend a hand with useful recommendations.

The overwhelming lunch buffet is a hit among office workers for hot, crispy samosas with sweet tamarind chutney, or fiery *tandoori* wings baked until smoky and juicy. The area takes a bit of a dive at sunset, but that doesn't curb this kitchen's appeal. Families keep coming to devour huge portions of *aloo gobi* in an onion-and-tomato masala along with intensely spicy lamb *vindaloo*—and inevitably leave toting leftovers.

Monsieur Benjamin

French ✗✗

C1

451 Gough St. (at Ivy St.)

Phone: 415-403-2233
Web: www.monsieurbenjamin.com
Prices: $$$

Lunch Sat – Sun
Dinner nightly

Chef Corey Lee's take on timeless bistro cuisine is as sleek and striking as the space it's served in. Fit for the cover of a magazine, this black-and-white dining room's minimalist, yet intimate décor is trumped only by its piece de resistance: an exhibition kitchen where you'll find the meticulous brigade of cooks hard at work, producing impressively authentic French food.

Begin with the *pâté de Campagne*, enhanced with liver and shallots and presented with strong mustard, cornichons, and country bread. The Arctic char amandine is excellent, dressed with fragrant *beurre noisette* and served over a bed of crispy haricot verts and sunchoke. For a sweet and fruity finish, purists will delight in the dessert menu's *crêpe façon gâteau*.

Nopa

Californian ✗✗

B2

560 Divisadero St. (at Hayes St.)

Phone: 415-864-8643
Web: www.nopasf.com
Prices: $$

Lunch Sat – Sun
Dinner nightly

Before you're able to enjoy a single forkful at this Bay Area sensation, you'll have to secure a table—and that takes some serious effort. Reservations are snapped up at lightning speed, and hopeful walk-ins must lineup prior to the start of service to add their name to the list.

The good news? Your efforts will be well rewarded. Inside, an open kitchen, soaring ceilings, and hordes of ravenous sophisticates produce a cacophonous setting in which to relish Nopa's wonderful, organic, wood-fired cuisine. Dig into a bruschetta of grilled *levain* spread with smashed avocado, pickled jalapeños, lemon-dressed arugula, and shaved *mezzo secco*, or go for the roasted King salmon fillet over creamed corn, smoky maitakes, crisp green beans, and sweet tomato confit.

Nopalito

B2

Mexican ✗

306 Broderick St. (bet. Fell & Oak Sts.)

Phone: 415-437-0303   Lunch & dinner daily
Web: www.nopalitosf.com
Prices: 🍛

Whether they're digging into a griddled corn *panucho* stuffed with earthy black beans and zesty citrus-marinated chicken or tender *mole* enchiladas garnished with tangy *queso fresco*, local couples and families adore this sustainable Mexican spot. Sister to Cal-cuisine icon Nopa, Nopalito is so beloved that an equally good and popular Inner Sunset location is thriving.

The small, cheerful space with reclaimed wood and bright green accents doesn't take reservations; call ahead to get on the list, or try takeout. Once seated, friendly servers will guide the way with house-made *horchata* for the kids and an extensive tequila selection for grown-ups. Both groups will certainly agree on a sweet finish: Mexican chocolate and seasonal fruit *paletas* are a favorite.

Pläj

D1

Scandinavian ✗✗

333 Fulton St. (bet. Franklin & Gough Sts.)

Phone: 415-294-8925   Dinner nightly
Web: www.plajrestaurant.com
Prices: $$

NorCal is short on the Scandinavian-inspired fare that's all the rage right now, so it's no wonder why Bay Area foodies flock to this upscale spot. Steps from the opera, symphony, and ballet, Plaj has caught on like wildfire with the pre-theater crowd, who congregate at the linen-topped tables and cozy bar for a taste of Californian cuisine mingled with Nordic flair. Swedish-born Chef/owner Roberth Sundell offers smart riffs on classic dishes, from a tender duo of potato dumplings accented with brown butter, caramelized onions, and bacon to deep-red seared elk medallions set in a woodsy juniper jus and accented by tart lingonberries. For dessert, a parfait-like take on princess cake, with layers of raspberry, sponge cake, and marzipan, is worthy of royalty.

The Progress

Contemporary ✗✗

B1

1525 Fillmore St. (bet. Geary Blvd. & O'Farrell St.)

Phone: 415-673-1294   Dinner nightly
Web: www.theprogress-sf.com
Prices: $$$

The sequel to mega-popular State Bird Provisions, located right next door, has retained all of its sibling's inventiveness while moving things forward (hence the name) in a more restrained, elegant way. Set in a 100-year-old former theater, the retro-industrial space is a real looker, with attentive, thoughtful service and exceptional wine and cocktails to boot.

Diners are encouraged to team up to savor the "choose-your-own-adventure" feast, which allows a choice of six courses from a list of about 20. The enticing array of dishes includes "potstickers" filled with triple-cream cheese and peas, spice-rubbed grilled squab with salted chili paste, and earthy poppy-seed cake with mascarpone, pistachio paste, and strawberries for dessert.

Rich Table

Contemporary ✗✗

C2

199 Gough St. (at Oak St.)

Phone: 415-355-9085   Dinner nightly
Web: www.richtablesf.com
Prices: $$

Its rustic-chic décor, highlighting reclaimed and raw wood, gives Rich Table a farmhouse feel, and the crowds that pack it are equally shabby-sleek. Reserve early or expect a long wait, as there's serious competition for seats that quickly fill with young professionals in designer casualwear.

The contemporary American food from Chef/owners Evan and Sarah Rich is highly engaging with menu mainstays like crispy sardine chips and porcini-salted doughnuts set alongside a warm raclette dip. Snap peas are arranged beside grapefruit segments, pecans, and nasturtium blossoms; while seasonal mains include a tangy strawberry gazpacho topped with crunchy chicken skin and burrata. Also irresistible is a smoky pork chop posed atop wheat berries and pork-*garum* jus.

Rusty's Southern

Southern ✗

D1

750 Ellis St. (bet. Larkin & Polk Sts.)

Phone: 415-638-6974   Lunch Tue – Sun
Web: www.rustyssf.com   Dinner Tue – Sat
Prices: $$

In the hard-charging techie wilds of San Francisco, homesick transplants can find Southern comfort at this Tenderloin newbie, which eschews fine-dining frills for rib-sticking simplicity. Its environs are a bit sketchy after dark, but that doesn't deter the young and stylish crowds, who swill craft beers at the front bar and congregate in groups in the casual, wood-accented dining room.

Rustic and homey treats arrive in abundant portions: tangy, smoky Brunswick stew is loaded with pork, chicken, collards, lima beans and tomatoes, while expertly brined fried chicken is encased in a crunchy, golden-brown breading. For a snack, the fluffy fried hush puppies come equipped with a decadent pimento-ranch dipping sauce, and pair nicely with an icy sweet tea.

Tadu

Ethiopian ✗

D1

484 Ellis St. (bet. Jones & Leavenworth Sts.)

Phone: 415-409-6649   Lunch & dinner daily
Web: www.taduethiopiankitchen.com
Prices:

Strength in numbers is the way to go when planning a visit to this charming Ethiopian newcomer: its neighborhood is one in which you won't want to walk alone, and besides, you'll need all the help you can get to tackle the hearty portions, all served family-style here. Despite its bleak environs, Tadu's cheerful décor and friendly, engaging staff make for a very warm welcome.

Rev up your palate with the spicy, golden-brown *sambussas*, filled with earthy lentils and caramelized onions. Then go full-throttle with the *kitfo*, a zippy mixture of ground beef, onion, jalapeño, and Ethiopian spices. There's plenty of fluffy, slightly sour *injera* to mellow the burn: you can even enjoy it cooked with spices and vegetables in the delightful *firfir*.

State Bird Provisions ✿

B1

American ✗✗

1529 Fillmore St. (bet. Geary Blvd. & O'Farrell St.)

Phone: 415-795-1272   Dinner nightly
Web: www.statebirdsf.com
Prices: **$$**

&

The crowds start queuing up long before State Bird Provisions swings open its doors, with excited guests hoping to score one of their few dozen walk-in spots (you can also make reservations, but the process is still a coup). The buzzing and open kitchen located up front is the focal point of the space. The energy is palpable, and a night out at this popular spot can feel (in the best way possible) like you've scored a ticket to a very cool party.

The bright, industrial-chic dining room features countrified yet sleek wooden tables; and playful pegboard walls highlighting intricate wire sculptures. The easygoing army of servers roll the kitchen's seasonal American small plates around dim sum-style on trolleys (or carry it by foot), showcasing each menu item with an accompanying price tag.

It's hard not to want a taste of everything on offer, which is probably even more reason to come with as many friends as you can rally. A quenelle of rich squab liver pâté is spread on sweet almond cakes; while plump guinea hen dumplings are served in a fragrant hen broth. Then, a flaky, croissant-like wheat bread gets a creamy hit of burrata and thump of crushed black pepper; and ultra-fresh sweet peas are paired with spicy horseradish cream and fried parsnip chips.

Thep Phanom

Thai ✕

C2

400 Waller St. (at Fillmore St.)

Phone: 415-431-2526
Web: www.thepphanom.com
Prices: $$

Dinner nightly

A good Thai spot is as essential to a SF neighborhood as air to breath, and Lower Haighters have long pledged their allegiance to Thep Phanom's interpretation of the sweet and spicy cuisine. Whether they crave sinfully crisp, golden-brown chicken wings with sweet-chili dipping sauce or a range of healthy vegetarian options, they've yet to be disappointed.
Tucked just off bustling Haight and Fillmore, the location is no friend to drivers (prepare to circle), but once inside, it's dimly lit and low-key, ideal for a quiet date night or even solo dining. Spice levels are adjustable—and hot means hot—for all the dishes ranging from creamy red pumpkin curry, to "Thaitanic" tofu, eggplant, and string beans in a lemongrass-ginger- and Thai basil-sauce.

Tycoon

Thai ✕

D1

620 O'Farrell St. (bet. Hyde & Leavenworth Sts.)

Phone: 415-796-3391
Web: N/A
Prices:

Lunch & dinner daily

Its location in the gritty Tenderloin doesn't offer much in terms of ambience, but this Thai newcomer makes up for it with flavorful, fragrant cooking that's a cut above the standard pad Thai racket. You'll swoon for the utterly perfect *sai ua*, juicy, smoky pork sausages bursting with the aromas of makrut lime, lemongrass, and chili, and the delectable *pad ped*, a spicy coconut-milk curry loaded with piquant green peppercorns, tender tofu, eggplant, and bell pepper.
For true culinary adventurers, there's a small selection of Laotian dishes, like *pad mee lao* or thin rice noodles with chicken, fresh mint, and a splash of earthy black bean sauce. Also notable is the unusual and authentic drink selection, which includes vibrant *pandan* and chrysanthemum juices.

Zuni Café

Mediterranean XX

D2

1658 Market St. (bet. Franklin & Gough Sts.)

Phone: 415-552-2522   Lunch & dinner Tue – Sun
Web: www.zunicafe.com
Prices: $$

Over thirty years young and still thriving as if it were newborn, locals and visitors remain drawn to this SF institution, famous for its laid-back California vibe and great, locally sourced eats. This iconic space embraces its unique shape, and is styled with bold artwork-covered walls, a copper bar counter, and wood-burning oven sending out delightful pizzas and filling the room with mouthwatering aromas.

Given its ace location, Zuni makes for a divine lunch destination—and proof is in the many business folk, trendy ladies-who-lunch, and tourists that fill its tables midday. Menu treasures include sliced persimmon scattered with shaved Jerusalem artichoke and baby arugula leaves, tailed by toothsome artisanal rigatoni clutching fragrant lamb sugo.

Feast for under $25 at all restaurants with ⊜.

Financial District

EMBARCADERO · UNION SQUARE

Booming with high-rises and large-scale companies, the Financial District is world-renowned. While the city itself is reputed for its easygoing vibe and cool 'tude, the financial sector is ever-bustling with the prominence of Fortune 500 companies, multi-national corporations, major banks, and law firms. Settled along the west of the waterfront, expect to see streetcars, pedestrians, and wildly tattooed bicycle messengers on weekdays clogging the routes of the triangle bounded by Kearny, Jackson, and Market streets. Come noon, lines snake out the doors of better grab-and-go sandwich shops and salad spots.

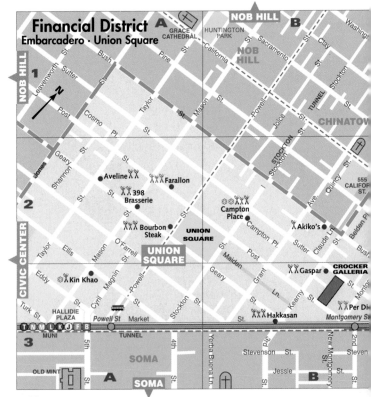

Financial District
Embarcadero · Union Square

NOB HILL

GRACE CATHEDRAL
HUNTINGTON PARK
NOB HILL
CHINATOWN

Aveline
Farallon
398 Brasserie
Campton Place
Akiko's
555 CALIFORNIA ST.
Bourbon Steak
UNION SQUARE
Kin Khao
Gaspar
CROCKER GALLERIA
HALLIDIE PLAZA
Powell St   Market
Hakkasan
Per Die
Montgomery St

MUNI
TUNNEL
SOMA
OLD MINT
SOMA

Of course, there is always a steady stream of expense-account clients who continuously patronize this neighborhood's host of fine-dining establishments; whereas along Market Street, casual cafés and chain restaurants keep the focus on families, tourists, and shoppers alike.

EMBARCARDERO

Despite all that this area has to offer, its greatest culinary treasures lies within the famed **Ferry Building**. This 1898 steel-reinforced sandstone structure is easily recognized by its 244-foot clock tower that rises up from Market Street and way above the waterfront promenade—**The Embarcadero**. It is among the few survivors of the 1906 earthquake and fire that destroyed most of this neighborhood. Thanks to a 2004 renovation, the soaring interior arcade makes a stunning showcase for regional products, artisanal foods, rare Chinese teas, and everything in between. Popularly referred to as the **Ferry Building Marketplace**, every diligent foodie is destined here for the likes of Lauren Kiino's **Il Cane Rosso,** a quick-serve rotisserie-cum-casual hangout serving weekday brunch (the olive oil-fried egg sandwich is a particular thrill); or lunch standbys

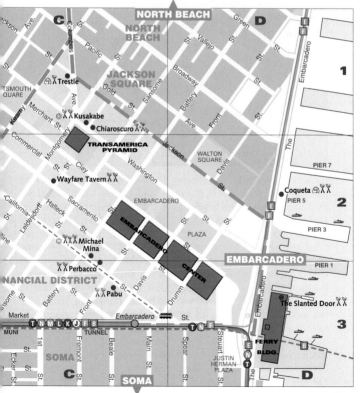

like salads, soups, and sammies. A three-course dinner here can be had for less than $30. This emporium also pays homage to the surrounding food community by highlighting small producers. Two of the most popular among them are **Cowgirl Creamery**'s farmstead cheeses, and Berkeley's **Acme Bread Company**—whose organic breads are a sight (and smell) to behold! Following this philosophy, find numerous organic and exotic mushrooms, medicinal herbs, and themed products at **Far West Fungi**. Here,

also includes an impressive array of olive oil-based products.

While such world-class food shopping may whet the appetite of many, more immediate cravings can be satisfied at the Building's more casual dining delights like **DELICA**, popular for beautifully prepared Japanese fusion food, from signature sushi rolls to savory croquettes. Join the corporate lunch rush seated at picnic tables in **Mijita** (run by Traci Des Jardins of **Jardinère** fame) to sample such treats as *queso fundido* or Baja-style fish tacos.

patient enthusiasts can even purchase logs on which to grow their own harvest. Legendary **Frog Hollow Farm** is also stationed nearby, offering pristine seasonal fruit alongside homemade chutneys, marmalade and fresh-baked pastries. Known for their Parisian-style chocolates and caramels, **Recchiuti Confections** has elevated their craft to an art form that can only be described as heavenly. And, completing this gourmet trend are gleaming bottles of **McEvoy Ranch Olive Oil** from their Petaluma ranch that

Or, perch atop a barstool at **Hog Island Oyster Company** to get first dibs on their plump bivalves, plucked fresh from Tomales Bay. While this is a great spot to sit, slurp, and take in the view, the most decadent takeout option is still **Boccalone Salumeria**, for their comprehensive charcuterie. Whether purchasing these salty eats by the platter, pound, or layered in a single-serving "cone," prepare for an unapologetically carnivorous treat. On Tuesday, Thursday, and Saturday mornings, high-minded chefs share laughs

with the locals at **Ferry Plaza Farmer's Market**, dealing in everything from organic produce and baked goods to fresh pastas and tons more. On market days, open-air stands and tents line the picturesque sidewalk in front of the Ferry Building and rear plaza overlooking the bay.

Tourists and unwearied locals are sure to enjoy some visual stimulation at The Bay Lights—an undulating light installation by artist Leo Villareal—illuminating the west span of the Bay Bridge. **The Embarcadero** boasts the best view of this beautiful piece. Meanwhile, groups of suits know to head to the **Embarcadero Center** (spanning five blocks and boasting reduced parking rates on weekends) to get their midday shopping fix in the sprawling three-story indoor mall, or to grab a quick lunch at one of the thirty-some eateries ranging from mini-chains to noodle shops. A speck of sweet from **See's Candies** or caffeine from **Peet's** makes for an ideal finale.

UNION SQUARE

Upscale department stores like Barneys, Neiman Marcus, and Saks preside over Union Square, where foodies gather for a gourmet experience and fashionistas flock to designer shops. Just as noodle lovers form a queue outside **KATANA-YA** for steaming bowls of slurp-worthy ramen, shopaholics and local bargain hunters pop into **Tout Sweet Patisserie** (housed inside Macy's) for a pick-me-up in the form of pastries, candies, and macarons. Take home a few extra goodies, if only to appreciate their beautiful packaging.

Akiko's

Japanese ✗

B2

431 Bush St. (bet. Grant & Kearny Sts.)

Phone: 415-397-3218
Web: www.akikosrestaurant.com
Prices: $$$

Lunch Mon – Fri
Dinner Mon – Sat

Akiko's is hard to find. In addition to sharing a name with a lesser nearby sushi bar, it's hidden just off an alleyway and has no sign. The cool clientele is probably happy to avoid any more competition for the mere handful of tables and seats at the small sushi bar.

Arrive at dinner, sit at the counter, toss aside that à la carte menu, and opt for an omakase feast created by the very talented chefs. Expect them to take liberties and leave tradition behind; yet the quality remains high with pristine nigiri featuring fluke, scallop, or geoduck clam minimally garnished and perched atop rice with a touch of nutty red rice vinegar. Bookend the meal with rich tuna poke with sesame, or a lightly torched slice of A5 Wagyu beef with black truffle shavings.

Aveline

Contemporary ✗✗

A2

490 Geary St. (at Taylor St.)

Phone: 415-345-2303
Web: www.avelinesf.com
Prices: $$$

Lunch Sat – Sun
Dinner Mon – Sat

Snap-happy Instagrammers will delight in this contemporary stunner in the Warwick Hotel, where the Hollywood Regency-style room and exquisitely arranged plates are picture-perfect. Located steps from the busy shopping corridor of Union Square, it's a great spot to unwind with a refreshing, bubbly cocktail—either over a full meal or a snack at adjoining bar, The European.

The kitchen's artful creations include a spiraling arrangement of house-smoked salmon with ribbons of lightly pickled vegetables and avocado purée, or a crispy duck leg resting atop charred Brussels sprouts, cherry, and parsnip. Don't miss the menu's chief attraction: delicate, buttery crab "macarons" or tiny sandwiches filled with an ample portion of creamy, herb-flecked crab salad.

Bourbon Steak

A2

Steakhouse ✗✗✗

335 Powell St. (bet. Geary & Post Sts.)

Phone: 415-397-3003   Dinner nightly
Web: www.bourbonsteaksf.com
Prices: $$$$

For soigné takes on steakhouse classics, it's hard to beat this Michael Mina affiliate in the Westin St. Francis hotel, which draws a steady stream of tourists and business diners for its dressed-up fare. The space is sophisticated and masculine, with dimly lit tables in a tan-and-chocolate color palette and soaring ceilings raised by dark Grecian pillars.

As the name implies, meat is a specialty here, and the prime cuts arrive cooked to a perfect medium-rare. Throw in a sweet, crunchy shrimp Louie topped with a fan of creamy avocado, and you'll be on cloud nine. If you can save room for something sweet, make it a point to order the maple-Bourbon panna cotta, a knockout dessert that's garnished with coffee cake and Bourbon ice cream, but of course.

Chiaroscuro

C1

Italian ✗✗

550 Washington St. (bet. Montgomery & Sansome Sts.)

Phone: 415-362-6012   Lunch Mon – Fri
Web: www.chiaroscurosf.com   Dinner Mon – Sat
Prices: $$

An upscale retreat for well-heeled FiDi deal-doers, Chiaroscuro brims with a lunchtime crowd tucking into memorable pastas. One such standout is the delicate house-made *tagliolini* with julienned winter vegetables and a light, truffle-scented sauce enriched with *Parmigiano*. If you can't choose a single dish, opt for the popular "trilogia" of three daily delights, then follow it with *pollo ai peperoni*, a delicious chicken roulade stuffed with roasted bell pepper and served over crisp vegetables.

While its food is classically Roman, Chiaroscuro's décor is modern, sleek, and chic, with pillow-topped concrete banquettes and modern glass-and-metal chandeliers. For a quieter meal, come at dinner, when the crowds dissipate and the menu goes prix-fixe.

Campton Place ✿ ✿

Indian XXX

B2

340 Stockton St. (bet. Post & Sutter Sts.)

Phone: 415-955-5555
Web: www.camptonplacesf.com
Prices: $$$$

Lunch & dinner daily

With its sleek booths, wall-to-wall windows, plush carpeting, and pristinely robed tables, this elegant oasis in the Taj Hotel is as formal and traditional as one would expect; even the dining room's pièce de résistance, a blown-glass floral chandelier that hangs from the coffered ceiling, is elegant and sophisticated. An odd mix of gourmands and hotel guests keep the vibe desultory inside, but by greeting each diner as they enter, the staff maintains a sense of refinery that is true to this contemporary Cal-Indian menu.

Courses, which arrive on charcoal-glazed ceramics, allude to Indian spices but honor outstanding skill and taste over drama or novelty. Lighter dishes cover all bases of flavor and texture as witnessed in a modern expression of *chaat* (carrots, peas, and tamarind tossed in "whey shorva" dotted with chutney); or spicy, pan-fried potato-corn *tikkis* lodged atop a bright salad of plum brunoise and cilantro. Dollops of tangy lime curd expertly complete this sublime, seasonal plate, while charred potatoes and leeks accentuate a decadent butter-poached Maine lobster.

Just as slow-cooked meat dishes have an elegant undertone of *garam masala*, for dessert, *tandoori* strawberries with lemon ice cream may under-promise on paper but will over-deliver on taste and flavor.

Coqueta

Spanish X X

D2

Pier 5 (at The Embarcadero)

Phone: 415-704-8866   Lunch Tue – Sun
Web: www.coquetasf.com   Dinner nightly
Prices: $$

Local diners have a full-blown infatuation with Michael Chiarello's city-side spot, though its name is Spanish for "flirt." The handsome dining room is a rustic-chic and masculine display of cowhides, distressed wood, and stone, with huge windows overlooking the Embarcadero. All this makes the crowded Pier 5 restaurant a highly coveted reservation.

The Spanish fare has some California lightness (order extra). Begin with oblong, crunchy fried and *chicharrón*-encrusted chicken croquetas filled with English pea mousse. Toasted sandwiches of smoked salmon with *queso fresco* and truffle honey are tasty little bites. Desserts are a slam dunk with a touch of sweet—don't miss the lush Manchego cheesecake dipped in caramel-white chocolate with caramel corn.

Farallon

Seafood X X X

A2

450 Post St. (bet. Mason & Powell Sts.)

Phone: 415-956-6969   Dinner nightly
Web: www.farallonrestaurant.com
Prices: $$$

Union Square's lauded seafood respite is an aquatic-themed fantasy at every turn. Dive in and enjoy an extravagant platter of *fruits de mer* while admiring their thematic, custom-made chandeliers and bar stools in The Jellyfish Lounge. Also known as the Jelly Bar, it's a San Francisco institution unto itself. Then head to the Pool Room (it once served as the pool room of the Elks Club) to dine on the kitchen's coastal cooking amid sparkling mosaics and a vaulted ceiling.

A raw first course unearths yellowtail sashimi adorned with garlicky aïoli, finely chopped piquillo peppers, and dollops of basil chantilly. Following that is an entrée of crisp-skinned grilled salmon, accompanied by torn croutons, heirloom tomatoes, red onions, and balsamic vinegar.

Gaspar

French 🍴🍴

B3

185 Sutter St. (bet. Kearny & Montgomery Sts.)

Phone: 415-576-8800
Web: www.gasparbrasserie.com
Prices: $$

Lunch Mon – Fri
Dinner nightly

In a sea of faux-rustic restaurant décor, this recruit stands out for its sexy, intimate vibe, complete with dark-tufted banquettes, soft lighting, and an intimate downstairs bar. It's the kind of place where you'll see FiDi brokers rehash deals over pre-dinner cocktails, before being joined by their well-dressed dates for a swanky dinner party upstairs.

The menu of French brasserie favorites is prepared with skill, from grand plateaux of *fruits de mer* to a perfectly cooked flatiron steak with well-seasoned pommes frites and red wine bordelaise. Don't miss the outstanding *Paris-Brest*, golden-hued pastry filled with creamy rose-mascarpone and juicy raspberries. Or if you'd rather skip sweets, opt for their well-curated cheese plate.

Hakkasan

Chinese 🍴🍴🍴

B3

1 Kearny St. (at Market St.)

Phone: 415-829-8148
Web: www.hakkasan.com
Prices: $$$$

Lunch & dinner daily

An eclectic crowd of business people, cocktailing hipsters, and fashionable Chinese tourists descend on the SF outpost of this upscale international chain. Housed on the second floor of the historic One Kearny building, the dining room's luxe design features carved wood screens, embroidered white leather, and a striking, V-shaped bar—it's a scene worth dressing up for.

Sample Hakkasan's mouthwatering Cantonese eats, however, and you'll see that its appeal transcends the décor. The menu's extensive array of artfully plated treats includes hits like braised chicken dressed with soy sauce, toasted sesame oil, ginger, and scallions. The French green beans, stir-fried with minced pork, dried shrimp, and an umami-packed brown sauce, are just as magical.

Kin Khao ☭

Thai ✗

A3

55 Cyril Magnin (entrance at Ellis & Mason Sts.)

Phone: 415-362-7456
Web: www.kinkhao.com
Prices: $$

Lunch Mon – Fri
Dinner Mon – Sat

Don't let its covert location fool you—Kin Khao is a flagrantly delicious and very distinctive dining room. The décor is unexceptional by no uncertain terms, but really nobody seems to care, as the cooking—punctuated by Californian elements and welcome seasonality—is the real deal.

Northern Thai is what this kitchen is all about and pad Thai-loving palates should vacate these premises…pronto. Of course, the unique menu reads like a veritable thesis on Isaan food mingled with California love. Then there's the easygoing and chill staff who never miss a beat—as they bestow tables with vibrant, product-driven plates. These have included crispy lima beans tossed in *nam tok* followed by crunchy albeit not as "hot" chicken wings massaged with tamarind and chili. Pork meatballs seasoned with garlic and lemongrass (*laab tod*) are enriched by a phenomenal chili (*jaew*) sauce; while a gorgeous platter of crunchy vegetables is accompanied by a jar of the incredible *nam prik* (potent with shrimp paste) layered with caramelized pork jowl, fried catfish, and a salted duck egg. Panang curry with tender-braised duck is a champ among palates less valiant.

Closing arguments may reveal that this is a truly Thai kitchen turning out insanely memorable food. All objections overruled.

Kusakabe ✿

Japanese ✗✗

C1

584 Washington St. (bet. Montgomery & Sansome Sts.)

Dinner Mon – Sat

Phone: 415-757-0155
Web: www.kusakabe-sf.com
Prices: $$$$

This is a place for dedicated sushi lovers. Serene with warm wood, clean lines, and a strong sense of minimalism, Kusakabe brings distinctive creativity to this sushi-focused operation. The stunning counter is crafted from a single piece of live-edge elm. Oyster-hued leather chairs and a ceiling of wood slats complete the Japan-chic look.

Of late, due to increased popularity (and ergo, demand), the nightly omakase tasting has felt more like a conveyor belt-style dining experience. However, by employing myriad cooking techniques, Chef Mitsunori Kusakabe ensures that every bite is deliciously balanced and memorable. After awakening the palate with a cup of warm kelp tea, embark on a sashimi parade starring thick slices of bluefin served over crushed ice and with a tangy yuzu- onion- and sesame oil-sauce. A soup course may feature fresh crabmeat in a delicate *tai* broth bobbing with *mitsuba*, tofu, and sweet corn-speckled fish cake. And finally, a top rendition of sushi yields *shima aji* with daikon as well as *ayu* that is torched just enough to blister the skin and impeccably contrasted with grated cucumber.

A single Shigoku oyster on the half shell served with a simple brushing of yuzu juice makes for a nice opening bite.

Michael Mina ❀

Contemporary ✕✕✕

C2

252 California St. (bet. Battery & Front Sts.)

Phone:	415-397-9222	Lunch Mon – Fri
Web:	www.michaelmina.net	Dinner nightly
Prices:	$$$$	

Chef Michael Mina's eponymous home base remains the crown jewel in his nationwide empire of restaurants. Housed in a stately grey stone building, it's a magnet for nearby business folk, who can be seen brokering deals over dinner or unwinding with a glass of the chef's private-label cabernet along with a bite from the bar menu. High-ceilinged and lively, the spacious dining room is elegantly appointed with huge foliage arrangements and oversized framed mirrors.

The French- and Asian-influenced cuisine emphasizes luxurious ingredients as found in seared abalone, divinely tender and presented with grilled cabbage heart, sticky rice, and a *togarashi*-spiced red miso broth poured tableside. Lobster is impeccably cooked and plated, bearing a seasonally appropriate mélange of produce and a dousing of savory ginger-lemongrass jus to complete the composition.

Mina's menu is constructed as a four-course prix-fixe, but diners are also invited to select the chef's tasting for an extended expression of the kitchen's talents. Regardless of your decision, there will always be dessert—followed by joy—when frozen nougat dressed with Earl Grey streusel and torched white grapefruit segments is set in front of you.

Pabu

Japanese ✗✗

C3

101 California St. (bet. Davis & Front Sts.)

Phone: 415-668-7228
Web: www.pabuizakaya.com
Prices: $$$

Lunch Mon – Fri
Dinner nightly

Michael Mina and Ken Tominaga have gone big with their Japanese offspring and baby boy is quite a looker. Encompassing a stunning, high-ceilinged bar, gleaming sushi counter, several dining rooms, and a casual ramen joint (The Ramen Bar, next door), Pabu is enormous in space but serene in atmosphere. The warm service is highly personal.

If you can fork over the requisite gobs of cash, the massive menu will accommodate seemingly any Japanese craving—from whole grilled squid and *izakaya*-style skewers of smoky chicken tails or thick trumpet mushrooms, to a sweet, salty, and savory burdock salad. Sushi fans can opt for the omakase or stick to à la carte treats like a tender *kanpyo* squash roll. The top-notch sake and Japanese whiskey lineup is worth exploring.

Perbacco

Italian ✗✗

C3

230 California St. (bet. Battery & Front Sts.)

Phone: 415-955-0663
Web: www.perbaccosf.com
Prices: $$

Lunch Mon – Fri
Dinner Mon – Sat

Slick financial types flex their expense accounts at this longtime Northern Italian favorite, whose polished décor belies an extensive menu of house-made pastas and comfort fare like roast chicken and meatballs at lunch, with slightly more refined takes at dinner. Dishes are executed with care—from mortadella-stuffed, black truffle-topped quail to handmade pastas, though portions can be a little scant.

The space is larger inside than it looks, with plenty of booths and seats at the marble bar up front, and buzzy tables in the back with a view of the open-plan kitchen. Well-versed servers will encourage saving room for the end of the meal—as the cheese display, an impressive selection of grappas, and the inventive, delicious desserts are all highlights.

Per Diem

American ✗✗

B3

43 Sutter St. (bet. Montgomery & Sansome Sts.)

Phone: 415-989-0300
Web: www.perdiemsf.com
Prices: $$

Lunch Mon – Fri
Dinner Mon – Sat

This aptly-named hot spot is a favorite among the well-heeled FiDi power players who fill its dramatic, bi-level space. Equal parts industrial loft and swanky Prohibition-era club, Per Diem is a vision of rich wood surfaces, dramatic pillars, exposed brick, and concrete. It's a sleek atmosphere for a sleek crowd—but the real draw here is the food.

A new chef has taken the menu in a seasonally inspired direction that's at once refined and approachable. Of-the-moment delights include a salty, smoky flatbread topped with slices of roasted porcini and hon shimeji mushrooms, shaved prosciutto, and crescenza cheese. This may be tailed by an equally impressive spinach-ricotta ravioli with roasted squash, a soft-poached egg, and sprinkle of lemon gremolata.

The Slanted Door

Vietnamese ✗✗

D3

1 Ferry Building (at The Embarcadero)

Phone: 415-861-8032
Web: www.slanteddoor.com
Prices: $$

Lunch & dinner daily

Reservations are a challenge at this modern stunner with a killer view of the Bay Bridge, which has managed to stay atop tourists' hit lists even as its NorCal spin on Vietnamese food has steadily become more uninspired and corporate. It's an efficient, professional place, but with little warmth; the hospitality is hit-or-miss at best.

Steer clear of the overpraised cellophane noodles with crab or overpriced shaking beef, and stick to more solid offerings like *gau choy gow*, pan-fried dumplings with Gulf shrimp and vibrant garlic chives accompanied by a zippy soy and fish-sauce dip. Half-orders are encouraged, so take advantage by sampling more than one of the delectable vegetable sides, like crisp, spicy broccoli with pressed tofu.

398 Brasserie

French ✕✕

A2

398 Geary St. (at Mason St.)

Phone: 415-654-5061
Web: www.398restaurantsf.com
Prices: $$$

Lunch & dinner daily

Skip the Union Square tourist traps and head for this newcomer in the Hotel G, where the French-accented fare is a step up from the neighboring options. Distressed pillars and ceiling panels give the interior a demolition-chic vibe, but contemporary chandeliers, sleek furniture, and a gleaming exhibition kitchen make the chaos feel flashy, not funky.

The cocktail crowd descends early here, and for good reason: the drinks are outstanding, and pair well with the kitchen's Euro-American cuisine. Try the classic Lyonnaise salad of frisée, poached egg, crisp bacon lardons, and duck prosciutto, or the tender duck confit with cremini mushroom fricassee. If it's available, the wood-roasted calamari with smoked peppers and chorizo is not to be missed.

Trestle 😊

American ✕

C1

531 Jackson St. (at Columbus Ave.)

Phone: 415-772-0922
Web: www.trestlesf.com
Prices: $$

Dinner nightly

In SF's dizzyingly expensive dining landscape, this rookie, which offers a three-course menu for $35, is an incredible steal—provided you're willing to sacrifice freedom of choice. Dishes are top-notch, with great ingredients: on a given night, you might sit down to a repast of silky slow-roasted pork belly with grilled peaches, pristine pan-roasted salmon with chickpeas and salsa verde, and a velvety dark chocolate *pot de crème* with Bourbon-whipped cream.

As with any killer deal, there are caveats: reservations are necessary and they are hard to score, and the noise level is through the roof. But, the historic brick space is lots of fun with cool, contemporary art and a namesake central trestle table. The fact that the price is right only adds to the lure.

Wayfare Tavern

Gastropub

C2

558 Sacramento St. (bet. Montgomery & Sansome Sts.)

Phone: 415-772-9060   Lunch & dinner daily
Web: www.wayfaretavern.com
Prices: $$

Though it feels like it's been around for decades, celebrity chef Tyler Florence's FiDi favorite is actually a toddler—at least in tavern years. Nonetheless, it's become a standby for business types doing deals or enjoying post-work cocktails. Complete with dark wood and leather furnishings, a private billiards room, and bustling bar, Wayfare Tavern has the air of a gastropub-turned-private club.

Hearty Americana with seasonal accents defines the menu, like a take on biscuits and gravy that integrates plump dayboat scallops and spicy chili oil. Buttermilk-brined fried chicken, grilled hanger steak, and baked macaroni and cheese are pure comfort, as is a decadent TCHO chocolate cream pie with salty caramel ganache and devil's food cake crumble.

Look for the symbol 🛏
for a brilliant breakfast to
start your day off right.

Marina

JAPANTOWN · PACIFIC HEIGHTS · PRESIDIO

Following the havoc wreaked by the 1906 earthquake, San Francisco began reconstructing this sandy marshland by selling it to private developers. They, in turn, transformed the Marina into one of the most charming residential bubbles in town. Picture young families, tech wealth, and an affluent vibe straight out of a 21st century edition of The Yuppy Handbook, and you're in the Marina! Pacific Heights is considered the area's upper echelon—known for older family money and members who couldn't care less about being edgy. Here, bronzed residents adore jogging with their dogs at Crissy Field, or sipping aromatic chocolate from the **Warming Hut**. Parents can be seen pushing Bugaboos in haute couture boutiques or vying for parking in German-engineered SUVs.

CASUAL EATS

Marina girls as well as Pac Heights socialites are always on the go, and quick-bite cafés are their calling card. Find these denizens gather at **Jane** for pastries and paninis to nibble along with sips from a range of excellent teas, coffees, and smoothies. **Cafe GoLo** brings to life a classic American coffeehouse replete with expected breakfast specials, salads, and sandwiches; and **The Tipsy Pig** is a welcoming gastropub boasting an impressive bevy of bites and brews. True burger buffs in the Marina seem

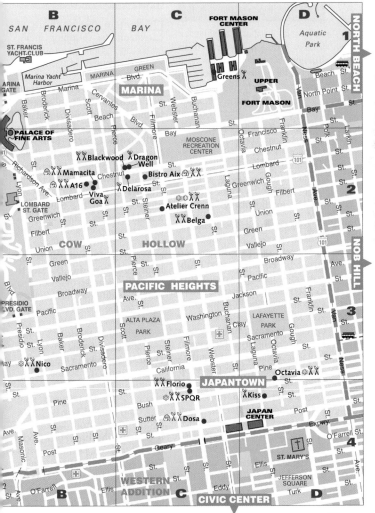

to have an insatiable appetite for locally founded **Roam Artisan Burgers**. Equally popular and sought-after are the contemporary, flavor-packed offerings at SoCal favorite, **Umami Burger**. In truth, quality cuisine has little to do with a Marina restaurant's success: the locals are unapologetically content to follow the buzz to the latest hot spot, where the clientele's beauty seems to be in direct proportion to its level of acclaim and popularity.

However, in the Presidio (home to Lucasfilm HQ) squads of tech geeks opt for convenience at nearby **Presidio Social Club**, cooking up tasty, regionally focused fare in a classic northern Californian setting. "**Off the Grid-Fort Mason**" is California's most coveted street food fair that gathers every Friday night and features a fantastic collection of vendors and food trucks—from **Curry Up Now** and **Magnolia Brewery** to **Rocko's Ice Cream Tacos** and everything in between. Then again, food is mere sustenance to some, and simply a sponge for the champagne and chardonnay flowing at the district's numerous watering holes. The bar scene here is not only fun but also varied, with a playground for

everyone. Oenophiles plan far in advance for the annual **ZAP Zinfandel Festival** in the winter; while preppy college kids swap European semester stories at sleek wine spots like **Ottimista Restaurant & Bar** or **Nectar**. Couples can find more romance by the fireplace at posh **MatrixFillmore**.

JAPANTOWN

Evident in the plethora of restaurants, shopping malls, banks, and others businesses, the Asian community in the Marina is burgeoning. Thanks to the prominent Japanese population and abundant cultural events, **Japantown** is an exceptional and unique destination. The **Northern California Cherry Blossom Festival** and **Nihonmachi Street Fair** bring to life every aspect of Asian-American heritage and living. Date night is always memorable at the **Sundance Kabuki Cinema**, which happens to be equipped with two full bars. For a post-work snack, prepared meals, or even authentic imported ingredients, **Super Mira** is a market that offers a host of traditional eats. But for lunch on the run, grab excellent sushi, sashimi, or bento boxes at nearby **Nijiya Market**. Visitors and laid-back locals sojourn to **Daikoku by Shiki** (in the Kintetsu Mall) if only to admire their assortment of beautiful Japanese ceramics, cast iron teapots, sake sets, and glazed bowls. Just a couple blocks from Japantown is perhaps the best spice shop in the country. Featuring walls lined with stacks of jars, **Spice Ace** boasts of extensively curated spices, extracts, and salts, that can all be sampled before purchase.

A16 😀

Italian 🍴🍴

B2

2355 Chestnut St. (bet. Divisadero & Scott Sts.)

Phone:	415-771-2216	Lunch Wed – Fri
Web:	www.a16sf.com	Dinner nightly
Prices:	$$	

An undying favorite of yuppies, families, and tourists alike, A16 is known for rustic Italian cooking and a vast selection of delicious, unusual wines from all over the boot. Dinner reservations are indispensable, especially if you want one of the prime counter seats facing the open kitchen and wood-burning pizza oven.

The menu's pies, pastas, and antipasti change with the season, so you could sample anything from perfectly al dente bucatini with roasted cherry tomatoes, garlic, and flaky white anchovies to grilled bruschetta piled with caramelized prosciutto, creamy ricotta, cherry tomatoes, and blistered shishito peppers. For dessert, look no further than the fig crostata with vanilla gelato, which tastes like the work of a particularly talented *nonna*.

Belga

Belgian 🍴🍴

C2

2000 Union St. (at Buchanan St.)

Phone:	415-872-7350	Lunch Sat – Sun
Web:	www.belgasf.com	Dinner nightly
Prices:	$$	

Belgian brews and bites are the cornerstones of this new recruit in the former Café des Amis, which has kept its brasserie look but pivoted from Paris to Brussels. All the classics are accounted for: well-salted frites with garlic aïoli; bowls of mussels; and of course, house-made sausages—try the combo board, which comes with andouille, *boudin noir*, *boudin blanc*, and *currywurst*, not to mention a generous bowl of spaetzle. Flatbreads and salads round things out.

The Euro-café vibe is fun with red banquettes, classic bistro chairs, and marble floors to complement the big beer selection (both European and domestic) and cocktails. Young Marinaites have, understandably, caught on quickly: the bar and dog-friendly patio are constantly abuzz.

Atelier Crenn ❀ ❀

C2
Contemporary ✗✗

3127 Fillmore St. (bet. Filbert & Pixley Sts.)

Phone: 415-440-0460
Web: www.ateliercrenn.com
Prices: $$$$

Dinner Tue – Sat

Neutral gray and very discreet, Atelier Crenn is almost camouflaged in plain sight. Inside, gracious servers keep the dining room low key and very serene. The décor follows suit with a ceiling comprised of a backlit reed canopy, twig-like fixtures, and unadorned wood tables. This is a place for celebrants as well as serious foodies. Warm and very competent servers explain dishes with the same painstaking detail and dexterity that the kitchen uses to place carrot jerky onto its mossy twig.

Chef Dominique Crenn's cooking is at once whimsical and deeply accomplished, based on elemental expressions of the earth or sea. While the idea of "poetic culinaria" may seem self-indulgent to some, this cuisine is undeniably authentic, deeply personal, and filled with brilliant grace notes of flavor and creativity.

Expect dishes that are light yet complex, such as fluke that seems ready to melt over tarragon ice, amid droplets of creamy smoked sturgeon, sea-cucumber dashi, and pickled Asian pears. Dark and intense spot prawn broth is so deeply flavored that it seems like you are tasting shellfish for the first time. A trio of aloe gelée, purée, and snow is incomparably refreshing and herbaceous.

Bistro Aix

Mediterranean XX

C2

3340 Steiner St. (bet. Chestnut & Lombard Sts.)

Phone: 415-202-0100   Dinner Mon – Sat
Web: www.bistroaix.com
Prices: $$

In the competitive Marina market, lovely Bistro Aix remains a charming and relatively affordable neighborhood option for thoughtfully made Southern French fare with a California touch. The dining room offers two distinct culinary experiences, beginning with seats in front at the convivial marble bar and small bistro tables. Beyond this, find the sunny bubble of the intimate back atrium, verdant with olive trees and flooded with natural light. A well-heeled crowd enlivens the space.

Dishes are simple and well executed, like roasted eggplant with grilled sesame seeds, gypsy peppers, and a topping of creamy burrata; or the perfectly grilled ahi tuna with fried baby spinach and a spicy Port reduction. Nicely chosen French wines complement each dish.

Blackwood

Fusion XX

C2

2150 Chestnut St. (bet. Pierce & Steiner Sts.)

Phone: 415-931-9663   Lunch & dinner daily
Web: www.blackwoodsf.com
Prices: $$

For a hip, fusion-y take on Thai fare, Marina locals beeline to this stylish spot, which offers classic dishes like shredded mango salad with cilantro, scallions, and smoky tiger prawns, as well as more mod items such as grilled Wagyu flank steak massaged with a five-spice sauce, set atop ginger rice and garlicky long beans. Empanada-like samosas come stuffed with potato, caramelized onions, and carrots, accompanied by a light and refreshing cucumber-avocado salad.

The sleek interior features tufted banquettes and enormous mirrors, but the prime perch is at their lovely front patio, with two fireside communal tables that face the hustle and bustle of Chestnut Street. Allow extra time for parking and expect a wait at weekend brunch—the most popular service.

The Commissary

Californian ✗✗

A2

101 Montgomery St. (in the Presidio)

Phone: 415-561-3600
Web: www.thecommissarysf.com
Prices: $$

Lunch Mon – Fri
Dinner Mon – Sat

Once an officer's mess for the soldiers of the Presidio, this historic space now offers more refined cooking, courtesy of superchef Traci Des Jardins. Inside, communal wood tables, a bustling chef's counter, and antique light fixtures honor the past while allowing for modern comfort. Dine alfresco on the big front porch, facing the former parade grounds, or grab cheese, wine, and charcuterie from the in-house shop.

The menu takes its cues from Spain, with richly seasoned chicken *basquaise* in a peppery tomato broth and *bacalao* salad strewn with fennel, olive, pomelo, and basil. *Jamón Ibérico*, gazpacho, and churros also make appearances.

For a double dose of Des Jardins, head to nearby Arguello, her Mexican concept in the Presidio Officer's Club.

Delarosa

Italian ✗

C2

2175 Chestnut St. (bet. Pierce & Steiner Sts.)

Phone: 415-673-7100
Web: www.delarosasf.com
Prices: $$

Lunch & dinner daily

People-watching aficionados will delight in this Marina favorite, where sidewalk tables afford a killer view of Chestnut Street's many stroller-pushing parents, awestruck tourists, and Pilates-toned socialites. Befitting the visual overload, bright orange is Delarosa's signature color and can be seen in light fixtures hanging over communal tables as well as eye-popping tiles in the kitchen.

Simple, rustic Italian food steals the show, like spicy-smoky thin-crust pizzas topped with salami, *coppa*, and chopped chilies, or a fresh, flavorful salad of young kale with a pecorino-Caesar dressing. The laid-back vibe extends to the signature dessert: a trio of puffy, sugar-dusted *bomboloni*, served warm with chocolate, raspberry, and mascarpone dipping sauces.

Dosa

Indian ✕✕

C4

1700 Fillmore St. (at Post St.)

Phone: 415-441-3672
Web: www.dosasf.com
Prices: $$

Lunch Wed – Sun
Dinner nightly

Grandeur and glamour infuse every inch of this stylish restaurant, whose soaring ceilings and glittering crystal chandeliers complement the boldly flavored, fragrantly spiced fare. As the name suggests, dosas are a highlight, with crisp exteriors, spicy fillings, and excellent accompanying *sambar* and chutney.

Welcoming servers will help translate street favorites like *bhel puri* (a delicious sweet-spicy blend of puffed rice, crispy noodles, green mango, and chutney); or shake up a tangy Bengali gimlet with gin, curried nectar, and lime. Desserts are every bit as exotic as the rest of the menu and include *rasmalai*—delicate patties of fresh cheese in sweet cream flavored with cardamom and rosewater.

Find a second, smaller location on Valencia Street.

Dragon Well

Chinese ✕

C2

2142 Chestnut St. (bet. Pierce & Steiner Sts.)

Phone: 415-474-6888
Web: www.dragonwell.com
Prices: ⊜⊜

Lunch & dinner daily

This Marina mainstay nestled among the posh boutiques of Chestnut Street has been at it for over a decade. Westernized classics crafted with fantastically fresh ingredients are the secret to their ongoing success. Inside, high ceilings with sunny skylights and butter-yellow walls evoke an airy feel, while framed photos depict the everyday life of the vast Chinese culture.

Pop in for a shopping break and nosh on tasty tea-smoked duck, served with hand-made steamed buns, thick hoisin sauce, and julienned leeks; or Chinese chicken salad, mixed with cilantro and a lemon-soy vinaigrette. The *Kung Pao* chicken, stir-fried with roasted peanuts and chili sauce, is fiery but never overpowering. Sweeten things up with a chocolate (or traditional) fortune cookie.

Florio

XX

C4

1915 Fillmore St. (bet. Bush & Pine Sts.)

Phone: 415-775-4300   Dinner nightly
Web: www.floriosf.com
Prices: $$

After a day of shopping in the neighboring boutiques, locals head to Florio to nurse a glass of wine at the bar or to meet friends for a casual dinner. Complete with linen-topped tables, wood floors, and relaxed furnishings, it has the cozy, romantic vibe of an authentic bistro, and you're likely to see plenty of couples (sometimes in duos) out for a date night.
The approachable French-cum-Italian menu is full of hearty crowd-pleasers, like a salad of shaved summer squash with mint, pea tendrils, and dollops of creamy ricotta; or a juicy, deep-brown roast chicken laid over caramelized onions and blistered mild peppers. For a delicate finish, try the buttery almond tea cake, accompanied by sweet corn ice cream and tart blackberry verjus.

Greens

Vegetarian X

C1

Building A, Fort Mason Center

Phone: 415-771-6222   Lunch Tue – Sun
Web: www.greensrestaurant.com   Dinner nightly
Prices: $$

Annie Somerville's pioneering vegetarian restaurant has been around since 1979, but neither the menu nor the surroundings show Greens' age. Instead, fresh, energetic cuisine abounds, with a light touch and a slight Italian bent. Brunch draws a big crowd, so be prepared to wait for those perfectly fried eggs over griddled potato cakes. Vegetarians and carnivores will rejoice after sampling the honest, colorful, down-to-earth seasonal entrées at dinner, followed by delightful desserts like an huckleberry upside down cake with a subtle kick from Meyer lemon.
Housed in historic Fort Mason, the warehouse-style space is rustic yet refined, with sweeping views of the Golden Gate Bridge and sailboats on the Bay.
For a quick lunch, there's also a to-go counter.

Hong Kong Lounge II

Chinese XX

A4

3300 Geary Blvd. (at Parker Ave.)

Phone: 415-668-8802
Web: www.hongkonglounge2.com
Prices: $$

Lunch & dinner daily

While lesser Chinese restaurants struggle to balance quality dim sum with equally tasty dinner entrées, Hong Kong Lounge II does it all. As a result, it's become one of the Richmond's biggest draws, with big crowds on weekends and Chinese families packing the round banquet tables at lunch and dinner. The pretty interior's rose walls, wood screens, and white tablecloths are another attractive step up from the competition.

Bring a group to fully sample the array of winning dishes, including handmade soup dumplings, tender honey-glazed barbecue pork, salt-and-pepper tofu fritters, and an excellent mushroom rice-noodle roll. Skip the steamed pork buns and opt for the fluffy baked ones—their crisp, slightly sweet, and very unique topping is a real highlight.

Kiss

Japanese X

D4

1700 Laguna St. (at Sutter St.)

Phone: 415-474-2866
Web: N/A
Prices: $$$

Dinner Wed – Sat

In a sea of trendy and flashy Japanese restaurants, this mom-and-pop standby sometimes gets drowned out—but one taste of its top-quality fish will have you hooked for life. Traditional nigiri, ranging from giant clam and halibut to bluefin tuna, arrives minimally dressed and served atop excellent rice. Appealing non-sushi options include a delicate *chawan mushi* filled with flaky white fish and buttery ginkgo berries, with an umami-rich dashi.

Adjacent to Japantown's Peace Plaza, tiny Kiss is easy to miss (look for the sign on the door), and reservations are recommended. Expect a quiet, sparse, and decorous atmosphere, with polite service from the husband-and-wife owners. The contemplative vibe encourages savoring each delicious morsel.

Mamacita

B2

Mexican 𝗫𝗫

2317 Chestnut St. (bet. Divisadero & Scott Sts.)

Phone: 415-346-8494   Dinner nightly
Web: www.mamacitasf.com
Prices: $$

An eclectic mix of young families, stylish hipsters, and see-and-be-seen Marinaites may pack its tables, but this hot ticket has more to offer than looks alone. The talented kitchen's creative takes on Mexican flavors are always on-point, from shrimp "al pastor" tacos with a sweet-spicy apple-mango salsa, to *molotes*, masa fritters oozing a delectable mixture of smoky ground beef and Monterey Jack cheese; as well as *esquites*, chile-inflected roasted corn with *cotija* and *crema*. Mamacita's food is deeply flavorful, varied, and made for sharing (but you'll want to make a reservation if you bring a big group, because just about everyone has the same idea). Stuck with a wait? Head to the front bar for a tasty mezcal cocktail or three to help ease the sting.

Sociale

A4

Italian 𝗫𝗫

3665 Sacramento St. (bet. Locust & Spruce Sts.)

Phone: 415-921-3200   Lunch Tue – Sat
Web: www.sfsociale.com   Dinner Mon – Sat
Prices: $$

Italian in name but Californian in spirit, Sociale is a go-to for comfort fare that blends the best of both worlds. Creamy burrata is served over pumpkin purée and garnished with pepitas and pecans, while braised pork belly with a wine sauce melts in the mouth. Dessert is a must; you'll be hard-pressed to find a table that can resist ordering the signature chocolate oblivion cake, a sinfully rich ganache accented with olive oil, sea salt, and amaretti cookie crumble.
Located at the end of an alley with a quiet heated patio, the vibe here is bistro-chic, with a hint of European flair accented by the warm, accommodating staff and the Italian and French chanteuses on the playlist. It's the kind of neighborhood gem that everyone wishes they had on their block.

Nico ❀

Contemporary 🍴🍴

B3

3228 Sacramento St. (bet. Lyon St. & Presidio Ave.)

Phone:	415-359-1000	Dinner Tue – Sat
Web:	www.nicosf.com	
Prices:	$$	

Pacific Heights is a dreamy little pocket of San Francisco, with its colorful Victorians and sweeping views of the Bay. It's one of those magical places that linger in the memory, and now the area has yet another reason to remember it by: the lovely, urbane Nico—a relaxed and sophisticated French bistro with a distinctly Californian vibe.

The space houses only a 40-seat restaurant and a small bar area, but feels wonderfully expansive with its high ceilings, gleaming glass windows, seats overlooking Sacramento Street, and intimate tables with a view of the glass-enclosed kitchen in the back.

Diners at Nico can choose between a three- or five-course dinner, listed off a menu that notes only the main ingredients. Co-owners Nicolas and Andrea Delaroque are essentially asking you to play a trust game—and you should not hesitate to jump. Razor-thin slices of crispy artichoke arrive fanned over cool green herb jus and topped with delicious minced escargot; while a dish of wildly fresh peas finds perfect pairing in basil, peaches and sweet ricotta. Tender seared duck breast, duck confit roulade, and duck liver mousse are plated with *lentilles du Puy*, fresh cabbage, and roasted hedgehog mushrooms for an earthy finish.

Octavia ✿

D3   Californian ✖✖

1701 Octavia St. (at Bush St.)

Phone: 415-408-7507   Dinner Tue – Sun
Web: www.octavia-sf.com
Prices: $$$

Chef/owner Melissa Perello, already a local culinary personality with Frances, shines even brighter at this new sequel in the tony Lower Pacific Heights neighborhood. Packed with a dynamic and diverse group of diners, the airy and open space is designed with a minimalist-chic eye, from the white-tiled kitchen to those raw-wood benches lined with wool-encased pillows. Service is enthusiastic and genuinely hospitable.

Chef Perello has a gift for elevating straightforward dishes through the use of pristine ingredients and technique, and her magic is in full force here with dishes like golden saffron fettuccine twirled with caramelized garlic, wilted fennel, and roasted tomatoes. Luscious roasted King salmon with fingerling potatoes in a dill-infused crème fraîche sauce may seem basic, but in her hands, it's anything but. Even a simple grilled toast, with warm, creamy house-made ricotta and charred spring onion, is revelatory.

At Octavia, the golden touch extends to the exquisite desserts, which might include a nectarine "float" with nectarine ice cream and soda, mint, and lavender, and the thoughtful wine list brims with unusual options. With food and furnishings this captivating, tables fill early, so be sure to reserve well in advance.

SPQR ⁂

Italian XX

C4

1911 Fillmore St. (bet. Bush & Pine Sts.)

Phone: 415-771-7779
Web: www.spqrsf.com
Prices: $$$

Lunch Sat – Sun
Dinner nightly

Pleasant and homey with excellent Italian cooking, there is little wonder why this destination is always bustling. Book in advance and assume that the dining counter reserved for walk-ins is already overflowing for the night. The space itself is narrow with tightly packed wood tables and furnishings; it would seem cramped were it not for the soaring ceiling, skylights, and open kitchen to brighten the mood. This is a place where passion and enthusiasm for Italian specialties are palpable—even contagious.

From *piccolo* (snacks) to *dolce*, the extensive menu evolves with the seasons, yet remains consistently good. Memorable pastas may include forest mushroom-stuffed *francobolli* ravioli tossed with more mushrooms and dark Umbrian lentils beneath a melting layer of espresso BellaVitano. Follow this with a tasting of goat, perhaps including fennel-infused sausage, roasted rib chops, and an exceptional roulade of smoked belly meat served with jammy-sweet quince saba, caramelized cippolini, bok choy, and quince *mostarda*.

Desserts may seem unassuming but are beautifully composed, like the persimmon torta with torched marshmallow, walnut-praline powder, and caramel ice cream.

Spruce ☙

Californian XX

3640 Sacramento St. (bet. Locust & Spruce Sts.)

Phone: 415-931-5100
Web: www.sprucesf.com
Prices: $$$

Lunch Mon – Fri
Dinner nightly

Set in one of San Francisco's snazziest neighborhoods, Spruce draws a regular crowd of wealthy retirees and corporate types by day; evening brings couples out for date night. The dining room is masculine yet modern, with velvet banquettes, studded leather chairs, and splashes of charcoal and chocolate. A small front café serves coffee and pastries, while the marble bar lures happy-hour crowds for a lengthy choice of cocktails or glass of wine from their extensive global list.

Micro-seasonal and delightfully Californian, Spruce's cuisine spotlights Mediterranean cooking that is at once simple and undeniably elegant. Rustic and homey starters may include a savory turkey soup stocked with thick, toothsome strands of tagliatelle, sliced carrots, and tender white meat. Pan-roasted black cod begins as a beautifully seared skin-on fillet, which is then topped with smoked cherry tomatoes and plump borlotti beans, further elevated with a quenelle of basil pesto and fresh herb leaves.

For dessert, miniature vanilla bean-speckled panna cotta is artistically plated alongside a swipe of silky crémeux infused with Kaffir lime, a neat scoop of blood orange sorbet, granola, and pomegranate arils.

Viva Goa

Indian ✗

B2

2420 Lombard St. (bet. Divisadero & Scott Sts.)

Phone: 415-440-2600
Web: www.vivagoaindiancuisine.com
Prices: 💰💰

Lunch & dinner daily

The Portuguese-influenced cuisine of Goa typically gets less play in the States than that of its northern neighbors. But Goan food takes center stage in this sparse, low-key dining room decked with burgundy booths. The kitchen is skilled at preparing delicious dishes like a spicy bronzed curry with prawns and coconut milk or *channa xacutti*, a creamy concoction of chickpeas, fresh coconut, onion, carrot, and poppy seeds.

The less adventurous can opt for more familiar Indian items like crisp, golden-brown samosas filled with potato and peas, and chewy, smoky naan studded with garlic and fresh cilantro. Takeout and delivery are the core of the restaurant's dinner business, so those in search of a lively scene might prefer the crowd-drawing (and budget-friendly) lunch buffet.

Bib Gourmand 😊
indicates our inspectors'
favorites for good value.

Mission

It's like the sun never goes down in the Mission, a bohemian paradise dotted with palm trees and doted on by scores of artists, activists, and a thriving Hispanic community. Here, urban life is illustrated through graffiti murals decorating the walls of funky galleries, thrift shops, and indie bookstores. Sidewalk stands burst with fresh plantains, nopales, and the juiciest limes this side of the border. Mission markets are known to be among the best in town and include **La Palma Mexicatessen** teeming with homemade *papusas*, chips, and fresh cheeses. **Lucca Ravioli** is loved for its legion of imported Italian goods; and the petite grocer, **Bi-Rite**, is big on prepared foods and fresh flowers. Across the street, **Bi-Rite Creamery** is a cult favorite for ice cream. Moving on from markets to hip coffee haunts, **Ritual Coffee Roasters** is the leader of the pack. Join their fan base in single file outside the door, order a special roast from the barista, and find yourself thoroughly in awe of this pleasing, very potent berry. Coffee connoisseurs also pay their respects at the original **Philz Coffee** for fresh brews that cannot be beat.

CLASSIC MEETS CUTTING-EDGE

The Mission is home to many contemporary hangouts, although those bargain *mercados* and dollar stores might suggest otherwise. **Dynamo Donuts** over on 24th Street is a dreamy retreat for these fried and sugary parcels of dough, complete with delectable flavors such as lemon-buttermilk and chocolate-star anise. **Walzwerk** charms with East German kitsch and is the go-to spot for traditional delights; while carb fiends know to stop by **The Sandwich Place** for freshly baked bread loaded with flavorful fillings. Here in the Mission, pizza reigns supreme and thin-crust lovers are happy to wait in line at **Pizzeria Delfina** for wickedly good slices with crisped edges. A destination in its own right, **Tartine Bakery's** exceptional breads, pastries, and pressed sandwiches are arguably unmissable. However, to best experience this region's range of culinary talents, forgo the table and chairs and pull up at a curb on Linda Street, where a vigilant street food scene is brimming with a wealth of international eats.

DAYTIME DELIGHTS

The city's hottest 'hood also offers a cool range of sweets. A banana split is downright retro-licious when served at the Formica counter of 90-year-old **St. Francis Fountain**, whose sundaes are made with Mitchell's Ice Cream, famous since 1953. Modish flavors like grasshopper pie and Kahlua mocha cream are in regular rotation at the newer **Humphrey Slocombe**; while **Mission Pie** is another local gem that tempts with a spectrum of pies—both sweet and savory. For more bold plates, **Plow** in Potrero Hill is a top breakfast and brunch hit. The space is small but insanely popular, so expect to wait a while before your first bite of lemon-ricotta pancake—there's even a menu for the little "plowers" who arrive by stroller. At lunch head to Peru by way of abuela-approved **Cholo Soy** for authentic, homemade, and always-affordable fare. **La Taqueria**'s carne asada burrito is arguably the most decadent around, but when it comes to tacos, it's a tossup on whether **El Gallo Giro** or **El Tonayense** takes the title for best truck in town.

NIGHT BITES

The **Monk's Kettle** brags a beer list beyond par, with over 200 rotating craft brews on their carte. But, if cocktails are what you crave, then dash over to **Trick Dog** for tantalizing concoctions and creative small plates. Sate a late-night appetite at **Pig & Pie**, offering an array of tasty eats including daily desserts, before dancing off these indulgences on Salsa Sunday at **El Rio**, the dive bar with a bustling back patio. Growling stomachs seem game to brave the harsh lighting at the many taquerias around, including **Cancún** for a veggie burrito or **El Farolito** for mind-blowing meats.

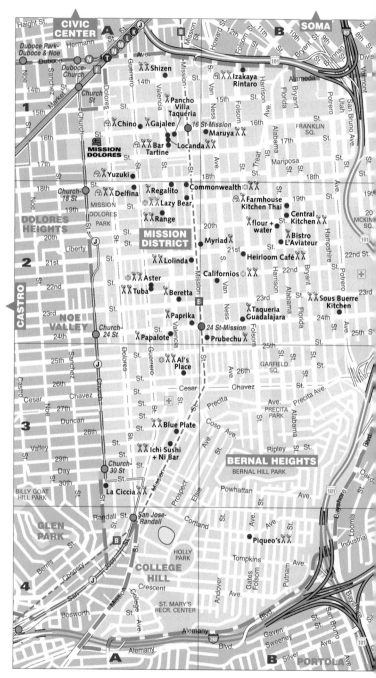

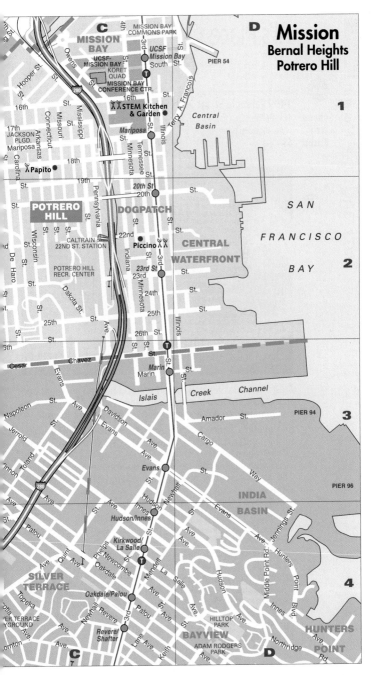

Mission
Bernal Heights
Potrero Hill

C   D

D 1

MISSION BAY COMMONS PARK

MISSION BAY

UCSF Mission Bay South St.

PIER 54

Hooper St.

Owens

UCSF-MISSION BAY
KORET QUAD

MISSION BAY CONFERENCE CTR.

16th St.

16th St.

Central Basin

STEM Kitchen & Garden

Mariposa St.

17th JACKSON PLGD.
Mariposa

Papito

18th St.

SAN

19th

20th St.
20th

FRANCISCO

POTRERO HILL

DOGPATCH

St.

BAY

CALTRAIN 22ND ST. STATION

22nd

CENTRAL

Piccino

POTRERO HILL RECR. CENTER

23rd St
23rd

WATERFRONT

2

24th St.

25th St.

26th St.

St.

Cesar

Chavez

Marin
Marin

St.

PIER 94

Islais

Creek

Channel

Napoleon St.

Davidson

Amador

St.

Jerrold

Evans

Cargo

Way

PIER 96

Evans
St.

Hudson

Innes

INDIA

Hudson/Innes

BASIN

Evans

Kirkwood/La Salle

SILVER TERRACE

Oakdale/Palou

HILLTOP PARK

4

ER TERRACE YGROUND

Revere/Shafter

BAYVIEW

HUNTERS

ADAM RODGERS PARK

POINT

C   D

Al's Place ❀

Californian ✕✕

1499 Valencia St. (at 26th St.)

Phone: 415-416-6136

Web: www.alsplacesf.com

Prices: $$

Dinner Wed – Sun

Fresh, seasonal vegetables and seafood headline this fantastic new Mission District restaurant, where Chef Aaron London has managed to deftly recast proteins in a supporting role.

Straddling a sunny corner, Al's Place sports a bright blue façade and a kind of cheery, seaside, and retro-chic interior where tables are set with kitchen towel napkins and pendant lights glint against the natural light flooding into every corner. The service staff is friendly and attentive, but delightfully unfussy.

The restaurant's mix-and-match menu is easily shared, and dishes are light, incredibly flavorful and informal in all the right ways. Chef London combines thought-provoking flavors (think sunchoke with black lime) with ease, layering dimensions you didn't know existed. A soft and creamy plate of burrata finds its match in a coat of crunchy potato chips, and is plated with nutty potato skin mousse, grilled young asparagus, currant *soffritto*, and Miner's lettuce; while *tonarelli* is paired with vibrant green garlic purée, citrusy bergamot and briny, grated *bottarga*. For dessert, don't miss the buttery Meyer lemon tart, studded with sweet strawberries and served with creamy lavender ice cream.

Aster ✿

Californian

A2

1001 Guerrero St. (at 22nd St.)

Dinner nightly

Phone: 415-875-9810
Web: www.astersf.com
Prices: $$$

Fine dining SF-style means hip soundtracks, spare spaces, and going to dinner in jeans, but this newcomer makes all of those trappings seem cool, never forced. Set in a quiet, residential corridor of the Mission, Aster's caramel-colored banquettes, wood tabletops, and strands of LED lights make for a studied, yet casual vibe. This is the kind of place where even the attentive, hospitable service manages to feel laid-back, but getting in will require some effort—if you can't score a reservation, line up early to snag a walk-in table.

Start with an aperitif as you peruse Chef Brett Cooper's elegant menu, which deftly interplays sweet, tangy, earthy, and salty elements in dishes like blanched asparagus with egg yolk, grilled spring onions, and shreds of ham hock. Packets of black cod, wrapped in chard leaves and steamed until tender, arrive in a complex, smoky bone broth, while deliriously rich pork head croquettes are balanced by a zippy arugula salad with blood orange *kosho.*

Aster's light food makes it easy to save room for the excellent desserts, including a decadent and refreshing beet-and-blood orange crémeux, or a raspberry meringue with just a hint of Sichuan peppercorn.

Bar Tartine 😊

A1

561 Valencia St. (bet. 16th & 17th Sts.)

Phone: 415-487-1600
Web: www.bartartine.com
Prices: **$$**

Lunch Sat – Sun
Dinner nightly

A little bit Eastern European, a little bit Californian, and a whole lot of delicious, this is a favorite among local gourmets. Now chef-owned and with an impending name change, the intensely satisfying menu continues to sate with everything from falafel-like sprouted lentil fritters with kefir and beet sauce, to roasted carrots with sumac yogurt and sunflower tahini. Wood-smoked, flash-fried potatoes, served with earthy black garlic aïoli and an herb salad, are unmissable.

The hearty, homey vibe extends to the rustic dining room, with well-worn floors and simple wood furnishings, as well as the gracious staff, who makes diners feel right at home. Be sure to sample the tasting menu, which shows promise of great things to come, along with a house-made soda, tea, or creative cocktail.

Beretta

A2

1199 Valencia St. (at 23rd St.)

Phone: 415-695-1199
Web: www.berettasf.com
Prices: **$$**

Lunch Sat – Sun
Dinner nightly

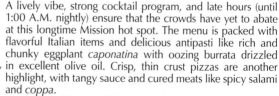

A lively vibe, strong cocktail program, and late hours (until 1:00 A.M. nightly) ensure that the crowds have yet to abate at this longtime Mission hot spot. The menu is packed with flavorful Italian items and delicious antipasti like rich and chunky eggplant *caponatina* with oozing burrata drizzled in excellent olive oil. Crisp, thin crust pizzas are another highlight, with tangy sauce and cured meats like spicy salami and *coppa*.

A handful of booths offer a more private experience, while a large communal table serves the walk-in crowd. Whether you're spending an evening amid the glow of Edison bulbs and the clink of cocktail shakers or munching on a brunch-time pizza carbonara at a sunny outdoor table, you'll exit both sated and energized.

Bistro L'Aviateur

Mediterranean ✗

B2

2850 21st St. (at Alabama St.)

Phone: 415-757-0270   Lunch Tue – Sun
Web: N/A
Prices: $$

Touch down for a meal at this family-run Mission newcomer. Though it boasts a veritable collection of aviation-related décor (think chrome propellers and model airplanes), L'Aviateur is no hobbyist's shop. With vases of fresh flowers, chalkboard menus, and big front windows offering prime people-watching, it gives off the feel of a cozy neighborhood café.

Depending on how you order from the Mediterranean-inspired menu, your palate could land in North Africa (piquant Tunisian lamb couscous), Burgundy (rich bœuf bourguignon), or Basque country (garlicky, herbaceous ratatouille and tender stewed chicken and sausage over buttery rice). But no matter how far-flung your journey, this is the kind of comforting fare that will make you feel right at home.

Blue Plate

American ✗✗

A3

3218 Mission St. (bet. 29th & Valencia Sts.)

Phone: 415-282-6777   Dinner nightly
Web: www.blueplatesf.com
Prices: $$

Wedged between the Mission and Bernal Heights, this casual and quirky charmer is constructed from reclaimed and repurposed materials all dripping with local art. This draws a relaxed and funky crowd for comfort-food favorites. Dig into a vibrant heirloom-tomato salad with wedges of ripe peaches, sourdough, and creamy pecorino vinaigrette. Move on to slow-cooked pork belly with a smoked oyster-Thousand Island sauce and velvety soft-cooked egg.

The American menu shifts with the seasons, but a few dishes are constants, like the blue-plate meatloaf or fried chicken with cornbread. At nightfall, large groups and couples pack this long and narrow space to share slices of tangy key lime pie. Warm up from the winter chill at tables near the vibrant open kitchen.

Californios ✿

Fusion 🍴🍴

3115 22nd St. (bet. Capp St. & Van Ness Ave.)

Phone:	415-757-0994
Web:	www.californiossf.com
Prices:	**$$$$**

Dinner Tue – Sat

In contrast to the bohemian posture of its neighborhood, this sterling debut by Chef Val M. Cantu is a luxurious oasis. A gleaming open kitchen and burnt caramel-hued banquettes pop against the dark lacquered walls, while sparkling chandeliers and shelves of cooking and design books further punctuate the upscale look of this intimate room. You'll feel as though you're dining in a chef's private atelier, complete with a polished, professional, and tight-knit staff that delivers truly impressive service.

While the feast set forth by Chef Cantu is inspired by Mexican flavors, it is modern Californian at its foundation. Produce plucked from nearby farms are transformed into stimulating bites to begin this tasting menu; highlights from which have included delicious interpretations of *menudo* featuring fresh raw hamachi slices doused with a succulent tripe broth; and *esquites* that top a creamy sweet corn pudding with charred kernels and decadent Santa Barbara uni. Fourteen-day dry-aged Wagyu ribeye cap is grilled over the *binchotan* and served with charred onion, dabs of avocado purée, tomatillo salsa, as well as puffy, griddled sourdough tortillas.

And for dessert, if the sound of foie gras-and-coffee ice cream drizzled with *cajeta* seems crazy, just trust us—it's brilliant.

Central Kitchen

Californian ✗✗

B2

3000 20th St. (at Florida St.)

Phone: 415-826-7004	Lunch Sun
Web: www.centralkitchensf.com	Dinner nightly
Prices: $$$	

A chic and sleek crowd of hip Mission foodies gathers at this trendy restaurant, nestled in a complex beside sister shop/deli Salumeria, cocktail bar Trick Dog, and coffee shop Sightglass. Wend your way to the central courtyard, with a trickling fountain and large glass doors leading into the main space, where a large open kitchen faces the simple wood tables.

Select inventive dishes à la carte, or opt for a five- or six-course tasting menu. Along the way, you might taste seared tuna topped with earthy matsutake mushrooms and a silky avocado purée, or hen roulade with confit radishes and *puntarelle*. Their delicious desserts—maybe white chocolate with kiwi and nasturtiums or strawberries and fennel with black-garlic ice cream—are compelling.

Chino

Asian ✗

A1

3198 16th St. (at Guerrero St.)

Phone: 415-552-5771	Lunch Sat – Sun
Web: www.chinosf.com	Dinner nightly
Prices: 🥜	

Pan-Asian dining comes to this hip district thanks to the team behind Tacolicious. Loud music fills this fun corner, along with colorful pops of avocado-green tile, turquoise booths, and pastel paper lanterns.

After ordering, a caddy of house-made chili garlic and spicy mustard sauces is brought to the table, so be prepared to dip, slather, and spice your own way to bliss once the scrumptious plates arrive. Yuba is presented as a salad of slender strips tossed with pickled shiitakes and cilantro-ginger spiked salsa verde. Skewers of lamb are served hot off the grill, appetizingly charred and seasoned with a hit of chili and cumin. Tasty *bao de chicharrón* arrive stuffed with crispy pork belly, avocado, pickled onion, cilantro, and spicy aïoli.

Commonwealth ✿

Contemporary ✗✗

2224 Mission St. (bet. 18th & 19th Sts.)

Phone: 415-355-1500   Dinner nightly
Web: www.commonwealthsf.com
Prices: $$$

&

Welcome to this cool food-cum-tech heaven, appropriately set in the heart of the Mission District. Inside, the dining room nails that Nordic-Cali sensibility with sleek filament light bulbs, bare wood, and frosted glass that allows sun but shields guests from the bustling (read gritty) surrounds. The hospitable team of servers shares that same informal style. And their long counter is the absolute best place to drink, dine, and chill with a few friends.

À la carte offerings are a welcome alternative to the fixed menu, and light portions encourage ordering four or more courses. The full tasting though lets guests thoroughly explore the kitchen's adept contemporary cooking. However, this meal may not be for everyone as the chefs' creativity can be more eclectic than crowd-pleasing.

Begin with a lush, layered presentation of decadent sea urchin with creamy cauliflower pudding, fennel, and trace of popcorn powder and kale juice. Then remarkably tender pork cheeks are infused with wood smoke and served with Brussels sprout leaves, shaved apple, and crisp daikon in a fermented chili-miso broth. Desserts are far out yet technically superb, as in the salty-sweet boilermaker of beer meringue with sweet chocolate ganache, salty pretzel crumble, and crème fraîche ice cream.

Delfina 😊

Italian ✗✗

A2

3621 18th St. (bet. Dolores & Guerrero Sts.)

Phone: 415-552-4055   Dinner nightly
Web: www.delfinasf.com
Prices: $$

♿ One of the city's greats for rustic Italian meals, Delfina is nestled on a block of gems for food lovers including Bi-Rite (and its creamery), Tartine Bakery, and sister spot Pizzeria Delfina. But even with this rarefied competition, Delfina books up well in advance and draws lines for its few walk-in seats.

The simple, yet lively dining room is attended to by a warm staff, and the bill of fare shifts with the seasons. Soul-satisfying dishes include house-made *fazzoletti* with garlicky basil pesto, tender potatoes, and crisp green beans, as well as a perfectly roasted half-chicken in a richly caramelized jus. For dessert, one spoonful of the creamy, delicate fig-leaf panna cotta, accented by macerated *pluots*, will have you floating home on a cloud.

Farmhouse Kitchen Thai 😊

Thai ✗

B2

710 Florida St. (bet. 19th & 20th Sts.)

Phone: 415-814-2920   Lunch & dinner daily
Web: www.farmhousesf.com
Prices: $$

♿ For authentic Thai flavors in a lively space, this Mission neophyte is hard to beat—and already has a dedicated following among the young techies and families who reside in the neighboring industrial lofts. Adorned with an accent wall covered in red and gold faucets and planter boxes full of Thai herbs, it's the kind of affordable weeknight spot that's designed for repeat business.

The array of classic dishes is prepared with quality ingredients, from the marinated flank steak rolled around crisp cucumber, cilantro and mint to the smoky coconut- and turmeric-marinated barbecue chicken with papaya salad and black sticky rice. A menu must: the herbal rice salad, a multidimensional blend of green mango, dried shrimp, chili, long beans, and much more.

flour + water

B2

Italian ✗

2401 Harrison St. (at 20th St.)

Phone: 415-826-7000   Dinner nightly
Web: www.flourandwater.com
Prices: $$

As the name implies, two ingredients create a world of possibilities at this always-packed Mission hot spot. Neapolitan pizzas and handmade pastas (like al dente *garganelli* with whole-grain mustard and braised pork) will have you sighing after each bite, and a new selection of more traditional mains (such as seared duck breast with chanterelles and pecorino-dusted charred Brussels sprouts), scores every bit as big as the noodles and pies.

Laid-back service, up-to-the-moment music, and a buzzy, effervescent vibe make flour + water the epitome of California cool. Throw in a glass of their refined Italian wine along with an alluring dessert like the salted caramel apple tart, and you can see why getting a table here is well worth the challenge.

Gajalee

A1

Indian ✗

525 Valencia St. (bet. 16th & 17th Sts.)

Phone: 415-552-9000   Lunch & dinner daily
Web: www.gajalee.net
Prices: $$

Don't let the neon signs out front color your opinion of Gajalee, whose dining room is a bright, cheery vision of yellow walls and colorful murals. Snag a window seat for great people-watching on one of Valencia Street's most bustling corners, and settle in for a South Indian feast.

Though the creations at this temple of seafood-centric cuisine may not appear lavish, they're heavy on traditional flavor and ingredients (think creamy, coconut-enriched curries and delicate spices). Portions are generous, as in the fish *Malvani*, a brick-red, roasted coconut-based sauce infused with a mélange of spices, or the *Varan dhal*, a spice-speckled, lushly textured lentil stew. For a light dessert, the meltingly sweet *gulab jamun* is just the ticket.

Heirloom Café

Californian ✖✖

B2

2500 Folsom St. (at 21st St.)

Phone: 415-821-2500   Dinner Mon – Sat
Web: www.heirloom-sf.com
Prices: $$$

Though a nice selection of European vintages is a boon to this charming bistro housed in a quiet corner of the Mission, the delicate and seasonal food keeps it bustling. Fresh and elegant Mediterranean-leaning dishes are pure expressions of California's bounty. Sample the likes of seared scallops on a bed of fava beans and frisée with minced bacon and shallot-butter; or pan-roasted cod with cauliflower purée, English peas, and ramps. Simple desserts display a gentle touch, as in the polenta cake with macerated strawberries and tarragon cream.

The dining room features communal tables, a marble counter with a close-up view of the open kitchen, whitewashed walls plastered with European wine labels, warm candlelight, and even warmer service.

Ichi Sushi + Ni Bar

Japanese ✖✖

A3

3282 Mission St. (bet. 29th & Valencia Sts.)

Phone: 415-525-4750   Dinner Mon – Sat
Web: www.ichisushi.com
Prices: $$$

Gone are the days when dining here was marred by the memory of how hard it was to score a table—this new space down the street is much bigger than the previous spot, now Ichi Kakiya Oyster Bar. Relaxed and casual, with a big, fun mural on one wall, it's an über-busy smash among tech types and hipsters. Hit the central sushi bar for nigiri, or opt for *izakaya* dishes and sake (but no sushi) at adjacent Ni Bar.

The cognoscenti opt for the omakase, which might kick off with oysters garnished with yuzu juice and bits of caviar, followed by piping hot grilled skewers of tender and juicy miso-glazed pork. The nigiri pack punches of flavor from *yuzu kosho* or ponzu sauces and unique garnishes. The fish (maybe sea bream, Hokkaido scallops, ocean trout, or uni) are always fresh and delicious.

Izakaya Rintaro 😊

Japanese ✗✗

82 14th St. (bet. Folsom & Trainor Sts.)

Phone: 415-589-7022   Dinner Mon – Sat
Web: www.izakayarintaro.com
Prices: $$

Delicate *izakaya* cuisine with a produce-centric NorCal sensibility awaits at this Japanese newcomer, which transforms even the most humble dishes into art. Freshly made soft tofu is infused with fragrant bergamot peel, while meaty king trumpet mushrooms join classic chicken thighs and tender *tsukune* on the menu of smoky, caramelized charcoal-grilled skewers. The blancmange, infused with white sesame and topped with sweet black soybeans, is particularly unmissable. Housed in the former Chez Spencer, which was destroyed in a fire, Rintaro has kept its predecessor's gorgeous (and charred) arched ceiling beams, but added a delicate, wood-framed bar and booths. The result is a serene environment perfect for sharing and sampling the exquisite food.

La Ciccia

Italian ✗✗

291 30th St. (at Church St.)

Phone: 415-550-8114   Dinner Tue – Sat
Web: www.laciccia.com
Prices: $$

Sardinian cuisine takes the spotlight at this family-run charmer, which draws a loyal crowd of Noe Valley regulars—particularly parents on a well-earned date night. The intimate, dark green dining room is always full, and nestled right up against the kitchen, from which the chef regularly pops out to greet guests in a blend of Italianenglish.
Start with the house-made bread and the home-cured *salumi* of the day (think citron-studded mortadella). The pasta *longa* with cured tuna heart slivers twirls fresh, delicious linguini with sea urchin and tomato, and an entrée of stewed goat is gamey but tender, served alongside braised cabbage, black olives, and fried capers. For a pleasant conclusion, cap it all off with the fluffy and airy ricotta-saffron cake.

Lazy Bear ✿

Contemporary ✗✗

A2

3416 19th St. (bet. Mission & San Carlos Sts.)

Phone:	415-874-9921	Dinner Tue – Sat
Web:	www.lazybearsf.com	
Prices:	**$$$$**	

Communal dining is the name of the game at this white-hot restaurant. Billed as a fine dining dinner party, Lazy Bear is an underground phenom "gone legit," meaning your average Joe can now score a seat. That is, if they can jump through a few hoops: you'll need to buy a ticket in advance, and once you do, you'll be e-mailed a list of house rules you should read in earnest.

Fortunately, this hip hottie delivers. The nightly tasting menu is dished out in a cool, bi-level warehouse and starts with aperitifs served alongside small bites upstairs in the loft, before moving downstairs to a dining room that boasts two giant tree slabs as communal tables, each lined with 20 chairs.

Diners are given a pamphlet with the menu (there's space for note-taking underneath) and are invited to walk into the kitchen to chat with the cooks themselves. The young crowd loves this kind of chef worship, and digging into David Barzelay's luscious fare, we're inclined to agree. A saffron dish of creamy Anson Mills grits arrives with fresh lobster, pickled chard, Tokyo turnips, and prawn roe crisps; while tender caramelized squab is paired with lightly roasted sweet pear, a reduced jus, and crushed spices for dipping.

Locanda

A1

557 Valencia St. (bet. 16th & 17th Sts.)

Phone: 415-863-6800   Dinner nightly
Web: www.locandasf.com
Prices: $$

This chic Roman-style *osteria* packs in the hipsters with a lively scene, killer cocktails, and inspired pastas, like radiatore tossed in tomato-lamb ragù with pecorino and hints of fresh mint. None of this is surprising, considering Locanda is from the team behind Mission favorite, Delfina. Classic chicken under a brick is characteristically on-point: smoky, tender, and served with a squeeze of lemon over nutty farro, Umbrian lentils, and red quinoa salad.

Reservations here are a tough ticket, but the attire and vibe are casual and welcoming (if noisy). Can't get a table? Seats at the bar, where the full menu is served, are a solid backup. Locanda's ultra-central address makes parking a challenge, so plan on using the valet or allotting extra time.

Lolinda

A2

2518 Mission St. (bet. 21st & 22nd Sts.)

Phone: 415-550-6970   Dinner nightly
Web: www.lolindasf.com
Prices: $$

Equal parts contemporary steakhouse and small plates spot, Argentine-inspired Lolinda is fun and sexy, loaded with twenty- and thirty-somethings gabbing over cocktails and sips of malbec. The soaring dining room with its wagon-wheel chandeliers and tufted-leather banquettes leads to a bustling second-floor mezzanine; whereas El Techo, a heated and more casual roof deck, offers sweeping views of the skyline. Sharing is encouraged and groups can be found divvying up plates of silky ono ceviche, flaky chicken empanadas, or sweet, caramelized pork belly.

Bull sculptures and murals remind diners that the chargrilled steak or crosscut beef short ribs with *chimichurri* are must-orders—tender and smoky, they'll transport you to Buenos Aires in a flash.

Maruya

Japanese ✕✕

B1

2931 16th St. (bet. Mission St. & Van Ness Ave.)

Phone: 415-503-0702   Dinner Tue – Sat
Web: www.maruyasf.com
Prices: $$$$

A new team has brought a more easygoing vibe to this sushi restaurant. Housed in a petite space that used to be quiet enough to hear a pin drop, the sushi chefs now joke with customers; for the best service, be sure to request a seat at the central L-shaped counter. The traditional, minimalistic room, decorated with delicate wood, keeps the focus on the fish.

Maruya's increased flexibility extends to the menu as well, where traditional dishes like warm, house-made *chawan mushi*-style tofu or blanched asparagus gets punch from the addition of black truffle and blue cheese sauce, respectively. But in the end, it's all about the nigiri: warm, well-seasoned rice is a cushion for palate-pleasers like custardy uni, luxurious king salmon, and fatty tuna.

Myriad

International ✕

B2

2491 Mission St. (bet. 20th & 21st Sts.)

Phone: 415-525-4335   Lunch Sat – Sun
Web: www.myriadsf.com   Dinner nightly
Prices: $$

Not sure what to eat tonight? Bring your indecision and your appetite to this globe-trotting gastropub, which turns out skillfully prepared dishes from across cultures. Whether you're feeling like a dose of Moroccan (roasted lamb sandwich with tomato jam and feta), Mexican (*cochinita pibil*), French (farm toast with *fromage blanc* and roasted plums), Italian (ricotta *zeppole* with caramel sauce), or any combination of the above, there's a dish that's sure to satisfy. And, there's also a selection of beer and wine to match every delightful bite.

A new arrival to the Mission, Myriad sprawls over two long, narrow rooms, where hipster couples and families with kids trade bites of the shareable dishes. If you're paralyzed by choice, friendly servers are happy to lend a hand.

Pancho Villa Taqueria

A1

Mexican   ✗

3071 16th St. (bet. Mission & Valencia Sts.)

Phone: 415-864-8840   Lunch & dinner daily
Web: www.sfpanchovilla.com
Prices:

Around the corner from the 16th and Mission BART stop, this long-running taqueria earns high marks from locals. Upon entering, take a moment to step back and examine the menu board; the vested attendants working the flat-tops and grills will be quizzing you on the beans, condiments, and choice of ten meats you desire. That line moves quickly, so be ready. After loading up your burrito, perhaps filled with thinly sliced steak and butterflied prawns, select an *agua fresca* from the glass barrels, and hit the salsa bar. It features award-winning varieties in every range of heat and sweet to complement their thin, ultra-crispy tortilla chips. Ambience is nil and tables can be hard to snag, but the reward is a fresh and flavorful taste of the Mission.

Papalote

A2

Mexican   ✗

3409 24th St. (bet. Poplar & Valencia Sts.)

Phone: 415-970-8815   Lunch & dinner daily
Web: www.papalote-sf.com
Prices:

Head to this little standout for a lighter take on the gut-busting taqueria treats that define the Mission. Papalote manages to deliver the goods without the guilt, and the difference is clear in the outstanding fish tacos: corn tortillas piled with fresh, flaky white fish (sautéed in butter and garlic) along with sliced romaine and chopped tomato.

Unlike the competition, Papalote doesn't have a salsa bar, but it doesn't need one: its defining feature is its gobsmackingly good, house-made roasted tomato salsa, which you'll want to slather on dishes like the pitch-perfect breakfast burrito, stuffed with scrambled eggs, chorizo, cheese, and guacamole. The space and service are bare-bones, but with food this good, you won't care.

Papito

Mexican ✗

C1

317 Connecticut St. (at 18th St.)

Phone: 415-695-0147   Lunch & dinner daily
Web: www.papitosf.com
Prices: ⊜⊜

Owned by the team behind nearby Chez Maman, this taqueria has a French touch that complements its sunny, bistro-like environs on the slope of Potrero Hill. The colorful walls and tightly packed tables lead to a semi-open kitchen full of energy and movement, where servers may be snappy without ever sacrificing timely presentations.

Start with the zippy *ensalada* Papito, packed with avocado, crispy tortilla strips, and cilantro dressing. Then, dig into the giant mushroom quesadilla with Oaxaca cheese or crisp rock cod tacos with chipotle mayo and cabbage slaw. Well-crafted Mexican entrées, a flavorful salsa selection, and a fully-stocked bar further cement Papito's status as a neighborhood favorite spot for a quiet lunch or bustling dinner.

Paprika

Eastern European ✗

A2

3324 24th St. (bet. Bartlett & Mission Sts.)

Phone: 415-375-1477   Lunch Sat
Web: N/A   Dinner nightly
Prices: ⊜⊜

Diners who set foot into Paprika, named for one of the most essential spices in Eastern European cooking, should prepare to feel as if they've been transported to Prague. It's a simple, no-frills, cash-only kind of place, but cheerful service, affordable fare, and a vast selection of European draft beers make for a relaxed, enjoyable atmosphere.

The small menu manages to cover all the bases, from tender, well-seasoned pork goulash packed with sweet tomatoes, caramelized onions, garlic, and zippy paprika, to a smoky, blistered Polish kielbasa over creamy mashed potatoes and paprika-infused gravy (you'll want some bread to soak up every last drop of this). Snag a table at one of the bay windows, then settle in to enjoy your meal with a stein of beer, of course.

Piccino

Pizza XX

C2

1001 Minnesota St. (at 22nd St.)

Phone:	415-824-4224	Lunch & dinner Tue – Sun
Web:	www.piccinocafe.com	
Prices:	$$	

A progenitor of the increasingly hot Dogpatch restaurant scene, Piccino embodies the neighborhood's many flavors, drawing families with kids in tow, young tech types, gregarious retirees, and more. Its memorable yellow exterior houses a relaxed, artsy-urban interior with lots of wood and natural light, a perfect venue for unwinding with friends.

Everyone comes here for deliciously blistered pizzas like the *funghi*, with roasted mushroom duxelles, sautéed wild mushrooms, *stracchino*, and slivers of garlic. Though pizza is a focus, Piccino excels in appetizers like tender, skillfully prepared *polpette* in tomato sauce, and must-order desserts such as a delectable hazelnut-cocoa nib cake. Their adjacent coffee bar is an area favorite.

Piqueo's

Peruvian XX

B4

830 Cortland Ave. (at Gates St.)

Phone:	415-282-8812	Dinner nightly
Web:	www.piqueos.com	
Prices:	$$	

Gather your friends for a trip to Peru (with a layover in Bernal Heights) at Piqueo's, where the menu of flavor-packed small plates is built for sharing. From crispy yucca balls stuffed with cheese to tender pork adobo over mashed sweet potatoes, hearty palate-pleasers abound. Sauces are a house specialty; the tender beef empanada boasts a trio of garlicky *huacatay*, creamy *huancaina*, and spicy *rocoto*. And where else can you sample a quinoa-blueberry flan?

While not as glamorous as upscale sister La Costanera, Piqueo's has its own charm, thanks to a quaint atmosphere with wood floors and an open kitchen. It's a standby for Bernal families, who stroll over in the evenings to catch up with the friendly servers and dig into their favorite dishes.

Prubechu

Chamorro ✗

B2

2847 Mission St. (bet. 24th & 25th Sts.)

Phone: 415-952-3654   Dinner Tue – Sat
Web: N/A
Prices: $$

Owned by two natives of Guam, Prubechu is the only Bay Area restaurant that serves the island's Chamorro cuisine. It's a shoebox-sized space without a full kitchen, but the intrepid staff manages to turn out utterly unique, utterly delicious meals like none you've ever had.

Diners can choose between a tasting menu offering intricate Chamorro interpretations, or a small selection of homey, à la carte dishes. Either way, the results are thrilling, from a flavorful chicken sausage steamed with luscious coconut milk in a banana leaf, to umami-rich dried pork shoulder with nettle purée. The nutty, creamy toasted rice porridge with caramel soy and a tempura-battered soft-cooked egg is a standout, as is a gently sweet and caramelized banana donut.

Range

American ✗✗

A2

842 Valencia St. (bet. 19th & 20th Sts.)

Phone: 415-282-8283   Dinner nightly
Web: www.rangesf.com
Prices: $$

Owner Phil West has returned to cooking at this Mission standby, whose menu has veered away from contemporary flourishes and back into straightforward American comfort. The results are sturdy and satisfying: tender roast chicken practically melts into a lovely asparagus, walnut, and kumquat bread salad, while a luscious chocolate peanut butter mousse cake gets an added boost from rich salted caramel ice cream. The drinks at Range continue to be as notable as the eats, and diners who skip cocktail hour are missing out on smart concoctions like the rum-based Wolf Moon, which boasts spicy, nutty notes from chili liqueur and sherry. Loyal regulars continue to fill the small, contemporary dining room, whose low, wood-beamed ceilings make every meal cozy.

Regalito

A2

3481 18th St. (at Valencia St.)

Phone: 415-503-0650
Web: www.sfregalito.com
Prices: $$

Lunch Sat – Sun
Dinner Tue – Sun

Regalito is Spanish for "little gift," and those who dine here will surely understand the choice of name. Instead of relying on the bold, spicy approach of local taquerias, Regalito takes a milder, ingredient-focused path, infusing dishes like chicken enchiladas with new life via handmade corn tortillas, fresh roast chicken, and a delicate green chili sauce. Familiar Mexican favorites get an upgrade here, from the super-sweet, fresh corn on the cob *elote* with tangy chili-lime mayo and *cotija*, to that silky vanilla flan bobbing in a pool of caramel sauce.

The cheery, colorful space and friendly servers are welcoming, but the real charmers are those smiling cooks, who happily interact with diners in prime seats overlooking the open kitchen.

Shizen

A1

370 14th St. (at Stevenson St.)

Phone: 415-678-5767
Web: N/A
Prices: $$

Dinner nightly

At first glance, this stylish *izakaya* and sushi bar could be another in a line of similar places that dot the San Francisco landscape, were it not for a major twist: everything on the menu is vegan. Purists and die-hard carnivores may scoff, but the food is exceptional, skillfully manipulating vegetables and starches to recreate seafood-centric Japanese favorites.

Spicy tuna gets a run for its money from the impressive spicy *tofuna* rolls, with chili-inflected minced tofu and cucumber crowned with creamy avocado and dusted in chili "tobiko." A yuba salad with miso dressing and tempura-battered shiitake mushrooms stuffed with faux-crab are equally compelling. Throw in a sleek, contemporary setting, and Shizen is a winner for eaters of all stripes.

Sous Beurre Kitchen

French ✗✗

B2

2704 24th St. (bet. Hampshire St. & Potrero Ave.)

Phone: 415-874-9831   Dinner Mon – Sat
Web: www.sousbeurrekitchen.com
Prices: $$

Largely Hispanic 24th Street might seem like an odd place to find this captivating Cal-French rookie, but it's quickly distinguishing itself as a classy-yet-casual alternative to the taqueria grind. The European vibe extends to the dining room, decked with delicate mismatched china and vintage sconces, and tax and tip are included in the prices—so what you see is what you'll pay.

The name may suggest dishes swimming in butter, but Sous Beurre's food is actually light and delicate. Silky house-smoked trout comes with a bright salad of arugula, golden beets, and shaved fennel; and spelt is dressed up with spring asparagus, creamy shallot soubise, and mint. Even the strawberry beignets, served over warm sabayon, feel fresh, balanced, and never too heavy.

STEM Kitchen & Garden

Mediterranean ✗✗

C1

499 Illinois St. (bet. 16th & Mariposa Sts.)

Phone: 415-915-1000   Lunch Mon – Fri
Web: www.stemkitchensf.com   Dinner Mon – Sat
Prices: $$

Plenty of restaurants boast about their garden-fresh menus, but this Mission Bay freshman means business: most of its ingredients come straight from the raised garden beds on the rooftop patio, which also double as decorative elements. With its buzzing bocce courts and stunning fire-pit seating overlooking the Bay, it's already become a favorite among the staff at the nearby UCSF complexes.

Simple, delicious food is the order of the day. A salad of garden lettuces in Meyer lemon vinaigrette is delicate and bright, while a blistered pizza comes loaded with *broccoli de ciccio*, *guanciale*, and mozzarella. Piquant *berbere*-spiced chicken plays surprisingly well with a tangy kale Caesar, and the tart, creamy, unmissable Meyer lemon verrine is like spring in a glass.

Taqueria Guadalajara

Mexican ✗

B2

3146 24th St. (at Shotwell St.)

Phone: 415-642-4892 Lunch & dinner daily
Web: N/A
Prices: 🪙

At this Mission mainstay for Cal-Mex treats, regulars place their order at the counter, watch the action unfold in the open kitchen located just beyond, and then settle into a vibrant mural-walled dining room that charmingly evokes the countryside and its way of life. Clay roof tiles, and handmade wood and leather seats stick to the rustic, very quaint theme that locals seem to have grown so fond of.

Any item ordered "super" is usually heaped with cheese, sour cream, and fresh avocado. Case in point: a *pollo asado* burrito packed with Mexican rice, pinto beans, and smoky, tender grilled chicken. These may be meals in themselves, but other classics like *al pastor* and *chile verde* tacos, enchiladas, and fajitas continue to thrive as tried and true favorites.

Tuba

Turkish ✗✗

A2

1007 Guerrero St. (bet. 22nd & 23rd Sts.)

Phone: 415-826-8822 Lunch Sun
Web: www.tubarestaurant.com Dinner nightly
Prices: $$

In a city where Turkish dishes are too often folded into in an unsatisfying "pan-Middle Eastern" menu, this bona fide charmer bursts with authentic flavor, as evidenced by its sizable clientele of handsome expats. Tuba's space is warm and welcoming, with crimson walls, soft, romantic lighting, and a friendly staff.

Start with a selection of meze like *sigara boregi* (thin phyllo-dough pastries filled with potatoes and peppery feta) and moist, fluffy falafel. Then dive into a smoky ground beef kebab with spicy chopped bell peppers and zesty spices. Desserts like the *künefe*, a mild white cheese wrapped in phyllo, soaked in syrup, and topped with pistachios, are worth saving room for, especially with a strong Turkish coffee or intensely flavored tea.

Culinary Agents

Connecting the industry

Find the best jobs. Find the best people.

CulinaryAgents.com

Culinary Agents

Connecting the industry

Find the best jobs. Find the best people.

CulinaryAgents.com

Yuzuki 😊

Japanese ✗

A1

598 Guerrero St. (at 18th St.)

Dinner Wed – Mon

Phone: 415-556-9898
Web: www.yuzukisf.com
Prices: $$

Formerly an *izakaya*, this elegant Japanese restaurant has changed chefs and focus, offering delicate Washoku-style fare (read: no sushi). A meal might begin with thin slices of lightly torched mackerel, artfully arranged on shiso leaves; then transition to tender Wagyu beef *tataki*, airy shredded vegetable and shrimp tempura, and a delicate sundae of azuki beans, mocha, and kelp gelée over vanilla ice cream.

With Tartine Bakery and other great gourmet spots sharing its block, there's no denying the fact that Yuzuki has a lot of competition. But with such an exquisite array of plates, not to mention outstanding organic sake and nutty buckwheat tea for sipping, it will transport you to Japan—provided you can snag a tough-to-get reservation.

Red=Particularly Pleasant.
Look for the red ✗ couverts!

Nob Hill

Thanks in large part to its connection to the Gold Rush industry magnates, Nob Hill is San Francisco's most privileged neighborhood. Its many plush mansions, strategic location complete with breathtaking views of the Bay, and accessible cable car lines that chug up to the top, ensure that it remains home to the upper crust. Speaking of which, note the familiar tinkle from wind chimes and postcard-perfect brass rails checking tourists who dare to lean out and take in the sights. Despite the large scale devastation following the 1906 earthquake, this iconic part of town bordering the gorgeous Golden Gate Bridge and Alamo Square's "Painted Ladies" was able to retain its wealthy reputation thanks to an upswell of swanky hotels, door-manned buildings, and opulent dining rooms. Unsurprisingly, "Snob Hill" today continues to echo of mighty egos and wealthy families who can be seen making the rounds at **Big 4**, cradled within The Huntington Hotel. Named after the 1800s railroad titans, this stately hermitage is known for antique memorabilia and nostalgic chicken potpie. A stop at **Swan Oyster Depot** for some of the finest seafood in town is a sure way to impress your out-of-town, tourist-trapped friends, but be prepared to wait up to several hours on busy days for one of their coveted few seats.

Cocktails and small plates ensure epic levels of enjoyment at the extravagant **Top of the Mark** restaurant, boasting a sleek, lounge-like vibe and panoramic vistas of the sun setting over the cityscape. Moving from day to night, a handful of food-centric saloons fortuitously sate the tastes of young professionals with pennies to spare. At the top is **Cheese Plus**, showcasing over 300 international varieties, artisan charcuterie, and of course, chocolate for added decadence. Just steps away, **The Jug Shop** is an old-time, reliable, and very personable destination among locals who can be seen lapping up micro-brew beers and global wines. For a total departure, kick back with a Mai Tai (purportedly invented at Oakland's Trader Vic's in 1944) at **Tonga Room & Hurricane Bar**—a tiki spot in the *très* chic

Fairmont, decked out with an indoor swimming pool that also functions as a floating stage.

RUSSIAN HILL

Slightly downhill and north toward Polk Street, the vibe mellows on the approach to Russian Hill, named after a Russian cemetery that was unearthed up top. Chockablock with cute boutiques, dive bars, and casual eateries, this neighborhood's staircase-like streets are scattered with predominantly un-Russian groups and singles that seem more than willing to mingle. Good, affordable fare abounds here, at such popular haunts as **Caffé Sapore** serving breakfast specials, sandwiches, soups, and salads; as well as **Street** for fine, seasonal American cuisine. Tacky taqueria-turned-nighttime disco, **Nick's Crispy Tacos**, is a perennial favorite. The downright sinful and delicious

chocolate earthquake from **Swensen's Ice Cream**'s flagship parlor (in business since 1948) is undoubtedly the town's most treasured dessert. From flashy finds to tastefully decorated destinations, **Bacchus Wine Bar** is an elegant and ever-alluring Italian-style spot lauded for both its beautiful interiors and exceptional wine, beer, and sake selections.

CHINATOWN

Scattered with large parks—Huntington Park is perhaps the city's most coveted stretch of greenery—Nob Hill's scene begins to change as you venture east to the country's oldest **Chinatown**. Here, authentic markets, dim sum palaces, souvenir emporiums, banks, and other businesses, which employ scores of the immigrant community, spill down the eastern slope of the Hill in a wash of color and vibrant Chinese characters. Amid these steep streets find some of the city's most addictive and crave-worthy barbecue pork buns at old, almost antique dim sum houses where jam-packed dining

is the name of the game. Even gastronomes flock here to scour the shelves at family-owned and operated **Wok Shop**, bursting with unique cookware, linens, tools, and all things Asian. Others may prefer to avoid the elbow-to-elbow experience and take home a slice of Chinatown by way of juicy dumplings, buns, and sweets from **Good Mong Kok Bakery**. Soldier on from this excellent and inexpensive take-out spot only to spin out a sugar-rush over creamy, oven-fresh custard tarts at **Golden Gate Bakery**; or prophetic little samples in the making at **Golden Gate Fortune Cookie Factory**. The amazing and very affordable **House of Nanking** is another rare (read: necessary) pleasure. Don't bother ordering from the menu—the owner will usually grab them from your hands and take over the ordering. But really, nobody is complaining. Finally, the **Mid-Autumn Moon Festival** brings friends and families together over mooncakes—a traditional pastry stuffed with egg yolk and lotus seed paste—and to reflect upon summer's bounty.

Acquerello ✿ ✿

A2

1722 Sacramento St. (bet. Polk St. & Van Ness Ave.)

Phone: 415-567-5432
Web: www.acquerello.com
Prices: $$$$

Dinner Tue – Sat

With its air of old-world sophistication, Acquerello is the kind of establishment where one dresses for dinner, which is always an occasion. The room feels embellished yet comfortable, with vaulted wood-beamed ceilings, warm terra-cotta walls, and contemporary paintings. It's the kind of place where celebrants of a certain age are happy to splurge on a white truffle-tasting menu.

Each prix-fixe here promises expertise and finesse, with a carefully curated wine list to match. Count yourself lucky if your meal begins with a silky parmesan *budino* topped with micro-herbs and lettuces in vinaigrette, surrounded by fragrant pearls of black truffle gelée. Pastas must not be missed, such as the lobster-filled *raviolo* in smoked butter-lobster jus. Decadent *risotti* may arrive topped with Taleggio, velvety egg yolk, compressed radicchio and herbaceous nasturtium leaves to cut the richness. A perfectly pink duck breast with sunflower seed-huckleberry relish, Nantes carrots, and pink peppercorn-duck jus adds just the right note of rusticity.

Save room for one of the best *mignardises* carts you will ever encounter, stocked with superlative house-made chocolates, macarons, *pâtes de fruits*, and caramels.

aliment

American 🍴

B3

786 Bush St. (bet. Mason & Powell Sts.)

Phone: 415-829-2737   Dinner nightly
Web: www.alimentsf.com
Prices: $$

Named for the Latin term for nourishment, this chic and comforting retreat feeds the soul as well as the body. Cheery, upbeat service, a small but compelling wine list, and an eye-catching stainless steel and wood design make it a pleasant retreat from the heart of Union Square, located just blocks away.

The menu may be short but is at once comforting and saturated with flavor-packed, hearty options like a thick and succulent grilled pork chop with pink peppercorn, set over roasted fingerling potatoes and apple chutney; or seared diver scallops in green curry cream topped with crunchy quinoa. For dessert, the homemade custardy cheesecake served on a delicately browned cookie-crumb base and coupled with chopped yuzu jelly and peel, is obligatory.

Belcampo

American 🍴

A2

1998 Polk St. (at Pacific Ave.)

Phone: 415-660-5573   Lunch & dinner daily
Web: www.belcampomeatco.com
Prices: $$

If dining in a butcher shop doesn't sound appealing, you haven't yet been to Belcampo. The space is downright elegant—all blue banquettes, rich paneled wood, and wide picture windows. Then imagine the local, organically raised meat, available to-go from a friendly butcher or cooked to perfection on your plate, which is bar none.

You'll taste the difference in the juicy, hand-chopped cheeseburger, swathed in melting cheddar and caramelized onions, and the tender smoked guinea hen with *chimichurri*. Herbivores will be pleased to know that meat isn't the only focus here (an escarole-arugula salad gets bite from an almond-anchovy vinaigrette), and even the wine list is thoughtful. For dessert, try an *alfajor*, crumbly cookies sandwiching dreamy dulce de leche.

All Spice ❀

International 𝗫𝗫𝗫

C3

648 Bush St. (bet. Powell & Stockton Sts.)

Phone:	415-874-9481	Dinner Tue – Sat
Web:	www.allspicerestaurant.com	
Prices:	**$$$**	

This baby boy of the elder statesman is gaining a cult-like following and for fitting reason. A friendly welcome awaits after you pass through the elevated lounge, and then descend a few steps to arrive at the spacious, stylish, and urbane All Spice. Covered in a warm palette of browns and sky-blue, and accoutered with pulled back curtains, this sultry lair feels like a hidden escape away from the buzz of Nob Hill.

Elegantly set linen-topped tables framed by colonial-style chairs are the perfect platform for Chef Sachin Chopra's globally inspired food. Brought to you at the hands of a professional and intent service team, courses are presented with careful explanations. Each element in the seared Maine scallops buried beneath a potato purée, lobster-citrus emulsion, and garnished with pearls of trout roe, is not just delicious but notable in its complex assortment of flavors. Then texture and global influences take the lead in supremely tender, perfectly seared medallions of lamb topped with anchovy-parsley butter and tailed by thinly sliced fingerling potatoes studded with spicy kimchi.

Need to turn down the heat? Cocoa-nib tortellini filled with lemon leaf-ricotta mousse and crowned by fresh coconut offer a cool *finis* to the festivities.

Frascati

Mediterranean ✗✗

A2

1901 Hyde St. (at Green St.)

Phone: 415-928-1406
Web: www.frascatisf.com
Prices: $$

Dinner nightly

Forget circling for parking and hop on a cable car instead to reach this quaint Mediterranean standby, where you'll see more of the iconic vehicles pass by their large front windows. Inside, closely-spaced tables are ideal for an intimate meal, and local residents definitely know it, because reservations are always hard to come by.

Frascati's fare may not be the city's most innovative, but it is very satisfying, thanks to well-made classics like tender potato gnocchi with asparagus and peas in thyme-white truffle butter, or grilled duck breast in pomegranate sauce over hearts of palm and herb spaetzle. Split the luscious *pain perdu*, caramelized sponge cake soaked in citrusy crème anglaise, and let the friendly servers and soft lighting work their magic.

Gioia

Pizza ✗

A2

2240 Polk St. (bet. Green & Vallejo Sts.)

Phone: 415-359-0971
Web: www.gioiapizzeria.com
Prices: $$

Lunch & dinner Tue – Sun

With its large space and casual vibe, Gioia has become a Russian Hill standby, drawing families with kids, groups of friends, and even solo diners (there's lots of counter seating). The rustic décor features white subway-tile walls, an open kitchen, and wood and metal furniture. Be warned: the noise level can be a bit high for any intimate conversation.

The highlight here is pizza, with creatively topped pies like summer squash with pesto, burrata, and Calabrian chili, or sausage, broccoli, leeks, pecorino, and olives. They're pricey, but worth it. A selection of salads and antipasti make for great starters. Otherwise, opt for *rigatoncini* in a meaty pork ragù with fresh, creamy ricotta and more Calabrian chili.

A second location dwells in Berkeley.

Helmand Palace

A2

Afghan

2424 Van Ness Ave. (bet. Green & Union Sts.)

Phone:	415-345-0072	Dinner nightly
Web:	www.helmandpalacesf.com	
Prices:	$$	

A drab exterior and an awkward Van Ness address haven't always worked in Helmand Palace's favor, but the food-savvy know it's one of the Bay Area's best for Afghan cuisine. The well-appointed interior is worlds away from the busy thoroughfare's steady stream of traffic, with linen-draped tables, big blue-cushioned armchairs, and warm, inviting service.

Every meal here kicks off with a basket of fluffy flatbread, served with three irresistible dipping sauces. The *kaddo*, caramelized baby pumpkin and ground beef in a garlic-yogurt sauce, is a perennial favorite, as is the *chapendaz*, marinated beef tenderloin over a tomato-pepper purée, rice, and lentils. Vegetarians will find numerous dishes to enjoy, all of them just as flavorful as the carnivorous feast.

Huxley

B3

American

846 Geary Blvd. (bet. Hyde & Larkin Sts.)

Phone:	415-800-8223	Lunch Sun
Web:	www.huxleysf.com	Dinner Tue – Sat
Prices:	$$	

Tattooed industry types can't get enough of this itsy-bitsy Tenderloin bistro, where the industrious young chef prepares every plate herself in the slip of a kitchen. With its warm wood surfaces, art deco accents, and vintage etched mirrors, it's an engaging place to pull up a counter seat—you'll feel like she's cooking just for you.

The menu is all about high-quality American comfort fare, like avocado toast with a creamy uni mousse and umami-rich nori powder; tender, caramelized pork belly tossed with sprouted lentils and pea tendrils; and a superb chicken pot pie, its flaky, buttery crust infused with black pepper. Desserts are limited, but a simple buttermilk-vanilla ice cream with caramelized honeycomb candy hits all the right notes.

Keiko à Nob Hill ✿

Fusion

B2

1250 Jones St. (at Clay St.)

Dinner Tue – Sun

Phone: 415-829-7141
Web: www.keikoanobhill.com
Prices: $$$$

Luxurious, discrete, and intimate, Keiko blends her own unique culinary style with traditional appeal. Cushioned banquettes wrap the square dining room, outfitted with subdued lighting, mustard-colored fabric walls, and heavy brown trim.

Just be prompt: the formal service team handles each night's single seating with military-like precision, and all guests are served at once. Arriving late means holding up the whole dining room (and making enemies). This place takes its service, its mission, and itself very seriously.

In the kitchen, Chef Keiko Takahashi performs her own superb feat of balancing pristine Japanese ingredients with classic French technique. Her success is undeniable from the first taste of impeccable sashimi such as cherry-smoked *sanma*—its pleasant oiliness countered with dried soy, pickles, and a bright dab of cucumber gelée. Hot, flaky, golden-brown puff pastry may encase a morsel of abalone baked in its pearlescent shell. Japanese Wagyu beef is meltingly tender, rich, and a highlight of the meal when served with yuzu-soy foam and grated wasabi.

Very good desserts may feature a Mont Blanc-like parfait layering candied chestnut purée and sweet whipped cream.

La Folie

A2

French   XXX

2316 Polk St. (bet. Green & Union Sts.)

Phone: 415-776-5577   Dinner Mon – Sat
Web: www.lafolie.com
Prices: $$$$

Few *grandes dames* of high-end French cuisine remain in the city, but this long-running spot from Chef/owner Roland Passot has held strong. With two formal dining rooms featuring starched tablecloths, polished servers, and a tall art deco wine case, it's a favorite among occasion-celebrating couples and the luxury-loving tourist crowd.

Diners can build their own three-to-five course prix-fixe, with old-school dishes like perfectly seared lamb rack with fava beans and green garlic, or delicate Dungeness crab bisque with English peas. Sumptuous supplements, from foie gras to lobster, are also offered, as is a chef's-choice tasting menu. For dessert, a clever baked Alaska blends bay leaf and rhubarb ice creams with vanilla chiffon.

Leopold's

A1

Austrian   XX

2400 Polk St. (at Union St.)

Phone: 415-474-2000   Lunch Sat – Sun
Web: www.leopoldssf.com   Dinner nightly
Prices: $$

The boisterous spirit of an Austrian *gasthaus* is alive and well in Russian Hill. All thanks are due to Leopold's, which draws a young crowd to its slice-of-Vienna dining room, adorned with wood booths, deer antlers, and attended to by cheerful female servers in dirndls. If dinner alone is your goal, go early; convivial groups lend the space a communal mien, but also get larger and louder as the night wears on and the boots of beer are drained.

The carte du jour is rife with well-executed classics like golden-brown pork wiener schnitzel with a cucumber salad, vegetable strudel, and delectable raspberry Linzer torte. If you've got a group in tow, the *choucroute garni* platter, laden with pork ribs, sausage, potatoes, and sauerkraut, is a crowd-pleaser.

Liholiho Yacht Club

Hawaiian ✗✗

B3

871 Sutter St. (bet. Jones & Leavenworth Sts.)

Phone:	415-440-5446
Web:	www.liholihoyachtclub.com
Prices:	$$$

Dinner Mon – Sat

This charming, highly personal newcomer delightfully reflects Chef/owner Ravi Kapur's patchwork upbringing—blending Hawaiian, Indian, Asian, and Californian influences into its own unique cuisine. Blue entryway tiles spelling "ALOHA" lead to a bustling bar, a sunny-yellow exhibition kitchen, as well as a sleek dining room, all attended to by exceptionally hospitable servers.

A refreshing Clifton special cocktail (with genever and coconut water) is the perfect counterpart to intriguing snacks like silky tuna poke atop crunchy nori crackers, smoky beef tongue wrapped in fluffy clamshell buns, and Flintstone-sized beef ribs in a sweet-spicy red chili sauce. Be sure to save room for the tangy, dense cardamom cheesecake with pistachio and Cara Cara oranges.

Mason Pacific

American ✗✗

B2

1358 Mason St. (at Pacific Ave.)

Phone:	415-374-7185
Web:	www.masonpacific.com
Prices:	$$

Dinner Tue – Sun

Since its debut in 2013, this smart American bistro is the darling of Nob Hill with swarms of Teslas and Maseratis lining up at the valet station. The stylish occupants, from tech millionaires to white-haired society matrons, stream into the light-filled dining room where they angle for a seat at the semi-private banquette facing the street or in the front room at the marble bar.

The menu is prepared with skill and top-notch ingredients, and includes a note-perfect fried chicken and caramelized Alaskan halibut with grated cauliflower and *peperoncini*. The burger, served on a pretzel bun with smoked tomato, is also a terrific choice. And while the friendly, smartly attired staff keeps the handful of tables moving, reservations are still a must.

Lord Stanley ❀

Californian ✕✕

A2

2065 Polk St. (at Broadway)

Phone: 415-872-5512
Web: www.lordstanleysf.com
Prices: $$$

Lunch Sat
Dinner Tue – Sat

You'll feast like a very refined lord at this outstanding newcomer, which, like its husband-and-wife chef/owners, is half Californian, half European. The West Coast vibe comes from the outstanding local ingredients and airy, light-flooded contemporary space, while across-the-pond touches (both chefs trained in the UK) include tip-free dining with all-inclusive dish prices and an intriguing wine list offering unusual Eastern European vintages.

Like its space, Lord Stanley's food is approachably refined, with stunning creations like a summer squash tart with almonds, summer squash, and herb aïoli. Silky black cod, pan-seared in butter and served in a spicy fava bean- and avocado-studded broth, is a showstopper. Even a seemingly simple dessert of grilled peaches with white Lillet sorbet and fruity olive oil gets an intriguing touch from slivers of Castelvetrano olives that add just the right amount of vibrancy.

In keeping with its San Franciscan ethos, Lord Stanley is a laid-back spot: the crowd of yupster couples often arrives on foot to the central Polk Street location, attired in casualwear. Be sure to quiz the attentive staff on the dishes—they'll happily explain each intricate layer.

Modern Thai

A3

1247 Polk St. (at Bush St.)

Phone: 415-922-8424

Web: www.modernthaisf.com

Prices: 💶

Lunch & dinner daily

♿

"Modern" is a bit of a misnomer, as this tropical Thai retreat actually feels like a step back in time with its whitewashed colonial façade, linen-topped tables, and rattan chairs. But the anachronism also applies to the portions (incredibly generous) and prices (incredibly reasonable), making it a favorite for nine-to-fivers seeking an affordable lunch break. Sweet and spicy Thai flavors abound here, from warm salads of glass noodles and minced chicken with a fish sauce-lime vinaigrette to comforting noodle soups like the *khao soy*, with chicken and egg noodles in a rich yellow coconut curry. And the MT sundae, a combo of coconut ice cream, sugar palm fruit, red beans, and jackfruit, is a refreshing dessert perfect for lunchtime dining.

Oriental Pearl

C2

760 Clay St. (bet. Grant Ave. & Kearny St.)

Phone: 415-433-1817

Web: www.orientalpearlsf.com

Prices: $$

Lunch & dinner daily

♿

Escape the cacophony of Chinatown at this calm upstairs retreat, where red ribbons hang in the light-filled windows and an attentive staff offers some of the neighborhood's best service. Though the crowd is decidedly non-Chinese with more than a few tourists mixed in, the food isn't overly Americanized and covers a range of regional specialties. Commence your culinary tour of China with an order of barbecue spareribs, lacquered on the outside and exceptionally tender on the inside, or a piece or two of dim sum. Then dive into the Chiuchow-style marinated duck, a plateful of sweet-and-salty meat beneath crisp, golden-brown skin. The Singapore-style rice noodles mixed with shrimp, pork, scallion, and yellow curry paste, are equally divine.

Parallel 37

Californian ✗✗✗

C2

600 Stockton St. (bet. California & Pine Sts.)

Phone: 415-773-6168
Web: www.parallel37sf.com
Prices: $$$

Dinner Tue – Sat

Housed in the stately, swanky San Francisco Ritz-Carlton, this modern Californian restaurant has the most laid-back vibe on the property, with a hopping front bar and a casual-chic dining room boasting leather banquettes in tasteful shades of brown and orange. But as relaxing as the atmosphere may be, you'll want to make like your fellow diners—a well-to-do crowd of couples and hotel guests—and dress up for date night.

With engaging offerings like roasted morel mushrooms over buttery marble potato purée and silky Alaskan halibut with broccoli pesto and clams, Parallel 37's cuisine is as refined as its haute address suggests. And if you leave without sampling the creamy, nutty black sesame panna cotta with strawberries, well, you're missing out.

Reverb

Californian ✗✗

A2

2323 Polk St. (bet. Green & Union Sts.)

Phone: 415-441-2323
Web: www.reverbsf.com
Prices: $$

Lunch Sat – Sun
Dinner nightly

The former home of Verbena has undergone a quiet revamp from the same owners, shifting from vegetable-centric haute cuisine to a more relaxed, omnivorous offering. Highlights include tender, smoky grilled octopus with spicy romesco and salsa verde; a delectable trio of heirloom carrots (caramelized, shaved, and pickled); and moist, flaky white bass with roasted artichoke purée, artichoke chips, and briny olive tapenade.

While Reverb's menu has shifted, its hip space was left mostly untouched, with dramatic antique wood doors, soaring ceilings, and a glowing tower of back-lit jars of homemade pickles. The bustling bar, which serves up punchy concoctions like the Tikal (with mezcal, pineapple, celery, and dry sherry), remains a neighborhood favorite.

Seven Hills

Italian

A2

1550 Hyde St. (at Pacific Ave.)

Phone: 415-775-1550
Web: www.sevenhillssf.com
Prices: $$

Dinner nightly

The dense sidewalk foliage, closely packed tables, and attentive service at this Russian Hill neighborhood hangout will transport you to Italy—that is, until you see the cable car rumbling its way up Hyde, and remember you're in San Francisco. The happy crowd of regulars wouldn't have it any other way.

They come to share bowls of house-made pasta, like a *tagliolini* mingled with asparagus and creamy buffalo ricotta (made fresh on-site). A thick grilled pork chop with gigante beans and charred Calçot onions sates heartier cravings, as do a few offal-centric dishes like rabbit tongues and roasted bone marrow. Finish with a creamy vanilla-blood orange panna cotta, or order a more superlative ricotta for dessert—this time drizzled with honey.

1760

Contemporary

A2

1760 Polk St. (at Washington St.)

Phone: 415-359-1212
Web: www.1760sf.com
Prices: $$$

Lunch Sat – Sun
Dinner nightly

The Acquerello team further enriches Nob Hill's dining-scape with the arrival of this darling and rousing adjunct to their upscale destination a block away. Awash in shades of grey, the dusky space closely seats a hip crowd, rife with bonhomie.

Creative plates that progress from lightest to heartiest start off with bracing tastes of hamachi crudo seasoned with diced Satsuma, *sriracha* meringues, and *bulgogi* vinaigrette. The unorthodox rendition of steak tartare is composed of zesty Thai-spiced dressing and a swipe of buttery Marcona almond purée. The carte goes on to reveal *maccheroni* tossed with a bright serrrano chili pesto and sweet Dungeness crab. The fried duck sandwich graced by slaw and pickles has become a house specialty.

Sons & Daughters ✿

C3

Contemporary XX

708 Bush St. (bet. Mason & Powell Sts.)

Phone: 415-391-8311
Web: www.sonsanddaughterssf.com
Prices: $$$$

Dinner Wed – Sun

Everyone at this inviting corner space is warmly professional, including the eager, well-paced staff. Add in the architecturally detailed dining room—a hybrid between your grandmother's home and a minimalist art gallery with its black-and-cream palette, leather banquettes, and vintage chandeliers—and you'll be counting down the days until your next visit.

Small but mighty, the kitchen turns out a seasonal, seven-course fixed menu that consistently pleases. A meal here might begin with candied limequat rind, briny sea beans, and light uni foam to flavor slices of sweet, silky scallops. Savory granola served with roasted cauliflower and creamy sweetbreads unites with trumpet mushrooms to form a perfect textural counterpoint to the smooth cauliflower soup poured tableside. And pork done three ways presents the loin dusted in pastrami spices; an exquisitely tender belly; and block of fried pork jowl set against pickled fennel and Satsuma segments.

Meyer lemon curd, sweet and tart with cranberry sauce, is a sublime dessert—but it's the intensely rich chocolate ganache, set over a bay leaf and chocolate cake crowned by pistachios, that showcases the technical prowess of this gifted kitchen.

Stones Throw

Contemporary X

A2

1896 Hyde St. (bet. Green & Vallejo Sts.)

Phone: 415-796-2901
Web: www.stonesthrowsf.com
Prices: $$

Lunch Sun
Dinner Tue – Sun

A good neighborhood restaurant should only be a stone's throw away, and this model has clearly hopscotched into Russian Hill's affections. Its terra-cotta floors, yellow walls, and chunky wood tables have a Mediterranean air, but the menu is more eclectically American, with a sizable beer and wine selection that makes the front bar great for a spur-of-the-moment drink and bite.

Clever takes on approachable dishes abound on the menu, from "toad in the hole" lasagna with a poached egg at dinner, to asparagus and duck confit hash at brunch. The creamy smoked salmon mousse, with bagel chips and crème fraîche, is rich and delicious. And pillowy doughnuts, topped with PB&J at dinner or pumpkin spice and pumpkin butter at brunch, are a delightful surprise.

Z & Y 😊

Chinese X

C2

655 Jackson St. (bet. Grant Ave. & Kearny St.)

Phone: 415-981-8988
Web: www.zandyrestaurant.com
Prices: $$

Lunch & dinner daily

Some like it hot, and here they are in heaven. Be forewarned: timid palates should steer clear of the super-spicy Sichuan dishes that have made Z & Y a Chinatown smash hit. Nearly every dish is crowned with chilies, from the huge mound of dried peppers that rest atop tender, garlicky bites of fried chicken to the flaming chili oil anointing tender, flaky fish fillets in a star anise-tinged broth with Sichuan peppercorns aplenty.

The well-worn dining room may seem unremarkable and the service perfunctory, but the crowds are undeterred. Plan to wait among eager fans for a seat, but then settle in for delicate pork-and-ginger wontons swimming in spicy peanut sauce and more chili oil. Allot time to navigate the challenging parking situation.

North Beach

Relatively compact yet filled with cool restaurants, casual cafeterias, and a hopping nightlife, North Beach has that authentic Californian vibe that makes it just as much a local scene as a tourist mecca. Steps from the docks and nestled between bustling **Fisherman's Wharf** and the steep slopes of Russian and Telegraph Hills, this neighborhood owes its vibrant nature to the Italian immigrants who passed through these shores in the late 1800s. Many were fishermen from the Ligurian coast, and their seafood stew (cioppino) that they prepared and perfected on the boats evolved into a quintessential San Francisco trademark. Though Italian-Americans may no longer be in the majority here, classic *ristorantes*, pizzerias, and coffee shops attest to their idea of the good life. At the annual **North Beach Festival** held in mid-June, a celebrity pizza toss, Assisi Animal

Blessings, and Arte di Gesso also pay homage to this region's Italian roots. Foodies however can rest assured that dining here isn't all about lasagna-loving, red-sauce joints. Brave the crowd

of locals and visitors for some of the most fantastic fish and chips this side of the pond and fish tacos this side of the border, at **The Codmother Fish and Chips**. This veritable local favorite is essentially a small kiosk with a window to place your order and a handful of tables on the front patio. Clearly, it isn't about the dining experience here, and most people get their fish and chips to-go—perhaps for a stroll along the wharf?

TELEGRAPH HILL

Cutting its angle through North Beach, Columbus Avenue is home to the neighborhood's most notable restaurants, bars, and lounges. Thanks to **Molinari's**, whose homemade salami has garnered a fanatic following since 1896, whimsical, old-world Italian delicatessens are a regular fixture along these streets. Pair their impressive range of imported meats and cheeses with some *vino* for a perfect picnic in

nearby Washington Square Park. Preparing wood-fired pizzas with classic combinations since 1935, **Tommaso's Ristorante Italiano** is another citywide institution, situated on the southern end of North Beach. The décor and ambience may be a vestige from the past, but that hasn't prevented devoted locals from cramping its quarters. Fine-dining can also come with a throwback feel and **Bix** is a grand example. This bi-level arena with a balconied dining room, classic cocktails, and jazz club ambience makes for date-night *extraordinaire*. Getting acquainted with North Beach is a never-ending but very telling experience. After all, these neighborhood venues were also home to a ragtag array of beret-wearing poets in the 1950s and remain a popular excursion for the Beat Generation. Those so-called beatniks—Allen Ginsberg and Jack Kerouac to name a few —were eventually driven out by busloads of tourists. Nonetheless, bohemian spirits still linger on here, at such landmarks as the City Lights bookstore and next door at **Vesuvio**, the quintessential boho bar.

FEASTING IN FISHERMAN'S WHARF

Fisherman's Wharf, that mile-long stretch of waterfront at the foot of Columbus Avenue, ranks as one of the city's most popular sites. There aren't many locals here and it teems with souvenir shops, street performers, and noisy rides, but you should go if only to feast on a sourdough bread bowl crammed with clam chowder, or fresh crabs cooked in huge steamers right on the street. Then, sample a bite of culinary history at **Boudin Bakery**. While this shop has bloomed into an operation complete with a museum and bakery tour, it stays true to its roots by crafting fresh sourdough bread every day, using the same mother first cultivated here in 1849 from local wild yeast. Not far behind, **Ghirardelli Square** preserves another taste of old San Francisco. This venerable chocolate company, founded by Domenico "Domingo" Ghirardelli in 1852, flaunts a host of delectable wares at the equally famous **Ghirardelli Ice Cream and Chocolate Manufactory**. When visiting here, don't forget to glimpse their original manufacturing equipment, while enjoying a creamy hot fudge sundae. On your way out, be sure to take away some sweet memories in the form of those chocolate squares.

Albona

Italian XX

B2

545 Francisco St. (bet. Mason & Taylor Sts.)

Phone: 415-441-1040
Web: www.albonarestaurant.com
Prices: $$

Dinner Tue – Sat

This brightly painted mid-century bungalow is nestled on a street with high-rises. Inside, find a petite, cozy, and brasserie-like dining room outfitted with velvet curtains and effusive waiters donning traditional waistcoats. Photographs on the walls depict the Istrian village from which the restaurant takes both its name and cuisine inspiration: the focus here is on the peninsula's cooking, where classic Roman and Venetian styles meet Croatian influences.

The menu reveals delicious but somewhat unfamiliar dishes like pork *involtini* stuffed with sauerkraut and enhanced by preserved-fruit sauce; or cured sardines with raisins and pine nuts. While presentations aren't overly refined, it's the ultimate in comfort fare—deeply satisfying and very flavorful.

Café Jacqueline

French X

C2

1454 Grant Ave. (bet. Green & Union Sts.)

Phone: 415-981-5565
Web: N/A
Prices: $$$$

Dinner Wed – Sun

You'll float away on a cloud at the first taste of Jacqueline Margulis' signature soufflés, light and fluffy masterworks that have kept her tables full for over 35 years. Since the chef makes each of her creations by hand, expect to spend three or so hours at the table—it's the perfect romantic escape for couples lingering over a bottle of wine.

To sate your appetite while you wait, a bowl of light carrot soup or a delicate cucumber salad in a champagne vinaigrette will do the trick. But the soufflés are the real draw, and keen diners plan on both a savory and a sweet course. For the former, a combination of flaky salmon, tender asparagus, and caramelized Gruyère is a delight. And the utterly perfect lemon soufflé will haunt any dessert lover's dreams.

Coi ✿ ✿

Contemporary ✗✗✗

373 Broadway (bet. Montgomery & Sansome Sts.)

Phone: 415-393-9000   Dinner Tue – Sat
Web: www.coirestaurant.com
Prices: $$$$

Even on the eve of its tenth anniversary, Coi manages to stay as fresh as the days when it first opened its doors. Its second decade is sure to be exciting as Daniel Patterson hands off his kitchen to a new and very talented brigade. The moniker translates to "silent" or "quiet"—and indeed the restaurant owns a serene, Zen-like atmosphere with branches arching across the foyer; soft grey upholstered banquettes; bare wooden tables; supple brown leather chairs; and beautiful, conversation-worthy earthenware dishes.

Service here is warm, refined and extraordinarily well trained—with a nearby sommelier at the ready with an impeccable wine list and a smile. Waiters quietly attend to every need of the stylish crowd.

The kitchen's contemporary cooking is a joy to experience and the multi-course tasting menu showcases both incredible technique and pristine seasonal ingredients. Picture thinly sliced geoduck sashimi paired with crunchy, seasoned cucumber, shavings of radish, and violet-hued edible flowers. Then a bright, chilled English pea soup is poured over creamy buttermilk, soft yellow nasturtium and whole spring peas picked at their peak. Tender, bite-sized slices of aged duck find perfect company in vibrant spring greens, sprouted wheat berry, and a rich duck broth.

Carmel Pizza Company

Pizza ✕

2826 Jones St. (bet. Beach & Jefferson Sts.)

Phone: 415-676-1185
Web: www.carmelpizzaco.com
Prices: 💰

Lunch & dinner Thu – Tue

Don't let the touristy Fisherman's Wharf address keep you from visiting as this ruby-red gem serves delicious wood-fired Neapolitan pies that belie its environs. (And in a bid to draw more patronage, the popular spot has covered and heated its rather special patio, a godsend on chilly afternoons.)

With eight to ten daily pies to choose from, there's something for everyone. Bring the kids and go to town on the zesty Diavola, topped with spicy *salame*, minced *pepperoncini*, and crisp arugula, or try the classic Americana, a tasty mix of ham, onion, sausage, mushrooms, and black olives. And the crust? Oh, the crust: it's thin, chewy, and well salted, with blistered, perfectly caramelized edges. Why should out-of-towners get to have all the fun?

Cotogna

Italian ✕✕

490 Pacific Ave. (at Montgomery St.)

Phone: 415-775-8508
Web: www.cotognasf.com
Prices: $$

Lunch Mon – Sat
Dinner nightly

Though rustic compared to Quince, its high-end sibling, Michael and Lindsay Tusk's casual Italian offshoot would be elegant by any other standard. Stylish, bright, and a hot ticket reservation-wise, the space centers around an exhibition kitchen, from which crisp pizzas and hearty roasted meats emerge.

Cotogna's absolutely delicious menu highlights Chef Tusk's pristine pastas, like rolled *casconcelli* stuffed with velvety pumpkin purée in sage butter, as well as seasonal starters that include a beautiful chicory salad with sweet red apple, pomegranate, and Piave cheese. And there's always that three-course prix-fixe delight: an exceptional value that features a dessert like pitch-perfect butterscotch *budino* with sea salt and *muscovado* custard.

Doc Ricketts

American 🍴

C3

124 Columbus Ave. (bet. Jackson St. & Pacific Ave.)

Phone: 415-649-6191
Web: www.docrickettssf.com
Prices: $$

Lunch Mon – Fri
Dinner nightly

♿ Nestled in a sea of spendy corporate hangouts and touristy Italian-American joints, Doc Ricketts is a welcome change of pace with its unique upstairs-downstairs vibe—the basement level is Doc's Lab, a comedy and music venue where the full menu is offered. The upstairs restaurant is simple and airy, with wood furnishings, wide windows, and engaging servers at the ready.

The American fare on the menu is unfussy and skillfully prepared, from butter-sautéed wild mushroom panzanella with chunks of torn sourdough and bacon-shallot vinaigrette, to a juicy, generously portioned half roast chicken, accompanied by toast slathered in chicken-liver mousse. Finish with a luscious chocolate *pot de crème*, topped with vanilla Chantilly and a chocolate cookie.

the house

Asian 🍴

C3

1230 Grant Ave. (bet. Columbus Ave. & Vallejo St.)

Phone: 415-986-8612
Web: www.thehse.com
Prices: $$

Lunch Mon – Sat
Dinner nightly

♿ This perennially popular Asian bistro provides a welcome alternative to the Italian-heavy streets in North Beach. The décor is minimal with blonde wood tables and there are always specials so listen closely to the efficient staff as they recite the bounties of the day. A versatile drinks list completes the enticing spread in addition to offering a happy reprieve to those who've endured a long wait for limited tables.

Dishes like delicately prepped scallops in saffron sauce, and crispy halibut tempura propped atop roasted cauliflower may vary by the day. But a playful, fusion element remains a steady feature in all items, including house specialties, of which warm wasabi noodles topped with flank steak or teriyaki-glazed salmon are perfect examples.

Gary Danko ✿

Contemporary ✕✕✕

A1

800 North Point St. (at Hyde St.)

Phone: 415-749-2060
Web: www.garydanko.com
Prices: $$$$

Dinner nightly

It is clear what all the fuss is about, right from the moment one enters this polished wood veneer sanctum of Chef Danko's revered dining room. Dressed-up occupants in the mood to celebrate are bathed in flattering light and surrounded by a rainforest's worth of orchids. Service is without reproach and displays an uncommon loyalty; diners here experience a level of hospitality usually reserved for luxury hotels.

Customizable tastings allow guests to mix and match their own three- to five-course meals from a menu of classic cooking layered with global inspiration. Pan-seared quail salad features a crispy rosemary-scented potato cake, sautéed maitake mushrooms, and wild greens—an eye-catching composition united by a warm pomegranate-sweetened dressing. Intensely crisp soft-shell crabs are even easier to love when nestled in a bed of white polenta scattered with black sesame seeds, enhanced with pickled ginger and zesty lime to cut the richness.

Banana tart with rum pastry cream, caramel sauce, and coconut sorbet is a fine choice for dessert, made even sweeter when paired with an after-dinner selection from the outstanding wine list boasting over 2,000 bottles from around the globe.

Il Casaro

Pizza ✗

C3

348 Columbus Ave. (bet. Grant Ave. & Vallejo St.)

Lunch & dinner daily

Phone: 415-677-9455
Web: www.ilcasarosf.com
Prices: $$

In a sea of too-touristy Italian joints, Il Casaro is the rare North Beach spot that delivers the goods: Neapolitan-style pizza cooked to crispy perfection in a bright red wood-fired oven. Whether you opt for the classic Margherita or the zippy *diavola* (with spicy salami and Calabrian chiles), you're sure to achieve carbohydrate bliss. Throw in an antipasto or salad and a silky panna cotta with raspberry coulis, and you're all set—at an affordable price, to boot.

Il Casaro's space is simple but hip, with reclaimed wood, polished concrete floors, and utensils in empty San Marzano tomato cans. Don't expect more than cursory service, as the restaurant is always packed and doesn't take reservations: waits can run an hour or more at peak times.

Kokkari Estiatorio

Greek ✗✗

D3

200 Jackson St. (at Front St.)

Lunch Mon – Fri
Dinner nightly

Phone: 415-981-0983
Web: www.kokkari.com
Prices: $$

Zeus himself would be satisfied after a soul-warming meal at this Greek favorite, which serves up San Francisco chic with a side of old-world taverna hospitality. Translation? Once you're seated at the bar or settled near one of the roaring fireplaces, the thoughtful staff will cater to your every need.

Kokkari's sophisticated menu leans heavily on the wood grill and rotisserie, which produce smoky, juicy lamb souvlaki with warm pita and tangy chickpea salad; as well as charcoal-kissed, feta-stuffed calamari over fennel, oranges, and olive tapenade. Resist the urge to conquer the Olympus-sized portions: you'll want to sample the *galaktoboureko*, crispy phyllo rolls filled with creamy custard and topped with honey, figs, and crème fraîche ice cream.

Park Tavern

American   𝐗𝐗

C2

1652 Stockton St. (bet. Filbert & Union Sts.)

Phone: 415-989-7300
Web: www.parktavernsf.com
Prices: $$$

Lunch Fri – Sun
Dinner nightly

North Beach favorite Park Tavern has a menu that spoils diners. Should you stick with the beloved Marlowe burger, or opt for a new plate like roasted sea bass with braised fennel and celeriac purée? The choices are plenty. Go another round with the time-honored Brussels sprout chips, or sample the newer lemon chips with burrata? Whatever you decide, you're unlikely to be disappointed.

Options also abound in terms of seating—the sidewalk tables, window seats, and marble-topped bar counter are equally appealing. In terms of drinking: the house-concocted cocktails, local beers, and varied global wines will each call your name. The good news is that a second visit will allow you to try more, provided you can snatch a table away from the other regulars.

Piperade

Basque   𝐗𝐗

D2

1015 Battery St. (bet. Green & Union Sts.)

Phone: 415-391-2555
Web: www.piperade.com
Prices: $$

Lunch Mon – Fri
Dinner Mon – Sat

Basque Chef Gerald Hirigoyen blends the region's French and Spanish roots at this popular restaurant and favorite for business lunches. His roasted lamb gets a touch of Middle Eastern flavor thanks to merguez sausage and a sweet-smoky cumin-date relish, served with tender and caramelized roasted fennel bulb. A solidly Gallic apple galette is deliciously none-too-sweet, combining puff pastry, finely shaved apple slices, and decadant caramel sauce.

Located among historic warehouses in a commercial district, this charming dining room features wood floors, brick walls, and chandeliers made from empty wine bottles. Hold a confab at the eight-person round table, or enjoy a solo glass of wine on the covered front patio and while away a warm afternoon.

Quince ✿ ✿

Italian

C3

470 Pacific Ave. (bet. Montgomery & Sansome Sts.)

Phone: 415-775-8500
Web: www.quincerestaurant.com
Prices: $$$$

Dinner Mon – Sat

Situated on a tree-lined street amid upscale galleries and design firms, Quince is elegant but never bogged down by formalities. Make your way through the champagne lounge to find this high-ceilinged, copper-hued room and its well-versed, passionate service team—clearly one of the best in the city. Solo diners may head to the bar, which is a warm gathering perch that also pours a lineup of standout drinks.

Each fixed menu option promises fine-tuned, elevated, and inspired cooking that aims beyond Italy. Pastas are a wow-inducing highlight here. Each handcrafted tortellini is a picture of perfect symmetry, stuffed with delicate pork, coated with cheese *fonduta*, and topped with slivers of white Alba truffles. Unique meat courses culminate in the distinctive *Cinta Senese* (heritage pork from Siena) prepared two ways. The first is *faggotini* bundling pork and wild nettles; the second is a chestnut flower *crispello* stuffed with a confit of belly and braised shoulder mixed with Swiss chard.

Desserts yield a very grand finale with dramatic presentations of Valrhona "Perigord" truffles filled with chocolate, citrus, and finished with a chestnut tuille and Satsuma orange.

127

Rose Pistola

Italian ✕✕

C2

532 Columbus Ave. (bet. Green & Union Sts)

Phone: 415-399-0499
Web: www.rosepistolasf.com
Prices: $$

Lunch & dinner daily

A new chef has enlivened the menu at this longtime North Beach spot, which stands out from the Disneyland-like crowd of tourist-baiting Italian restaurants along Columbus Avenue. The kitchen can satisfy the pasta-and-wine grind, but it's capable of a lot more. Perfectly tender and crisp-fried calamari gets a punch from an almond salsa verde dip, garlic-sautéed fresh spinach is bright and delicate, and the pan-fried chicken Milanese is a crisp, well-seasoned work of art.

Rose Pistola is also a cut above in terms of décor, thanks to huge front windowpanes, subdued mosaic-tile floors, and a large, dark wood bar. Linger over a slice of buttery, cream-filled *sacripantina* cake, and engage in some great people-watching on the busy thoroughfare outside.

Tony's Pizza Napoletana

Pizza ✕

C2

1570 Stockton St. (at Union St.)

Phone: 415-835-9888
Web: www.tonyspizzanapoletana.com
Prices: $$

Lunch & dinner Wed — Mon

A veritable polymath of pizza, Tony Gemignani serves every variety imaginable at his North Beach institution, from wood-fired Neapolitan to gas-cooked New York to 1,000-degree coal-fired. Tucked into the ground floor of a quaint Victorian, the sparse décor directs focus to the 12 styles of pizza on offer. It's always crowded, so expect a wait—and don't bring a big group.

Pies and Italian-American dishes are as rich and complex as the space is simple, from the tangy, herbaceous tomato sauce lapping tender beef meatballs to the delicious interplay of soft quail eggs, smooth potato, and crisp *guanciale* atop a wood-fired pie. Can't wait? Gemignani also owns a quick-fix slice shop right next door, plus nearby Capo's, which focuses on Chicago-style pies.

Tosca Café

Italian XX

C3

242 Columbus Ave. (bet. Broadway & Pacific Ave.)

Phone: 415-986-9651
Web: www.toscacafesf.com
Prices: $$$

Dinner nightly

This historic bar has been expertly revived under NYC stars, April Bloomfield and Ken Friedman, who spent millions to add a kitchen and make its old-school charm seem untouched. White-coated bartenders shake and stir behind the glorious carved wood bar, while diners feast in the cushy red leather booths. Reservations aren't accepted and tables are few, so expect a wait.

The food is Italian-American with Bloomfield's signature meaty influences, like flavorful, gamey grilled lamb ribs that nearly fall off the bone. Pastas are strong, from creamy *gemelli cacio e pepe* to rich, spicy *bucatini all'Amatriciana*, but don't neglect their vegetables: a dish of tender cauliflower and potatoes in a rich taleggio sauce with crunchy breadcrumbs is a showstopper.

Look for our symbol,
spotlighting restaurants
with a notable
cocktail list.

Richmond & Sunset

Named after an Australian art dealer and his home (The Richmond House), quiet yet urban Richmond is hailed for the surf that washes right up to its historic Cliff House and Sutro Baths. Springtime adds to the area's beauty with Golden Gate Park's blushing cherry blossoms and whimsical topiaries—nevermind those bordering pastel row houses in desperate need of a lick of paint. More than anywhere else in the city, this sequestered northwest enclave is ruled by a sense of Zen, and residents seem deeply impacted by it—from that incredibly stealthy sushi chef to über-cool Sunset surfer dudes. Given its multicultural immigrant community, Richmond's authentic cuisine options are both delicious and very varied. Begin with an array of European specialty items at **Seakor Polish Delikatessen and Sausage Factory**, proffering an outstanding selection of smoked, cured meats, sausages, pickles, sauerkraut, and more.

NEW CHINATOWN

While Richmond does cradle some western spots, it is mostly renowned for steaming bowls of piping-hot *pho*, as thick as the marine layer itself. This area has earned the nickname "New Chinatown" for good reason—deliciously moist and juicy plates of *siu mai* are meant to be devoured at **Shanghai Dumpling King** or **Good Luck Dim Sum**. Speaking to this neighborhood's new nickname, **Wing Lee Bakery** is famed for a comprehensive selection of dim sum—both sweet and savory. And while you're at it, don't miss out on Frisco's finest roast duck, on display at **Wing Lee BBQ** next door. Those looking to replicate this Asian extravaganza at home should start with a perfect wok, stockpot, noodle bowl, and rice cooker among other stellar housewares and kitchen supplies available at **Kamei**. If that doesn't make you feel like a kid in a candy store, Hong

Kong–style delights (on offer even late at night) at **Kowloon Tong Dessert Café** will do a bang-up job. Clement Street, also an inviting exposition for the adventurous home cook and curious chef, features poky sidewalk markets where clusters of bananas sway from awnings and the spices and produce on display are as vibrant as the nearby **Japanese Tea Garden** in bloom. While the Bay Area mantra "eat local" may not be entirely pertinent here, a medley of global goodies abound and everything from tamarind and eel, to live fish and pork buns are available for less than a buck. There is a mom-and-pop joint for every corner and culture. In fact, this is *the* 'hood to source that 100-year-old egg or homemade kimchi by the pound. The décor in these divey stops is far from remarkable and at times downright seedy, but really, you're here for the food, which is always authentic and on-point. Buses of Korean tourists routinely pull up to **Han Il Kwan** for a taste of home. The space may be congested and service can be a disaster, but the kitchen's nostalgic cooking keeps the homesick coming back for more. Native-born aficionados can be found combing the wares at **First Korean Market**, poised on Geary Boulevard and packed with every prepared food and snack under the sun. Meanwhile, culture vultures gather for an intense Burmese feast at **B Star Bar**, after which a refreshing sip at **Aroma Tea Shop** is nothing if not obligatory. Their owners even encourage free tastings of exclusive custom blends of individually sourced teas from around the world.

SUNSET

A dash more updated than bordering Richmond, Sunset—once a heap of sand dunes—retains a small-town vibe that's refined but still rough around the edges. Here, locals start their day with fresh-baked pastries at **Arizmendi Bakery** and then stroll around the corner for some much-needed caffeine at the **Beanery**. Asian appetites routinely patronize **Izakaya Sozai** for juicy *yakitori*, followed by cooling and fresh sashimi. Tourists taking in the sights at the de Young Museum or Academy of Sciences love to linger over lunch at **Wooly Pig Café**. Their namesake "Wooly Pig" sandwich, crafted from toasted challah and overflowing with pork belly, mizuna greens, and pickled shallots, is guaranteed to knock your socks off. Yes, the space is tiny with only a smattering of tables, but with gorgeous

Richmond & Sunset

A   **B**   **C**

South Bay

CHINA BEACH

1

LAND'S END

PACIFIC

COASTAL TRAIL

LINCOLN

SEA CLIFF

THE PRESID

Washington

Lincoln Blvd.

THE LEGION OF HONOR

PARK

Lake St.

Lake

25th St.

23rd St.

21st St.

19th St.

17th St.

California

Pizzetta 211

Dragon Beaux

Clement

OCEAN

27th

Aziza

Kappou Gomi

SUTRO BATHS RUINS

Seal Rock Dr.

35th

33rd

31st

29th

Clement St.

Sichua Home

Sutro's

CLIFF HOUSE

Point Lobos Ave.

Geary

Khan Toke Thai House

43rd

41st

39th

37th

St.

RICHMOND

SUTRO HEIGHTS PARK

47th

45th

Anza

Balboa

Ave.

Ave.

Ave.

Ave.

Cabrillo

Ave.

RICHMOND

Balboa

St.

Cabrillo Ave.

La Playa

Ave.

Cabrillo

2

OCEAN BEACH

Ave.

Ave.

Ave.

Fulton

Spreckels Lake

John F. Kennedy Dr.

park Presidio B

Stov Lake

47th Ave.

Chain of

Kennedy Dr.

GOLDEN GATE PARK

West Dr.

John F. Kennedy

Lakes

Middle Dr.

Martin Luther King Jr. Dr.

Great Highway

Martin Luther King Jr. Dr.

Way

Martin Luther King Jr. Dr.

Lincoln

Lincoln

45th

43rd

41st

37th

35th

31st

29th

27th

25th

23rd

21st

19th

Irving

La Playa

48th

Irving

Ocean Beach

Sunset

33rd

St.

Judah

17th

Irving

Judah

N

Judah

Judah-Sunset

N

Judah 19 Av

Kirkha

3

Outerlands

Kirkham

Ave.

Ave.

Ave.

22nd

Ave.

Ave.

Lawton

Lawton

Ave.

Ave.

Lawton

Moraga

36th

St.

Moraga

St.

OCEAN BEACH

Noriega

Noriega

St.

Ortega

SUNSET

43rd

37th

Ortega

Sunset Reservoir

Ave.

Pacheco

48th

St.

Pacheco

24th

Quintara

45th

41st

Quintara

35th

33rd

31st

29th

27th

25th

21st

Quintara

4

PACIFIC

Rivera

39th

Rivera

Santiago

Taraval 22 Av

OCEAN

47th

Ave.

Santiago Ave.

Taraval-Sunset

L

L

Tara

Taraval

L

L

St.

PARKSIDE

23rd

19th

Ulloa

Ave.

Ave.

Ulloa

Ave.

Ave.

GOLDEN GATE NATIONAL RECREATION AREA

Vicente

Sunset Blvd.

Vicente

Ave.

Ave.

Ave.

Wawona

SF Zoo

Wawona

L

PINE LAKE PARK

Sloat

Yorba

St.

Crestlake Dr.

Sloat Blvd.

A   **B**   **C**

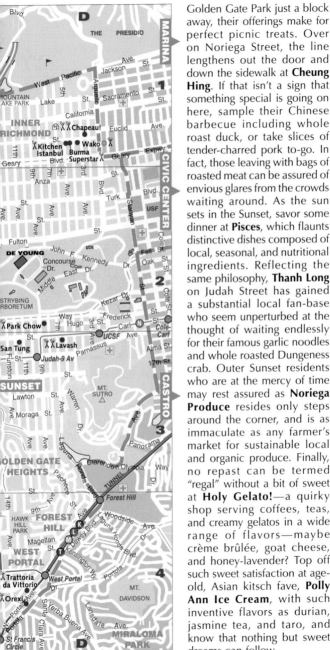

Golden Gate Park just a block away, their offerings make for perfect picnic treats. Over on Noriega Street, the line lengthens out the door and down the sidewalk at **Cheung Hing**. If that isn't a sign that something special is going on here, sample their Chinese barbecue including whole roast duck, or take slices of tender-charred pork to-go. In fact, those leaving with bags of roasted meat can be assured of envious glares from the crowds waiting around. As the sun sets in the Sunset, savor some dinner at **Pisces**, which flaunts distinctive dishes composed of local, seasonal, and nutritional ingredients. Reflecting the same philosophy, **Thanh Long** on Judah Street has gained a substantial local fan-base who seem unperturbed at the thought of waiting endlessly for their famous garlic noodles and whole roasted Dungeness crab. Outer Sunset residents who are at the mercy of time may rest assured as **Noriega Produce** resides only steps around the corner, and is as immaculate as any farmer's market for sustainable local and organic produce. Finally, no repast can be termed "regal" without a bit of sweet at **Holy Gelato!**—a quirky shop serving coffees, teas, and creamy gelatos in a wide range of flavors—maybe crème brûlée, goat cheese, and honey-lavender? Top off such sweet satisfaction at age-old, Asian kitsch fave, **Polly Ann Ice Cream**, with such inventive flavors as durian, jasmine tea, and taro, and know that nothing but sweet dreams can follow.

Aziza ✿

C1

Moroccan ✗✗

5800 Geary Blvd. (at 22nd Ave.)

Phone: 415-752-2222
Web: www.aziza-sf.com
Prices: **$$$**

Dinner Wed – Sun

Nestled in a quiet corner of outer Richmond, along a street peppered with little ethnic grocery stores, Mourad Lahlou's lovely Aziza doesn't knock you over upon arrival. But duck inside its worn blue door, and you'll find a warm hostess at the ready; a charming and softly lit interior lined with cozy booths; as well as a Moroccan-style lounge in the back, featuring low-slung seating and couches.

The result is exotic but accessible—a spot as perfectly appropriate for lively young families with kids in tow as it is for a sultry rendezvous with your steady.

Chef/owner Mourad Lahlou loves to turn traditional Moroccan cooking on its head, (in fact, there's not a tagine in sight) infusing irresistible dishes with a palpable Californian sensibility. The outcome is quite incredible, with sweet and savory flavors tangling in perfect harmony. It's hard to go wrong on this menu and you'll surely want to try a little bit of everything. But whatever you do, don't miss the kitchen's elegantly plated trio of dips. These may include silky cucumber yogurt and dill, smoky eggplant and a nutty piquillo pepper-almond dip; or the perfectly seared lamb loin and belly paired with creamy, green garlic-infused barley, grilled summer squash, and a flutter of fresh, peppery arugula.

Burma Superstar

Burmese ✗

D1

309 Clement St. (bet. 4th & 5th Aves.)

Phone: 415-387-2147
Web: www.burmasuperstar.com
Prices: $$

Lunch & dinner daily

Like any celebrity, it's easy to recognize this unusual dark wood superstar from the eager crowds swarming like paparazzi. Everyone endures this no-reservations policy to Instagram their favorite Burmese dishes. See the iPhones poised over the famed rainbow and tea-leaf salads or *samusa* soup (also available as a lunchtime combo). Regulars stick to traditional items, marked by asterisks on the menu. Palate-tingling options include rice noodles with pickled daikon and tofu in a spicy tomato-garlic sauce, or pork and kabocha squash stewed in a gingery broth with coconut sticky rice. A creamy Thai iced tea is the perfect counterbalance to the spicy, boldly flavored fare.

Hipper digs, a cooler crowd, but renovated favorites can be found at sib—Burma Love.

Chapeau! 😊

French ✗✗

D1

126 Clement St. (bet. 2nd & 3rd Aves.)

Phone: 415-750-9787
Web: www.chapeausf.com
Prices: $$

Dinner nightly

For an oh-so-French experience on Asian food-centric Clement, denizens head to Philippe Gardelle's authentic bistro, where tightly spaced tables and paintings of the titular hats create a convivial atmosphere. Packed with regulars receiving *bisous* from the chef, Chapeau! is warm and generous, a vibe that's aided by its strong Gallic wine list.

Dishes are traditional with a bit of Californian flair, like fingerling potato chips in a frisée and duck confit salad or salted-caramel ice cream that tops the *pain perdu*. The cassoulet, wholesome with braised lamb, rich with smoky sausage, and earthy with white beans, is perfect for a foggy night in the Avenues. Come before 6:00 P.M. on weeknights for a $36.95 early bird prix-fixe, or create your own from their many set menus.

Dragon Beaux

C1

Chinese ✗✗

5700 Geary Blvd. (at 21st Ave.)

Phone: 415-333-8899
Web: www.dragonbeaux.com
Prices: $$

Lunch & dinner daily

This Richmond Chinese newbie has a split personality that food fiends will adore: by day, it offers dim sum delights from the same owners as Daly City's acclaimed Koi Palace, while at night, it segues into spicy hot pot offerings. The dramatic, over-the-top space is lively in any light, thanks to its lit stone pillars, dark wood furnishings, and soaring ceilings.

Dim sum seekers will have to take a number and wait (only parties of eight or more can reserve), but the rewards are numerous—think fluffy-sweet-smoky-salty barbecue pork buns, tender crab roe-topped *siu mai*, and exquisite roasted pork belly with crackly skin. Classic and ultra-flaky egg custard tarts and crunchy sesame balls offer a sweet finish, and pair nicely with the fragrant jasmine tea.

Kappou Gomi 🈑

C1

Japanese ✗

5524 Geary Blvd. (bet. 19th & 20th Aves.)

Phone: 415-221-5353
Web: N/A
Prices: $$

Dinner Tue – Sun

Sushi-seekers should take a pass, but those yearning for elegant, traditional Japanese food will find kindred spirits at this precious gem. The serene, ultra-minimalist dining room isn't fancy, with only a few shelves of ceramics as décor. But, older Japanese women in traditional garb who run the show are endlessly polite and attentive so long as you're not raising a din—or requesting a spicy tuna roll.

If you're able to go with the flow, you'll find much to adore on their menu, like umami-rich wilted mizuna salad with fresh fava beans and bonito sauce, or pale green edamame tofu with fresh cherries, cherry blossom noodles, and a sour-salty cherry paste. The exquisitely moist and flaky black cod, grilled with a slightly sweet sake marinade, is revelatory.

Khan Toke Thai House

Thai ✗

C2

5937 Geary Blvd. (bet. 23rd & 24th Aves.)

Phone: 415-668-6654   Lunch & dinner daily
Web: www.khantokethai.com
Prices:

Don your best dinner socks for this traditional Thai restaurant, where diners are asked to remove their shoes before perching on low cushions at the intricately carved tables. Service is as slow as a glacier, making it more suited to casual dining than business lunch. Still, Khan Toke is worth the wait.

Awaken the senses with a bowl of enticingly pungent and spicy-sour *tom yum* soup, loaded with tomato, onion, and sliced lemongrass, finished with fresh cilantro. Then dive into *gai ga prou*, a delicious stir-fry of chicken and bell peppers studded with sliced Thai chilies. Indeed, chili-lovers who order dishes "very spicy" will get what they want. There is no shortage of firepower in the bamboo shoots with chili sauce and excellent Panang curry.

Kitchen Istanbul

Turkish ✗

D1

349 Clement St. (at 5th Ave.)

Phone: 415-753-9479   Lunch & dinner daily
Web: www.kitchenistanbulsf.com
Prices: $$

This cheerful Inner Richmond spot has retained the chef, managing team, and décor of previous occupant Troya, but taken its menu in a more exclusively Turkish direction. The results—like a sublime lentil soup richly puréed and made slightly tart with lemon, or a juicy, perfectly grilled duo of lamb meatballs over basmati rice—will transport you to the Aegean sea.

A Mediterranean oasis surrounded by dozens of Chinese restaurants, Kitchen Istanbul is bright and well-lit with red walls donning sleek black-and-white framed photos. The friendly staff is quick to recommend an unusual Turkish wine; if you're willing to put yourself in their hands, they're also happy to whip up a mini tasting menu of highlights, from creamy hummus to briny sardines.

Lavash

D3

511 Irving St. (bet. 6th & 7th Aves.)

Phone: 415-664-5555
Web: www.lavashsf.com
Prices: $$

Lunch & dinner Tue – Sun

You'll feel like you've dined in a Persian home after leaving family-run Lavash, which has become a neighborhood fixture thanks to warm service and sizable portions. Painted in hues of orange, gold, and rose, the casual and flower-filled space is inviting, and throughout a meal here, you'll see locals dropping in for takeout or just to chat.

Begin your feast with *sabzi panir*, a plate of fresh herbs, feta, cucumber, tomato, walnuts, and grapes that's perfect for ad hoc toppings on the cracker-like namesake bread. Then order up a skewer or two of tender and smoky ground beef and lamb *koobideh*, served over fluffy basmati rice. Finally, don't miss the crispy, sticky-sweet *baghlava*—it's available in traditional pistachio or as a chocolate "choclava."

Orexi

D4

243 W. Portal Ave. (bet. 14th Ave. & Vicente St.)

Phone: 415-664-6739
Web: www.orexisanfrancisco.com
Prices: $$

Lunch Sat – Sun
Dinner Tue – Sun

Nestled away from the hustle and bustle in charming, village-like West Portal, Orexi offers a future-perfect twist on the classic Greek taverna. The long, narrow space, with its rustic wood beams, wood furnishings, and oversized mirrors, has a contemporary vibe that contrasts nicely with the homey food.

The lunch menu is full of light, yet satisfying dishes, like a Greek salad packed with crunchy cucumber, ripe tomato, and tangy feta. A juicy, well-seasoned lamb burger is topped with goat cheese, tomato, and crunchy red onion. Dinner is heartier with moussaka, slow-braised lamb shank with orzo, and lamb chops among other options. At either meal, be sure to sample the *kataifi*, a baklava-like phyllo pastry filled with chopped toasted almonds.

Outerlands

A3

4001 Judah St. (at 45th Ave.)

Phone: 415-661-6140   Lunch & dinner daily
Web: www.outerlandssf.com
Prices: $$

For the residents of this foggy beachside community, this new hotspot is an ideal hangout. The salvaged wood-dominated décor is perfectly cozy, and all-day hours ensure crowds flock here for breakfast and Bloody Marys to start their day. A friendly staff, good, locally roasted coffee, and a nicely stocked bar with a fine listing of beers on tap persuade further lingering.

Stop in for fresh baked pastries like coffee cake, scones, and glazed doughnuts; or dig into heartier fare like an open-faced sandwich topped with black eye pea purée, green tomato, and griddled ham slices. Once the sun sets over Ocean Beach, expect more ambitious cooking from the dinner menu, like smoked chicken with tomato panzanella and charred gem lettuce.

Park Chow

D2

1240 9th Ave. (bet. Irving St. & Lincoln Way)

Phone: 415-665-9912   Lunch & dinner daily
Web: www.chowfoodbar.com
Prices: $$

Steps from the Golden Gate Park museums, Park Chow draws locals and tourists alike with its approachable and well-priced organic American comfort food. No matter the mood or time of day, something here will appeal. Options abound from kid-friendly mini-pizzas to lighter and healthier fare like a tangy beet and endive salad with creamy avocado and salty goat cheese. Find straightforward pleasure in the grilled free-range chicken BLT on a griddled bun with crisp fries. For dessert, don't miss the rustic ginger cake with pumpkin ice cream and caramel.

The homey space is full of appealing nooks, including a dog-friendly front patio and sunny roof deck. Remember to call ahead to get your name on the wait list (especially for weekend brunch).

Pizzetta 211

C1

211 23rd Ave. (at California St.)

Phone: 415-379-9880   Lunch & dinner Wed – Mon
Web: www.pizzetta211.com
Prices: $$

This shoebox-sized pizzeria may reside in the far reaches of the Outer Richmond, but it's easily identifiable by the crowds hovering on the sidewalk to score a table. Once inside, you'll be greeted by *pizzaiolos* throwing pies in the tiny exhibition kitchen—ask for a counter seat to get a better view.

The thin, chewy, blistered *pizzettas* each serve one, making it easy to share several varieties. Weekly specials utilize ingredients like seasonal produce, house-made sausage, and fresh farm eggs, while standbys include a pie topped with wild arugula, creamy mascarpone, and San Marzano tomato sauce. Whatever you do, arrive early: once the kitchen's out of dough, they close for the day, and the omnipresent lines mean the goods never last too long.

San Tung

D3

1031 Irving St. (bet. 11th & 12th Aves.)

Phone: 415-242-0828   Lunch & dinner Thu – Tue
Web: www.santungchineserestaurant.com
Prices: $$

If you don't know what to order, just repeat after us: dry-fried chicken wings. Tossed in a chili-flecked ginger glaze, they're the reason foodies flock to this tasty, Americanized Chinese spot, write their names on a whiteboard, endure a long wait on the sidewalk, and finally eat at a communal table with strangers. It's all part of the restaurant's ramshackle appeal (as are the ultra-affordable prices).

Even if poultry's not your thing, the menu's other offerings are well worth the effort it takes to eat here: dry-fried prawns are tossed in a sweet-and-spicy chili-garlic sauce, and hot and salty twice-cooked pork is fried with a heap of bell peppers and dried red chilies. Tables turn fast, so don't plan to linger—but for a filling meal, this one's a winner.

Sichuan Home 😊

Chinese ✗

C2

5037 Geary Blvd. (bet. 14th & 15th Aves.)

Phone: 415-221-3288
Web: N/A
Prices: $$

Lunch & dinner daily

One of the brightest offerings on Geary Boulevard, Sichuan Home lures diners far and wide. Its spotless dining room is a vision of varnished wood panels and mirrors, with plexiglass-topped tables for easy chili oil clean-up and menus that feature tempting photos of each item.

A sampling of the wide-ranging Sichuan cuisine should include tender, bone-in rabbit with scallions, peanuts, and a perfect dab of scorching hot peppercorns. Fish with pickled cabbage gets a delightfully restorative hit of bold flavors from mustard greens and fresh green chilies, and red chilies star in aromatic dry-fried string beans with minced pork. For dessert, rich and velvety mango pudding, topped with grapefruit sorbet and fresh pineapple, is a tropical treat.

Sutro's

Californian ✗✗

A2

1090 Point Lobos Ave. (at Ocean Beach)

Phone: 415-386-3330
Web: www.cliffhouse.com
Prices: $$$

Lunch & dinner daily

Set in the historic Cliff House, perched above the roaring Pacific, Sutro's would be worth a trip just for its commanding views of the rugged California coastline. But this SF landmark doesn't rest on its laurels; instead, it serves surprisingly good food. In season, Dungeness crab is unmissable here, whether in a terrifically colossal crab Louie with avocado mousse and hard-boiled eggs, or shatteringly crisp panko-crusted crab cakes over carrot hummus and lemon-tarragon aïoli. The tasty seafood-focused fare goes on to include mussels steamed in Anchor Steam beer and *harissa*; as well as a sautéed red trout sandwich with fennel, cucumber, and yogurt.

After your meal, stroll the beach or visit the windswept ruins of the Sutro Baths next door.

Wako ⭐

Japanese ✖

D1

211 Clement St. (bet. 3rd & 4th Aves.)

Phone: 415-682-4875
Web: www.sushiwakosf.com
Prices: $$$

Dinner Tue – Sun

The area feels workaday and the exterior is understated from first glance, with a simple noren over the door and dark wood blinds. Yet Wako is a truly lovely little *sushi-ya* that vies to be among the city's best.

The buzz here has been rightly earned and spread quickly. Don't bother showing up without a reservation—these tables and stools are packed well in advance. Still the vibe remains fun with foodies and chefs chatting along the blonde wood bar.

Both omakase and à la carte offerings underscore the talented kitchen's vision of approachable, well-crafted dishes that satisfy Eastern and Western palates. Begin with a progression of superb small plates like house-made sesame tofu with dashi gelée, or small-bodied firefly squid in uni sauce with a touch of yuzu. Deliciously thick, precise cuts of toro, amberjack, and golden eye snapper arrive with a smoky house-brewed soy sauce, grated yuzu, and wasabi. Tempura does not disappoint as light and crunchy morsels of tiny smelts, sweet potato, and green beans with sea salt and fresh lemon. Wako's excellent quality sushi is downright sublime—whether brushed with salty-sweet soy, tucked with shiso, or topped with tobiko over pitch-perfect rice.

Trattoria da Vittorio

Italian ✗✗

D4

150 W. Portal Ave. (bet. 14th Ave. & Vicente St.)

Phone:	415-742-0300	Lunch & dinner daily
Web:	www.trattoriadavittorio.com	
Prices:	$$	

Mamma knows best at this West Portal hot spot, with home cooking imported straight from the kitchen of the owner's Italian mother, Mamma Francesca. One bite of her lasagna, rich with creamy ricotta and hearty Bolognese, will have you cheering "Mamma mia," while oversized portions have some crying "basta!" A semi-open kitchen and cheerful staff add to the sense of homey hospitality. A kids' menu makes it an extra popular choice for families.

Start meals with an immaculately fresh caprese salad, then sample a crisp pie from the Neapolitan wood-burning pizza oven. Don't miss the outstanding tiramisu: ultra-creamy and not overly sweet, these layers of espresso-soaked cake with whipped mascarpone and shaved chocolate won't require coaxing to scrape clean.

Remember, stars
(✿✿✿... ✿) are awarded
for cuisine only! Elements
such as service and décor
are not a factor.

SoMa

Once the city's locus of industry, sprawling SoMa (short for South of Market) has entered a post-industrial era that's as diverse and energetic as San Francisco itself. From its sleek office towers and museums near Market, to the spare converted warehouses that house the city's hottest startups, SoMa teems with vitality, offering memorable experiences around every turn. Tourists may skip it for its lack of Victorians, but SoMa's culinary riches and cultural cachet are of a different, authentically urban kind—the neighborhood equivalent of a treasured flea-market find.

FINE ARTS & EATS

Most visitors to SoMa tend to cluster in the artsy northeast corridor (bordering downtown) for trips to the Museum of Modern Art (now closed for renovations), Yerba Buena Center for the Arts, Contemporary Jewish Museum, and a profusion of other galleries and studios. For a pit stop, join the tech workers snagging a caffeinated "Gibraltar" from local coffee phenomenon **Blue Bottle**, housed in the back of Mint Plaza (there is also a rotating schedule of food trucks that visit Mint Plaza). For a more serene setting, gaze over Yerba Buena Gardens with a cup of rare green tea and

spa cuisine at **Samovar Tea Lounge**.

In a city where everyone loves to eat, even the **Westfield San Francisco Centre** mall is a surprisingly strong dining destination, offering cream puffs, fresh fish, and *bi bim bap* in its downstairs food court. Local chain **Buckhorn Grill**, in the Metreon Mall, is another treasure for deliciously marinated, wood-fired tri-tip. A hard day's shopping done, hit happy hour on Yerba Buena Lane with the yupsters fresh from their offices, indulging in a strong margarita at festive Mexican cantina, **Tropisueño**, or a more sedate sip at chic **Press Club**, which focuses on Californian wine and beer. In the midst of it all, the Moscone Center may draw conventioneers to overpriced hotel restaurants and clumsy chains, but the savvier ones beeline to **ThirstyBear Brewing Company**, where classic Spanish tapas and organic brews come without the crowds or crazy prices. Alternatively, stroll over to the Rincon Center for a unique meal at **Amawele's South African Kitchen**, which has won the hearts of local office workers with unique and tasty food like "bunny chow"—a curry-filled bread bowl.

PLAY BALL

SoMa's southeast quarter has undergone a revival in the last decade, with baseball fans flooding AT&T Park to watch the Giants, perennial World Series contenders. The park's food options are equally luring and include craft beer, sushi, and Ghirardelli sundaes. Crabcake sandwiches at **Crazy Crab'z** have a fan club nearly as sizable as the team itself. Off the field, this corridor is dominated by the tech scene, which has transformed the area's former factories and warehouses into humming open-plan offices. An oasis of green amid the corporate environs, South Park is a lovely retreat, particularly with a burrito from cheerful taqueria **Mexico au Parc** in hand. Just outside the park, legions of young engineers in their matching company hoodies form long lines every lunchtime outside **HRD Coffee Shop**—it may look like a greasy spoon but serves tasty Korean-influenced fare like spicy pork and kimchi burritos. Hip graphic designers can be seen speeding their fixed-gear bikes towards Market to pick up desktop fuel from **The Sentinel**, where former Canteen Chef Dennis Leary offers house-roasted coffee in the mornings and excellent corned-beef sandwiches for lunch.

Silicon Valley commuters begin pouring out of the Caltrain station around 5:00 P.M., giving the area's nightlife an extra shot in the arm. **21st Amendment**, a brewpub with

hearty food and popular beers like Back in Black, is a favorite for a relaxed lunch; whereas Farmerbrown's **Little Skillet** might serve *the* best fried chicken and waffles in town. For those in need of an understated retreat, the 700-label selection at ripped-out-of-France wine bar, **Terroir**, will enchant natural-wine junkies.

BEST OF THE WEST

SoMa's western half may be grittier, but is still a must for those in search of great eats. After a closure and remodel, Vietnamese standby **Tú Lan** is once again drawing lines of customers for its killer imperial rolls, despite the drug-addled environs of its Sixth Street digs. Crowds also cluster at neighboring **Montesacro Pinseria Romana**, billed as the first restaurant in the United States to specialize in *pinsa*, a type of Roman flatbread similar to pizza.

Indeed, very little is same old-same old on this side of the city, whether it's the tattooed skateboarders practicing their moves, the omnipresent cranes constructing new condo towers, or the drag performers who entertain bachelorette parties over Asian-fusion fare at bumping nightspot **AsiaSF**. Amidst the edgy bars, kitschy boutiques, and design start-ups of Folsom, **Citizen's Band** turns out seasonal "diner-inspired cuisine" like a killer burger on buns from next-door **Pinkie's Bakery**, while Ethiopian stews on spongy *injera* fuel a booming takeout business at **Moya**. Feast on fragrant Thai curries at **Basil Canteen** in the original Jackson Brewery building. Then hit the 11th Street bars for hours of drinking and dancing, before soaking up all the evening's sins with a rich Nutella-banana triangle from late-night perma-cart, **Crêpes a Go Go**.

SoMa

NOB HILL

CHINATOWN

NOB HILL

MARINA

UNION SQUARE

UNION SQUARE

M.Y. China

The Cavalier

OLD MINT

54 Mint

MOSCONE CENTER

Lu

Tin Vietnamese

TENDERLOIN

CIVIC CENTER

CIVIC CENTER

ASIAN ART MUSEUM

CITY HALL

UN PLAZA

SF PUBLIC LIBRARY

SF WAR MEMORIAL & PERFORMING ARTS CENTER

Civic Center

AQ

Pampalasa

Una Pizza Napoletana

Bar Agricole

1601 Bar & Kitchen

Manora's Thai Cuisine

MISSION

Ame ✿

Contemporary XxX

C2

689 Mission St. (at 3rd St.)

Phone: 415-284-4040

Dinner nightly

Web: www.amerestaurant.com

Prices: $$$

True, it is located off a hotel lobby, but the smart design employing frosted glass, wood slats, and sheer curtains have made this modern dining room a world unto itself since opening. The interior offers both a comfortable counter and more formal area with cloth-covered tables, angular black vases, and bursts of seasonal flowers. Service is both anticipatory and extremely pleasant.

The contemporary menu maintains a clear, consistent focus on Japanese cuisine with a nod to local Californian ingredients. Seafood is treated with great care and skill, through offerings like cubes of tuna poke wrapped in nori, then panko-coated and pan-seared until crisp and topped with a bright julienne of radish and daikon. Porcelain bowls of *chawan mushi* reveal savory dashi over steaming, pale-yellow custard so airy that it seems almost imperceptible on the tongue, juxtaposed with enticingly chewy shiitake, tender lobster, and creamy uni. Firm and buttery Alaskan cod fillet is first marinated then broiled to gently charred perfection.

Light and fresh desserts may feature a nutty and milky sesame panna cotta served with pear slices and pomegranate arils underscored by a swipe of fragrant basil purée.

AQ

Contemporary XX

B3

1085 Mission St. (bet. 6th & 7th Sts.)

Phone: 415-341-9000
Web: www.aq-sf.com
Prices: $$$

Dinner Tue – Sat

Like its once-sketchy, increasingly tech-centric SoMa corridor, this chic Californian restaurant is aiming for the stars—and even if it doesn't always succeed, it's certainly never a dull ride. Whether you opt for the four-course or tasting menu, you'll be wowed by flavor combos that are always intriguing and often breathtaking: think silky-sweet scallop crudo with white sesame and pineapple, earthy beets with snap peas and lavender ice cream, and black cod with clam butter.

AQ's hyperseasonal menus are gently accented by a quarterly décor shakeup; depending on the time of year, you'll find cherry blossoms or fall leaves accenting the sleek, neutral space. Be sure to come early to enjoy one of the exceptional cocktails at the front bar.

Bar Agricole

Californian XX

B4

355 11th St. (bet. Folsom & Harrison Sts.)

Phone: 415-355-9400
Web: www.baragricole.com
Prices: $$

Lunch Sat – Sun
Dinner nightly

Cocktails and conversation are always a pleasure at Bar Agricole, which is known for having one of the city's best drink programs. Its narrow, industrial-modern dining room boasts soaring ceilings from which huge acrylic sculptures hang, while mod concrete booths line the side wall. An outdoor patio, with plant beds and a trickling fountain, is particularly popular for brunch.

The menu is thoroughly Californian and loaded with the season's best, showcased in dishes like a frisée, arugula, and radish salad with a *citronette* dressing; halibut *brandade* with asparagus; as well as roast pork leg and belly with Canario beans, greens, and horseradish. At brunch, opt for flavorful, tender, and homemade lamb sausage served over fried eggs and wilted kale.

151

Benu ✿ ✿ ✿

C2

22 Hawthorne St. (bet. Folsom & Howard Sts.)

Phone:	415-685-4860
Web:	www.benusf.com
Prices:	$$$$

Dinner Tue – Sat

Don't miss the street views directly into this kitchen as you enter—the chefs here are preparing a series of masterpieces. Outside in the courtyard, benches are exactly the kind of place to linger, after a regal repast. The interior is awash in earthy colors, sleek banquettes, and oversized cushions. The slate-gray dining room is serene with clean lines drawing the eye across the meticulous design, while the staff is impressively warm and relaxed for a restaurant of this caliber.

Chef Corey Lee's nightly tasting menu is a unique marriage of contemporary American and Korean influences and Master Sommelier Yoon Ha oversees an exceptional beverage program. Dishes promise a fascinating interplay of ingredients, as seen in the potato salad crowned with mirin-glazed anchovies and spirals of mild red chili. Find subtlety and elegance in raw fluke seasoned with sesame oil and sandwiched between crisp sesame leaves; while sea bream served in an aged tangerine jus with black trumpet mushrooms is royally decadent. Rich, marbled beef reaches a new height of excellence when prepared with charred scallion sauce, ramps, and meaty morels.

Finally, a striking dessert of luscious coconut cream with strawberry gelée, tapioca pearls, and topped with a thin disc of meringue, will have you seeing stars.

Boulevard

Californian ✕✕

D1

1 Mission St. (at Steuart St.)

Phone: 415-543 6084
Web: www.boulevardrestaurant.com
Prices: $$$

Lunch Mon – Fri
Dinner nightly

Housed in one of the city's most historic buildings, this Belle Époque stunner is still breathtaking after more than 20 years, with glamorous mosaic floors, colorful glass, and polished bronze at every turn. The Embarcadero-adjacent location offers lovely views of the Bay Bridge and the water, and business lunchers as well as evening romance-seekers adore its transporting vibe.

Chef/owner Nancy Oakes is known as a pioneer of Californian cooking, with comforting takes on standards like Dungeness crab with avocado and ruby-red grapefruit, burrata served with a side of shaved kale, and flaky halibut over a mashed potato cake. Sweets are notable: try the pear- and apple-studded winter symphony crisp or creamy butterscotch pudding with pecan granola for a bit of bliss.

The Cavalier

Gastropub ✕✕

B2

360 Jessie St. (at 5th St.)

Phone: 415-321-6000
Web: www.thecavaliersf.com
Prices: $$

Lunch & dinner daily

One of the city's high-profile openings, this is the third effort from the team behind Marlowe and Park Tavern. Everything here has a British bent, echoed in the hunting-lodge-gone-sophisticated décor with red-and-blue walls accented by taxidermied trophies and tufted banquettes. Across-the-pond classics have Californian twists like a deep-fried Scotch duck egg wrapped in truffled duck rillettes. The restaurant has quickly become a see-and-be-seen haunt of the tech oligarchy (complete with a private club). However, the food is comforting and homey as seen in a caramelized roast chicken set atop horseradish mash.

Though reservations are a must, its location in Hotel Zetta means service runs from morning to night, giving diners plenty of options.

Cockscomb

C3

564 4th St. (at Freelon St.)

Phone: 415-974-0700
Web: www.cockscombsf.com
Prices: $$$

Dinner Mon — Sat

Carnivores will thrill to the offerings at this newcomer from offal-loving *Top Chef Masters* champ Chris Cosentino. And, largely because it doesn't shy away from aggressively rich fare like wood-grilled bruschetta topped with uni butter, sweet Dungeness crab, and buttery *lardo*; or smoky butterflied roast quail in a rich, salty tetrazzini gravy. Even veggie-centric celery Victor gets a meaty spin, its tangy vinaigrette accented by crisp chicken-skin *chicharrónes*.

Thanks to the hearty menu and location in a tech-centric corridor, Cockscomb draws a mostly male crowd that packs in for shellfish platters and intense, boozy cocktails named for SF landmarks. Laid-back, yet attentive service and a soaring, industrial space make it the very picture of a hot spot.

Epic Steak

D1

369 The Embarcadero (at Folsom St.)

Phone: 415-369-9955
Web: www.epicroasthousesf.com
Prices: $$$

Lunch & dinner daily

A meal at Epic is a ticket to a wondrous view—the Bay Bridge arching over the gentle water with Treasure Island across the way, plus the twinkle from The Bay Lights installation, which promises to shine again in early 2016. It's so pretty that you might struggle to keep your eyes on the plate. This roast house's surroundings are no slouch either, with a clubby, leather-clad dining room leading to a terrace designed for sunny afternoons.

As the name promises, meat is the big draw here, with juicy, tender cuts of everything from American prime beef to Japanese Wagyu. An old-school shrimp cocktail, fish dishes, and even venison round out the offerings, and a wine list rich with bold reds complements the cooking. At night, prices can get high; consider lunch for a more affordable visit.

54 Mint

Italian ✗✗

B2

16 Mint Plaza (at Jessie St.)

Phone: 415-543-5100
Web: www.54mint.com
Prices: $$

Lunch Mon – Fri
Dinner nightly

With its largely Italian waitstaff and clientele, a meal at 54 Mint is the next best thing to a plane ticket to Rome. A happy respite from the neighborhood's hustle and bustle, the space boasts a contemporary dining room stocked with shelves of Italian ingredients and a surprisingly tranquil front patio facing Mint Plaza.

The food is an authentic culinary journey through the Eternal City, with favorites like perfectly al dente *bucatini all'amatriciana*, twirled with smoked pancetta, sweet onion, tomato, and chili. The must-order *suppli*, fried balls of tomato risotto stuffed with smoked mozzarella, are best described as arancini on steroids. For dessert? The buttery, dark chocolate-flecked ricotta tart will leave you feeling *molto buono*.

Fly Trap

Middle Eastern ✗✗

C2

606 Folsom St. (bet. 2nd & 3rd Sts.)

Phone: 415-243-0580
Web: www.flytrapsf.com
Prices: $$

Dinner Mon – Sat

This contemporary Middle Eastern restaurant is definitely a trap for corporate folk from neighboring offices, who often end up turning "just one" delicious after-work cocktail into a meal inside this warm and inviting dining room. Here, old architectural and botanical sketches as well as vintage maps abound; and the staff is attentive, efficient and kind, never fussy or intrusive.

The unique food has a strong Persian influence that is showcased in tender meatballs with *harissa*, pomegranate, and pistachios. But even the more contemporary fare boasts a nuanced blend of spices, like the black cardamom in a braised short rib with quinoa, cranberry beans, and salsa verde. A tangy goat cheesecake with eggplant jam may sound strange, but is utterly satisfying.

Fringale 🐶

French 🍴🍴

C3

570 4th St. (bet. Brannan & Bryant Sts.)

Phone: 415-543-0573
Web: www.fringalesf.com
Prices: $$

Lunch Tue – Fri
Dinner nightly

This tech-centric corner of SoMa has seen booms and busts aplenty since the restaurant's opening in 1991, but Fringale has held strong, with a loyal squad of regulars who come for a taste of its Basque-inflected French cooking. The timeless décor starring clean wood furnishings and soft lighting is ideal for a business lunch or date night.

Start with the tasty calamari *à la plancha*—its topping of briny black olives and sliced jalapeños clearly differentiates Fringale from its tired bistro competition. After the mostly French staff recommends a wine, dive into the juicy roasted chicken breast over fluffy Israeli couscous and crunchy fennel. Finish with a creamy, nutty hazelnut-and-roasted almond mousse cake, drizzled with rich dark chocolate, of course!

Manora's Thai Cuisine

Thai 🍴

A4

1600 Folsom St. (at 12th St.)

Phone: 415-861-6224
Web: www.manorathai.com
Prices: 🪙🪙

Lunch Mon – Fri
Dinner Mon – Sat

A firmly rooted dining destination in this otherwise underdeveloped part of town, Manora's has been a source for authentic Thai dishes since the '80s. Crowds flock here for the affordable lunch specials, which include gems like pad Thai topped with plump shrimp and a golden fried egg, fragrant lemon chicken soup, and moist, perfectly charred satay skewers surrounded by fresh vegetables.

The pace at dinner is more relaxed, with endearing service that makes customers truly feel at home amid the wood carvings of the dining room. The fresh, zingy flavors of dishes like spicy green papaya salad draw diners through the well-aged wooden door again and again. Meals are all the better when cooled off with a creamy cold coffee or sweet Thai iced tea.

Luce

B3

888 Howard St. (at 5th St.)

Phone:	415-616-6566
Web:	www.lucewinerestaurant.com
Prices:	$$$

Lunch & dinner daily

San Francisco ▶ SoMa

Know that the ambience is pleasant, the space is elegant, the service team operates at the highest level, and the food is consistently excellent. Also, know that you probably won't have a hard time getting a reservation—Luce is often inexplicably empty. Let its lack of popularity be your reminder to come here when privacy is desired.

Dark and dramatic spherical lights, a wall of wine on display, and cushioned banquettes give the dining room a sumptuous, airy feel that promises the high level of luxury echoed in the cuisine.

Luce does serve breakfast, lunch, and brunch; but dinner is when the serious diner arrives for an entirely different experience. Pops of bitter coffee, bright young sage leaves, and dollops of toasted almond foam do not merely enliven an earthy and sweet pear-celery velouté, but prove this kitchen's skill with refined flavor combinations. Autumnal tastes are at the forefront of beautifully roasted lamb loin with cubes of crisped belly, butter-glazed carrots, sweet fuyu persimmons, and toasted buckwheat for nutty crunch.

Artistic presentation is paramount in the rectangular tranche of pumpkin cheesecake served on slate drizzled with tangy pomegranate gastrique.

Mourad ✿

Moroccan ✕✕✕

C2

140 New Montgomery St. (bet. Minna & Natoma Sts.)

Phone:	415-660-2500	Lunch Mon – Fri
Web:	www.mouradsf.com	Dinner nightly
Prices:	**$$$**	

With the debut of this glamorous outpost at the base of the PacBell building, Aziza Chef/owner Mourad Lahlou has become a big-city slicker. The area's young, food-obsessed techies practically flock to this grand space, replete with soaring ceilings, glowing central columns, and a glass-enclosed wine cellar catwalk.

Chef Lahlou's food retains the influence of his Moroccan upbringing, with dishes like duck confit basteeya rolled in thin sheets of flaky pastry. However, diners can also look forward to new levels of creativity using ingredients from around the globe. Even a simple dish of carrots gets unexpected heft from meaty dates and crunchy pecans, not to mention a hit of spice from urfa pepper. Then a wreath of eggplant packs a punch of texture and flavor into one beautiful dish; while tender, smoky octopus, served in a spicy lamb merguez broth with chickpea purée, is Californian and Moroccan all at once.

The visionary chef's attention to detail extends to the exceptional drinks. But, those travelling in groups may also want to consider the larger La'Acha menu, which offers family-style Moroccan dishes. Imagine roast chicken or lamb shoulder, rife with sides and sauces, and you'll get the picture.

M. Y. China 🏮

Chinese ✕✕

B2

845 Market St. (bet. 4th & 5th Sts.)

Phone:	415-580-3001	Lunch & dinner daily
Web:	www.tastemychina.com	
Prices:	$$	

♿ 🚫

Need proof that Yan Can Cook? Just snag a table at the famed PBS chef's elegant restaurant. Housed under the dome of the Westfield San Francisco Centre shopping mall, M.Y. China is a dark, sultry space full of posh Chinese furniture, antiques, and dramatic lighting. Shopping-weary patrons fill the dining room; whereas chowhounds hit the exhibition counter to watch the staff masterfully hand-pull noodles and toss woks. The menu reads like an ode to regional Chinese cuisine, spanning chewy scissor-cut noodles with wild boar, fluffy *bao* stuffed with sweet and smoky barbecue pork, and, when it's in season, delectable pepper-dusted whole crab. Be sure to order strategically, as you'll want room for the flaky, buttery, creamy, and outright superb Macanese egg tarts.

One Market

Californian ✕✕

C1

1 Market St. (at Steuart St.)

Phone:	415-777-5577	Lunch Mon – Fri
Web:	www.onemarket.com	Dinner Mon – Sat
Prices:	$$	

♿ 🍽️

Located at the very end of Market Street facing the Ferry Building, this perennial power-lunch spot draws crowds for its bright, bustling vibe and Bay views. High ceilings and a busy open kitchen catch the eye, while efficient bow-tied waiters attend to the booths and banquettes.

Chef Mark Dommen's contemporary Californian food is fresh and seasonal, starting with Nantucket Bay scallops sautéed in brown butter with baby mustard greens in a pool of fermented black bean sauce, garnished with apple and puffed rice. This might lead to a colorful composition of seared flounder over flavorful black-eyed peas with smoky bacon and tart *sofrito* vinaigrette. Signature desserts like pear galette are sized as "traditional" or "singular" (half) portions.

159

Omakase ✿

C4

665 Townsend St. (bet. 7th & 8th Sts.)

Phone: 415-865-0633
Web: www.omakasesf.com
Prices: **$$$$**

Dinner Tue – Sat

An "omakase" places the guests in the hands of the chef—and indeed the only dining option at this tiny new Edomae-style restaurant are three chef-designed tasting menus, clocking in at $100, $150, or $200. Sound risky? It isn't: trust us, this is an experience worth relinquishing all control for.

Housed in an area of SoMa popping with big tech companies and modern lofts, Omakase is a quiet little oasis of elegant minimalism. The tiny dining room consists of an L-shaped counter offering 14 seats (so yes, you'll definitely want to make reservations) facing the chefs. But, while all eyes are focused on the food, you won't get the impression these chefs think they're rock stars. On the contrary, it's not uncommon for them to inquire if the size of the sushi rice is appropriate for each guest's mouth; and the chefs and servers both bow profusely and offer their gratitude upon exit.

A night in their capable hands will reveal plate after plate of fresh sushi and sashimi (flown in three times a week from the Tsukiji fish market) and unique little dishes like a seaweed and fresh herb salad, laced with lovely strands of Okinawan sea grapes, served over cured whitefish and accompanied by white tuna *temarizushi*.

Pampalasa

✗

B4

1261 Folsom St. (bet. 8th & 9th Sts.)

Phone: 415-590-3251
Web: www.pampalasa.com
Prices: 💲💲

Lunch Tue – Sun
Dinner Fri – Sat

"Pampalasa" is Tagalog for "to add flavor," and that's precisely what this new Filipino restaurant has done to this industrial stretch of Folsom Street. With sunny yellow walls and lots of Filipino artwork, it has a casual, island-party vibe. Adding to the fun, you're encouraged to dine *kamayan*-style (with your hands); there's a sink in the center of the room for easy cleanup.

Kick things off with the *tocino* sliders, rich vinegar-soy marinated pork topped with garlicky *lechon* sauce on a pillowy *pan de sal* bun. From there, the savory, moist chicken adobo awaits, atop garlic rice with tiny dried shrimp. (Ask for a side of hot sauce and banana ketchup for even more flavor.) Deep-fried banana spring rolls with calamansi coconut cream are a sweet finish.

Prospect

American 🍴🍴🍴

D1

300 Spear St. (at Folsom St.)

Phone: 415-247-7770
Web: www.prospectsf.com
Prices: $$$

Lunch Mon – Fri
Dinner Mon – Sat

For a polished and contemporary experience that doesn't sacrifice approachability, FiDi denizens turn to Prospect, a crowd-pleaser for the full-pocketbook crowd. Set on the ground floor of a soaring high-rise, its airy space offers attractive, roomy tables, adept service, and a popular, well-stocked cocktail bar.

Simple, well-constructed American fare abounds, with menu mainstays like an heirloom tomato salad with creamy dollops of burrata and crisp, garlicky breadcrumbs; or a perfectly flaky Coho salmon fillet set over earthy black rice, sweet yellow corn, and caramelized summer squash. Dessert should not be missed: the butter brickle icebox cake with honey-glazed plums and toasted pecan butter crunch is a truly memorable treat.

RN74

C1

301 Mission St. (at Beale St.)

Phone: 415-543-7474
Web: www.rn74.com
Prices: $$$

Lunch Mon – Fri
Dinner nightly

Named for Burgundy's most famous road, RN74 draws a crowd of suited corporate types who pack this high-ceilinged room for lunch. Come sunset, the lounge is equally busy for after-work drinks, but dinner is sedate. Burgundy is, of course, the house specialty here, and an array of high-end bottles is listed on a train station-style board, which clicks over as each one sells out.

The food is playful and globally inspired, from pastrami-style salmon tartare with warm brioche and creamy dill crème fraîche to a panzanella with arugula, cherry tomatoes, and pan-fried chicken breast. Each plate is artistically constructed, like the "peach mille feuille," which combines pretty dollops of vanilla cream and peach sorbet with peaches and shards of puff pastry.

Salt House

C2

545 Mission St. (bet. 1st & 2nd Sts.)

Phone: 415-543-8900
Web: www.salthousesf.com
Prices: $$

Lunch Mon – Fri
Dinner nightly

With a roster of restaurants including nearby Town Hall and Anchor & Hope, the owners of this Mission Street favorite know exactly what diners want. Attractive and comfortable, the industrial setting embraces its past as a former printing warehouse with details like wide plank and exposed brick flooring. While the atmosphere is business-friendly at lunchtime, with elegant fare like a bruschetta of grilled sourdough bread and decadent burrata drizzled with quality olive oil and syrupy balsamic, it amplifies when the after-work crowd streams in.

Mains may include golden-skinned chicken confit atop a mélange of spring vegetables. Of course, such inventive desserts as salted caramel chocolate cake with German chocolate cake ice cream are not to be missed.

Saison ✿ ✿ ✿

D3

178 Townsend St. (bet. 2nd & 3rd Sts.)

Dinner Tue – Sat

Phone: 415-828-7990
Web: www.saisonsf.com
Prices: $$$$

San Francisco ▲ SoMa

No expense has ever been spared in this massive wow-inducing space. There are enough shining copper pots to supply a village of restaurants in France; wood tables, smart chairs, and faux-fur rugs mean that someone has recently been to Scandinavia. There is also a refreshing breakdown of traditional barriers between the kitchen and dining areas—underscored by the chefs' visits to each table, personally presenting and describing dishes.

Dining here is gorgeous; some find the service personalities to be pompous, while others regard them as warm and convivial. However, the blaring 80's soundtrack (if indeed that is your era) keeps the mood lively.

One thing that is undeniable is the level of extraordinary skill and detail that Chef Joshua Skenes uses to craft each item on his spontaneous menu. Expect cultured butters and cream, light and infused broths, as well as the smoke of a wood-fired oven to feature prominently. Meals may highlight luscious white sturgeon caviar with crisp potatoes *tourné* and a dab of cultured cream. Then, sample sweet, tender lobster barely warmed over coals with a savory seaweed dressing and rich lobster-brain sauce. Dry-aged duck is grilled "near the fire," served with giblet-confit ragù, wood-roasted date, a dark jus, and is absolutely delicious.

1601 Bar & Kitchen 😊

Sri Lankan ✗✗

1601 Howard St. (at 12th St.)

Phone: 415-552-1601
Web: www.1601sf.com
Prices: $$

Dinner Tue – Sat

♿ The flavors of India and Asia infuse the creative dishes at this quiet winner, which blends Eastern and Western ingredients to arrive at its very own delicious concoctions. A decidedly untraditional *lamprais* might stuff a classically French bacon-wrapped rabbit loin, toasted buckwheat, and eggplant curry into a banana leaf. Meanwhile, the halibut "ceviche" is more like a flavored sashimi, with hints of coconut milk and rings of serrano chilies.

The sleek, contemporary space with its wraparound windows, lovely art, and slate walls, is a perfect showcase for the food. Dine solo at the bar with a bittersweet Dubonnet sangria, or come with a group to share dishes and bottles of wine at the communal table—the polished staff makes either experience enjoyable.

Tin Vietnamese

Vietnamese ✗

937 Howard St. (bet. 5th & 6th Sts.)

Phone: 415-882-7188
Web: www.tinsf.com
Prices: $$

Lunch & dinner Mon – Sat

♿ The modern atmosphere at this hip downtowner might conjure thoughts of misguided fusion fare, but rest assured: when it comes to food, Tin is as traditional as it gets. Nonetheless, the dark wood walls, sleek glass pendant lights, and rich wood furnishings are a welcome change, making the spot a draw for groups residing far beyond its gritty, largely industrial neighborhood.

High-quality ingredients are the secret that sets this kitchen's cooking apart—from crunchy threads of banana blossom tossed with fried eel, shallots, peanuts, and herbs, to smoky soy-lemongrass pork shoulder atop rice noodles with a spicy lime-chili dipping sauce. Throw in some crunchy imperial rolls and garlicky, peppery wok-tossed shaking beef, and you'll have an affordable feast.

Trou Normand

M e d i t e r r a n e a n

C2

140 New Montgomery St. (at Natoma St.)

Phone:	415-975-0876	Lunch & dinner daily
Web:	www.trounormandsf.com	
Prices:	$$	

Named for the Norman tradition of drinking a glass of Calvados to revive the palate during a heavy meal, Bar Agricole's SoMa sequel shares its predecessor's skill with outstanding cocktails. They're perfect palate-cleansers for the expansive and delightful house charcuterie like rich duck pâté with plum and Armagnac or garlicky *finocchiona* kissed with fennel seeds.

While their *salumi* and selection of spirits are huge draws, Trou Normand is an all-day menu of shareable French- and Italian-leaning plates. Come for a croque madame with ramps and locally roasted coffee at brunch, sausage sandwiches with homemade sauerkraut at lunch, and pastas or roasted meats at dinner.

This large and glamorous space is a major hit among hipster tech types.

Twenty Five Lusk

American XXX

C3

25 Lusk St. (bet. 3rd & 4th Sts.)

Phone:	415-495-5875	Lunch Sun
Web:	www.25lusk.com	Dinner nightly
Prices:	$$$	

Nestled in the center of SoMa's dynamic startup scene, this high-design stunner draws an equally high-powered crowd. They stream in at happy hour to catch up on the latest tech gossip in the swinging lounge, then head upstairs to wheel and deal in the refined dining room, which boasts an impressive glassed-in exhibition kitchen.

Lusk's food is American with contemporary touches, from the *togarashi* and carrot coulis that spikes a highbrow take on shrimp and grits, to the ginger vinaigrette that accents a summery salad of little gem lettuce and heirloom cucumbers. Dessert aficionados will thrill to the freedom from choice offered by the "sampling" trio, featuring creamy lime posset, spiced carrot cake, and a decadent salted-caramel brownie.

Una Pizza Napoletana

A4

Pizza ✗

210 11th St. (at Howard St.)

Phone: 415-861-3444
Web: www.unapizza.com
Prices: $$

Dinner Wed – Sat

In keeping with owner Anthony Mangieri's monastic devotion to the perfect pie, Una Pizza Napoletana is a spare space, housed in a chilly former garage on an industrial corner of SoMa. The vibe is completely casual yet alluring with crowds riveted by the altar—a tiled turquoise oven, where Mangieri stretches dough and deftly coaxes the crackling wood fire to produce his perfect pies. Their blistered and puffy crusts sport a delicious char as well as an addictively chewy texture thanks to tangy fermentation.

Waits are long, but the hassle is well worth it after one bite of the Filetti, slathered with creamy buffalo mozzarella and juicy cherry tomatoes. Mangieri is unquestionably a master of his craft, and his pies are a cut above local competition.

Waterbar

D1

Seafood ✗✗

399 The Embarcadero (bet. Folsom & Harrison Sts.)

Phone: 415-284-9922
Web: www.waterbarsf.com
Prices: $$$

Lunch & dinner daily

Stunning views of the Bay Bridge are the chief draw at this Embarcadero fave for sipping wine on the lovely terrace and slurping oysters at the enormous raw bar. Though the polished, modern dining room can seem serious (as can the expense account-rocking prices), warm and thoughtful service brings things back down to earth.

Seafood-centric entrées make global use of the local waters' bounty by way of tender squid almost bursting with chorizo alongside candy-like chickpeas. Perfectly crisp pan-roasted striped bass atop flavorful wild rice oozes with delectable flavors and textures; and an Americana-influenced dessert menu (think carrot cake ice-cream sandwiches with rum-raisin sauce) is the final touch in ensuring that Waterbar stays packed to the gills.

Yank Sing 😊

Chinese XX

D1

101 Spear St. (bet. Howard & Mission Sts.)

Phone: 415-781-1111   Lunch daily
Web: www.yanksing.com
Prices: $$

With a higher price tag than the average Chinatown joint, Yank Sing is arguably *the* place in town for dim sum. While peak hours entail a wait, one can be assured of quality and abundant variety from these rolling carts. The signature Peking duck with its lacquered skin and fluffy buns is a memorable treat, as are the equally sweet and salty *char siu bao*. Of course, dumplings here are the true highlight, from plump and fragrant pork *xiao long bao*, to paper-thin *har gao* concealing chunks of fresh, sweet shrimp. Don't see favorites like the flaky egg custard tarts? Just ask the cheerful staff, who'll radio the kitchen for help via headsets.

The upscale setting is cheaper by day, but the zigzagging carts can get hectic. Things calm down a bit at dinnertime.

Zero Zero 😊

Pizza XX

C3

826 Folsom St. (bet. 4th & 5th Sts.)

Phone: 415-348-8800   Lunch & dinner daily
Web: www.zerozerosf.com
Prices: $$

Zero Zero may be named for the superlative flour used in its enticingly blistered, thin-crust pies, but this is much more than a pizzeria. While pies like the Geary with chewy clams, caramelized bacon, and Calabrian chilies, are delicious, this casual spot offers much more than a good slice. Absolute knockouts include tomato-braised chickpea bruschetta, oozing with melted burrata; and a salad of smoky grilled radicchio hearts cut by creamy Pt. Reyes blue cheese.

A mix of families, hipsters, and business people fresh from the Moscone Center fill the warm, bi-level space. Group dining is ideal for sharing and sampling more of the menu, and the sizable bar will ensure that everyone's equipped with a terrific cocktail or pint of local draft root beer.

East Bay

A signature mash-up of wealthy families, senior bohemians, and college kids, Berkeley is extolled for its liberal politics and lush university campus. Snooty gourmands and reverential foodies consider it to be the Garden of Eden that sprouted American gastronomy's leading purist, Alice Waters. Her Chez Panisse Foundation continues to nurture the **Edible Schoolyard**, an organic garden-cum-kitchen classroom for students. Waters' also founded **Slow Food Nation**, the country's largest celebration of sustainable foods; and her influence can be tasted in numerous establishments serving Californian cuisine.

flavors mingle with creative techniques. Every Thursday, the **North Shattuck Organic Farmer's Market** draws cooking enthusiasts looking to expand their repertoire with a vast range of regionally sourced produce.

GOURMET GHETTO

B udget-conscious Berkeleyites needn't look to restaurants alone for pristine, local, and organic food. Their very own **North Shattuck** corridor (also known as the "gourmet ghetto") gratifies with garden-fresh produce as well as takeout from **Grégoire** and **Epicurious**. This area is also home to aficionados who frequent co-ops like the **Cheese Board Collective**, **Cheese Board Pizza Collective**, and **Acme Bread Company** for first-rate produce and variety. **The Juice Bar Collective** keeps diet-conscious droves coming back for more; whereas meat addicts can't get enough of Chef Paul Bertolli's **Fra'Mani Salumi**, where traditional Italian

M eanwhile, hungover scholars can't imagine beginning a day without brunch at **La Note**, where the cinnamon-brioche *pain perdu* packs a walloping punch. Too rich? Test the spread at **Tomate Cafe**, churning out an amazing Cuban breakfast followed by lunch on the pup-friendly patio. Cooks on a mission collect routinely at ingredient-driven **Berkeley Bowl**, a grocery store-farmer's market hybrid, to scan their offering of fresh produce, cooked items, and health foods. Named after a region in Southwest India, **Udupi Palace** is equally revolutionary in concept, with cooking that is wildly popular for that region's delicacies. Sample the likes of *dosas*, packed with spiced mashed potatoes and paired with fiery *sambar*, for an undoubtedly satisfying meal.

OAKLAND

Located across the bridge from the city, Oakland may not exude the same culinary flamboyance. Nevertheless, this earnest and enterprising city has seen a resurgence of its own, thanks to an influx of businesses and residences. With panoramic views of the Bay, terrific restaurants, shops, and a hopping nightlife, Jack London Square is not only a tourist draw but equally revered by locals for sun-soaked docks and a **Sunday Farmers' and Artisan Market**. Routine-loving locals cherish mornings at **La Farine**, a European-style bakery, serving pastries, cakes, and buttery croissants. As noon sets in, downtown crowds nosh on po'boys from **Café 15**. But over in Temescal, **Bakesale Betty** caters to big appetites with bulky chicken sandwiches served atop ironing-board tables. Post-work revelry reaches epic status at the **Trappist**, pouring over 160 Belgian and other specialty beers. However, if dessert is the most divine way to end a day, then convene at **Fentons Creamery**, churning handmade ice creams for over 120 delicious years. Similarly, **Lush Gelato** spotlights homegrown ingredients like Cowgirl Creamery Fromage Blanc or McEvoy Ranch Olive Oil in some of the city's most decadent flavors. **Tara's Organic Ice Cream** continues the craze with unique licks like beet-balsamic in compostable cups.

HOME IS WHERE THE HEART IS

Down-home Mexican food fans get their fiesta on at taco trucks parked along International Boulevard. However, local joints like **Tacos Sinaloa** remain the real deal for these treats. The **Art & Soul Festival** in August brings a buffet of world flavors; and **Chinatown Streetfest** adds to the lure with fragrant curries served alongside flavorful barbecue. Bonus bites await at **Market Hall**, a shopper's paradise presenting fresh, sustainable seafood at **Hapuku Fish Shop**; specialty eats at **Pasta Shop**; and delicious blends from **Highwire Coffee Roasters**. Set between Oakland and Berkeley, Rockridge boasts of plethora of quaint boutiques and tasty eateries—namely **Oaktown Spice Shop** on Grand Avenue, showcasing excellent herbs and exotic spices, available in both small amounts and bulk bags.

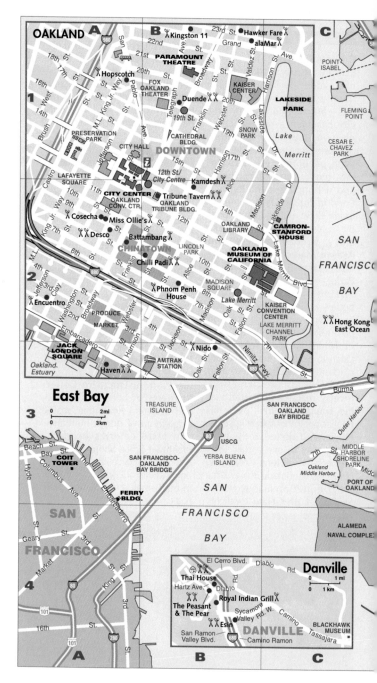

OAKLAND

A • 980 • San Pablo Ave.

B • Kingston 11 • 23rd St. • Hawker Fare X • Grand • alaMar X

C

18th St.
17th St.
16th St.
14th St.
West St.

M.L. King Jr. Way

X Hopscotch

22nd
21st St.
20th St.
19th St.

Broadway
Telegraph Ave.
Franklin St.

PARAMOUNT THEATRE

FOX OAKLAND THEATER

Duende X X

KAISER CENTER

Webster St.
Harrison St.
Valdez St.
Lakeside Dr.

POINT ISABEL

FLEMING POINT

LAKESIDE PARK

Lake Merritt

CESAR E. CHAVEZ PARK

Brush St.
Jefferson St.
Castro St.

PRESERVATION PARK

CITY HALL

CATHEDRAL BLDG.

DOWNTOWN

15th St.

12th St/ City Centre

Kamdesh X

20th St.
19th St.
17th St.

SNOW PARK

LAFAYETTE SQUARE

M.L. King Jr. Way
9th St.
10th St.
11th St.

CITY CENTER
OAKLAND CONV. CTR.

Tribune Tavern X X
OAKLAND TRIBUNE BLDG.

14th St.

Alice St.
Madison St.

OAKLAND LIBRARY

Lakeside Dr.

CAMRON-STANFORD HOUSE

SAN

FRANCISCO

BAY

X Cosecha
X X Desco

Miss Ollie's X

Battambang X

CHINATOWN

LINCOLN PARK

12th St.
10th St.

OAKLAND MUSEUM OF CALIFORNIA

K ing Jr. Way
4th
3rd
Jefferson St.
Clay St.
Washington St.
Broadway
Webster St.

2nd St.

X Encuentro

Chilli Padi X X

X Phnom Penh House

MADISON SQUARE

8th
7th
Oak St.
Fallon St.
Madison St.
Lake Merritt Blvd.

Lake Merritt

KAISER CONVENTION CENTER

X X Hong Kong East Ocean

PRODUCE MARKET

Embarcadero

JACK LONDON SQUARE

Oakland Estuary

Haven X X

Harrison St.
3rd St.
4th St.
Jackson St.

X Nido

AMTRAK STATION

Oak St.
Fallon St.

Nimitz Fwy.
880

East Bay

3
0 ———— 2mi
0 ———— 3km

Beach St.
Bay St.
The Embarcadero
Hyde St.
Columbus Ave.

COIT TOWER

FERRY BLDG.

SAN

FRANCISCO

Geary St.
Market St.
3rd St.
King St.

TREASURE ISLAND

USCG

SAN FRANCISCO-OAKLAND BAY BRIDGE

YERBA BUENA ISLAND

SAN

FRANCISCO

BAY

4

101
80
280
16th St.

SAN FRANCISCO-OAKLAND BAY BRIDGE

Burma

Outer Harbor

7th St.

MIDDLE HARBOR SHORELINE PARK

Oakland Middle Harbor

Middle

PORT OF OAKLAND

ALAMEDA NAVAL COMPLEX

80

81

Danville inset

El Cerro Blvd.

Diablo Rd.

Danville

0 ———— 1mi
0 ———— 1 km

X X Thai House

Hartz Ave.
Diablo Rd.

Royal Indian Grill X

X X The Peasant & The Pear

Sycamore Valley Rd. W.
Camino Ramon
San Ramon Valley Blvd.

X X Esin

DANVILLE

BLACKHAWK MUSEUM

Camino Tassajara

680

172

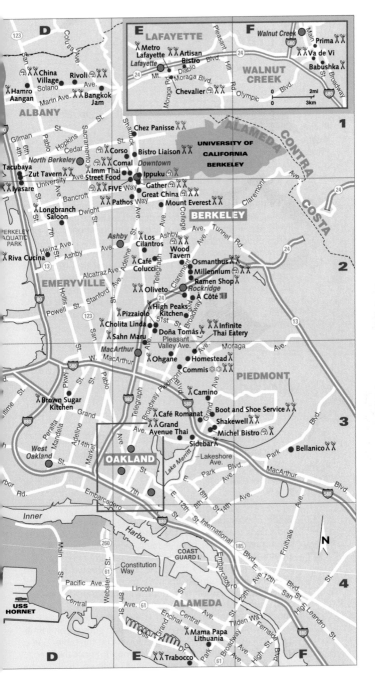

D

123
Colusa Ave.
Solano Ave.

⚲ 🍴🍴 **China Village** **Rivoli** 🍴🍴
🍴 **Hamro** Marin Ave. 🍴🍴 **Bangkok**
Aangan **Jam**

ALBANY

St.
Sacramento St.
Shattuck St.

Gilman St.
Hopkins St.
4th Cedar St.
Pablo

🍴 **Chez Panisse** 🍴🍴

North Berkeley ⚲ 🍴 **Corso** ● **Bistro Liaison** 🍴🍴
Tacubaya ⚲ 🍴🍴 **Comal** *Downtown*
🍴 **Zut Tavern** 🍴🍴 **Imm Thai** **Ippuku** 🍴
🍴🍴 **Iyasare** University Ave. **Street Food**
🍴🍴 **FIVE** **Gather** ⚲ 🍴🍴 **Way**
Bancroft 🍴🍴 **Pathos** **Great China** ⚲ 🍴
🍴 **Longbranch** Dwight St. **Way** 🍴 **Mount Everest** 🍴🍴
Saloon

UNIVERSITY OF
CALIFORNIA
BERKELEY

BERKELEY

ALAMEDA
CONTRA
COSTA

BERKELEY
AQUATIC
PARK

🍴 **Riva Cucina** Heinz Ave.
Ashby Ave.

Ashby ⚲ 🍴 **Los**
Cilantros Ashby Ave.
College Ave.
Tunnel Rd.

🍴 **Café** **Wood**
Colucci **Tavern**

EMERYVILLE Adeline St. 🍴🍴 **Oliveto** Telegraph Ave. Claremont Ave.
Alcatraz Ave.
Stanford

Hollis St.
Powell St.
123

🍴 **Osmanthus** 🍴🍴
● **Millennium** 🍴🍴
● **Ramen Shop** 🍴
Rockridge ⚲
● **À Côté** 🍴

🍴 **High Peaks** 51st St.
Kitchen Broadway

🍴 **Pizzaiolo**
🍴 **Cholita Linda**
🍴 **Sahn Maru**

🍴🍴 **Infinite**
Thai Eatery

Doña Tomás 🍴

MacArthur ⚲
W. MacArthur Blvd.
580

🍴 **Ohgane** ● **Homestead** 🍴🍴
● **Commis** ⚲ 🍴🍴

PIEDMONT
Piedmont Ave.
Grand Ave.

🍴 **Brown Sugar** Grand Ave.
Kitchen

🍴 **Camino**

880
Telegraph Ave.
Broadway

🍴 **Café Romanat** 🍴🍴 **Boot and Shoe Service** 🍴🍴
🍴🍴 **Grand** 🍴🍴 **Shakewell** 🍴🍴
Avenue Thai 🍴 **Michel Bistro** 🍴

Peralta St.
Mandela Pkwy.
A14th St.
Market St.

West
Oakland ⚲
St.

OAKLAND ⚲

Lake Merritt

🍴 **Sidebar**

● **Bellanico** 🍴🍴

Lakeshore Ave.
Park Blvd.
MacArthur Blvd.
580

rbor Rd.
7th St.
Embarcadero

Inner
Harbor
260

COAST
GUARD I.
880
E. 12th St.
International Blvd.
185
Fruitvale Ave.

N

USS
HORNET

Main St.
Pacific Ave.
Webster St.
61
Constitution
Way
Lincoln Ave.
8th St.
61
Central Ave.

ALAMEDA
Encinal Ave.
Grand
Central Ave.
Otis

🍴 **Mama Papa**
Lithuania

Park St.
Broadway
High St.
Tilden Way
Fernside Blvd.
580

🍴🍴 **Trabocco**
61

E

LAFAYETTE

🍴 **Metro**
Lafayette
Lafayette ⚲
🍴🍴 **Artisan**
Bistro
Pleasant Hill Rd.

24 Mt. Diablo Blvd.
Moraga Blvd.
Moraga Rd.
Olympic Blvd.

🍴🍴 **Chevalier**

F

Walnut Creek ● 680 Main St.
● **Prima** 🍴🍴
🍴 🍴🍴 **Va de Vi**
Babushka 🍴🍴
Broadway

WALNUT
CREEK

0 ___ 2mi
0 ___ 3km

173

À Côté

E2

M e d i t e r r a n e a n

5478 College Ave. (bet. Lawton & Taft Aves.), Oakland

Phone: 510-655-6469
Web: www.acoterestaurant.com
Prices: $$

Dinner nightly

A long-running small-plates icon set within the posh stores of Rockridge, À Côté nearly always requires a wait—only a handful of seats are available for reservations. But, after settling into a cozy wood table or perhaps at the granite bar, a lively, very communal vibe will ease any irritation. Forty-plus wines offered by the glass augment the appeal.

The seasonal menu has a French affect, discernable in plump fava bean falafel set atop tart tahini and pickled turnips; or green-garlic soup with a *fromage blanc* crouton. Entrées like seared yellowtail Jack brightened with asparagus, spring onion, and a Meyer lemon-blood orange relish perk up the palate; while a wood-fired oven and heated patio provide comforting warmth for indoor and outdoor meals.

alaMar

B1

S e a f o o d

100 Grand Ave., Ste. 111 (at Valdez St.), Oakland

Phone: 510-907-7555
Web: www.alamaroakland.com
Prices: $$

Lunch Tue – Fri
Dinner Mon – Sat

While alaMar does a steady business serving sandwiches and salads to downtown Oakland office workers, the food-savvy prefer to dine here at night, when the menu flips to a memorable array of seafood dishes—many offered by the pound in low-country boil style. Golden-brown blue crab poppers boast a punchy anchovy-piquillo aïoli, while a boil of fresh local crawfish is studded with house-made sausage, corn on the cob, and spring garlic.

The space, with aqua-painted walls and rope elements, is tastefully nautical and designed to cater to guests' comfort as they peel apart dinner—there are towels on the tables and a special hand-washing sink. Bring a group to shoot the breeze as you work; then split some beignets with caramel-mocha sauce as a reward.

Artisan Bistro

French XX

E1

1005 Brown Ave. (at Mt. Diablo Blvd.), Lafayette

Lunch & dinner Tue – Sun

Phone: 925-962-0882
Web: www.artisanlafayette.com
Prices: $$

From the warm welcome to top-notch service, Artisan Bistro's staff makes dining here a genuine pleasure. They're aided by the quaint setting of a Craftsman-style cottage featuring a garden patio, romantic interior, and trickling fountain amongst the flora.

Arrive early to kick things off with a creative cocktail at the tiny front bar, then move to a table to enjoy Chef/owner John Marquez's Cal-French fare. This may reveal a bright Cobb salad draped with delicately poached Maine lobster, or seared John Dory over artichokes, asparagus, and capers. Ladies who lunch swear by the chicken and avocado sandwich, served with shoestring fries. And for a fantastic finish, don't miss the outstanding butterscotch panna cotta with candied lemon and blueberry sauce.

Babushka

Eastern European X

F1

1475 Newell Ave. (bet. Main St. & Maria Ln.), Walnut Creek

Lunch & dinner Wed – Sun

Phone: 925-210-0779
Web: www.babushkafood.com
Prices: $$

Home to the best Russian food this side of Moscow, this Walnut Creek fixture has been a local favorite for two decades. Don't be misled by the deli of the same name in front—a door inside will transport you to a lovely white-tablecloth dining room, complete with charming servers and a full wine selection.

Rib-sticking classics are all perfectly executed here. Buttery and super-crispy chicken Kiev is made to order; thick borscht brims with rich beet flavor; beef stroganoff is an aromatic delight; and pork- and beef-stuffed *pelmeni* dance in an herbaceous broth. Keep your eye out for the refrigerated case of gorgeous, house-made desserts. But, if you're too full, be sure to take home a slice or two of their insanely delicious Napoleon sheet cake.

Bangkok Jam

D1

Thai

1892 Solano Ave. (bet. Fresno Ave. & The Alameda), Berkeley

Phone: 510-525-3625
Web: www.bangkok-jam.com
Prices: 💰💰

Lunch & dinner daily

Do not be deterred by the plain façade sandwiched amid retail stores. Inside, this long and narrow space is contemporary and stylish with glittering chandeliers, dark wood tables, and brick wainscoting. A sweet, attentive staff keeps things casual and kid-friendly.

Whet the appetite with a plate of crispy vegetable spring rolls stuffed with carrots, cabbage, and onion, served with a tangy sweet and sour dipping sauce. Follow this with organic lemongrass chicken breast, tender and smoky, served over rice and complemented by a duo of spicy lime and sweet tamarind sauces. However, curries are the true standout here, with choices ranging from succulent pumpkin to sweet and spicy mango stewed in coconut red curry with cabbage, peas, carrots, bell peppers, and tofu.

Battambang

A2

Cambodian

850 Broadway (bet. 8th & 9th Sts.), Oakland

Phone: 510-839-8815
Web: N/A
Prices: 💰💰

Lunch Mon – Sat
Dinner nightly

Embrace the unknown at one of the Bay Area's very few Cambodian restaurants. Though the menu may be unfamiliar to Western palates, Battambang boasts warm, hands-on service that will make any diner feel at ease. Don't let its gaudy exterior deter you: the interior is pleasant and tastefully adorned.

The must-order here is the *amok trei,* a hard-to-find dish of catfish steamed in a fragrant banana leaf. Layered with red lemongrass sauce and coconut milk, it's utterly beguiling. Equally good is the spicy-sour *yihoeur char tumpaing,* a stir-fry of calamari and bamboo shoots with lemongrass and ground chili. Adventurous diners should also sample the omelet-like *num banchev,* an eggy rice-flour crêpe with chicken, prawns, sprouts, and a strong, funky fish sauce.

Bellanico

Italian ✗✗

 F3

4238 Park Blvd. (at Wellington St.), Oakland

Phone:	510-336-1180	Lunch & dinner daily
Web:	www.bellanico.net	
Prices:	$$	

Considering Bellanico is named for its owners' daughters, it's no surprise that this resto is a hit with families. The sibling of Potrero Hill's Aperto, it fills day and night with local couples (dining with or without their children), enjoying the cheery, persimmon-accented dining room, bustling open kitchen, and wall of windows overlooking Park Boulevard.

Kick off a meal with kid-friendly antipasti like cauliflower fritters with garlic *aglioli* or fresh burrata with grilled bread. Then dig into a pasta like the *tagliolini pepati*, full of smoky bacon, chopped hot peppers, wilted arugula, chili, and garlic. The pan-roasted chicken breast is also a favorite for all ages, with tasty seasonal accompaniments like roasted sweet corn and toybox squash.

Bistro Liaison

French ✗✗

E1

1849 Shattuck Ave. (at Hearst Ave.), Berkeley

Phone:	510-849-2155	Lunch Sun – Fri
Web:	www.liaisonbistro.com	Dinner nightly
Prices:	$$	

This slice of Paris in Berkeley, just two blocks from campus, draws regulars with its authentic bistro vibe, complete with closely spaced tables and cheerful yellow walls displaying vintage French posters and artwork. On warm days, diners scramble to score one of the sidewalk tables, though the traffic on busy Shattuck Avenue might dispel any fantasies of the Champs-Élysées.

The fare, like the décor, is classic French, with dishes like escargots in garlic butter and a croque monsieur oozing with Emmenthaler cheese. At dinner, hearty bœuf bourguignon and steamed mussels in garlic and white wine send diners into Gallic reveries. Finish with a buttery, flaky apple tarte Tatin, drowned in caramel and topped with a scoop of rum-raisin ice cream.

Boot and Shoe Service

E3

Pizza 🍴🍴

3308 Grand Ave. (bet. Lake Park Ave. & Mandana Blvd.), Oakland

Phone: 510-763-2668   Lunch & dinner Tue – Sun
Web: www.bootandshoeservice.com
Prices: $$

Named for its former incarnation as a shoe-repair shop, this very accommodating Grand Avenue standby brings stellar pizzas and a totally relaxed vibe to its hungry neighborhood. The light, bright space suits every configuration, from the solo dining counter to gregarious communal tables and a semi-private room for large groups. Adept servers cater to the whims of hipsters and families alike.

Dig into blistered Californian pies like wild nettle and *ricotta salata*; or try bacon, Calabrian chili, and cream. Other menu offerings should also be explored, especially the chili-inflected heirloom bean ragù with a velvety soft-cooked egg, smoky from the wood-fired oven. Healthier options feature a nutty farro salad with tender marinated beets and fresh herbs.

Brown Sugar Kitchen

D3

American 🍴

2534 Mandela Pkwy. (at 26th St.), Oakland

Phone: 510-839-7685   Lunch Tue – Sun
Web: www.brownsugarkitchen.com
Prices: 💰💰

Its industrial West Oakland location is far from any sort of restaurant row, but visitors to this soul-food palace (open for breakfast and lunch only) will find plenty of company—mostly ahead of them in line. Over the years, Chef/owner Tanya Holland has built a loyal following of families as well as foodies who arrive early to avoid those long waits for tender, flaky biscuits and signature buttermilk fried chicken with a cornmeal waffle. Others go for the juicy jerk chicken with a kick of heat, cooled by mashed yams and pineapple-red onion salsa. The earthy, well-seasoned black-eyed pea salad is another favorite—and fittingly so.

Casual and welcoming with a chill vibe and colorful look, BSK may be a crowd magnet, but it's earned the hype.

Café Colucci

E2 **Ethiopian** ✗

6427 Telegraph Ave. (at 65th St.), Oakland

Phone: 510-601-7999   Lunch & dinner daily
Web: www.cafecolucci.com
Prices: 🍲

On a stretch of Telegraph that's something of an Ethiopian restaurant row, Colucci stands out for its eye-catching décor, including a plant-laden terrace, fabric-draped ceiling, and selection of African art. As with all Ethiopian restaurants, bring clean hands and leave your fork at home: you'll be dining exclusively with *injera*, the spongy-sour bread that's traditional to the country.

The menu offers many appealing options to scoop, from mild *begue tibs* (lamb with onions, garlic, and rosemary), to spicy eggplant *wot* stewed in a piquant *berbere* sauce. Fried potato slices called *dentich tibs* are great on their own, but extra tasty when paired with *assa tibs*, a whole baked fish. Save room for a buttery pistachio baklava and house-roasted Ethiopian coffee.

Café Romanat

E3 **Ethiopian** ✗

462 Santa Clara Ave. (near Grand Ave.), Oakland

Phone: 510-444-1800   Lunch & dinner Tue – Sun
Web: www.caferomanat.com
Prices: 🍲

In a stretch of Oakland that teems with Ethiopian restaurants, Romanat is a standout, thanks to deliciously spiced dishes served in generous portions. Locals (including some Ethiopian families) fill the small room, set with traditional low stools and woven tables and featuring colorful fabric curtains and artwork.

Order up an Ethiopian beer, honey wine, or a nutty ground flax or sesame seed juice to pair with the *sambussas*, triangular pastries stuffed with piquant, chile-flecked ground beef. All the combo platters, served on spongy, slightly sour *injera*, are perfect for sharing. And the veggie combo, with dishes like sautéed collard greens, lentils in smoky *berbere*, and split peas with turmeric and ginger, will delight any crowd.

Camino

Californian ✗

E3

3917 Grand Ave. (bet. Jean St. & Sunnyslope Ave.), Oakland

Phone: 510-547-5035
Web: www.caminorestaurant.com
Prices: $$

Lunch Sat – Sun
Dinner Wed – Mon

With its look of a medieval refectory and that central wood-burning hearth, Camino can seem like a trip to the days of yore—but the cool crowd, fun cocktails, and innovative food are decidedly modern. Take a seat under wrought-iron chandeliers at one of the long, communal tables (one of them is cut from a single redwood tree!) and expect to make some new friends.

Chef-owner Russell Moore worked at Chez Panisse for many years, and his food is appropriately hyper-seasonal. An egg baked in the wood oven, its yolk still creamy, is nestled in leeks, herbs, and cream, while slices of char-grilled sourdough provide the base for a sandwich of juicy pancetta and rustic sauerkraut. Moist, sticky Lardy cake is also grilled, and topped with rich ricotta and honey.

Chevalier 😊

French ✗✗

E1

960 Moraga Rd. (at Moraga Blvd.), Lafayette

Phone: 925-385-0793
Web: www.chevalierrestaurant.com
Prices: $$

Dinner Wed – Sun

From the flowers that dot its outdoor patio to the trickling water fountains and chic curtains, everything about Chevalier radiates French charm. Inside, you'll find a cadre of friendly servers gliding effortlessly between tables, with the chef drifting out to chat up guests from time to time.

Chevalier's three-course prix-fixe offers traditional French fare at exceptional value. Meaty *escargots de Bourgogne* arrive pooled in a delicious garlic- and parsley-butter, with chewy baguette slices for dipping; while a tender Piedmontese-style flat iron steak is laced with a heavenly Bordelaise sauce and served with hand-cut fries and field green. At the end, a softly-poached meringue floating island is paired with crème Anglaise and drizzled with delicious caramel and toasted almonds.

Chez Panisse

Californian ✗✗

E1

1517 Shattuck Ave. (bet. Cedar & Vine Sts.), Berkeley

Phone:	510-548-5525	Dinner Mon – Sat
Web:	www.chezpanisse.com	
Prices:	**$$$$**	

For avid gourmets, Alice Waters' mecca of Californian cuisine needs no introduction. Housed in a beautiful Craftsman-style home, it's divided in two: the upstairs café offers more casual fare, while the elegant downstairs restaurant serves a nightly prix-fixe menu. Both spaces teem with copper light fixtures, displays of seasonal foliage, and vintage glassware.

The restaurant prides itself on serving every ingredient at peak season, from the raspberries in a prosecco aperitif to the delicate Black Prince tomato that tops handmade roasted eggplant ravioli. Many dishes are cooked at the wood-fired hearth, like a delectably smoky pork loin with sweet corn and fried squash blossoms. This icon books up early; be sure to reserve a month in advance.

Chilli Padi

Malaysian ✗✗

B2

366 8th St. (bet. Franklin & Webster Sts.), Oakland

Phone:	510-891-8862	Lunch & dinner daily
Web:	www.chillipadimalaysiancuisine.com	
Prices:	**$$**	

Shake up your Oakland Chinatown routine with a trip to this contemporary newcomer, which blends Malaysian and Chinese flavors into an interesting menu that's jam-packed with flavor. Kick things off with the terrific Chilli Padi Sampler, which features tangy green papaya salad, moist chicken satay, samosas, tofu fritters, and a delicious Malaysian-style roti with warm curry dipping sauce.

From there, the mindful servers can recommend dishes like chili-soy chicken and vegetables served in a crisp taro nest, or classic *char kway teow*, flat rice noodles with shrimp, squid, and shrimp paste. With its dark wood floors and undulating fuchsia walls, the space is sleek and clean, which may explain why it has caught on with the largely local crowd.

China Village

Chinese ✕✕

1335 Solano Ave. (at Ramona Ave.), Albany

Phone: 510-525-2285
Web: www.chinavillagealbany.com
Prices:

Lunch & dinner daily

It takes a village to feed a big group, and this laid-back spot is a favorite with families. A stylish recent renovation has added a sleek front bar, contemporary chandeliers, and dramatic Chinese art, but one look at the scorching-hot menu options—think spicy Sichuan frog and flaky sautéed fish with pickled chili peppers—confirms the authenticity factor.

Skip the Hunan, Mandarin, and Cantonese offerings in favor of the Sichuan specialties, like dry-fried, bone-in chicken laced with ground chili and numbing peppercorns. And be sure to order the five-spice hot and spicy pork shoulder. A house specialty, this mouthwatering dish is fork- (or chopstick) tender and rests atop a deliciously piquant chili-oil jus with baby bok choy, scallions, and garlic.

Cholita Linda

E2

Latin American ✕

4923 Telegraph Ave. (bet. 48th & 51st Sts.), Oakland

Phone: 510-594-7610
Web: www.cholitalinda.com
Prices:

Lunch & dinner Mon – Sat

The old Bay Area saw of farm-to-table gets a tasty spin at this purveyor of Latin fare, which transformed from a megapopular farmer's market stand into a packed house of communal tables. Bright, colorfully decorated, and flooded with natural light, it's a casual space where diners order and pay at the counter, then sip drinks from glass Mason jars under the potted palms.

The outstanding Baja fish tacos are the source of Cholita Linda's reputation, but its dishes traverse Latin America, from a hearty Cubano to a plate of slow-braised, well-seasoned carnitas with black beans and fried plantains. With such reasonable prices, there's no excuse not to order a sweet, smooth mango *agua fresca* to wash down the tender, tangy *pollo al pastor* tacos.

Comal 😊

Mexican ✕✕

E1

2020 Shattuck Ave. (bet. Addison St. & University Ave.), Berkeley

Phone: 510-926-6300   Dinner nightly
Web: www.comalberkeley.com
Prices: $$

For bold, zesty Mexican food crafted with pristine ingredients, Berkeleyites throng this industrial-chic hot spot, where an excellent cocktail program and an extensive tequila plus mezcal selection keep things buzzing. The large flat tortilla griddles for which it's named are on full display in the open kitchen, while a covered, heated back patio draws locals for year-round outdoor dining.

Comal's fryer-fresh warm tortilla chips, paired with perfect, creamy guacamole, are irresistible; summon an order as you peruse options like the refreshing white shrimp ceviche and earthy hen-of-the-woods mushroom quesadilla. Just make sure the smoky wood-grilled rock cod tacos, with creamy avocado aïoli and spicy cabbage slaw, are on your must-order list.

Corso 😊

Italian ✕

E1

1788 Shattuck Ave. (bet. Delaware & Francisco Sts.), Berkeley

Phone: 510-704-8004   Dinner nightly
Web: www.corsoberkeley.com
Prices: $$

A Tuscan follow-up from the couple behind nearby Rivoli, Corso is every bit the equal of its big sister, thanks to generous, Florentine-inspired dishes like a roasted squid panzanella with torn flatbread, buttery white beans, and bright dashes of lemon juice and chili oil. Pasta fiends will swoon for house-made tagliatelle in a meaty beef and pork sugo, while butter-roasted chicken boasts juicy meat, golden-brown skin as well as fresh peas and asparagus alongside.

Soul-warming in its hospitality, Corso is the kind of place where servers will bring complimentary pistachio biscotti simply because they're "so good when they're warm." It's no surprise that the tiny trattoria is a favorite among new couples, so be sure to reserve in advance and come hungry.

Commis ❀ ❀

3859 Piedmont Ave. (at Rio Vista Ave.), Oakland

Phone: 510-653-3902   Dinner Wed – Sun
Web: www.commisrestaurant.com
Prices: $$$$

Chef/owner James Syhabout may be keeping busy outside of Commis at his other popular restaurants, but this sparse Oakland original is still turning out elegant and creatively complex seasonal dishes to a packed house every night.

Tucked into colorful, boutique-strewn Piedmont Avenue, this dining space is a long, clean, minimalist number with a smattering of tables up front; intimate banquette seating in the back; and a lively counter overlooking the humming kitchen. Soft hip-hop music and a vibrant service staff set the mood—cool and contemporary; relaxed but serious.

In the kitchen, Chef Syhabout pairs well-sourced, local ingredients with precise technique to create his sophisticated nightly tasting, which continues to be exciting even for jaded gourmands. Dinner might unveil a plate of silky scallops paired with tangy crème fraîche, poached asparagus, and charred lemon granité; warm, roasted abalone with artichoke heart, fried artichoke slivers, and chicken sabayon; or a chilled fava bean soup laced with tarragon-infused crème fraîche, green tomato gelée, and smoked trout roe. A perfectly poached halibut confit with spring pea "porridge" and ginger foam is another beautifully composed plate that reflects the kitchen's attention to detail.

Cosecha

Mexican ⛼

A2

907 Washington St. (at 9th St.), Oakland

Phone: 510-452-5900
Web: www.cosechacafe.com
Prices: ♿♿

Lunch & dinner Mon – Sat

Even the pickiest Mexican *abuela* would be hard-pressed to turn down a meal at Cosecha, where the heartwarming blue-plate specials are made from scratch daily. Handmade tortillas stuffed with roasted yams and creamy Oaxaca cheese, or flaky fish and smoky chipotle *crema* are a cut above typical taqueria fare, while the chicken *torta ahogada* nearly bursts with tender grilled meat, soft pinto beans, garlicky guacamole, and spicy *guajillo* chile.

Housed in Old Oakland's historic Swan's Marketplace, Cosecha draws a loyal crowd of business people at lunchtime and local residents in the evenings. They order at the counter, take a seat at the communal tables, and sip tangy, refreshing lime *aguas frescas* as they await the delicious creations in store.

Desco

Italian ⛼⛼

A2

499 9th St. (at Washington St.), Oakland

Phone: 510-663-9000
Web: www.descooakland.com
Prices: $$

Lunch Mon – Fri
Dinner nightly

After a tumultuous series of turnovers, this beautiful Old Oakland space has found a solid owner in Donato Scotti (of Redwood City's Donato Enoteca), who's given it an Italian spin. Inside, the exposed brick walls, copper-topped bar, wood-burning oven, and mosaic floors in the 1870s-era building are as captivating as the food is delicious.

Desco's simple offerings are full of flavor, from a house-made charcuterie board of smoked duck, roasted *porchetta*, and rabbit terrine to golden pappardelle bathed in a thick lamb, red onion, and tomato *sugo*. For dessert, the pear-almond torta with hazelnut gelato is a must. The wine list boasts 50 Italian selections, half of which are available by the glass—no wonder the bar is so popular for happy hour.

Doña Tomás

E2

5004 Telegraph Ave. (bet. 49th & 51st Sts.), Oakland

Phone: 510-450-0522   Lunch Sat – Sun
Web: www.donatomas.com   Dinner Tue – Sat
Prices: $$

Californian ingredients and Mexican flavors combine to create magic at this Temescal neighborhood standby, where regulars pour in at happy hour to chat with their favorite bartenders, and families savor warm Oakland nights on the spacious patio. In fact, Doña (and Berkeley sibling Tacubaya) is enough of a draw that you'll regret not making reservations, particularly on weekends.

Hearty but never heavy, meals here commence with fresh-fried chips and appetizers like a butternut squash quesadilla packed with caramelized onions, corn, and poblano chile. Delightfully smoky *mole negro* stars in the shredded chicken enchiladas, served with braised kale and black beans. For dessert, a traditional *tres leches* is light as air—and heavy on flavor.

Duende

B1

468 19th St. (bet. Broadway & Telegraph Ave.), Oakland

Phone: 510-230-7350   Dinner Wed – Mon
Web: www.duendeoakland.com
Prices: $$$

Savor the flavors and sounds of Spain at this novel restaurant in developing Uptown Oakland, where Chef/owner Paul Canales turns out everything from *pintxos* to paella. The voluminous bi-level space set in the historic Floral Depot is packed with large windows, exposed brick, and colorful murals which contribute a fun vibe attracting groups of hip, urban types.

The food is authentic with seasonal accents and has included rabbit and lobster sausage with blistered Padrón peppers; and seafood-studded *arroz negro*, thick with rockfish, scallops, cherry tomatoes, and garlic aïoli. The crowd is loud and festive, especially when one of the rotating local musicians hits the stage for a set. Like the food and ambience, the music lends Duende a casual, warm energy.

Encuentro

Vegetarian 🍴

A2

550 2nd St. (at Clay St.), Oakland

Phone: 510-832-9463   Dinner Tue – Sun
Web: www.encuentrooakland.com
Prices: $$

Recently relocated, Encuentro is now sitting pretty in an industrial-chic space fitted with large windows, lofty ceilings, and an easy-breezy front bar. Though it's minimal in a California-meets-Manhattan way, the kitchen promises maximum satisfaction via its haute (read: heavenly) take on vegan treats. Avocado bruschetta drizzled with olive oil and chili jam entices with a kick of spice, while baby kale and roasted veggies are enriched with toasted quinoa and a lemon-tahini dressing.

Here, each menu item is so carefully composed and appetizingly prepared (think of empanadas stuffed with pumpkin seed *piccadillo* served atop pinto beans with cashew *crema*) that you won't miss the meat—which explains why the dining room is peppered with carnivores.

Esin

Mediterranean 🍴🍴

B4

750 Camino Ramon (at Sycamore Valley Rd.), Danville

Phone: 925-314-0974   Lunch & dinner daily
Web: www.esinrestaurant.com
Prices: $$

Esin brings tasty Mediterranean and American inspiration to this boutique-filled Danville shopping complex. The spacious restaurant outfitted with a front bar combines several dining areas trimmed in dark wood, nicely contrasted with soft beige walls and bright windows. Lunchtime service efficiently accommodates groups of area business people, while evenings draw locals who soak in the ambience.

Meals here might begin with a hearty Tuscan-style kale and white bean soup flavored with oregano and garlic, liberally sprinkled with parmesan cheese. Then, sample the tender pot roast in reduced jus over a generous mound of garlicky mashed potatoes and roasted root vegetables. Homemade dessert specials are sure to beckon, as in the warm fig and almond galette.

FIVE 😊

E2

2086 Allston Way (at Shattuck Ave.), Berkeley

Phone: 510-225-6055   Lunch & dinner daily
Web: www.five-berkeley.com
Prices: $$

Right off Berkeley's main drag, this pre-cinema and pre-theater favorite in the historic Hotel Shattuck Plaza boasts a seriously impressive dining room, with airy high ceilings, dramatic pillars, and a gorgeous statement chandelier. Locals and hotel guests seem to be equally in love with its large front bar.

Fine dining it isn't, but FIVE has become a favorite for approachable American food—including items designed for Berkeley's sizable vegetarian crowd. A golden beet salad is a cornucopia of Californian ingredients including fresh ricotta, tomato, and cucumber, while the juicy, delicious house-ground burger is accompanied by addictive parmesan fries. For dessert, persimmon sorbet gives a burst of freshness to dense, intense chocolate lava cake.

Gather 😊

E2

2200 Oxford St. (at Allston Way), Berkeley

Phone: 510-809-0400   Lunch & dinner daily
Web: www.gatherrestaurant.com
Prices: $$

With its heavily vegetarian bill of fare, reclaimed and repurposed décor, and local Berkeley crowd, Gather is a must for mostly-meatless diners of all ages. This aptly-named hit offers a relaxed vibe for a light lunch, cocktails at the bar, dinner on the patio, and everything in between.

Surprisingly hearty dishes like chicory salad tossed with sliced fennel and fines herbes vinaigrette won't leave you craving meat, nor will the gourmet Wagon Wheel grilled cheese with braised greens and chanterelle mushrooms. Dinner is more complex, with ambitious offerings like the vegan "charcuterie," a platter of four delicious vegetable preparations. Should you venture into San Francisco City, be sure to visit its new—and already acclaimed—sister restaurant, Verbena.

Grand Avenue Thai

Thai XX

E3

384 Grand Ave. (bet. Perkins St. & Staten Ave.), Oakland

Phone: 510-444-1507

Web: www.grandavethai.net

Prices: 🍘

Lunch Mon – Fri
Dinner nightly

Thanks to its charming décor, friendly service, and flavorful cuisine, Grand Avenue Thai is a winning standout—just one block from picturesque Lake Merritt. The space is small with bright walls, fresh flowers, and colorful local artwork. Service is prompt even with a steady to-go business.

Be sure to try one of the house favorites like the sweet and fragrant coconut curry with chunks of pumpkin, eggplant, broccoli, and string beans. Summer rolls neatly wrap up fresh veggies and garlicky rice noodles for a dip in peanut-chili sauce, while the ever-popular pad Thai combines plump prawns stir-fried with egg, bean sprouts, scallions, and peanuts in a tasty tamarind-Thai fish sauce. Spice can be tame, but the kitchen is happy to indulge the fire fiends.

Great China 🙂

Chinese XX

E2

2190 Bancroft Way (at Fulton St.), Berkeley

Phone: 510-843-7996

Web: www.greatchinaberkeley.com

Prices: $$

Lunch & dinner Wed – Mon

Great China may have moved a block away following a catastrophic fire, but that hasn't dimmed its appeal. Chic enough for the style-savvy, cheap enough for Cal students, and authentic enough for local Chinese families, it's one of the few local restaurants everyone can—and does—agree on.

Fresh and flavorful meat and produce set Great China's food apart. And while it's not super-spicy, it's also not reliant on chili oil and Sichuan peppercorns to mask low-quality ingredients. Bring a group and savor it all: tender and aromatic twice-cooked pork, piquant *mapo* tofu, beautifully lacquered tea-smoked duck with fluffy steamed buns, and tender-crisp *ong choy* (water spinach) with fermented tofu paste. Generous portions and ample seating seal this savory deal.

Hamro Aangan

D1

Nepali

856 San Pablo Ave. (bet. Solano & Washington Aves.), Albany

Phone: 510-524-2220
Web: www.hamroaangan.com
Prices:

Lunch & dinner Thu – Tue

Nepali restaurants have proliferated in the East Bay of late, but Hamro Aangan remains at the top of the heap thanks to its rustic, flavorful, generously portioned dishes. The handmade *momos* (steamed dumplings filled with spiced cabbage, carrot, and onion) are accompanied by a garlicky curry sauce, while the fluffy, layered chicken biryani is rich with caramelized onions and ground cardamom. Goat stew with tomato and an intensely-spiced gravy is another delicious option.

Located on busy San Pablo Avenue, Hamro is low-key, with red, rose, and copper décor and a beautiful mural from a local Nepali artist on the wall. It attracts a steady stream of regulars, particularly families, making it an excellent choice for a casual meal with kids in tow.

Haven

Contemporary

44 Webster St. (at Jack London Sq.), Oakland

Phone: 510-663-4440
Web: www.havenoakland.com
Prices: $$

Dinner nightly

Locals continue to rely on this delight (part of the Daniel Patterson Group) for good food and a sleek, industrial-chic setting in prime Jack London Square. With windows facing the Square and counter seats offering great views into the open kitchen, it's hard to pick a perch; in either case, kick things off with one of the intriguing barrel-aged cocktails. The food is contemporary and seasonal, with exquisite ingredients in dishes like roasted Monterey squid with smoked fingerling potatoes, chorizo, and green olives, or lamb roulade with warm lentils and roasted fennel. For dessert, cinnamon churros with caramelized peaches and nasturtium whipped cream are quite divine.

Haven now offers a fixed three- or four-course menu in the dining room as well as a limited à la carte at the bar.

Hawker Fare

Asian ✗

B1

2300 Webster St. (at 23rd St.), Oakland

Phone: 510-832-8896
Web: www.hawkerfare.com
Prices: 💰

Lunch Mon – Fri
Dinner Tue – Sat

Those hawker stalls across Southeast Asia may not qualify as trendy, but here in uptown Oakland, hipsters in oversized eyeglasses and skinny jeans clamor for humble and tasty (if toned-down) street food. Groups of hard-drinking twenty- and thirty-something's are everywhere at Hawker Fare, sharing plates, perusing the faux-graffiti on the walls, and bobbing their heads to the beat of their own soundtrack.

They come for well-made Thai like arugula salad with lotus root, jicama, and Chinese sausage; or spicy *gang dang* tofu curry with pumpkin over steamed rice. Indeed, rice is everywhere on the menu, from lunchtime bowl combos to a coconut pudding with banana jam and sesame—a treat that merits the long waits.

A second location in the Mission is equally popular.

High Peaks Kitchen

Indian ✗

E2

5299 College Ave. (bet. Clifton St. & Manila Ave.), Oakland

Phone: 510-450-0644
Web: www.hipeaks.com
Prices: $$

Lunch & dinner Wed – Mon

The Himalayan-inspired name and Dalai Lama headshot might have you guessing correctly that this retreat is owned by Tibetans, but there's a twist: they were raised in India, and South Asian cooking is their specialty. The simple space, with its bright colors, small open kitchen, and inviting patio, is a cheerful setting for enjoying the delicious, affordable food.

A range of well-spiced dishes boast layers of aroma and flavor, from the whole cardamom, shredded ginger, and star anise in a fiery potato *vindaloo*, to the potent yellow curry in a stewed chicken *jalfrezi*. The clientele is largely Indian, a testament to the kitchen's authenticity, and they can be found filling up on potato-stuffed naan with toasted coriander and cumin as well as smoky, moist ground lamb kebabs with mint chutney.

Homestead

E3

4029 Piedmont Ave. (bet. 40th & 41st Sts.), Oakland

Phone: 510-420-6962   Dinner Tue – Sun
Web: www.homesteadoakland.com
Prices: $$

If it wasn't housed in a beautiful Julia Morgan-designed building, this farm-to-table jewel would be defined by the enticing smells that engulf you upon entrance. It's a rustic space, full of large windows peering onto Piedmont Avenue, and the jars of dry ingredients, pickling vegetables, and Julia Child cookbooks on the counter create an upscale country-kitchen vibe.

The menu focuses on the best and freshest of local produce such as a panzanella with shaved carrot and crunchy asparagus. Braised octopus with Marcona almonds is light and fresh, allowing room for the star of the show: incredible wood-roasted pork, tender and moist, with potato gratin alongside. For a bright breakfast, look no further than the house-baked pastries and quiche.

Hong Kong East Ocean

C2

3199 Powell St. (at Emeryville Marina), Emeryville

Phone: 510-655-3388   Lunch & dinner daily
Web: N/A
Prices: 👝👝

Primo panoramic views of the Bay Bridge and cityscape give this two-story favorite well-deserved attention. The spacious dining rooms may appear slightly dated, but who cares, given the stunning waterfront scene?

Lunchtime here at Hong Kong East Ocean is a dim sum affair. The place is packed with business folks savoring their *xiao long bao* (pork soup dumplings with fragrant, ginger-infused pork broth); fluffy pork buns; delicious rice noodle-crêpes filled with garlicky beef and cilantro; or steamed vegetable rolls, stuffed with sautéed mushrooms and wrapped in tofu. Nights draw a large crowd of local families who show up for seafood offerings such as wok-fried Dungeness crab with spicy herbs, or rock cod with ginger and scallions.

Hopscotch

American ✗

A1

1915 San Pablo Ave. (at 19th St.), Oakland

Phone: 510-788-6217   Lunch & dinner daily
Web: www.hopscotchoakland.com
Prices: $$

A stone's throw from the heart of transitioning (read: gentrifying) uptown Oakland, Hopscotch's Kickstarter buzz may have died down, but its small size means that reservations are a must. Checkered floors and red-and-chrome chairs lend a retro diner vibe, but you'd be hard-pressed to find cocktails as intriguing as a Domino (combining Scotch, amaro, blackberry, and jalapeño) at some local greasy spoon. The winning American cooking boasts subtle Japanese influences like the kabocha pumpkin cake with fresh pomegranate seeds. In the same vein, a tangy and bright pomegranate-and-sunchoke salad offers a refreshing counterpoint to heartier options like the cheekily named "first base" burger topped with sesame aïoli and griddled beef tongue.

Imm Thai Street Food

Thai ✗

E1

2068 University Ave. (bet. Milvia St. & Shattuck Ave.), Berkeley

Phone: 510-898-1123   Lunch & dinner daily
Web: N/A
Prices: 💰💰

While you won't actually be eating on the street, this bitty Berkeley spot isn't much more than a sidewalk stand with a handful of tables and counter seats. But what Imm lacks in glitz it more than makes up for in its bold, intensely spiced Thai cooking.

Bring the gang for an insanely affordable spread: start with thin slices of kabocha squash, battered and deep-fried until tender and served with a sweet-sour dipping sauce, or a tangy green papaya salad with fresh shrimp and a spicy chili-lime vinaigrette. Creamy red coconut curry is loaded with zucchini, bell peppers, bamboo shoots, and cubes of fresh tofu. And, don't skip out before trying the *suki*, a Thai-style hot pot packed with beef, chicken, prawns, tofu, veggies, glass noodles, and plenty of herbs.

Infinite Thai Eatery

Thai XX

E3

4301 Piedmont Ave. (at John St.), Oakland

Phone: 510-817-4816

Web: N/A

Prices: 🥜

Lunch & dinner Tue – Sun

Infinitely warm service is the hallmark of this engaging Thai newcomer, where the attentive owner checks in on each customer to ensure they're enjoying their meal (an easy task, as the food is fresh, fragrant, and prepared with top-notch ingredients). And, if you like things spicy don't worry—western palates aren't shortchanged here.

Kick things off with a classic *larb gai,* a cool salad of ground chicken mixed with lots of herbs and sliced shallots in a zippy lime dressing. Then turn up the temperature with the drunken rice noodles, packed with chicken and crisp vegetables in a fiery red chili-garlic sauce. If there's still room, opt for *moo yang,* grilled marinated pork boasting a rich smokiness and a tangy lime-chili dipping sauce.

Ippuku 😊

Japanese X

E1

2130 Center St. (bet. Oxford St. & Shattuck Ave.), Berkeley

Phone: 510-665-1969

Web: www.ippukuberkeley.com

Prices: $$

Dinner nightly

Can't swing a ticket to Tokyo? Dinner at Ippuku is the next best thing. With its low Japanese-style tables, extensive woodwork, and enormous selection of sake and shochu, it feels like an authentic *izakaya* transplanted into a corner of downtown Berkeley. The low-profile entrance adds to the feeling you've lucked upon a special dining secret—assuming you don't stroll right past it, that is.

Yakitori are the big draw here, with smoky, salty chicken thighs, necks, hearts, and gizzards arriving fresh off the *binchotan.* Other excellent small plates include *korokke* or golden-brown Dungeness crab croquettes, crisp on the outside and with a creamy interior, or *yaki imo,* caramelized white sweet potato with a sweet-and-salty glaze.

Iyasare

Japanese XX

D2

1830 4th St. (bet. Hearst Ave. & Virginia St.), Berkeley

Phone: 510-845-8100
Web: www.iyasare-berkeley.com
Prices: $$$

Lunch daily
Dinner Wed – Mon

Japanese technique and Californian ingredients blend harmoniously at this charming Berkeley getaway, which flaunts a buzzing dining room and a delightful (heated) patio. Start the evening off right with an excellent (and reasonably-priced) local wine on tap or a selection from the well-edited sake list. Then, order a variety of their exquisite small plates for sharing.

Every dish is a carefully crafted delight for the senses. Baby kale and mustard greens might not sound very Japanese, but they blend beautifully in a salad with Fuji apple and a sesame-miso dressing. The superb hamachi crudo is dusted with a sprinkle of wasabi snow and lemon-tamari oil, while fresh Manila clams arrive in an aromatic broth of sake, bacon, potatoes, and earthy shiitakes.

Kamdesh

Afghan X

B2

346 14th St. (at Webster St.), Oakland

Phone: 510-286-1900
Web: N/A
Prices: 🄐🄐

Lunch & dinner daily

Cheerfully perched on a commercial corner in downtown Oakland, Kamdesh's sunny yellow façade is a welcome sight. Expect to find business folks at lunch, locals at dinner, and a take-out clientele all day long.

Afghan *kabobs* are all the rage here—perfectly seasoned, marinated, charbroiled, and absolutely mouthwatering. Try the lamb *tikka kabab*, moist and smoky with cumin, piled over fluffy *pallow* (brown basmati rice) infused with lamb jus and completed with a spicy cilantro chutney and salad. Other delicious options include tender *mantoo* stuffed with seasoned ground beef and onions, then drizzled with tangy yogurt sauce; or the flavorful charbroiled chicken wrap with yogurt, cucumber, tomato, mint, and red onion in a chewy, thick *naan*.

195

Kingston 11

East Bay

B1

Caribbean 🍴

2270 Telegraph Ave. (bet. 23rd St. & Grand Ave.), Oakland

Phone: 510-465-2558
Web: www.kingston11eats.com
Prices: $$

Lunch Tue – Fri & Sun
Dinner Tue – Sat

Thanks to this lively Jamaican pop-up gone permanent, authentic island flavors have arrived in uptown Oakland. Its environs remain a bit dicey, but once inside, the smiling servers, boisterous crowds of families and friends, and reggae beats will transport you to the Caribbean—with a dose of California-chic from the modern interior design.

Boldly flavored fare includes tender, smoky jerk chicken with an intense and peppery spice rub, and a milder (but wildly delicious) curried goat stew with potato, carrots, and onion. Crisp and flaky salt-fish fritters are mouthwateringly delicious, and ideal for dunking in an herbaceous *chimichurri*. Skip the forgettable desserts and save your calories for a refreshing rum cocktail from the Fern Gully bar.

Longbranch Saloon

D2

Gastropub 🍴

2512 San Pablo Ave. (bet. Dwight Way & Parker St.), Berkeley

Phone: 510-984-0518
Web: www.longbranchberkeley.com
Prices: $$

Dinner Tue – Sun

The wonders of whiskey are on full display at this relatively recent gastropub, which stocks a sizable selection of Bourbon, Scotch, and rye. If you're new to the brown elixir, never fear: well-chosen tasting flights will help you gain proficiency, and the laid-back crew of locals is engaging, never snobby.

The kitchen's signatures are worthy of the bar's spirits selection, which explains why the space fills quickly with a local crowd. Order up a cocktail and half-dozen Tomales Bay oysters with mignonette. Then tuck into the hearty bangers and mash featuring a juicy house-made white sausage and buttery potato purée. Lighter appetites will love the asparagus *sformato*, a custardy, savory pudding accompanied by a tangy fennel salad with pickled grapes.

Los Cilantros

Mexican ✗

E2

3105 Shattuck Ave. (bet. Prince & Woolsey Sts.), Berkeley

Phone: 510-230-7350
Web: N/A
Prices: 💰

Lunch Tue – Sun
Dinner Wed – Sun

If there's no Mexican grandma in your life, Los Cilantros will show you what you've been missing: homey, authentic south-of-the-border fare (and if there is, it might just give her a run for her money). Whether you're biting into a crunchy tostada topped with chipotle chicken, black beans, sour cream, and avocado, or savoring rustic chicken enchiladas in a tangy green chile-tomatillo salsa, this is comfort food at its best.

Cute and simple, the Berkeley newbie features tiled floors, pops of yellow and orange, and colorful paintings by Mexican artists. Settle in at one of the wooden tables and let the gracious staff make you feel right at home, or, if the weather's nice, grab a seat on the tiny front patio and catch some rays.

Mama Papa Lithuania

Eastern European ✗

E4

1241 Park St. (bet. Encinal & San Antonio Aves.), Alameda

Phone: 510-522-4100
Web: www.mamapapalithuania.com
Prices: $$

Lunch & dinner daily

Even highly avid diners may be unacquainted with Lithuanian food, but they won't be for long if this Alameda charmer—reputed to be the only one of its kind on the West Coast—is any indication. With exceptionally hospitable service and a cozy, brick-walled room full of rustic wooden tables, it's the next best thing to a home-cooked meal in Vilnius.

Lithuania's iconic dumpling dish, *cepelinai*, is a must for newbies: the potato dough, filled with pork, caramelized onion, and a little cinnamon, is rib-stickingly rich. Refresh your palate with a cooling summer borscht, creamy with beets and yogurt; then go for broke with the meaty, yet delicate stuffed cabbage. Try and leave room for dessert, as the sweet cherry dumplings with sour cream are to die for.

Metro Lafayette

Californian ✗

3524 Mt. Diablo Blvd. (bet. 1st St. & Oak Hill Rd.), Lafayette

Phone: 925-284-4422
Web: www.metrolafayette.com
Prices: $$

Lunch & dinner daily

The signs and framed vintage map hint of the Paris Metro, but this longtime hot spot could be renamed "The Patio." Both cuisine and dining are decidedly Californian and that means enjoying this flavor-packed fare out on the patio, or inside the sophisticated space fitted with a bar and sunroom overlooking local scenesters dining alfresco.

The oft-changing menu embraces global flavors, so a meal might start with a surprisingly light and complex rendition of onion soup that is perfectly seasoned, silky from a dash of cream, and presented with parmesan toast. Follow this with two tacos loaded with tender grilled fish, salsa verde, avocado, drizzles of lime *crema*, and fresh tomato salsa. Seasonal desserts may reveal a warm organic plum crisp.

Michel Bistro 😊

French ✗

3343 Lakeshore Ave. (at Trestle Glen Rd.), Oakland

Phone: 510-836-8737
Web: www.michelbistro.com
Prices: $$

Lunch Sat – Sun
Dinner Tue – Sun

A slice of France on a prime block of Lakeshore Avenue, this bistro boasts a heavily Gallic waitstaff and clientele chatting away in their native tongue. With its exposed brick, soaring ceilings, and cute touches like an excerpt from a Marcel Pagnol play inscribed on the wall, it's a simple but pleasant spot to enjoy a delicious, low-key meal.

The food is authentic, with some modern touches like the green almonds in a trout *amandine* with Lyonnaise-style potato salad, or the bison in a tartare with a quail egg. Brunch is a highlight with a gourmet eggs Benedict over artisan *levain* and butter-basted asparagus that steals the show. At either meal, the vanilla crème brûlée is a rich treasure—too often jumbled on other menus, it's perfectly rendered here.

Millennium

Vegan ✗✗

E2

5912 College Ave. (bet. Chabot Rd. & Harwood Ave.), Oakland

Phone: 510-735-9459   Dinner nightly
Web: www.millenniumrestaurant.com
Prices: $$

After more than 20 years in San Francisco, this vegan paradise recently relocated to Oakland, where it's continuing to put out some of the most unique, delicious plant-based cuisine in the country. The rustic-chic new space is laid-back and unfussy, with lots of dark wood, a patio for alfresco dining, and a crowd of young families and professionals attended by welcoming servers.

While dedicated vegans are sure to swoon, even hardcore carnivores might reconsider the lifestyle after a dose of Chef/owner Eric Tucker's culinary creativity, showcased best on a five-course "Taste of Millennium" menu. Spicy *sopes* with a smoked eggplant *picadillo* and pumpkin seed cream are knockouts, as is the take on a Thai *larb* salad made with ripe red plums.

Miss Ollie's

Caribbean ✗

A2

901 Washington St. (at 9th St.), Oakland

Phone: 510-285-6188   Lunch & dinner Tue – Sat
Web: www.realmissolliesoakland.com
Prices: $$

Raised in Barbados, Chef/owner Sarah Kirnon brings a taste of the Caribbean to her novel home in Old Oakland. Named after her grandmother, Miss Ollie's features an utilitarian-chic space, enlivened by corner windows, cheerful paintings, and deep orange bottles of house-made habanero sauce. Watch out—it rings with spice and packs a punch.

Callaloo, ackee, chow chow, and *giromon* may not be words in the average foodie's vernacular, but Chef Kirnon presents them here, as part of a pleasing roster of dishes like *phulourie*—crisp *garam masala*-tinged split-pea fritters served with *shado beni* or tamarind chutney—washed down with sorrel, a sweet hibiscus punch. But, it's that familiar, moist, crispy fried chicken that takes the crown, so grab it if available.

Mount Everest

E2

2598 Telegraph Ave. (at Parker St.), Berkeley

Phone: 510-843-3951   Lunch & dinner daily
Web: www.themounteverestrestaurant.com
Prices: ☜

Lured by the wafting scents of spices just a few blocks south of UC Berkeley's campus, students, professors, and local corporate types flock to Mount Everest. The corner spot has plenty of light, cheery yellow walls, friendly service, and a relaxed atmosphere. Students appreciate the inexpensive *thali* at lunch, while overflow crowds settle on the balcony.

The menu offers Indian cuisine, but specializes in traditional Nepali dishes like steamed *momos* filled with minced cabbage, carrot, and onion, with a deeply spiced dipping sauce of sesame, turmeric, and ginger. *Channa masala* boasts chickpeas seasoned with subtle Nepali spices; and the creamy tomato sauce in chicken *tikka masala* is infused with pungent aromatics. Both beg to be sopped up with naan and rice.

Nido

B3

444 Oak St. (at 5th St.), Oakland

Phone: 510-444-6436   Lunch Tue – Sun
Web: www.nidooakland.com   Dinner Tue – Sat
Prices: $$

The industrial area west of the I-880 freeway doesn't boast many good restaurants, but this hidden Mexican gem is an exception. Complete with hip reclaimed-wood décor and a local clientele of business people along with trendy foodies, it's definitely a cut above a taqueria in terms of quality and price, with fresher, lighter food in smaller—but by no means stingy—portions.

At lunch, a trio of tacos includes moist pork *adobado* with a sweet-and-spicy pineapple salsa, grilled chicken with *chamoy* glaze, and smoky beef *barbacoa* with caramelized onions. Dinner brings pozole with chicken and *chile negro*, and a grilled pork chop with braised greens and almond *mole*. With a truly relaxed vibe and home cooked feel to the food, it's worth the extra effort to drop by.

Ohgane

Korean ✗

E3

3915 Broadway (bet. 38th & 40th Sts.), Oakland

Phone: 510-594-8300   Lunch & dinner daily
Web: www.ohgane.com
Prices: ⊕⊕

♿ Ohgane still beats out the local Korean competition thanks to its delicious food, contemporary dining rooms, and private parking lot (huge bonus in this area!). Business crowds appreciate the all-you-can-eat lunch buffet. Meals here start with an assortment of *banchan*—sixteen small bites including spicy kimchi, glazed sweet yam, and mild egg cake. Other kitchen-prepared dishes include *mandoo* and *dolsot bibimbap*.

At night, Korean families gather beneath the ventilation hoods for tabletop mesquite grilling (*soot-bool*)—a specialty that is absolutely the way to go for dinner. During lunch, have the kitchen grill it for you and still enjoy the likes of smoky and tender *galbee*—beef short ribs marinated for 72 hours in garlic, soy, and sesame oil.

Oliveto

Italian ✗✗

E2

5655 College Ave. (at Shafter Ave.), Oakland

Phone: 510-547-5356   Lunch Mon – Fri
Web: www.oliveto.com   Dinner nightly
Prices: $$$

♿ Its memorable location in a prime corner of Rockridge is only
🍇 the first hint of Oliveto's good looks: diners enter through
a delightful mini-market and café—selling everything from pasta to Maine lobster—before climbing the spiral staircase
🍽 into this elegant dining room, where a huge wood-burning oven, linen-topped tables, and bunches of fresh flowers delight the eye.

Nothing about Oliveto screams "Italian," from the décor to the all-American staff; yet its menu is completely authentic. Crisp, pan-roasted chicken breast rests on juicy herbed barley and asparagus, while charred Brussels sprouts get a kick from sweet *saba* and chopped walnuts. Barbaresco and Barolo, perfect with the strong selection of pastas and roasted meats, dominate the wine list.

Osmanthus

Asian ✗✗

6048 College Ave. (bet. Florio St. & Harwood Ave.), Oakland

Phone: 510-923-1233   Lunch & dinner Tue – Sun
Web: www.osmanthusrestaurant.com
Prices: $$

Chef-owner Julia Klein has brought her cooking experience at Napa's Terra to bear on this "modern-classic Asian" restaurant. Osmanthus offers some fun bites that recall the '80s heyday of Asian fusion (shrimp toast or ginger-soy tuna tartare with avocado, maybe?) and some with more current touches like the *sriracha*-honey glaze served atop superlative fried Brussels sprouts with bacon. Sichuan influences abound, but chili-hounds beware: the cooking is more about flavor than fire.

Inside, the former Nan Yang space has been updated with a serene look and boasts a dark tiled floor, colorful paper lanterns, and colonial-style ceiling fans. Drinkers should sample the house cocktail, while teetotalers enjoy a Thai iced tea—in regular or crème brûlée form.

Pathos

Greek ✗✗

2430 Shattuck Ave. (bet. Channing Way & Haste St.), Berkeley

Phone: 510-981-8339   Lunch Sat – Sun
Web: www.pathosrestaurant.com   Dinner Wed – Sun
Prices: $$

Forget the flaming *saganaki* and cries of "Opa!"; Pathos is a sophisticated newcomer that will dispel any tired conceptions of Greek food. You'll want to dress up and bring a date to match its stylish décor, all hammered copper bar, oversized framed windows, and patterned banquettes.

Most dishes come straight from the wood-fired oven, including a lighter take on moussaka, with nutmeg-infused Greek yogurt béchamel baked over ground beef and eggplant; or a roasted red bell pepper stuffed with ground beef and rice. The *htapodi*, tenderly grilled octopus over shaved red onion and fried capers, is another hit for its full, smoky flavor. Turn to the friendly staff for help in selecting from among the many Greek wines, or try an ouzo or *metaxa* cocktail.

Phnom Penh House

Cambodian ✕

B2

251 8th St. (bet. Alice & Harrison Sts.), Oakland

Phone: 510-893-3825   Lunch & dinner Mon – Sat
Web: www.phnompenhhouse.com
Prices: 💰💰

Devotees in the know pray to the parking gods and push through Oakland's Chinatown crowds to get to one of the best Cambodian restaurants in the Bay Area. While the outside appears unassuming, the interior is a calm respite with colorful, native artwork and temple tiles. Expect a warm welcome from the family who runs this simple but pleasant place.

The menu is full of flavorful, fragrant, and fresh dishes such as a vibrant salad of shredded green papaya, carrots, and delicious herbs tossed in a garlicky house-made vinaigrette. The spicy flavors of lemongrass permeate tofu cubes sautéed with onion, button mushrooms, and red bell pepper; and infuse the *sach chhrouk ann kreun*—charbroiled and glazed pork with crunchy, tangy pickled vegetables.

Pizzaiolo

Pizza ✕

E2

5008 Telegraph Ave. (bet. 49th & 51st Sts.), Oakland

Phone: 510-652-4888   Dinner Mon – Sat
Web: www.pizzaiolooakland.com
Prices: $$

Lines are still a given at Temescal's pizza palace. In fact, find eager patrons arriving before the doors even open. A smattering of entrées and hearty plates like king salmon baked on a fig leaf with asparagus and mint yogurt evoke spring on a plate. But, crowds are here for their pies, crisp from the wood-burning oven and topped with the finest and freshest of ingredients like tangy tomato sauce, house-made sausage, and decadent *panna*.

The large dining room with handsome plank floors and dark wood tables centers around the exhibition kitchen lined with bowls of pristine local produce. Couples and groups gather at tables or pack the polished wood bar. Add on a rich caramel *pot de crème* and the endless queues will start to make sense.

Prima

F1

Italian ✖✖

1522 N. Main St. (bet. Bonanza St. & Lincoln Ave.), Walnut Creek

Phone: 925-935-7780
Web: www.primawine.com
Prices: $$$

Lunch Mon – Sat
Dinner nightly

With a premier location amid high-end boutiques, this contemporary Italian Romeo is a draw for business folk and local shoppers alike. The spacious interior wears a contemporary style accentuated by smart tables.

There are three distinct seating areas: a glass-enclosed porch framed in dark wood, a front room with views of the wood-fired oven, and another dining haven just past the bar with a fireplace and vaulted ceilings. The food is authentically Italian, from a refreshing panzanella tossed with sweet basil and ripe heirloom tomatoes; to al dente *tagliatelle* swirled with a meaty ragù. Considering the hefty prices, service may be lacking. But, all blemishes quickly fade away thanks to their distinguished atmosphere and notable food.

Ramen Shop

E2

Japanese ✗

5812 College Ave. (bet. Chabot Rd & Birch Ct.), Oakland

Phone: 510-788-6370
Web: www.ramenshop.com
Prices: $$

Dinner nightly

The ramen is non-traditional and the staff non-Japanese at this hip Oakland noodle joint, but that doesn't keep an onslaught of young locals from flooding in for a California-style take on Japan's iconic dish. Chewy, springy noodles and fresh vegetables like maitake mushrooms and tomato confit fill each bowl, with a choice of rich, savory pork or veggie Meyer lemon broths.

With only three rotating ramens on the menu, appetizers actually make up most of the offering, and boy, they're killer—a shaved summer squash salad with creamy avocado and fried squash blossoms is to die for. The fun hipster vibe and delicious cocktails at the bar ensure this no-reservations spot fills up fast, so be sure to arrive early—or steel yourself for an inevitable wait.

Riva Cucina

Italian ✗

D2

800 Heinz Ave. (at 7th St.), Berkeley

Phone:	510-841-7482
Web:	www.rivacucina.com
Prices:	$$

Lunch Tue – Fri
Dinner Tue – Sat

A labor of love from an Italian chef and his American wife, this Berkeley favorite overflows with families and their *bambini* (who get their own special menu). While he turns out the rustic, flavorful dishes of his youth in the kitchen, she attends to guests in the high-ceilinged, brick-walled dining room or on the flower-decked front patio.

Kick off a meal here with a fresh and vibrant panzanella packed with sweet heirloom tomatoes, diced cucumber, and shaved salty *ricotta salata*. Parsley-infused fettuccine is equally delightful, twirled with garlicky olive oil, mushrooms, and a dusting of truffled pecorino cheese. Finish with another study in delicious simplicity: the *torta della nonna*, with lemon cream and pine nuts in a cookie crust.

Rivoli 😊

Californian ✗✗

D1

1539 Solano Ave. (bet. Neilson St. & Peralta Ave.), Berkeley

Phone:	510-526-2542
Web:	www.rivolirestaurant.com
Prices:	$$

Dinner nightly

Northern Californian cooking with a trace of Italian flavor is the main draw at this lush charmer on the Albany-Berkeley border, serving up delectable and seasonal dishes. Rivoli is always popular and a winner among its patrons, who come here to savor undeniably excellent items like a crisp endive salad tossing peppery arugula, sweet plums, and blue cheese. Tender braised lamb-stuffed ravioli topped with tomato sauce, spiced chickpeas, and garlic-mint yogurt is another jewel.

Set in an adorable cottage, the dining room also features enormous picture windows overlooking a lush "secret" garden blooming with tender fronds and climbing ivy. The greenery is a stunning contrast to the crisp, white-linen tables, smartly serviced by an engaging waitstaff.

205

Royal Indian Grill

B4

Indian

629 San Ramon Valley Blvd. (at Boone Ct.), Danville

Phone: 925-743-1747 Lunch & dinner daily
Web: www.royalindiangrill.net
Prices: $$

Some of the East Bay's best Indian food can be found at this casual joint in a sprawling Danville strip mall, which is always packed with local families chatting, playing with kids, or catching Bollywood flicks on the overhead TVs. While it's not suited for those in a rush as service redefines slow, those who wait will be rewarded with fare worthy of royalty.

Many of the kitchen's best dishes pack a spicy punch like the hot, tangy lamb *vindaloo*, flavored with pungent ginger, cilantro, and onion; or the classic *aloo gobi*, a turmeric-based curry with cubed potatoes and florets of cauliflower. Ease the burn with some smoky, caramelized, and pillowy naan, before diving into superb chicken *kofta* stewed in a spice-laden, delicious cashew-tomato sauce.

Sahn Maru

E2

Korean

4315 Telegraph Ave. (bet. 43rd & 44th Sts.), Oakland

Phone: 510-653-3366 Lunch & dinner Wed – Mon
Web: www.sahnmarukoreanbbq.com
Prices: $$

As one of East Bay's top Korean restaurants, Sahn Maru's name (which translates as "top of the mountain") is perfectly fitting. Its casual vibe, large size, and friendly service make it a good choice for groups. Never mind the wainscoting and country-quaint chairs that juxtapose walls covered with pictures of Korean dishes—this is a place for authentic food.

Meals start with barley tea and tasty *banchan* like daikon kimchi, bean sprout salad in sesame oil, and fish cakes, alongside a bowl of delicately flavored kelp and daikon soup. Lunchtime might feature a deliciously unexpected combination of beef *bulgogi* stir-fried with *jap chae*. While the spot earns raves for Korean barbecue, the kitchen prepares it for you, as there are no tabletop grills.

Shakewell

Mediterranean ✕✕

E3

3407 Lakeshore Ave. (bet. Longridge & Trestle Glen Rds.), Oakland

Phone: 510-251-0329
Web: www.shakewelloakland.com
Prices: $$

Lunch Wed – Sun
Dinner Tue – Sun

This trendy eatery, the brainchild of *Top Chef* alums Jennifer Biesty and Tim Nugent, was made for sipping and supping. Donning a bar up front and several dining nooks on either side of a central walkway, Shakewell keeps things Medichic with Moorish accents, reclaimed wood, and organic elements.

Service is particularly warm, and an even warmer teal-green wood-fired oven in the back turns out deliciously smoked items like crisp falafel topped with chorizo aïoli. A summer squash salad with heirloom tomatoes, fried bread, and feta offers an inspired blend of Greek and Tuscan flavors, and Bomba rice with braised fennel, *piperade*, chicken, and prawns is a fluffy take on paella. For a party in your mouth, finish with the caramel syrup-spiked flan Catalan.

Sidebar

Gastropub ✕

E3

542 Grand Ave. (bet. Euclid Ave. & MacArthur Blvd.), Oakland

Phone: 510-452-9500
Web: www.sidebar-oaktown.com
Prices: $$

Lunch Mon – Fri
Dinner Mon – Sat

A loyal crowd of regulars flocks to this lively Oakland gastropub, located right across Grand Avenue from Lake Merritt. Though it offers only a handful of tables, Sidebar makes eating at the spacious rectangular bar a delight, with attentive servers and a view of the action in the semi-open kitchen.

The cuisine is hearty and varied with starters like a chopped romaine salad with fennel salami and creamy garlic-herb dressing; braised chicken thighs with curried coconut-lime cream; and deviled eggs with smoky bacon and cheddar. Themed evenings include Mussel Madness Mondays and Goat Cheese Soufflé Wednesdays, but there's no shame in sticking to the excellent Niman Ranch burger, with house-pickled onions and chipotle-Thousand Island dressing.

Tacubaya

East Bay

Mexican ✗

1788 4th St. (bet. Hearst Ave. & Virginia St.), Berkeley

Phone: 510-525-5160   Lunch & dinner daily
Web: www.tacubaya.net
Prices: 😊

Megapopular Oakland Mexican restaurant Doña Tomas is reincarnated in taqueria form at this Berkeley shopping complex, where families grab a bite before or after errands. A line of people extends out the door from morning until night, ordering tangy limeade at the counter and claiming seats in the festive pink-and-orange dining room or on the sunny front patio.

The crowds come for *chilaquiles* and churros at breakfast, then transition into flavorful chorizo-and-potato *sopes* with black bean purée at lunch. Moist, well-seasoned beef enchiladas are doused in a smoky, tangy *guajillo*-tomatillo sauce and covered with melted cheese. For a sweet finish, tamales filled with cranberry jam and drizzled with goat-milk caramel are both beguiling and unusual.

Thai House 😊

Thai ✗✗

254 Rose Ave. (bet. Diablo Rd. & Linda Mesa Ave.), Danville

Phone: 925-820-0635   Lunch Mon – Fri
Web: www.thaihousedanville.net   Dinner nightly
Prices: $$

Many a warm evening has been spent on the garden patio of this fantastic Thai restaurant, where potted plants create a leafy retreat. Whether you're dining alfresco or tucked inside the tiny, colorful bungalow, you can be assured of a warm welcome and boldly flavorful food—a secret that's out with the locals, making this house a packed one from noon to night.

The consistently outstanding menu makes it hard to go wrong, but you can't miss with the creamy red pumpkin curry, full of tender scallops and prawns and perfectly balanced notes of sweet, spicy, salty, and sour. Other showstoppers may reveal *pad prig khing*, chicken in a spicy peanut-tamarind sauce, or the aromatic basil tofu, chockablock with fresh vegetables, chili, and garlic.

The Peasant & The Pear

International XX

B4

267 Hartz Ave. (at Linda Mesa Ave.), Danville

Phone: 925-820-6611
Web: www.rodneyworth.com
Prices: $$

Lunch & dinner daily

Peasants are hard to come by at this upscale Danville bistro, which draws ladies who lunch for long, leisurely meals in its cozy environs. But despite its wealthy clientele, The Pear (named for a nearby orchard that was once the world's largest) isn't the least bit stuffy, thanks to a friendly staff working the dining room and a relaxed California spirit in the kitchen.

The playful and eclectic menu offers some fun nods to the name, like a white cheddar-and-garlic fondue accompanied by slices of delicate Anjou pears. A succulent piece of cod bathed in lemon beurre blanc and encrusted in puff pastry shows a balanced touch, and even pear obsessives might have to concede that the bubbling strawberry rhubarb cobbler is the height of fruity goodness.

Trabocco

Italian XX

E4

2213 South Shore Center (bet. Otis & Shoreline Drs.), Alameda

Phone: 510-521-1152
Web: www.trabocco.com
Prices: $$$

Lunch & dinner daily

Big-city style and rustic Italian authenticity combine to create magic at this Alameda favorite, which is owned by a native of Abruzzo. Its location in a shopping center isn't the greatest, but the sleek and sophisticated dining room and spacious front patio are transporting enough that you won't mind. Also of assistance: killer cocktails starring Alameda craft distiller St. George Spirits.

The hearty food is a true taste of Italy, with lovingly hand-made dishes like *chitarrine* pasta swirled with a tender, tomato-flecked rabbit ragù. The massive wood-grilled pork chop is smoky, juicy, and accompanied by tender-crisp broccoli rabe. And for dessert, an airy *zabaglione*, delicately infused with a hint of Marsala, is served with fresh strawberries.

Tribune Tavern

B2

401 13th St. (at Franklin St.), Oakland

Phone: 510-452-8742
Web: www.tribunetavern.com
Prices: $$

Lunch & dinner daily

The team behind foodie-mobbed Chop Bar resurrected an Oakland landmark for their latest project: the former newsroom of the iconic *Tribune* building. And baby boy is quite the looker, featuring luxe leather sofas, wine barrels, and stained glass casting an elegant light onto the horseshoe-shaped bar.

Corporate types pack the bar for hearty, English-inspired items like a whole rabbit cooked down and presented as a jar of spreadable delight; Shepherd's pie bubbling with ground meat and topped with parmesan-potato mash; and a strawberry trifle sundae. Happy hour brings bites such as house pickled vegetables, smoked pork belly-stuffed dates, or the Tavern burger. Cocktails are stellar, while teetotalers are kept happy with house-made sodas.

Va de Vi

F1

1511 Mt. Diablo Blvd. (near Main St.), Walnut Creek

Phone: 925-979-0100
Web: www.vadevi.com
Prices: $$

Lunch & dinner daily

"Va de vi" is a Catalan phrase that roughly means "It's all about wine." Here you'll find no dissent from the moneyed locals who gather for flights with such cheeky names as "There's No Place Like Rhone." The fountain-enhanced, bucolic patio is a treasured sipping destination, as is the L-shaped counter with a view of the open kitchen set amid rich polished woods.

Good wine demands good food, and the global menu offered here entices with ultra-fresh choices like ahi tuna tartare topped with wasabi tobiko; or roasted asparagus in romesco, crowned with baked prosciutto chips. Asian influences abound, particularly in soy-glazed black cod, or pork belly with sticky rice and a chili glaze. Add on a sweet staff and easy vibe—no wonder it's such a hit.

Wood Tavern 😎

American ✗✗

E2

6317 College Ave. (bet. Alcatraz Ave. & 63rd St.), Oakland

Phone: 510-654-6607   Lunch Mon – Sat
Web: www.woodtavern.net   Dinner nightly
Prices: $$

There's always a crowd at this lively neighborhood standby, where groups of friends, parents on date night, and hip couples congregate for drinks at the copper-topped bar. Flanked by organic groceries, indie bookstores, and antique shops, its surroundings reek of peace, weaving a pleasantly bohemian spell that captivates both regulars and newcomers alike.

Rustic American food with a hint of Italian flair dominates the menu and the local Belfiore burrata—served atop diced pears, honey-cashew cream, and peppery arugula—is a surefire hit. Then pappardelle may arrive tangled in an intensely flavored veal ragù, enriched with spicy chili flakes and parmesan. For dessert, an apple-oatmeal crumble with sour cream ice cream is just the ticket.

Zut Tavern

Mediterranean ✗✗

D1

1820 4th St. (bet. Hearst Ave. & Virginia St.), Berkeley

Phone: 510-644-0444   Lunch & dinner daily
Web: www.zutonfourth.com
Prices: $$

Berkeley's beloved bistro is better than ever thanks to Chef Shotaro Kamio of Iyasare (just a few steps away) who has taken over and instilled a brand-new energy. Comfortable, inviting, and ever-popular, Zut Tavern features a skylight-brightened dining room enhanced with colorful artwork, front doors that open onto the patio, and waiting patrons spilling out onto busy Fourth Street.

One thing that hasn't changed, however, is the enticing spirit of the Mediterranean-meets-American menu. Diners here dig into plates of mouthwatering fare like panzanella with burrata, aged balsamic, chunks of melon, and heirloom tomatoes; or sweet basil and pine nut pesto-slicked rigatoni tossed with Romano beans and tender slices of fingerling potatoes.

Marin

Marin

Meandering Marin is located north of the Golden Gate Bridge and draped along breathtaking Highway 1. Coastal climates shower this county with abounding agricultural advantages, which in turn become abundantly apparent as you snake your way through its food oases, always filled with fresh, luscious seafood, slurpable oysters, and cold beer. Farm-to-table cuisine is de rigueur in this liberal-leaning and affluent county, boasting an avalanche of local food suppliers. One of the most celebrated purveyors is the quaint and rustic **Cowgirl Creamery**, whose "cowgirls" are charged with churning out delicious, distinctive, and hand-crafted cheeses. By specializing in farmstead cheeses alone, they have refined the process of artisan cheese-making, and garnered national respect along the way. Continue exploring these fromageries at **Point Reyes Farmstead Cheese Co.**, a popular destination among natives for the "Original Blue" and its famously lush and heady satisfaction. Thanks to such driven, enterprising cheese-makers (who live by terroir or taste of the earth), surrounding restaurants follow the European standard by offering cheese before or in lieu of a dessert course. After such a savory spread, get your candy crush going at **Munchies of Sausalito**; or opt for a more creamy scoop at **Noci Gelato**.

If cheese and meat are a match made in heaven, then North Bay must be a thriving intermediary with its myriad ranches. At the crest is **Marin Sun Farms**, a glorified and dedicated butcher

shop whose heart and soul lies in the production of locally raised, natural-fed meats for fine restaurants, small-scale grocers, and everything in between. Championing local eating is **Mill Valley Market**, a can't-miss commitment among gourmands for top-quality foods, deli items, and other organic goods.

STOP, SIP & SAVOR

To gratify those inevitable pangs of hunger after miles of scenic driving complete with ocean breezes, **The Pelican Inn** makes for an ideal retreat. Serving hearty English country cooking and a range of brews from the classic "bar," this nostalgic and ever-charming rest stop will leave you yearning for more. Continue your hiatus by strolling into **Spanish Table**, a shopper's paradise settled in Mill Valley, only to find foodies reveling in unique Spanish cookbooks, cookware, specialty foods, and drool-worthy wines. Peckish travelers should swing by **Three Twins Ice Cream** for organically produced creamy goodness that leaves an everlasting memory.

Waters off the coast here provide divers with exceptional hunting ground, and restaurants throughout Marin count on supremely fresh oysters, plump clams, and meaty mussels. The difficulty in (legally) sourcing these large, savory mollusks makes red abalone a treasured species in area Asian establishments, though seafood does seem to be the accepted norm among restaurants in this town. If fish doesn't float your boat, **Fred's Coffee Shop** in Sausalito is a no-frills find for outrageously fulfilling breakfast signatures like deep-fried French toast with a side of calorie-heavy, crazy-good caramelized 'Millionaire's bacon.' Carb addicts routinely pay their respects at **M.H. Bread & Butter**, said to be the best bakery in the area. Their crusty loaves make for fantastic sandwiches, but are equally divine just slathered with butter. If that's too tame for your tastes, enticing Puerto Rican flavors and *especiales* abound at **Sol Food**, settled in San Rafael. While this fertile county's regional and natural ingredients are sold in countless farmers' markets, many other celebrations of food and wine continue to pop up throughout this area during the spring and summer months. Given its culinary chops and panoramic views, Marin is one of the most sought after stops for celebrities and visitors alike. True, some places can seem crowded or touristy; however, its area chefs and restaurants are lauded for good reason, and know how to make the most of their choice homegrown produce and food purveyors.

Arti

Indian ✗

A1

7282 Sir Francis Drake Blvd. (at Cintura Ave.), Lagunitas

Lunch & dinner daily

Phone: 415-488-4700
Web: www.articafe.com
Prices:

In sleepy Lagunitas, locals spice things up with a trip to this itty-bitty Indian favorite, where yellow walls and flowers liven the handful of tables. Set in a strip mall that also plays host to a hippie bookstore and yoga studio, this is a comforting den of peace and love for your palate, down to the fluffy basmati rice, creamy raita, and gluten-free naan (made with rice flour).

Warm up a chilly night with with hot and tangy lamb *vindaloo* mingling tender cubes of lamb with fork-tender potatoes; or go for the full comfort effect with creamy chicken korma. Finish with an order of *gulab jamun*, homemade cheese dumplings soaked in sweet syrup. If you're in for lunch, be sure to sample the Indian wraps, also available in whole-wheat and gluten-free versions.

Arun

Thai ✗

C1

385 Bel Marin Keys Blvd. (near Hamilton Dr.), Novato

Lunch Tue – Fri
Dinner Tue – Sat

Phone: 415-883-8017
Web: www.arunnovato.com
Prices:

Don't be fooled by its location in an industrial park: this Thai restaurant is completely transporting, thanks to the small, well-tended garden in front, bubbling fountain, colorful walls, and dark wood tables. Dinner is more formal than lunch, but either service offers a calming air.

The standards are all present and accounted for: satays, curries (like a delicious, mildly spiced red curry with prawns, squash, and bell pepper), and heaps of fragrant jasmine rice. At dinner, Thai barbecue is king and unveils an appealing Islamic lamb dish. Vibrant in appearance and fresh in flavor, all items are strong, but the moneybag-like curry pouches are particularly memorable, thanks to their golden exterior, tie of leek at the top, and rich ground chicken filling.

Baan

B2

726 San Anselmo Ave. (bet. San Rafael & Tamalpais Aves.), San Anselmo

Phone: 415-457-9470
Web: www.baanthaimarin.com
Prices: $$

Lunch & dinner daily

Baan is Thai for "home" and this cozy space, full of warmth and laughter, will make you feel like you've found one—with better Thai food than your own, to boot. Local families regularly fill the bustling dining room, which features simple furnishings, cushioned banquettes, plenty of greenery, and authentic art on the walls.

Come for a quick lunch of tender pumpkin and plump prawns in a creamy, fiery red curry, or bring a crowd and share the spicy crying tiger salad, packed with grilled beef, red onion, tomatoes, and fresh herbs in a zippy lime dressing. Portions are absurdly generous, so plan on enjoying seconds of your moist green curry fried rice, spicy green beans, or charred yet tender *moo yang* (barbecue pork) for lunch the next day.

Bar Bocce

A3

1250 Bridgeway (bet. Pine & Turney Sts.), Sausalito

Phone: 415-331-0555
Web: www.barbocce.com
Prices: $$

Lunch & dinner daily

As chill a hangout spot as they come, Bar Bocce is seemingly designed to while away the hours with its pretty view of the water, namesake bocce courts, and roaring fire pit. Friendly and casual, it's a place where an afternoon glass of wine can easily fade into a multi-hour dinner, shared with a group of friends on the heated patio overlooking Sausalito's harbor.

Wood-fired sourdough pizzas, like a marble potato pie with fontina, bacon, and a fresh farm egg, are the heart of the menu, accented by antipasti such as shaved Brussels sprouts and pecorino salad or golden cod *brandade* fritters with a tangy citrus aïoli. Cheerful servers are always happy to recommend a bottle of *vino* (or three) to keep the festivities humming in the inviting little bungalow.

Barrel House Tavern

Californian XX

A3

660 Bridgeway (at Princess St.), Sausalito

Phone: 415-729-9593
Web: www.barrelhousetavern.com
Prices: $$

Lunch & dinner daily

The former San Francisco-Sausalito ferry terminal has found new life as this lovely Californian restaurant, which gets its name from its barrel-like arched wood ceiling. A front lounge with a crackling fireplace and well-stocked bar is popular with locals, while tourists can't resist the expansive dining room and back deck, which boasts spectacular views of the Bay.

The cocktail and wine offerings are strong, as is the house-made soda program, which produces intriguing, never-too-sweet combinations like yellow peach, basil, and ginger. These pair beautifully with meaty Dungeness crab sliders coupled with watermelon-jicama slaw; though they might be too tasty to keep around by the time grilled swordfish and pork belly with white beans hit the table.

Brick & Bottle

American XX

C2

55 Tamal Vista Blvd. (bet. Madera Blvd. & Wornum Dr.), Corte Madera

Phone: 415-924-3366
Web: www.brickandbottle.com
Prices: $$

Dinner nightly

Its strip-mall location may put you off the hunt, but Marin locals know that Brick & Bottle is one of the area's best for fuss-free, skillfully prepared American food that's packed with flavor. Grab a drink at the rollicking bar, complete with TVs for catching a game, then squeeze into a comfortable booth in the quieter back dining room.

The wide-ranging and perfectly executed menu dazzles as readily with Italian fare (like fluffy, well-caramelized potato gnocchi in a pitch perfect pesto) as it does with barbecue (try the smoky, tender pork shoulder in a cider-based sauce with jalapeño slaw). For dessert, a moist, buttery rum cake—complete with caramel sauce, rum raisin ice cream, and toasted pecans—rivals the Caribbean's best.

Buckeye Roadhouse

American XX

15 Shoreline Hwy. (off Hwy. 101), Mill Valley

Phone: 415-331-2600
Web: www.buckeyeroadhouse.com
Prices: $$

Lunch & dinner daily

This Marin hideout has welcomed generations of locals through its doors since 1937, even as its location on Highway 1 gave way to the more bustling 101. Enter the whitewashed craftsman building, and you'll be given your choice of dining in either the clubby bar or their grand dining room (complete with wood-paneled walls, red leather banquettes, and a tall fireplace).

The food here is classical but never dull, with a simple menu of salads, sandwiches, barbecue, and meat from the wood grill. A brunchtime meal of eggs Benedict boasts tender rosemary ham and rich potato croquettes, while plump asparagus ravioli with lemon olive oil stars in the evening. Finish up with a slice of pie—the famous s'mores version or a tart Key lime are both winners.

Bungalow 44

B2

American XX

44 E. Blithedale Ave. (at Sunnyside Ave.), Mill Valley

Phone: 415-381-2500
Web: www.bungalow44.com
Prices: $$

Dinner nightly

Nestled amid the fancy stores of quaint Mill Valley, vibrant Bungalow 44 draws a varied crew to its casual, contemporary environs. It's always busy at the bustling bar and slightly more subdued dining room, so for some peace and quiet, retire to the tented outer room with its glowing fireplace. Some prefer the counter to soak up the sizzle from the open kitchen.

Playful American cuisine is their dictum which shines through in tuna carpaccio—an homage to Italian antipasto—here starring tissue-thin slices of tuna served with citrusy *mizuna* and creamy mustard sauce. The whiff of cayenne from kickin' fried chicken is as tempting as the juicy meat—add the rich mashed potatoes. Local draft wines paired with pillowy-soft beignets make for a rewarding finish.

Burmatown

Burmese ✗

C2

60 Corte Madera Ave. (bet. Bahr Ln. & Redwood Ave.), Corte Madera

Phone: 415-945-9096

Dinner Tue – Sun

Web: www.burmatown.com

Prices: $$

Bypass the tired Asian-fusion offerings and head straight for the authentic Burmese dishes at this out-of-the-way cutie. A nutty, crunchy, and flavorful tea-leaf salad is the perfect answer to a hot summer day, while hearty potato-stuffed samosas and fresh, springy egg noodles tossed with barbecue pork and fried garlic chips will warm your soul in the cooler months.

Given the high quality of its food, it's no surprise that Burmatown is Corte Madera's most popular novel neighbor: it's big with local families from the surrounding residences, who pack every single table, attended to by warm servers. If you're willing to make a special trip to this charming bright-orange bungalow, the laid-back vibe will have you feeling right at home.

Copita

Mexican ✗✗

A3

739 Bridgeway (at Anchor St.), Sausalito

Phone: 415-331-7400

Lunch & dinner daily

Web: www.copitarestaurant.com

Prices: $$

Set sail aboard the Sausalito ferry for dinner at this Mexican smash, just steps from the harbor's bobbing yachts. Colorful and casual, Copita's most coveted seats are on the sidewalk patio (complete with partial views of the water and the quaint downtown), but a spot at the exceptionally well-stocked tequila bar or in the brightly tiled dining room is no disappointment.

A light meal of tacos could include seared mahi mahi with pineapple *pico de gallo* and tomatillo salsa or tomato-accented chicken *tinga* with avocado and Mexican *crema*. Options abound for heartier appetites, like 24-hour carnitas and chicken *mole enchiladas*. And the lively surrounds are a hit with kids, who love sipping on the sweet house-made almond *horchata*.

El Huarache Loco

C2

Mexican

1803 Larkspur Landing Circle (off Sir Francis Drake Blvd.), Larkspur

Phone: 415-925-1403

Web: N/A

Prices:

Lunch & dinner daily

In Mexico City, a *huarache* can be two things: a sandal, or a sandal-shaped disk of masa with delicious toppings—and talented native Chef/owner Veronica Salazar is definitely no cobbler. Though El Huarache Loco is housed in the tony Marin Country Mart, its crowd is largely Mexican, with many locals visiting this bright, airy counter-service spot for a taste of their homeland.

Served on beautiful hand-painted Mexican plates, these *huaraches* are unsurprisingly exceptional (try the version topped with nopales, tomato, onion, and *crema*). So, too, are regional specialties like *tlacoyito*, a cheese-stuffed blue corn masa cake layered with chicken *tinga*, onion, and cilantro, or *sopes* with tender potatoes and spicy chorizo.

El Paseo

B2

Steakhouse

17 Throckmorton Ave. (at Blithedale Ave.), Mill Valley

Phone: 415-388-0741

Web: www.elpaseomillvalley.com

Prices: $$$

Dinner nightly

"Rockstar chef" is a term that often gets tossed around, but it's all too true at this rustic steakhouse, co-owned by celebrity toque Tyler Florence and rocker Sammy Hagar. Hidden down an alley off the shopping arcade of Mill Valley, El Paseo reeks of old-world charm with rustic wood-beamed ceilings and brick walls. Adding a dose of romance are cool high-backed leather chairs warmed up by a live fireplace.

Once seated, the tuxedoed staff will present a cast iron tray of roasted bone marrow topped with a mild horseradish crust and turnip marmalade. A Heritage pork chop is grilled to smoky perfection and coddled with pea purée; while the béarnaise burger makes for a primally satisfying meal, especially if paired with a Napa red from the cavernous cellar.

Fish

Seafood 🍴

A3

350 Harbor Dr. (off Bridgeway), Sausalito

Lunch & dinner daily

Phone: 415-331-3474
Web: www.331fish.com
Prices: $$

Casual and family-friendly, this Sausalito seafood spot offers diners the choice of a bright and airy dining room with simple wood furnishings or an alfresco picnic table, both with great views of the harbor. If you dine outdoors, watch out for the local seagulls and crows, who are always ready to snag a snack from your plate (but provide great entertainment for the younger set).

The cooking is fresh and flavorful, from a Dungeness crab roll with butter and chives to crisp Anchor Steam-battered halibut served with house-made wedge fries and tartar sauce. Check the chalkboard for the latest specials, like mussels with chorizo and fennel or grilled Monterey sardines. After dining, visit the raw seafood counter for a selection of items to cook at home.

Frantoio

Italian 🍴🍴

A2

152 Shoreline Hwy. (off Hwy. 101), Mill Valley

Lunch Mon – Fri
Dinner nightly

Phone: 415-289-5777
Web: www.frantoio.com
Prices: $$

Named after the olive press used in olive oil production throughout Italy, Frantoio is distinguished by its own house-made olive oil, cold-pressed in a hefty granite contraption displayed just off the dining room. Bottled and sold on-site, this stellar product beams atop shavings of *Prosciutto di Parma* with arugula and *Mozzarella di Bufala*. Baked sea bass fillets are spread with an herbaceous horseradish crust—big on flavor but gentle on garnishes like chive-infused olive oil. Though its proximity to Highway 101 and roadside hotels isn't pleasant, an orange-and-charcoal color scheme and lofty ceilings ensure that the surrounds become a quickly fading memory. Also of assistance: perfectly crisp Neapolitan pizzas, quenched by some fine wines.

Insalata's 😊

B2

120 Sir Francis Drake Blvd. (at Barber Ave.), San Anselmo

Phone: 415-457-7700
Web: www.insalatas.com
Prices: $$

Lunch & dinner daily

San Anselmo restaurateur Chef Heidi Krahling honors her late father, Italo Insalata, at this crowd-pleasing Marin hangout. The *zucca*-orange stucco exterior alludes to the Mediterranean air within. Insalata's upscale setting is framed by lemon-yellow walls hung with grand depictions of nature's bounty setting the scene for the array of fresh and flavorful cuisine to come.

Sparked by Middle Eastern flavors, Insalata's specialties include velvety smooth potato-leek soup made brilliantly green from watercress purée. Also sample grilled lamb skewers drizzled with cumin-yogurt atop crunchy salad and flatbread. The takeout area in the back is stocked with salads, sides, and sandwiches made with house-baked bread. Boxed lunches are a fun, tasty convenience.

Left Bank

B2

507 Magnolia Ave. (at Ward St.), Larkspur

Phone: 415-927-3331
Web: www.leftbank.com
Prices: $$

Lunch & dinner daily

The very picture of a neighborhood bistro, Left Bank's breezy ambience and oh-so-French fare have really hit home with Larkspur locals. Inside, a lovely stone hearth is surrounded by cheery yellow walls and vintage French posters, while the wraparound terrace outdoors is the place to dine on a lazy summer afternoon.

The kitchen does French classics to perfection, including a charcuterie board groaning with hefty portions of truffle-flecked chicken liver mousse, duck and pork rillettes, and country pâté. Tender rainbow trout Grenobloise arrives with grilled Provençal country bread, soaked in savory herb-and-garlic butter. Finish with fresh profiteroles, stuffed with vanilla ice cream and topped with rich, not-too-sweet dark chocolate sauce.

Le Garage 😊

French 🍴

A3

85 Liberty Ship Way, Ste.109 (off Marinship Way), Sausalito

Phone: 415-332-5625
Web: www.legaragebistrosausalito.com
Prices: $$

Lunch daily
Dinner Mon – Sat

Cultivated French technique meets bold California tastes at this petite canteen, which, as advertised, is housed in a former garage (complete with roll-up doors). Flavorful bouillabaisse packed with fresh dorade, plump scallops, and local shellfish; or a beet-and-apple salad with mandarinquats and goat cheese; sealed by a tangy, buttery lemon tart are only some of the appealing menu options.

Le Garage's building was used to construct World War II battleships, but these days, it's more likely to house well-dressed sailors fresh off their yachts in the harbor, as well as lunching locals from the neighboring businesses. With coffee and croissants each morning, brunch on the weekends, and a thoughtful Cal-French wine list, it's a standby at any time of day.

Marché aux Fleurs

Mediterranean 🍴🍴

B2

23 Ross Common (off Lagunitas Rd.), Ross

Phone: 415-925-9200
Web: www.marcheauxfleursrestaurant.com
Prices: $$

Dinner Tue – Sat

Its dark wood dining room is charming, but Marché aux Fleurs truly comes alive on warm spring and summer evenings, when Marin residents flock to the picturesque hamlet of Ross to enjoy a meal on its front patio. Mediterranean-inspired eats with a California twist are what these patrons are after—imagine soft gnocchi with corn and chanterelles or squash blossom tempura with fresh ricotta and you will start to grasp the picture.

Local couples love it here and though many are regulars, even first-timers receive a friendly welcome from the engaging staff. Groups are everywhere and their smiles omniscient as they savor bacon-wrapped king salmon over sweet corn and green garbanzo succotash; or split bites of warm chocolate cake with vanilla bean ice cream.

225

Marinitas ☺

Latin American 🍴🍴

B2

218 Sir Francis Drake Blvd. (at Bank St.), San Anselmo

Phone: 415-454-8900
Web: www.marinitas.net
Prices: $$

Lunch & dinner daily

Thanks to its audible buzz and crowds spilling out onto the placid sidewalks of San Anselmo, this vast cantina can be spotted from a block away. Diners come in big groups to feast on Mexican and Latin cooking, aided by freshly squeezed margaritas and 101 tequilas. The décor is comfortable, with booths that boast a view of Marinitas' fun knickknacks and huge angled mirrors donning the walls.

Considering the crowds, the food here is still made with great care, from that cocktail glass of creamy Peruvian-style salmon ceviche with *aji amarillo* and citrus, to tender braised pork *tinga* over sweet corn polenta. Many items pack a surprising kick, so be sure to have a bowl of guacamole on hand. The moist *tres leches* cake with mango offers a delectable finish.

Molina

Californian 🍴🍴

B2

17 Madrona St. (bet. Lovell & Throckmorton Aves.), Mill Valley

Phone: 415-383-4200
Web: www.molinarestaurant.com
Prices: $$

Dinner nightly

Small and deeply personal, this Mill Valley destination is a showcase for Chef Todd Shoberg, who simultaneously mans the wood-fired oven and flips vinyl records that provide the soundtrack (and double as art). With a funky design full of wood and texture, it's almost like eating in the home of a friend—albeit one with great taste in music who really knows his way around the kitchen.

The best of Marin produce stars on the ever-changing menu, which might include gold rice with prawns, pork belly, and a green tomato gazpacho; or tender, crisp-skinned game hen over a Waldorf-esque salad of romaine, blue cheese, walnuts, and Bing cherries. From the wine to the bread, everything is local, yet inventive and compelling: it's a gift both to and from the community.

Nick's Cove

American ✗✗

A1

23240 Hwy. 1, Marshall

Phone: 415-663-1033
Web: www.nickscove.com
Prices: $$

Lunch & dinner daily

It's hard not to fall for this sweet waterside retreat in adorable Tomales Bay, which has served as a refuge for city-dwellers for decades. The vintage fuel pump outside is just for looks in this era of hybrid cars, and the updated interior has a lodge-like feel complete with vaulted ceilings, wood-paneled walls, a fireplace, and smattering of hunting trophies.

Unsurprisingly for northern California's oyster capital, the menu is heavy on seafood, from bivalves both raw and grilled to golden-brown Dungeness crab cakes. The white shrimp enchiladas with *salsa roja* and cilantro cream are soft and succulent. Longing for more even after you've finished your meal? Stay the night on their grounds in one of several cozy cottages with a wood-burning stove.

Osteria Stellina

Italian ✗✗

A1

11285 Hwy. 1 (at 3rd St.), Point Reyes Station

Phone: 415-663-9988
Web: www.osteriastellina.com
Prices: $$

Lunch & dinner daily

Its name is Italian for "little star," and this cutie spot does indeed shine in the heart of tiny Point Reyes Station, a one-horse clapboard town with little more than a filling station and a post office to its name. But the Wild West it's not: this frontier village is Marin-chic, and its saloon is a soothing retreat with soft sage walls, wide windows, and local produce on the menu.

You'll taste the difference in the pillowy house-made focaccia, the soothing chicken *brodo*, and the crisp salad of little gem lettuce with blue cheese, toasted walnuts, and honeycrisp apples. Organic, grass-fed beef stew is packed with spices and served over herbed polenta. Finish with a chocolate sponge cake with mocha mousse that's as unforgettable as the setting.

Picco

B2 Italian XX

320 Magnolia Ave. (at King St.), Larkspur

Phone: 415-924-0300 Dinner nightly
Web: www.restaurantpicco.com
Prices: $$

Picco is Italian for "summit," and this charming Larkspur hilltop home has long been a beacon among Marin county diners. Chef/owner Bruce Hill is a true local-food devotee; his Italian-influenced fare heaps on Marin ingredients like the fresh turnips that dot his silky-smooth duck *tortelli*; or the Meyer lemon yogurt and beets that sit atop a nourishing kale salad. The three-course "Marin Mondays" menu is a particular steal.

The precise staff moves ably through the busy dining room, carrying bowls of creamy risotto made on the half-hour. With a high ceiling and exposed brick walls, the vibe is graceful but never fussy, making this the perfect setting for couples and groups of friends who congregate here.

Also check out Pizzeria Picco next door.

Poggio

A3 Italian XX

777 Bridgeway (at Bay St.), Sausalito

Phone: 415-332-7771 Lunch & dinner daily
Web: www.poggiotrattoria.com
Prices: $$

You might forget you're not on the Adriatic coast midway through a meal at this Sausalito standby, where the Italian flavors are authentic and the views of yachts bobbing in the harbor add to the charm. Local regulars and tourists alike arrive early to snag one of the prime sidewalk seats overlooking the main drag; inside, the elegant dining room boasts a roaring pizza oven.

California-influenced appetizers like seared scallops with sunchoke purée and aromatic veal jus segue into comforting pastas—pappardelle tossed with braised pork ragout and *parmigiano*, anyone? Half-portions are available on every pasta and risotto, a bonus for those who want to save room for entrées like grilled yellowfin tuna with asparagus, green olives, and caramelized fennel.

Prabh

B2

Indian ✗✗

24 Sunnyside Ave. (at Parkwood St.), Mill Valley

Phone: 415-384-8241
Web: www.prabhindiankitchen.com
Prices: $$

Lunch & dinner daily

Located in a converted house and a welcome addition to Mill Valley's dining scene, this casual yet stylish Indian restaurant is a cut above the rest. South Asian art and sculpture, fresh flowers, and copper accents add splashes of color to the mahogany furnishings and granite tabletops, while the glass-enclosed front porch is a sunny spot to enjoy an easygoing lunch, kids included.

Bring a group and explore the menu family-style, as you won't want to miss the tender, well-spiced, and *garam masala*-redolent lamb *rogan josh* or the sizzling kebab of chicken tikka in its tangy, delectable yogurt marinade. Flaky samosas filled with a flavorful blend of potatoes, peas, caramelized onions, and served with a trio of tasty chutneys, are quite perfect.

R'Noh Thai

B2

Thai ✗✗

1000 Magnolia Ave. (bet. Frances & Murray Aves.), Larkspur

Phone: 415-925-0599
Web: www.rnohthai.com
Prices: ☜☜

Lunch Mon – Sat
Dinner nightly

Generous portions and thoughtful preparations are the key ingredients at this Thai restaurant, which occupies a long wooden building overlooking a small creek. The interior is warm and inviting, with bright skylights, oil paintings of water lilies, and a fireplace crackling away.

R'Noh's popularity is most evident at lunch, when local business people drop in for the daily special of a light curry with salad and rice. Ginger chicken, packed with mushrooms and tender meat, is a more mild but still flavorful option. The menu expands slightly at dinner, offering delicious plates like a crispy shrimp roll filled with plump prawns. Highly attentive servers can recommend a wine from the short list, or try their supremely thirst-quenching homemade lemonade.

Sir and Star 😀

A1

American ✖️✖️

10000 Sir Francis Drake Blvd. (at Hwy. 1), Olema

Phone: 415-663-1034
Web: www.sirandstar.com
Prices: $$

Dinner Wed – Sun

The dynamic duo of Chef/owners Daniel DeLong and Margaret Gradé have been missed in Marin's culinary scene since their previous restaurant, Manka's Inverness Lodge, was destroyed in a fire. Now, they're cooking again in this quaint yet quirky dining room, this time situated in the historic Olema Inn. It's a roadhouse, but a very quiet one—so don't bring your rowdy pals.

Simplicity and hyper-local fare are the focus here with dishes like Tomales Bay oyster shooters with wee ribbons of kohlrabi; spring onion soup with *gougères*; or luscious pork tenderloin with Bolinas beets and artichokes. A medieval fireplace (in winter) or tree-shaded patio (in summer) provides a romantic setting to unplug and relax over a wine list dominated by Marin grapes.

Sushi Ran 😀

A3

Japanese ✖️✖️

107 Caledonia St. (bet. Pine & Turney Sts.), Sausalito

Phone: 415-332-3620
Web: www.sushiran.com
Prices: $$

Lunch Mon – Fri
Dinner nightly

Chefs have come and gone at this Sausalito staple, but its Zen-like atmosphere and exquisite selection of raw fish haven't changed for upwards of a decade—and that's just how the regulars like it. With its charming beachside-bungalow ambience, attentive staff, and thoughtfully curated sake selection, Sushi Ran is as dependable as a restaurant can get.

Start off with a small bite like shrimp tempura over crisp veggies, tobiko, and asparagus, or a steamed red crab salad with seaweed, cucumber, and sweet soy dressing. Then move on to the main event: meticulously sourced, extraordinarily fresh hamachi, big-eye tuna, steamed blue prawns, and Santa Barbara uni. Whether you choose sashimi or nigiri, the talented chefs will steer you right.

Thai Aroi-Dee

Thai ✗

C2

1518 4th St. (bet. E & F Sts.), San Rafael

Lunch & dinner daily

Phone: 415-295-7464
Web: www.thaiaroi-dee.com
Prices: $$

Marin isn't known for a preponderance of great Thai restaurants, but Aroi-Dee is so outstanding that it would be destination-worthy even for those who live outside the charming enclave. Though its San Rafael space may be small and spare, the welcome is warm and the flavors are bold and exciting.

Americanized staples are available, but they're best skipped in favor of intense, authentic plates that aren't toned down for Western palates. Try the knockout duck *larb* with bright herbs, sharp sliced red onion, and smoky, rich meat, or salmon steamed in banana leaves with a fragrant, mousse-like coconut curry custard. If you like it hot, opt for the spicy spare ribs, stir-fried with house-made chili paste, young green peppercorns, and silky eggplant.

Valenti & Co.

Italian ✗✗

B2

337 San Anselmo Ave. (bet. Pine St. & Woodland Ave.), San Anselmo

Dinner Tue – Sun

Phone: 415-454-7800
Web: www.valentico.com
Prices: $$$

Guests leave both their hearts and their hunger behind after a meal at this utterly captivating spot in cozy San Anselmo, where the chef busily prepares each dish from scratch in the back as his bubbly wife hugs regulars and ushers them inside. Adding to the quaint trattoria feel, fragrant blooms from the window boxes release their delicate scents into the dining room.

The bill of fare is largely Italian, with a few fun twists: house-made fettuccine is twirled in a shrimp bisque and topped with plump, sweet Hawaiian prawns, and tiramisu becomes "crunchymisu" when puff pastry is subbed for ladyfingers. But even simpler dishes, like flaky, moist griddled Mt. Lassen trout with braised fennel, radicchio, and tangy lemon emulsion, are full of flavor.

Peninsula

Peninsula

A COLLISION OF CULTURES

Situated to the south of the city, the San Francisco Peninsula separates the Bay from the expansive Pacific Ocean. While it may not be known across the globe for stellar chefs and pioneering Californian cooking, the Peninsula boasts an incredibly diverse and rich Asian culture. Area eateries and numerous markets reflect this region's melting-pot and continue to draw locals for authentic international cuisines. Those in need of a taste from the East should join Korean natives at **Kukje Super Market** as they scoop up fresh seafood, rolls of *gimbap*, and a host of other prepared delicacies. Or practice the art of chopstick wielding at one of the many Japanese sushi bars, ramen houses, and *izakayas*. Filipino foodies tickle their fancy with an impressive selection of traditional breads and pastries at **Valerio's Tropical Bake Shop** in Daly City. Fittingly set in a Filipino-dominated quarter referred to as "**Little Manila**," Valerio's is famously revered as *the* best bakery around. Beyond the Far East, sugar junkies of the Western variety savor classic Danish pastries at Burlingame's **Copenhagen Bakery**, also applauded for creamy special occasion cakes. Over in San Mateo, Italians can't miss a stop

at **pasta pasta** for freshly made shapes, homemade sauces, and salads that are both fulfilling and easy to put together at home. If your domestic skills leave much to be desired, charming **La Biscotteria** has premium, hand-crafted Italian pastries and cookies, including cannoli, *amaretti*, *sfogliatelle*, and biscotti in an assortment of flavors. This precious gem in Redwood City also sells beautiful hand-painted Deruta ceramics imported from Umbria.

The Peninsula is also home to a large Mexican-American population. Their taste for home can be gratified at such authentic taquerias as **El Grullense** in Redwood City; **El Palenque** in San Mateo; and **Mexcal Taqueria** in Menlo Park. Just as **Gabriel & Daniel's Mexican Grill** in the Burlingame Golf Center clubhouse is an ideal place to unwind after playing a round out on the plush course, dive-y **Back A Yard** in Menlo Park is forever popular among foodies craving flavorful Caribbean cuisine. Pescetarians know that **Barbara's Fishtrap** in Princeton by the Sea is a sought-after "catch" for fish 'n chips by the harbor, whereas pig trumps fish at **Gorilla Barbeque**. Here, fat-frilled pork ribs are all the rage, especially when served out of an orange railroad car parked on Cabrillo Highway in Pacifica.

SUMMER'S BOUNTY

In addition to harboring some of the Bay Area's most authentic Cantonese dens and dim sum houses, Millbrae is a lovely spot to raise one last toast to summer. In fact, **The Millbrae Art & Wine Festival** is a profusion of wicked fairground eats—from meltingly tender cheesesteaks and Cajun-style corndogs, to fennel-infused sausages and everything in between. Motivated home chefs head to **Draeger's Market** in San Mateo to pick up some wine and cheese for dinner, and perhaps even sign up for cooking classes in a range of basic to highly specialized subjects. When in this 'hood, be sure to revel in a riot of Japanese goods at **Suruki Market**. Half Moon Bay is a coastal city big on sustainable produce; and in keeping with this philosophy, residents prepare for cozy evenings indoors by loading up on local fruits and vegetables from one of the many roadside stands on Route 92. Find them also scanning the bounty at **Coastside Farmer's Market**, known to unveil such Pescadero treasures as Harley Farms goat cheese and organic eggs from **Early Bird Ranch**.

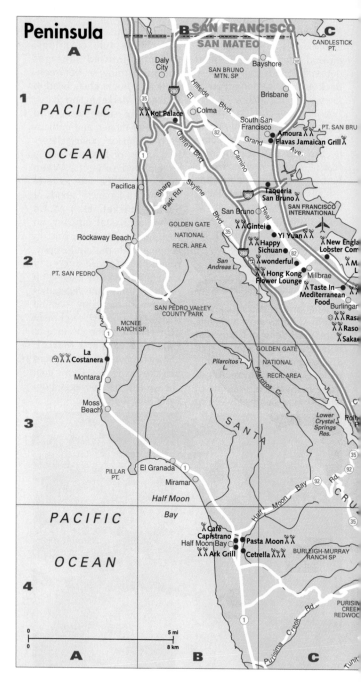

Peninsula

A

PACIFIC

OCEAN

B SAN FRANCISCO

SAN MATEO

C

CANDLESTICK
PT.

Daly
City

SAN BRUNO
MTN. SP

Bayshore

Brisbane

Hillside Blvd.

El Camino

280

35

Kol Palace

Colma

Gellert Blvd.

82

South San
Francisco

PT. SAN BRU

Amoura

Flavas Jamaican Grill

Grand Ave.

1

Pacifica

Sharp Park Rd.

Skyline Blvd.

380

Taqueria
San Bruno

San Bruno

Real

SAN FRANCISCO
INTERNATIONAL

Rockaway Beach

GOLDEN GATE
NATIONAL
RECR. AREA

35

Gintei

Yi Yuan

PT. SAN PEDRO

San
Andreas L.

Happy
Sichuan

82

New Engla
Lobster Com

wonderful

M
L

2

Hong Kong
Flower Lounge

Millbrae

SAN PEDRO VALLEY
COUNTY PARK

Taste In
Mediterranean
Food

Burlingan

MCNEE
RANCH SP

280

Rasa

Raso

Saka

1

La
Costanera

GOLDEN GATE
NATIONAL
RECR. AREA

Pilarcitos
L.

Montara

Moss
Beach

Pilarcitos Cr.

Lower
Crystal
Springs
Res.

S A N T A

Rolb
R

3

PILLAR
PT.

El Granada

1

35

92

92

C

Miramar

Half Moon

Bay

Half Moon Bay Rd.

C R U

PACIFIC

OCEAN

Bay

Café
Capistrano

Half Moon Bay

Pasta Moon

35

4

Ark Grill

Cetrella

BURLEIGH-MURRAY
RANCH SP

PURISIN
CREEK
REDWO

0   5 mi
0   8 km

Purisima Creek Rd.

Tunil

A   **B**   **C**

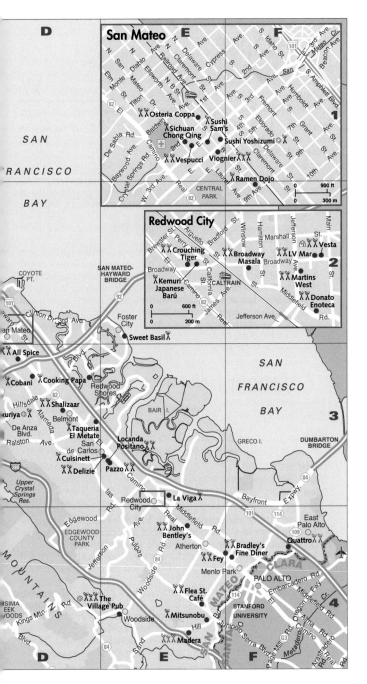

San Mateo

- Osteria Coppa
- Sichuan Chong Qing
- Sushi Sam's
- Vespucci
- Sushi Yoshizumi
- Viognier
- Ramen Dojo

CENTRAL PARK

0 — 900 ft
0 — 300 m

Redwood City

- Crouching Tiger
- Broadway Masala
- Vesta
- LV Mar
- Kemuri Japanese Barú
- Martins West
- Donato Enoteca
- CALTRAIN

Jefferson Ave.

0 — 600 ft
0 — 200 m

SAN FRANCISCO BAY

- Sweet Basil
- All Spice
- Cobani
- Cooking Papa
- Shalizaar
- kuriya
- Taqueria El Metate
- Locanda Positano
- Cuisinett
- Delizie
- Pazzo
- La Viga
- John Bentley's
- Bradley's Fine Diner
- Quattro
- Fey
- The Village Pub
- Flea St. Café
- Mitsunobu
- Madera

COYOTE PT.

SAN MATEO-HAYWARD BRIDGE

Foster City

Redwood Shores

BAIR I.

GRECO I.

DUMBARTON BRIDGE

Belmont

San Carlos

Redwood City

East Palo Alto

Atherton

Menlo Park

PALO ALTO

STANFORD UNIVERSITY

Woodside

EDGEWOOD COUNTY PARK

Upper Crystal Springs Res.

MOUNTAINS

SIMA EEK OODS

237

All Spice

D3

1602 El Camino Real (bet. Barneson & Borel Aves.), San Mateo

Phone: 650-627-4303   Dinner Tue – Sat
Web: www.allspicerestaurant.com
Prices: $$$

Set in a beautifully restored Victorian, walking into quaint All Spice feels like you've landed at the most exquisite home of a friend. Each small, brightly colored room is set with fine linens, and the big windows usher in translucent light. It's a magical setting for a date, though the fun-loving crowd never lets things get too serious.

Chef Sachin Chopra and wife, Shoshana Wolff, have set out to create a "New American Exotic" menu here. It may sound a bit too conceptual, but fits the unique dining experience perfectly. Begin with golden-crusted scallops basted in brown butter and plated with chipotle-saffron *sofrito* and asparagus. Then savor perfectly rendered lamb, paired with a slow-cooked egg yolk, cardamom-flavored milk foam, and a minty herb "cake."

Amoura

C1

713 Linden Ave. (bet. Aspen & Pine Aves.), South San Francisco

Phone: 650-754-6891   Lunch Mon – Fri
Web: www.amourasf.com   Dinner Mon – Sat
Prices: $$

In largely underserved South San Francisco, the arrival of this spacious Mediterranean spot was cause for celebration. With lots of tile and stonework, its polished vibe can run a bit corporate—but that's ideal for the large local office crowd who pack it at lunchtime. (Dinner, on the other hand, can be a bit sleepy.)

Here, classic Mediterranean dishes come with modern twists: tender, smoky grilled lamb skewers are draped over tabbouleh with butternut squash and arugula, while a perfectly cooked roast chicken is drizzled with garlicky basil pesto. The notable drink menu includes a wine list rich with unusual Lebanese and Croatian vintages, as well as an impressive selection of *arak*, an anise-flavored liquor popular in the Middle East.

Ark Grill

Indian ✗✗

724 Main St. (bet. Correas & Filbert St.), Half Moon Bay

Phone: 650-560-8152
Web: www.arkgrill.com
Prices: $$

Lunch Fri – Sun
Dinner Tue – Sun

Like Indiana Jones' coveted treasure, this Ark can only be found by those in the know—and since it's off the main tourist drag in Half Moon Bay, the locals mostly have it to themselves. It's the kind of place where bringing a group (kids included) pays dividends, as you'll be able to sample more of the delicious North Indian fare, which boasts exceptionally high-quality ingredients.

Check out the Bollywood films projected on the wall as you savor crisp and flaky potato samosas; smoky, and caramelized *tandoori* chicken; plump shrimp in a tangy, richly spiced *vindaloo*; and creamy *dal* fry starring yellow lentils and stewed tomatoes. Spice levels can be adjusted, but most dishes are mild—and fluffy naan is at hand to scoop up the curries.

Bradley's Fine Diner

American ✗✗

1165 Merrill St. (at Oak Grove Ave.), Menlo Park

Phone: 650-494-4342
Web: www.bradleysfinediner.com
Prices: $$$

Lunch & dinner daily

Like a grown-up greasy spoon, this newcomer from award-winning chef, Bradley Ogden, updates American favorites with quality ingredients and a dash of creativity. A delightful riff on Buffalo wings pairs crispy chunks of pork belly with a luscious Maytag blue cheese soufflé, while free-range chicken breast arrives moist and juicy, accompanied by a squash-centric panzanella. A piping-hot apple cobbler and killer butterscotch pudding are some of the stars on the dessert menu.

The sizable space has hip touches that appeal to the crowd of affluent Atherton locals, like a wood art piece embedded with chef's knives, a glowing neon sign, and wraparound porches for warm nights. For a classy yet unfussy night out, Bradley's is a fine choice indeed.

Broadway Masala

F2

Indian ✗✗

2397 Broadway (at Winslow St.), Redwood City

Phone: 650-369-9000   Lunch & dinner daily
Web: www.broadwaymasala.net
Prices: $$

Indian food gets its name in lights at Broadway Masala, offering both traditional and modern interpretations of the country's cuisine. The kitchen serves up a fine chicken biryani full of flavorful spices, tender chicken, and fluffy rice; and the spicy lamb *rogan josh* is equally sumptuous. The menu is full of quirky twists: think Cajun chicken *tikka*, spinach-tofu *kofta*, and a smoky *kulcha* filled with finely chopped aplewood-smoked bacon.

The long, narrow space boasts a stylish décor, with contemporary light fixtures, stacked stone pillars, and decorative wine barrels here and there. A side bar offers a solid selection of draft beer and wines, and when the sun is shining, a few tables out front offer people-watching on the namesake thoroughfare.

Café Capistrano

B4

Mexican ✗

523 Church St. (at Miramontes St.), Half Moon Bay

Phone: 650-726-7699   Lunch & dinner daily
Web: N/A
Prices: ⊗

Chef/owner Arturo Mul grew up on the Yucatán peninsula, and the traditional Mayan dishes of his youth are now the backbone of this cute café in the heart of Half Moon Bay. Housed in an older home surrounded by gardens and a small side deck, the spot is warm, homey, and, to the delight of local families, off most tourists' radars.

Start with a Yucatecan appetizer plate of *salbutes* (fried tortillas topped with grilled chicken, pickled onion, and cabbage slaw) and empanadas. Then dig into the smoky pork enchiladas, crowned with cheese and garlicky red chili sauce, or the tender grilled chicken adobo. Be cautious with the house-made habanero sauce: its Mayan name, *xni-pec*, means "dog nose" and it'll have yours running if you exceed a few drops.

Cetrella

Mediterranean XXX

B4

845 Main St. (at Monte Vista Ln.), Half Moon Bay

Phone: 650-726-4090
Web: www.cetrella.com
Prices: $$$

Lunch Sun
Dinner Tue – Sun

What it lacks in million-dollar ocean views, Cetrella more than makes up for in charm. One of the most elegant and stylish restaurants along the coast, it's housed in a stunning Mediterranean-style villa with exposed trusses and skylights, a roaring central fireplace, and a humming exhibition kitchen. Throw in warm, welcoming service, and you'll never want to leave.

Seasonal Californian ingredients get a Mediterranean spin here, and nightly specials like a warm Brussels sprouts salad with wood-smoked salmon or roasted pork chop with porcini mushrooms, heirloom carrots, and smoked ham jus are transcendent. This is definitely a meal worth dressing up for, so be sure to swap your beachwear for something more sophisticated before setting foot inside.

Cobani

Mediterranean X

D3

8 W. 25th Ave. (bet. El Camino Real & Flores St.), San Mateo

Phone: 650-389-6861
Web: www.cobanigyro.com
Prices: 🪙

Lunch & dinner daily

New to downtown San Mateo, this fast-casual Turkish spot is already a favorite with the locals. Lunch hour brings a crowd—think nine-to-fivers and families with kids—and the modus operandi is simple: order at the counter, grab a number and utensils, and take a seat in the cheerful dining room, adorned with a colorful mural depicting a Turkish village.

The kitchen churns out a mix of Turkish, Mediterranean, and Middle Eastern items: you'll find an *adana* kebab—made of spicy, charbroiled minced lamb and beef—that's worthy of Istanbul. Then, look forward to shaved chicken gyros wrapped in lavash, followed by crispy falafel with baba ganoush. And the skilled kitchen's take on *künefe*, a traditional dessert of mild white cheese broiled with syrupy pastry, is superlative.

Cooking Papa

Chinese ✗

Chinese ✗

949 Edgewater Blvd., Ste. A (at Beach Park Blvd.), Foster City

Phone: 650-577-1830

Web: www.mycookingpapa.com

Prices: 💰

Lunch & dinner daily

Cantonese and Hong Kong-style dishes draw weekend crowds to the sleek and minimally adorned Cooking Papa, set back in a shopping center alongside one of the Foster City canals. Inside, find expats clustered around faux-granite tables armed with dark wood chairs and framed by a wall of windows running the length of the space—every seat has a glorious water view.

A vast menu features all types of dishes, from simple yet heart-warming *congee* and soft tofu braised with vegetables, to sweet and salty barbecued pork—honey-glazed and intensely moist. Americanized standards like hot-and-sour soup may disappoint, so it's best to think outside the box and get the crispy, beignet-like egg puffs for dessert: they're perfect with strong black tea.

Crouching Tiger

2644 Broadway St. (bet. El Camino Real & Perry St.), Redwood City

Phone: 650-298-8881

Web: www.crouchingtigerrestaurant.com

Prices: 💰

Lunch & dinner daily

The heat is on at Redwood City's palace of Sichuan fare, where spice-hounds come for a dose of the chili-packed Chongqing chicken, *mapo* tofu, and other regional specialties. Sure, there may be blander options, but steaming platters of green chili-topped, richly flavored cumin lamb or plump prawns and crisp sautéed vegetables in hot garlic sauce are enough to induce a love of spice.

Crouching Tiger's midday crowd can be its own fire-breathing dragon, with droves of local workers packing the tables for reasonably priced lunch specials with soup, salad, and rice. Large, round tables are great for big groups (kids too). The chic interior with its dark wood furnishings, art, and drum lanterns, is definitely a step up from the standard Chinese joint.

Cuisinett

E3

1105 San Carlos Ave. (at El Camino Real), San Carlos

Phone:	650-453-3390
Web:	www.cuisinett.com
Prices:	$$

Lunch daily
Dinner Mon – Sat

French restaurants aren't often known for their chill vibe or affordability, but this casual counter-service charmer proves otherwise, with comforting quiches, salads, and *plats* at down-to-earth prices. Diners customize with mix-and-match sauces like Dijon mustard or Cognac black pepper to pair with a steak and choice of sides.

Families, kids, and those with dogs in tow can be seen noshing on a refreshing beet, endive, and blue cheese salad with a walnut vinaigrette; or the perfectly cooked roasted chicken with red wine sauce and herbed peas and carrots, all skillfully prepared with the French chef's authentic hand. Note: there will be butter.

Save room for the luscious, flaky *tarte au citron*, or beautiful raspberry and salted caramel macarons.

Delizie

Italian   ✗✗

E3

1107 San Carlos Ave. (bet. El Camino Real & Laurel St.), San Carlos

Phone:	650-486-1539
Web:	www.deliziesc.com
Prices:	$$

Lunch & dinner Mon – Sat

The name of this Southern Italian gem means "delicious," and its authentic fare delivers on the moniker. All credit goes to the owner, a native of Calabria who works hard to ensure that the welcome here is as warm and the house-made pastas as delectable as those of the Old Country.

Settle in under the twinkling chandeliers in the intimate space—nestled in the heart of San Carlos just steps from the Caltrain station—then summon a plate of perfectly cooked pappardelle in a tomato-kissed wild boar ragù. Move on to an indulgently cheesy gratin of baked cauliflower (under its crisp breadcrumb topping lies a touch of cream sauce), before finishing with bittersweet cappuccino mousse, served over coffee sponge cake and crowned by a chocolate-coated coffee bean.

243

Donato Enoteca

F2

Italian ✗✗

1041 Middlefield Rd. (bet. Jefferson Ave. & Main St.), Redwood City

Phone: 650-701-1000
Web: www.donatoenoteca.com
Prices: $$

Lunch & dinner daily

Set in Redwood City's sleek downtown, this Italian jewel draws lunching lawyers and civic workers from the nearby courthouses by day, and couples as well as families at dusk. The restaurant is spacious, with a patio boasting Sunbrellas and heat lamps, two dining rooms, and a large bar. Meanwhile its rustic, wood-centric décor is glammed up with thick rugs and gilded mirrors.

An array of pastas, wood-fired pizzas, salads, and meat dishes will please diners of all stripes, whether they opt for the house-made *agnolotti del plin* in a tomato-onion ragù, or the roasted chicken in a buttery jus with green Bosana olives. Lingering in the laid-back environs is always encouraged, especially to savor the creamy melon semifreddo with candied almonds.

Fey

E4

Chinese ✗✗

1368 El Camino Real (bet. Glenwood & Oak Grove Aves.), Menlo Park

Phone: 650-324-8888
Web: www.feyrestaurant.com
Prices: $$

Lunch & dinner daily

"Glitzy" isn't a word commonly used to describe Sichuan restaurants, but with its glamorous chandeliers and metallic wall art, Fey's interior is exactly that. The crowd follows suit, with Chinese investors conducting big negotiations alongside families dressed to the nines.

Though Westernized food is on offer, diners who order Sichuan dishes—like wok-fried Chongqing chicken buried under piles of dried chilies, or chili oil-drenched *mapo* tofu topped with ground pork—are rewarded with exceptional service and traditional spice. Ease the burn with hot black tea, then dive back into cold wheat noodles tossed with pork, cucumber, ground peanuts, and more chili oil, before heading to your car in the lot out back (an asset on this busy stretch of El Camino).

Flavas Jamaican Grill

Caribbean ✗

C1

314 Linden Ave. (at 4th Ln.), South San Francisco

Phone: 650-244-9785
Web: www.flavasjamaicangrill.com
Prices: 🪙

Lunch & dinner Mon – Sat

♿ South San Francisco has never been a restaurant hot spot, but this rookie could be a sign of things to come. The secret is already out with local residents and Genentech employees, who fill the casual space for its good food, gracious service, and soundtrack of reggae beats.

Flavas is simply decorated with basic furnishings and ocean-themed art, but its appeal is right there in the name. Authentic dishes brim with herbs, garlic, and Scotch Bonnet peppers, like the smoky, boldly spiced jerk chicken with caramelized fried plantains; or the fork-tender curried goat stew with coconut milk and chilies. Don't forget to keep an eye out for the intriguing daily specials, which can include jerk shrimp and snapper, saltfish and ackee, and other island favorites.

Flea St. Café

Californian ✗✗

E4

3607 Alameda de las Pulgas (at Avy Ave.), Menlo Park

Phone: 650-854-1226
Web: www.cooleatz.com
Prices: $$$

Dinner Tue – Sun

⛱ A pioneer in the locally sourced, sustainable movement, this intimate spot remains a die-hard darling with the older, moneyed Atherton crowd, who flood the space for special occasions and date nights. The petite dining rooms are quaint and homey, with linen-covered tabletops and flickering votive candles, and those alfresco sidewalk tables are hot tickets whenever the mercury rises.

Prepare to ponder "which came first?" with a dish of pasture-raised roast chicken over sautéed fiddlehead ferns, accompanied by a rich, soft-poached farm egg that enlivens its sherry jus. Moist, flaky house-smoked trout with horseradish crème fraîche begs to be scooped up by the accompanying waffle potato chips, and tangy lemon cake is a must for dessert.

Gintei

C2

235 El Camino Real (bet. Crystal Springs & San Felipe Aves.), San Bruno

Phone: 650-636-4135
Web: www.gintei.co
Prices: $$$

Lunch Tue – Fri
Dinner Tue – Sun

San Bruno's rep as a dining wasteland is due for a re-evaluation with the arrival of this sleek, stylish new sushi spot, whose offerings can hang with the best in San Francisco. Bright and contemporary, with dramatic pressed-tin ceilings and a coveted eight-seat sushi counter, it's already becoming known as a reservations-required must for omakase enthusiasts, with deeply hospitable service.

Newbies to nigiri should make a beeline for the omakase, but the more experienced palate will revel in market specials like silky Hokkaido scallops, sweet and succulent live spot prawns (with the traditional deep-fried heads alongside), and firm yet tender octopus. Everything is minimally dressed—all, the better to accentuate the fish's outstanding quality.

Happy Sichuan

C2

1055 El Camino Real (at Meadow Glenn Ave.), Millbrae

Phone: 650-692-8858
Web: N/A
Prices: $$

Lunch & dinner daily

The closure of several top Sichuan spots have saddened Peninsula diners in recent years, but newcomer Happy Sichuan is a worthy successor. Simply and minimally decorated, it won't win prizes for looks or surroundings (it's housed in a Millbrae strip mall), but servers are friendly and flavors appropriately bold.

Skip the milquetoast Americanized dishes and head straight for the menu's "Specialties" section, where you'll encounter the absolutely enormous hot pot—a flavorful, rich broth full of beef, chicken, lamb, and soft tofu. The magic chicken earns its name thanks to a crisp, chili-inflected coating, and the spicy cold wheat noodles with cucumber are a delight. With fiery fare this good and plentiful, you're sure to leave, well, happy.

Hong Kong Flower Lounge

Chinese

C2

51 Millbrae Ave. (at El Camino Real), Millbrae

Phone:	650-692-6666
Web:	www.mayflower-seafood.com
Prices:	$$

Lunch & dinner daily

Generations of dim sum diehards have patronized this palace of pork buns, where a small army of servers will throng you with carts from the moment you take your seat. They bear innumerable delights: rich barbecue pork belly with crispy skin, pan-fried pork-and-chive wontons steamed to order and doused in oyster sauce, delicate vegetable dumplings, and a best-in-class baked egg custard bun. Evenings are a bit more sedate, emphasizing Cantonese seafood straight from the on-site tanks.

As with all dim sum spots, the early bird gets the best selection (and avoids the non-negligible weekend waits). Thankfully, the super-central Millbrae location, towering over El Camino Real, boasts plenty of parking—and a machine-like staff that knows how to pack them in.

John Bentley's

Contemporary

E4

2915 El Camino Real (bet. Berkshire Ave. & Selby Ln.), Redwood City

Phone:	650-365-7777
Web:	www.johnbentleys.com
Prices:	$$

Lunch Mon – Fri
Dinner Mon – Sat

A vine-covered trellis walkway leads to this stately spot, located on a quiet, somewhat hidden stretch of El Camino Real. Inside the quaint tavern, whose dark wood wainscoting and oil paintings recall an earlier era of power-lunching, business people and locals alike can be found savoring the contemporary American cooking.

The grilled watermelon Napoleon, layered with avocado, spicy jicama, and rich crab salad, is a favorite for lovers of lighter food, while those seeking richer sustenance should beeline for the sweetbreads in a rich, creamy veal sauce, accompanied by mashed potatoes and green beans. For dessert, a classic puff-pastry apple tart with a scoop of homemade ice cream—boasting a dried cherry surprise—hits the spot.

247

Kabul

C2

Afghan ✗✗

1101 Burlingame Ave. (at California Dr.), Burlingame

Phone: 650-343-2075
Web: www.kabulafghancuisine.org
Prices: $$

Lunch & dinner daily

Though it's settled on a hopping corner in Burlingame's main shopping district and steps from the Caltrain station, this bright, light-filled Afghan spot is evocative of the desert country and its unique and hearty cooking. Dishes include *sambosa-e-goushti* (fried dough pockets filled with lamb and chickpeas); *kabab-e-murgh* (tender chicken skewers atop *pallaw*); or sautéed pumpkin with yogurt sauce, all of which draw business types at lunch and families for dinner.

Diners must exercise care not to load up on the fluffy flatbread with a green chili-and-herb chutney that's served at first, lest they miss out on a final course of syrup-soaked baklava studded with chopped walnuts. Service is casual at all times, despite the white tablecloths.

Kemuri Japanese Barú

E2

Asian ✗

2616 Broadway (bet. El Camino Real & Perry St.), Redwood City

Phone: 650-257-7653
Web: www.kemuri-baru.com
Prices: $$

Lunch Tue – Fri
Dinner Tue – Sun

You'll feel like you've strolled into a hip Tokyo nightspot when you enter Kemuri, which blends funky takes on *izakaya* dishes and a selection of Japanese-influenced craft beer and cocktails into a young, lively package. The spacious, industrial room—think bar shelves made of pipes and water spouts—is always abuzz with twenty-somethings who pack in at the communal wooden tables.

The menu is loaded with Japanese mashups that seem unusual but taste terrific, like a burger with "buns" made of griddled rice balls and stuffed with seared albacore and a creamy sauce. Chilled poke udon, featuring marinated fish and sliced avocado, comes atop cold noodles complete with a barely poached egg, and even the crème brûlée is spiked with green tea.

Koi Palace

B1

365 Gellert Blvd. (bet. Hickey & Serramonte Blvds.), Daly City

Lunch & dinner daily

Phone: 650-992-9000
Web: www.koipalace.com
Prices: $$

Long regarded as one of the Bay Area's best spots for dim sum, Koi Palace continues to earn its serious waits (guaranteed on weekends, and common at weekday lunch). The dining room is a step up from its competition, with shallow koi ponds weaving between tables, high ceilings, and huge tables to accommodate the Chinese-American families celebrating big occasions.

They come to share plates of perfectly lacquered, smoky-salty roasted suckling pig or sticky rice noodle rolls encasing plump shrimp, sesame oil, and minced ginger. Not far behind, find lotus leaves stuffed with glutinous rice, dried scallop, and roast pork, as well as big pots of jasmine tea. Save room for desserts like the fluffy almond cream steamed buns and flaky, caramelized custard tarts.

La Costanera 😊

A3

8150 Cabrillo Hwy. (bet. 1st & 2nd Sts.), Montara

Dinner Tue – Sun

Phone: 650-728-1600
Web: www.lacostanerarestaurant.com
Prices: $$

Set atop one of the most beautiful perches in the entire Bay Area, this bungalow boasts a gorgeous patio and a dining room that's walled with windows.

While the panoramas are amazing—endless ocean, spectacular sunsets, and even frolicking dolphins if you're lucky—so are the boldly flavored plates produced by Chef Carlos Altamirano and his team. A *cebiche* tasting is the best way to experience Peru's national dish; while cool and creamy *causas*, perhaps topped with lobster and salmon roe, or garlicky *anticucho de camarones* hit with zesty *aji amarillo* and salsa verde are other treasures worth devouring.

Be sure to sample the creative cocktails. Alternatively, try a delicious and refreshing *chicha morada*, which is safer for the drive home.

La Viga

E3

1772 Broadway (bet. Beech & Maple Sts.), Redwood City

Phone: 650-679-8141   Lunch & dinner Tue – Sun
Web: www.lavigarestaurant.com
Prices: 🅥🅥

Named after Mexico City's massive seafood market, La Viga is a Redwood City favorite for oceanic fare with a Latin twist. Wedged between an industrial area and downtown, the basic but cheerful dining room draws both blue- and white-collar workers for heaping tacos—soft white corn tortillas stuffed with fried snapper fillet, cabbage, and chipotle *crema*; or crisp prawns with tomatillo-garlic sauce and *pico de gallo*. At the dinner hour, local residents stream in for the famed *camarones picantes*, a sizable mound of al dente *fideos* studded with plump prawns bathed in a spicy tomato sauce. With such fresh ingredients and bold flavors, the low prices and generous portions are particularly pleasing—be sure to allow room for a creamy, delicate flan to finish.

Locanda Positano

E3

617 Laurel St. (bet. Cherry St. & San Carlos Ave.), San Carlos

Phone: 650-591-5700   Lunch & dinner daily
Web: www.locanda-positano.com
Prices: $$

Take a trip to Napoli with a casual Italian meal along the quaint San Carlos strip. Owned by a native and staffed mostly by Italians, it's a perennial favorite among locals for savoring seasonal starters like peaches with burrata, then digging into Neapolitan-style pies like the *pizza con uovo* with salty pancetta, earthy wild mushrooms, and a luscious slow-cooked egg. Toothsome *scialatelli* tossed with tender clams and cherry tomatoes in a white wine sauce is another simple yet tasty choice. Desserts shouldn't be missed, especially Mamma's tiramisu and the traditional ricotta cheesecake. The *bambini* are courted with their own menu of mini pizzas and simple pastas.

The sleek space with contemporary furnishings is grown-up, but not overly upscale.

LV Mar

Latin American ✗✗

F2

2042 Broadway (bet. Jefferson & Main Sts.), Redwood City

Phone: 650-241-3111
Web: www.lvmar.com
Prices: $$

Lunch & dinner Mon – Sat

Located just a few blocks from its casual cousin La Viga, LV Mar is worlds away in terms of cuisine, offering sophisticated contemporary Latin American fare. The space is appropriately stylish, with slate floors, high ceilings, and paintings of ingredients on the walls. Business lunchers fill the tables by day, giving way to couples and families in the evening.

Local produce shines in dishes like the *pescado con pepitas*, a flaky sea bass fillet encrusted in pumpkin seeds and served over buttery *huitlacoche*-potato purée. The *gordita de pato* encases rich duck meat in a golden puff pastry with port and dried cherries, while caramelized Brussels sprouts boast a Manchego-and-*arbol chile* vinaigrette. For the time-pressed, tortas are available at lunch.

Madera

Contemporary ✗✗✗

E4

2825 Sand Hill Rd. (at I-280), Menlo Park

Phone: 650-561-1540
Web: www.maderasandhill.com
Prices: $$$$

Lunch & dinner daily

As evidenced by the dozens of Teslas parked out front, this swanky spot in the Rosewood Sand Hill, adjacent to Silicon Valley's venture-capital row, is a second living room for wealthy techies. It's attired appropriately for the slick, moneyed crowd, with a grand open kitchen, roaring fireplace, and large outdoor patio complete with gorgeous views of the Santa Cruz mountains.

Dishes are equally stunning, yet approachable: silky Alaskan halibut arrives with tangy green strawberries and makrut lime-infused cream, while meaty yellowfin tuna crudo with cucumber and avocado is sprinkled with caviar. The wine list brims with rare, pricey bottles, and desserts are divine—an inspired take on the Boston cream pie with salted caramel and Pop Rocks cannot be missed.

251

Magda Luna

C2

1199 Broadway, Ste. 2 (bet. Chula Vista & Laguna Aves.), Burlingame

Phone: 650-393-4207
Lunch & dinner Tue – Sun
Web: www.magdalunacafe.com
Prices: 🍳

"Mexican food with a conscience" is on the menu at this café in Burlingame, which prides itself on vegetable-heavy, oil-light dishes made with hormone-free, sustainably raised meats. Located on the busy main drag, the restaurant is full of vibrant color and authentic details like decorative murals of Dia de los Muertos-style skulls.

Though healthy, the food here doesn't skimp on flavor. Start with a bowl of warm tortilla chips and a duo of salsas, then dive into a selection of tacos, burritos, and quesadillas. Entrées include *enchiladas Michoacanas* in a spicy-smoky *guajillo* chile sauce, which pair nicely with a fruity house-made *agua fresca*. A welcoming staff and a special menu for *los niños* also make this a great choice for families.

Martins West

F2

831 Main St. (bet. Broadway & Stambaugh St.), Redwood City

Phone: 650-366-4366
Lunch & dinner Mon – Sat
Web: www.martinswestgp.com
Prices: $$

British pub culture meets NorCal flavor at one of Redwood City's favorite after-work spots, where professionals gather for a pint and bite before snagging the Caltrain home. Named for a Scottish restaurateur (and childhood friend of the owner), Martins West has a comfy-chic feel with wax-dripping candelabras, wood floors, brick walls, and a well-stocked bar—including plenty of Scotch, of course.

The gastropub food is appropriately hearty and includes not-to-be-missed Scotch quail eggs with a crispy exterior, inner layer of flavorful ground sausage, and runny center yolk. Ale-battered Pacific cod is accompanied by Indian-spiced fries and celery root-tartar sauce, while creamy ham and cheese croquettes sing with a dash of tamarind chutney.

Mitsunobu

Japanese 🍴

E4

325 Sharon Park Dr., Ste. 2a (at Sand Hill Rd.), Menlo Park

Phone: 650-234-1084
Web: www.rmitsunobu.com
Prices: $$$

Lunch Tue – Fri
Dinner Tue – Sun

 ♿

This tiny, nondescript spot may seem a bit plain amidst the ritzy shops and restaurants of Menlo Park but it's well worth checking out for authentic Japanese fare. The top-notch nigiri selection includes sweet, creamy *ebi*, ultra-fresh uni, and buttery scallops, while a small offering of seasonal maki includes a "spring roll" packed with salmon, shrimp, squid, striped jack, and avocado, then topped with Japanese "Hollandaise."

Time-pressed lunchers should opt for the affordable prix-fixe sets with sashimi or *chirashi*, while a more luxurious experience can be had in the evening, when a seasonal kaiseki is offered alongside the à la carte menu. Sweet, professional service at all times only adds to Mitsunobu's hidden-gem vibe.

New England Lobster Company

Seafood 🍴

C2

824 Cowan Rd. (off Old Bayshore Hwy.), Burlingame

Phone: 650-443-1559
Web: www.newenglandlobster.net
Prices: $$

Lunch & dinner daily

♿

A wholesale supplier of lobster, crab, and other seafood to the Bay Area since 1986, this semi-industrial complex now offers irreproachably fresh, Californian-influenced fare. The freeway-adjacent space is enormous, with tanks of crabs and lobsters, oysters and clams for shucking, and picnic tables both inside and out.

Begin with house-made potato chip "nachos" heaped with fresh crab meat, black beans, and Monterey Jack cheese. Or, just dive into a pitch-perfect lobster roll accented by creamy avocado and crumbled bacon. New England classics include silky, smoky lobster corn chowder and fluffy whoopie pies.

Be sure to check out the flat-screen TV, broadcasting their seafood as it arrives in the huge central holding tanks, just outside.

Osteria Coppa

E1

Italian ✗✗

139 S. B St. (bet. 1st & 2nd Aves.), San Mateo

Phone: 650-579-6021
Web: www.osteriacoppa.com
Prices: $$

Lunch & dinner daily

In a sea of San Mateo restaurants, Osteria Coppa's skillfully prepared, rustic, and seasonally influenced Italian cooking stands above the pack. Filled with corporate sorts at lunchtime and families for casual dinners or brunch, the wood space is rustic and always flooded with natural light. The back hallway brings glimpses into the kitchen, where blistered, chewy pies topped with garlicky housemade pork sausage, smoky speck, and earthy crimini mushrooms are emerging. While wood-fired pizzas are popular here, also try pastas like house-made *tagliolini* full of chopped Early Girl tomatoes, olive oil, garlic, and basil.

An L-shaped bar is a nice perch to dine solo with a glass of wine, or savor a dessert like the mascarpone-rich butterscotch *budino*.

Pasta Moon

B4

Italian ✗✗

315 Main St. (at Mill St.), Half Moon Bay

Phone: 650-726-5125
Web: www.pastamoon.com
Prices: $$

Lunch & dinner daily

One of Half Moon Bay's most popular restaurants, Pasta Moon is always packed to the gills with locals and tourists filling up on massive portions of hearty Italian-American fare. With its vaulted ceilings, pops of bright red, and multiple intimate dining rooms, it's a hit with diners of all ages, especially those seated at tables with a view of the lovely side garden.

House-made pastas steal the show, with tempting options like the delicate 30-layer lasagna filled with ricotta, parmesan, and house Sicilian sausage. A grilled pork chop stuffed with peaches, pancetta, and caramelized onions arrives with mascarpone mashed potatoes. The butterscotch pudding (with shards of Ghirardelli chocolate, natch) is bound to send you over the moon.

Pazzo

Pizza ✗✗

E3

1179 Laurel St. (bet. Brittan & Greenwood Aves.), San Carlos

Phone: 650-591-1075   Dinner Mon – Sat
Web: www.pazzosancarlos.com
Prices: $$

New Haven transplants longing for the region's signature chewy, charred *apizz* will find a taste of home at this San Carlos jewel, which churns out authentically blistered pies. Keep it traditional with red sauce topped with house-made fennel sausage and crimini mushrooms. Or go slightly Californian with the garlicky asparagus pie, draped with creamy crescenza cheese.

Pazzo (Italian for "crazy") is anything but, thanks to a relaxed, family-friendly vibe. Kids of all ages will delight in the back counter, with a great view of the chef slipping pizzas into the cherry-red, wood-fired oven. And don't sleep through the house-made pastas: pillowy ricotta gnocchi, tucked into a lemony mascarpone and artichoke sauce, are good enough to steal the *apizzas'* show.

Quattro

Italian ✗✗

F4

2050 University Ave. (at I-101), East Palo Alto

Phone: 650-470-2889   Lunch & dinner daily
Web: www.quattrorestaurant.com
Prices: $$$

As is to be expected from a restaurant housed inside the Four Seasons, Quattro comes with a hefty price tag. But it's nothing that deal-doing tech moguls can't handle—even at lunchtime, when it's often bustling. With a sleek, airy atmosphere full of natural light (check out the impressive sculptures that line the stone walls), this is a swanky retreat worthy of its high-dollar clientele.

The Italian-influenced menu has something for everyone, from a light pea, zucchini, and watercress "garden bisque" to a hearty seafood salad full of octopus, grilled prawns, and squid. Drinks are also notable: whether you seek tasty "mocktails" for lunchtime teetotaling or a pricey dinnertime bottle from the fully stocked iPad wine list, you'll find your match.

Ramen Dojo

Japanese

805 S. B St. (bet. 8th & 9th Aves.), San Mateo

Phone:	650-401-6568
Web:	N/A
Prices:	🪙

Lunch & dinner Wed – Mon

The two-hour lines may have died down, but a 40-minute wait on the sidewalk is still standard at this noodle hot spot. The interior, when you finally reach it, is utterly spare—the better to showcase steaming bowls of tasty and satisfying soup. Customize your broth (soy sauce, garlic pork, soybean), spiciness, and toppings (like spicy cod roe and kikurage mushrooms), then dive in.

The ramen arrives in minutes, loaded with the standard fried garlic cloves, hard-boiled quail egg, scallion, chili, and two slices of roast pork. Your job is to slurp the chewy, delicious noodles (and maybe some seaweed salad or edamame), then hit the road—the hyper-efficient staff needs to keep the line moving, after all. But for one of the best bowls in town, it's worth it.

Rasoi

Indian 🍴🍴

1425 Burlingame Ave. (bet. El Camino Real & Primrose Rd.), Burlingame

Phone:	650-579-5661
Web:	www.rasoiburlingame.com
Prices:	$$

Dinner nightly

Mission District standby Aslam's Rasoi has expanded to the 'burbs with this sleek and contemporary outpost, featuring glimmering metallic floor tiles, tufted ottomans, and dark wood furnishings. Come early to enjoy a drink in the swank front lounge, which features a flickering gas fireplace.

While Rasoi looks ultra-modern, its food is blessedly traditional, with standards like samosas, tangy-tender lamb *rogan josh* and soft, fluffy garlic naan. Warm and welcoming servers bustle cheerfully among the tables, offering tips on their favorite dishes. One suggestion you should plan to take them up on is the chicken korma, loaded with super-smoky pieces of tender chicken in a creamy, well-spiced, buttery sauce. It may be the best rendition you'll ever taste.

Rasa ✿

209 Park Rd. (bet. Burlingame & Howard Aves.), Burlingame

Phone: 650-340-7272
Web: www.rasaindian.com
Prices: $$

Lunch & dinner daily

In a bustling tech corridor that's also home to Indian expats with high culinary standards, Rasa has managed to find the perfect middle ground. No-joke dishes that aren't toned down for Western palates cater to the likes of software execs and area couples, and though the bi-level space boasts a gorgeous, minimalist-mod décor with bright splashes of orange, sleek pendant lights, and stylish dark wood fittings, the focus here is on food.

The kitchen excels in elevating the cuisine of South India with solid technique and superlative ingredients. Get the party started with *dahi vada* (crispy fried lentil fritters buried in smooth yogurt), before savoring a basil-chutney *dosa* starring a crisp rice-lentil crêpe stuffed with potato masala and served with basil chutney as well as an ultra-spicy ghost chili version—to be risked by hardcore hotheads only.

Each plate is carefully composed, as shown in the complex Andhra chicken curry, enriched with coconut and bobbing with tender dark meat. Sop up the pungent sauce with a flaky Kerala *paratha*, and then cool down over a creamy and smooth *chikku* frappe, which blends the eponymous pear-like fruit with vanilla ice cream and candied rice puffs for a captivating finale.

Sakae

Japanese ✕

243 California Dr. (at Highland Ave.), Burlingame

Phone: 650-348-4064
Web: www.sakaesushi.com
Prices: $$

Lunch Mon – Sat
Dinner nightly

Its glory days of crowds packed to the rafters have passed, but Sakae is still a solid option for elegant sushi and other Japanese specialties. Adjacent to downtown Burlingame and the Caltrain station, this is a sleek space clad in varying shades of wood, Japanese pottery, and fresh flowers. Local families enjoy sitting at the bar, where a friendly and engaging sushi chef is a hit with kids.

Skip the specialty rolls and stick to fresh and neat nigiri topped with the likes of albacore, yellowtail, crab, salmon, or daily featured fish. Otherwise, go for the whiteboard's changing specials like maitake mushroom tempura or grilled baby octopus.

Be sure to order a pot of *hoji cha*, a roasted green tea that nicely complements their impressive range of fish.

Shalizaar

Persian ✕✕

300 El Camino Real (bet. Anita & Belmont Aves.), Belmont

Phone: 650-596-9000
Web: www.shalizaar.com
Prices: $$

Lunch & dinner daily

A perennial favorite for Persian flavors, Shalizaar is friendly, charming, and authentic. Lunchtime draws a large business crowd, while dinners cater to couples on dates. The upscale space features chandeliers, linen-topped tables, Persian carpets, and walls of framed windows that flood everything with light.

Meals here are always a pleasure, thanks to the high quality of every ingredient. Try the signature *koobideh*, smoky ground beef and chicken kebabs served with char-broiled whole tomatoes and rice. Or, tuck into *baghali polo*, a fork-tender lamb shank over bright green rice full of dill and young fava beans. For dessert, take the friendly servers' advice and order the *zoolbia barnieh*, sticky-crisp squiggles of fried cake soaked in rosewater syrup.

Sichuan Chong Qing

Chinese ✗

E1

211 S. San Mateo Dr. (bet. 2nd & 3rd Aves.), San Mateo

Phone: 650-343-1144
Web: N/A
Prices: $$

Lunch & dinner Tue – Sun

The medical staff at the Mills Health Center take plenty of heat in an average day, but that doesn't stop them from piling into this compact neighboring Sichuan restaurant for their fix of spicy chili oil and numbing peppercorns. Both ingredients are featured in the crispy Chong Qing chicken and shrimp, each laden with chili peppers (be sure to watch out for shards of bone in the cleaver-chopped chicken).

Skip the mild Mandarin dishes and stick to the house's fiery specialties, like the nutty, smoky cumin lamb with sliced onion and still more chilies and chili oil. Aside from a few contemporary touches, the décor isn't newsworthy and the staff is more efficient than engaging—but you'll likely be too busy enjoying the flavor-packed food to mind.

Sushi Sam's

Japanese ✗

E1

218 E. 3rd Ave. (bet. B St. & Ellsworth Ave.), San Mateo

Phone: 650-344-0888
Web: www.sushisams.com
Prices: $$

Lunch Thu – Sat
Dinner Tue – Sat

Fresh sushi in San Mateo means a trip to Sushi Sam's, which is no secret among connoisseurs and neighborhood folk who regularly flock here the moment it opens to avoid a wait. Service is fast and efficient, though stark white walls, Formica tables, and simple wood chairs do little for the no-frills décor. Check the daily specials on the board for the best and freshest fish, which are mostly from Japan. Selections might include silky salmon placed atop neat mounds of rice with a light grating of wasabi; rich, firm mackerel brushed with a dab of ponzu; and buttery toro lightly seared and unembellished to enhance the delicate flavor. The spicy pickled ginger is house-made.

For those who don't feel like choosing, order one of the chef's menus.

Sushi Yoshizumi ❀

E1

Japanese ✗

325 E. 4th Ave. (bet. B St. & Railroad Ave.), San Mateo
Dinner Wed – Sun

Phone: 650-437-2282
Web: www.sushiyoshizumi.com
Prices: $$$$

Run, don't walk to this wonderful new Edomae-style gem, for Sushi Yoshizumi might be flying under the radar at the moment, but that won't last long. For now, you'll find a fun mix of Japanese expats and foodies-in-the-know (snapping iPhone pictures faster than you can say omakase) filling this immaculate little interior, fitted out in blonde wood and beige accents.

The menu here centers on Edomae-style sushi, a style that Akira Yoshizumi spent years perfecting, both in Japan and in New York. The long tutorial clearly paid off, for his food is refined, delicate, and beautifully balanced. Employing wild, sustainable, and often local seafood to craft an intimate omakase experience, Chef Yoshizumi serves each course with a detailed explanation, welcoming questions with his warm and open demeanor.

In addition to the mind-blowing parade of sashimi and sushi that awaits, look for dishes like a wispy seaweed salad featuring bits of strawberries and apples in a vinegary broth; or a soft, peppery *chawan mushi* tucked with black cod. Then smoky barracuda, gently salted and redolent of spicy wasabi, may be tailed by a bowl of rice studded with sesame, salmon roe, and two gorgeous lobes of uni from Hokkaido and Santa Barbara.

Sweet Basil

Thai

E2

1473 Beach Park Blvd. (at Marlin Ave.), Foster City

Phone: 650-212-5788
Lunch & dinner daily
Web: www.sweetbasilfoster.com
Prices: $$

Set near a charming bayside walking and biking trail on Foster City's perimeter, Sweet Basil makes for a great meal after a stroll or ride. Inside, the space is snazzy and contemporary-looking with bamboo floors and rustic tables, but the vibe is casual with the waitstaff hustling to serve the daytime rush of office workers as well as families for dinner.

Though you may have to wait for a table, the signature kabocha pumpkin and beef in a deeply flavorful red curry will merit your patience. Other faves include well-marinated chicken *satay*; spicy tofu stir-fried with bell peppers, garlic, and basil; and sticky rice topped with mango. You can choose your own spice level, but watch out—when they say hot, they're not kidding around.

Taqueria El Metate

Mexican

D3

120 Harbor Blvd. (at Hwy. 101), Belmont

Phone: 650-595-1110
Lunch & dinner daily
Web: N/A
Prices:

Industrial and no-frills, El Metate isn't a looker—but taqueria connoisseurs know it's the place to go for a great meal. Sidle up to the counter and order a round of street-style tacos, topped with well-seasoned carne asada or piquant shredded chicken, then crowned with onions and cilantro. Or go big with an enormous super burrito, stuffed with caramelized, pineapple-studded *al pastor*, fluffy rice, pinto beans, avocado, cheese, sour cream, and *pico de gallo*.

Located right off the 101, the restaurant's minimal room has lines of both white- and blue-collar lunchtime workers streaming out the door, and crowds of Mexican families on weekends (kids adore it). A well-stocked salsa bar, crisp chips, and a refreshing melon *agua fresca* help ease the wait.

Taqueria San Bruno

1045 San Mateo Ave. (bet. Hermosa & Scott Sts.), San Bruno

Phone: 650-873-1752
Web: N/A
Prices: 😊

Lunch & dinner daily

If you're willing to forgive its divey, industrial location in San Bruno's auto-repair corridor, this taqueria will reward you with flavor-packed food that's worthy of the largely Mexican clientele that congregates here at lunchtime. Expect to sit elbow-to-elbow with them at communal tables, where options range from authentically Mexican to delightfully Americanized (hello, hefty super burritos).

Every type of taco served here is perfection—from fresh, plump marinated shrimp to sweet, caramelized *al pastor*. The superior chicken enchiladas sub smoky grilled chicken for the traditional boiled variety, then get added zest from a garlicky red chile sauce. Throw in warm, well-salted tortilla chips and piquant salsa, and you'll be a happy camper.

Taste In Mediterranean Food

1199 Broadway, Ste. 1 (bet. Chula Vista & Laguna Aves.), Burlingame

Phone: 650-348-3097
Web: www.tasteinbroadway.com
Prices: 😊

Lunch & dinner Mon – Sat

Taste In Mediterranean Food could easily get lost along Broadway's blocks of cafés and boutiques, but this tiny restaurant is truly not to be missed. Beyond the deli cases of baklava and salads, find the open kitchen where rotating lamb, chicken, and beef slowly turn and roast to become gyros, shawarma platters, and wraps.

About half of the guests grab take out; the others sit in the small dining room to enjoy the likes of combo platters spanning the Mediterranean from Greece to Lebanon. Chewy pita bread scoops up nutty hummus, smoky-garlicky baba ghanoush, and herbaceous Moroccan eggplant salad. Or try thin slices of lamb shawarma in a pita wrap with homemade garlic sauce, cabbage, and fried potatoes. Don't forget the baklava from the counter.

Vespucci

Italian ✗✗

E1

147 E. 3rd St. (bet. Ellsworth Ave. & San Mateo Dr.), San Mateo

Phone: 650-685-6151
Web: www.vespucciristorante.com
Prices: $$

Lunch Fri – Sat
Dinner Tue – Sun

When a Southern Italian couple with extensive restaurant experience moves to the New World, the result is nothing less than promising—it may even become one of the most popular spots in town. Intricate white wainscoting, a gilded ceiling, and travertine floors ensure that Vespucci's interior is as charming and classically Italian as the wonderfully warm and hospitable service.

Start with tasty salads like the caprese, fanning fresh mozzarella with tomatoes. Beautifully composed hand-made pastas may showcase linguine twirled with plump, sweet scallops, cherry tomatoes, garlic, and white wine. Don't miss dessert, particularly a world-class panna cotta, perfumed with vanilla bean and topped with tangy raspberry coulis as well as a dollop of whipped cream.

Vesta

Pizza ✗✗

F2

2022 Broadway St. (bet. Jefferson Ave. & Main St.), Redwood City

Phone: 650-362-5052
Web: www.vestarwc.com
Prices: $$

Lunch & dinner Tue – Sat

Whether they're rolling in from their offices at lunch or their condos at dinner, Redwood City locals are always up for a wood-fired pie at this stylish downtown pizzeria. With an airy, mosaic-filled dining room extending into a large front patio, it's a relaxed, roomy space perfect for groups and families.

The menu is divided into red and white pies, and they're equally delicious: zesty tomato sauce enlivens a combo of peppery *soppressata*, smoked mozzarella, and spinach, while a white version with crumbled French feta, fresh slices of garlic, cherry tomatoes, and chopped applewood-smoked bacon is irresistible. Get your greens in with the arugula salad, tossed with shaved *Parmigiano Reggiano*, toasted hazelnuts, and a delicious apricot vinaigrette.

The Village Pub ✿

E4

2967 Woodside Rd. (off Whiskey Hill Rd.), Woodside

Phone: 650-851-9888
Web: www.thevillagepub.net
Prices: $$$

Lunch Sun – Fri
Dinner nightly

Though it has the feel of a chichi private club, this attractive New American restaurant is open to all—provided they can live up to the style standards set by its fan base of tech tycoons and ladies-who-lunch. Draw your eyes away from those Teslas in the lot and head inside for fine dining that exceeds this sophisticated restaurant's humble name.

That said, the cuisine is surprisingly approachable, with offerings like house charcuterie and a superb Pub burger available in the lounge and main dining areas. A crisp, lunchtime flatbread is loaded with flavor and all too easy to devour. The kitchen shines its brightest at dinner, with starters like octopus carpaccio adorned with shaved radish, tomato confit, cucumber brunoise, and a drizzle of paprika oil.

Service is a priority, and this staff readily attends to every need—even grinding coffee to order as an accompaniment for warm, fluffy, sugar-dusted beignets served with creamy almond anglaise and tangy cranberry compote. The wine list is similarly designed to court the deepest of pockets, with an outstanding selection of French vintages and aged Bordeaux. On a budget? Aim for lunch, which is lighter not only in approach, but also on the wallet.

Viognier

Contemporary XXX

E1

222 E. 4th Ave. (at B St.), San Mateo

Phone: 650-685-3727
Web: www.viognierrestaurant.com
Prices: $$$

Dinner Mon – Sat

One of the few remaining special-occasion spots in an increasingly casual dining landscape, this refined restaurant is full of guests dressed in their best; and the charming dining room with its roaring central fireplace is their equal. Service is attentive, and the semi-open exhibition kitchen is perpetually abuzz.

Sip on a glass of Viognier's namesake wine before embarking on their five-course tasting menu, full of beautifully plated fare like a pungent spiced carrot soup with smoked *ricotta salata*; delicate winter squash tortellini in a brown butter-sage emulsion; as well as meaty 72-hour braised short ribs. Desserts are particularly exquisite—the white chocolate cheesecake, accented by tangy citrus curd and mandarin sorbet, is quite divine.

wonderful

Chinese X

C2

270 Broadway (bet. La Cruz & Victoria Aves.), Millbrae

Phone: 650-692-2829
Web: www.wonderful.restaurant
Prices: $$

Lunch & dinner daily

Hunanese cuisine often takes a backseat to the Bay Area's bumper crop of Cantonese and Sichuanese restaurants, so this hot spot is a welcome addition to the Chinese-food landscape. It's already caught on with the area's Chinese transplants, so you can expect a wait at peak meal hours—especially for large parties as the dining room is tiny.

The boldly flavored dishes incorporate oodles of smoked, cured, and fermented ingredients—from the bacon-like pork wok-tossed with leeks, garlic, and soy, to the pungent pork, black bean, and pickled chili mixture that tops those spicy, chewy, hand-cut Godfather's noodles. The whole chili-braised fish, fresh and flaky in its bath of bright red mild chili sauce flecked with scallions and garlic, is an absolute must.

Wakuriya ✿

D3

115 De Anza Blvd. (at Parrot Dr.), San Mateo

Dinner Wed – Sun

Phone: 650-286-0410
Web: www.wakuriya.com
Prices: $$$$

Innovative, serious, and very well-established, Wakuriya is the rare restaurant that successfully combines deep respect for kaiseki tradition with a contemporary touch. This is largely thanks to the lone chef behind the counter, Katsuhiro Yamasaki; his wife is the one so deftly managing and serving the entire dining room. The location is charmless and the décor verges on nonexistent, but there is a sober elegance here to balance the low-key vibe. The room is fully booked on a nightly basis so reserve in advance.

Each month brings a new set menu, perhaps beginning with fresh New Caledonian blue shrimp and squid seasoned with soy, grilled tableside over a heated stone. This may lead to appetizers that highlight pristine ingredients and jewel-like presentation, as in Tasmanian ocean trout sushi topped with mascarpone cheese and olives, or barbecued unagi rolled into an omelet. Comforting and fragrant soups may brim with fine noodles, shimeji mushrooms and duck magret that finishes cooking in the warm broth.

Once you are halfway through the clay pot filled with madai snapper and hot dashi, go ahead and empty the rest of your rice into the broth—it is the best way to ensure you do not miss a drop.

Yi Yuan

Chinese XX

C2

1711 El Camino Real (at Park Pl.), Millbrae

Phone: 650-869-6222
Web: www.yy1711.com
Prices: $$

Lunch & dinner daily

Millbrae boasts no end of Chinese restaurants, but this fire-hot spot stands out for its tasty Sichuan-style dishes laden with chilies, peppercorns, and chili oil, as well as its attempts to bring some decorative polish to the oft-dumpy area landscape. Sure, the faux-pagoda ceilings and strings of red lanterns are a bit tacky, but the food is worth it.

Try to score a table near the glass-enclosed kitchen, where you can watch a cook expertly hand-pull the chewy, thick noodles in your *dan dan mien*, a spicy blend of ground pork and chili paste. Fatty, rich smoked pork is sautéed with leeks, garlic, and plenty of spice, just as crispy, tongue-numbing Chongqing chicken arrives under a pile of still more peppers. If you like your food fiery, look no further.

Look for our symbol ⃝, spotlighting restaurants with a notable sake list.

South Bay

South Bay

SILICON VALLEY

Silicon Valley has for long been revered as the tech capital of the world, but it's really so much more. Combine all that tech money with a diverse, international population and get a very dynamic culinary scene. If that doesn't sound like an outrageously successful formula on its own, think of the area's rich wine culture descending from the Santa Cruz Mountains, where a burgeoning vintner community takes great pride in its work, and realize that the South Bay may as well be sitting on a gold mine. Visitors should be sure to see everything the area has to offer, with a sojourn at **The Mountain Winery** in Saratoga—part-outdoor concert venue, part-event space, and part-winery—that offers stunning views of the vineyards and valley below.

FESTIVALS GALORE

The Valley is proud of its tech-minded reputation, but don't judge this book by its cover as South Bay locals definitely know how to party. In San Jose, celebrations kick off in May at the wildly popular **South Bay Greek Festival** featuring music, eats, drinks, and dancing. With little time to recover, buckets of cornhusks wait to be stuffed and sold at the **Story Road Tamale Festival**, held every summer within the gorgeous grounds

of Emma Prusch Farm Park. In July, **Japantown** breathes new life for the two-day **Obon/Bazaar**, and come August, the Italian-American Heritage Foundation celebrates its annual **Family Festa**. It's a year-round shindig, and **Santana Row** (a sleek shopping village housing numerous upscale restaurants and a fantastic farmer's market) plays a pivotal role in these festivities. One of San Jose's most notable destinations is **San Pedro Square Market**, whose four walls harbor a spectrum of artisanal merchants at historic Peralta Adobe downtown. Farmers and specialty markets are a way of

life for South Bay residents and these locals cannot imagine living elsewhere.

CULTURAL DYNASTY

As further testimony to its international repute, the capital of Silicon Valley is also a melting pot of global culinary influences. Neighborhood *pho* shops and *bánh mì* hangouts like **Huong Lan**, gratify the growing Vietnamese community. They can also be found gracing the intersection of King and Tully streets (home to some of the city's finest Vietnamese flavors) sampling decadent cream puffs at **Hong-Van Bakery** or crispy green waffles flavored with *pandan* paste at **Century Bakery** just a few blocks away. **Lion Plaza** is yet another hub for bakeries, markets, and canteens paying homage to this eighth most populated Asian country. Neighboring Cambodia makes an appearance through delicious noodle soups like **Nam Vang Restaurant** or **F&D Yummy**. Chinese food makes its formidable presence known at lofty **Dynasty Chinese Seafood Restaurant**. Located on Story Road, this is a popular arena for big parties and favored destination for dim sum. **Nijiya**

Market is a Japanese jewel with several locations, all of which sparkle with specialty goods, top ingredients, and other things Far East. Long before it was cool to be organic in America, Nijiya was focused on bringing the taste of Japan by way of high-quality, seasonal, and local ingredients to the California coast. Today, it continues to tantalize with some of the area's most pristine seafood and meat, as well as an array of tasty sushi and bento boxes. Also available via their website are sumptuous, homespun recipes for a variety of noodle dishes, fried rice signatures, and other regional specialties. Encompassing the globe and travelling from this Eastern tip to South America, Mexican food enthusiasts in San Jose seem eternally smitten by the still-warm tortillas at **Tropicana**, or the surprisingly delish tacos from one of the area's many **Mi Pueblo Food Centers**.

A STUDENT'S DREAM

And yet there is more to the South Bay than just San Jose. Los Gatos is home to prized patisseries like **Fleur de Cocoa** as well as such historic, continually operating, and specialized wineries like **Testarossa**. Meanwhile, cool and casual Palo Alto is home base for celebrated Stanford University, its countless students, and impressive faculty. Find locals lining up for homemade fresh and frozen yogurt at **Fraîche**. Others fulfill a Korean fantasy in Santa Clara, where these same settlers enjoy a range of authentic nibbles and tasty spreads at food court favorite—

Lawrence Plaza. Just as foodies favor the *soondubu jjigae* at **SGD Tofu House**, conservative palates have a field day over caramelized and roasted sweet potatoes at **Sweet Potato Stall**, just outside the Galleria. Fill a belly with impeccable produce along El Camino Real near the Lawrence Expressway intersection. Then treat your senses to a feast at Mountain View's **Milk Pail Market**, showcasing over 300 varieties of cheese. Have your pick among such splendid choices as Camembert, Bleu d'Auvergne, Morbier, and Cabriquet, as well as imported Mamie Nova Yogurt.

Despite the fast pace of technology in Silicon Valley, **Slow Food**—the grassroots movement dedicated to local food traditions—has a thriving South Bay chapter. Even Google in Mountain View feeds its large staff three organic, square meals a day. For a wider range of delicacies, they may frequent surrounding eateries or stores selling ethnic eats. Residents of Los Altos have their German food cravings covered between **Esther's German Bakery** and **Dittmer's Gourmet Meats & Wurst-Haus**. In fact, Dittmer's delectable sausages are made extra special when served on a salted pretzel roll from Esther's. **Los Gatos Meats & Smokehouse** is another age-old, culinary stalwart serving these meat-loving mortals an embarrassment of riches. Think poultry, fish, and freshly butchered meat sandwiches presented alongside savory specialties like beef jerky, prime rib roasts, juicy pork loin, beef jerky, corned beef, and of course, bacon...but, wait... did you want it regular, pepper, country-style or Canadian? Pair all these salt licks with a sip from Mountain View's famous **Savvy Cellar Wine Bar & Wine Shop** only to discover that it's a picnic in the making. Smokers looking to wind down in luxury may head to the handsome, upscale, and members-only Los Gatos Cigar Club, where the choices are exceptional and conversation, intriguing.

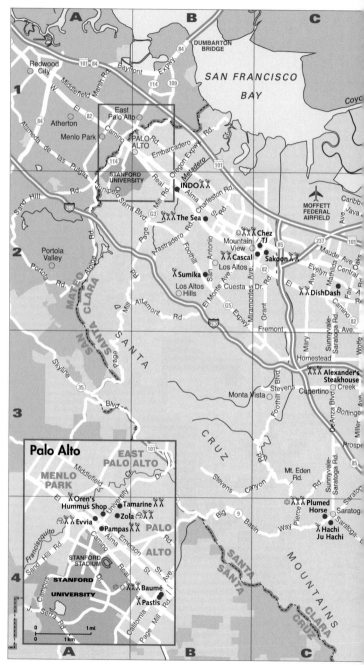

274

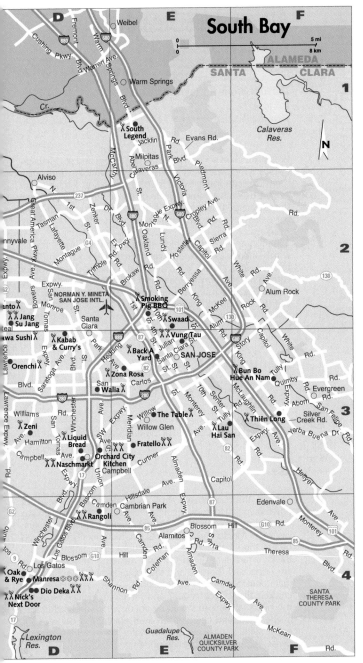

South Bay

D · E · F

5 mi
8 km

ALAMEDA
SANTA CLARA

1

N

Weibel

Fremont
Cushing Pkwy.
680
Warm Springs Blvd.
Cr.

Warm Springs

Calaveras Res.

South Legend
Jacklin Rd.
Evans Rd.

Milpitas
Abel
Calaveras
Piedmont Rd.
Victoria
Park Blvd.

Alviso
237
1st
Zanker Dr.
McCarthy Blvd.
880
Montague Expwy.
Oakland Rd.
Cropley Ave.
Rd.
Rd.

Great America Pkwy.
Tasman
Lafayette
Montague
Expwy.
Trimble Rd.
Brokaw Rd.
Berryessa Rd.
King
McKee Rd.
White Rd.
Rd.
130
Alum Rock
2

Bowers Ave.
San Tomas Expwy.
Monroe St.
NORMAN Y. MINETA SAN JOSE INTL.
Santa Clara
101
Smoking Pig BBQ
Swaad
Vung Tau
Alum Rock Ave.
Capitol Ave.
Sierra Rd.
White Rd.
Rd.

nto X
X Jang Su Jang
teal
awa Sushi X
Orenchi
Kabab & Curry's
Park Ave.
Hedding
880
87
Julian
Santa Clara St.
Back A Yard
SAN JOSE
King Rd.
Story Rd.
680
Bun Bo Hue An Nam
Quimby Rd.
Evergreen
Rd.
San Felipe Rd.

Lawrence Expwy.
Saratoga Ave.
Zona Rosa
Walia X
82
San Carlos
280
St.
St.
Monterey
10th St.
Senter
Tully Rd.
McLaughlin Rd.
Aborn Rd.
Silver Creek Rd.
Yerba Buena Dr.

Blvd.
Williams Rd.
Zeni
Hamilton
Campbell
Liquid Bread
San Tomas Expwy.
Winchester Blvd.
SW Expwy.
Ave.
Meridian Ave.
Willow
Willow Glen
The Table X
Fratello X X
Thiên Long
Lau Hai San
82
Rd.

Lawrence Expwy.
Rd.
Orchard City Kitchen
Naschmarkt
Campbell Ave.
Union Ave.
280
17
Curtner
Almaden Expwy.
Capitol

G2
Bascom Ave.
Rangoli
Camden Ave.
Cambrian Park
Hillsdale Ave.
87
Edenvale
Monterey
101

Winchester Blvd.
Los Gatos Blvd.
85
Blossom
Alamitos
Blossom Hill
Rd.
Sta.
Almaden Expwy.
Hwy.
G10 Rd.
85
Theresa
Blvd.

9
tos
Blossom
G10
Hill
Coleman Rd.
Almaden Rd.
Camden Ave.
Los Gatos
Oak & Rye
Manresa ❀❀❀ X X X
Dio Deka X X
Nick's Next Door
Shannon Rd.
Rd.
Camden Expwy.
Ave.
SANTA THERESA COUNTY PARK
4

17
Lexington Res.
Guadalupe Res.
ALMADEN QUICKSILVER COUNTY PARK
McKean Rd.
Rd.

D · E · F

275

Alexander's Steakhouse

Steakhouse ✕✕✕

C3

10330 N. Wolfe Rd. (at I-280), Cupertino

Phone: 408-446-2222
Web: www.alexanderssteakhouse.com
Prices: $$$$

Lunch Tue – Fri
Dinner nightly

Wealthy techies set down their smartphones and plug in face-to-face at this swank steakhouse, where a double-wide dining room, fireside lounge, and duo of exhibition kitchens aim to sate executives doing deals on the company tab. Pricey steaks emerge from the glass-enclosed aging room, while the bar is the place to go for high-dollar Napa cabernets and rare whiskeys.

The flash at Alexander's extends to the more-is-more menu, which often piles on overpowering ingredients to diminishing returns—and those with sensitive palates should order carefully. If you're not dining with a group, opt for the more sedate bar, which boasts friendlier, less-scripted service (you can skip the upsold hamachi shots) and a cast of interesting Silicon Valley characters.

Back A Yard

Caribbean ✕

E3

80 N. Market St. (bet. Santa Clara & St. John Sts.), San Jose

Phone: 408-294-8626
Web: www.backayard.net
Prices:

Lunch & dinner Mon – Sat

Though this Caribbean spot is located in the heart of downtown San Jose, dining here feels like a vacation thanks to cheerful murals, a lively soundtrack, and hospitable servers. Unlike its Menlo Park predecessor, which mainly does to-go orders, this location boasts a capacious brick dining room.

Back A Yard is a Jamaican term meaning "the way things are done back home," and the food doesn't disappoint on that count. Specialties include smoky, spicy, and tender jerk chicken, flavorful curry goat, and vinegar-marinated *escovitch* fish fillets, all accompanied by coconut rice and red beans, a side salad, and caramelized fried plantains. Cool off your palate with a glass of coconut water, then order a slice of dense, flan-like sweet potato pudding.

Baumé

Contemporary

B4

201 S. California Ave. (at Park Blvd.), Palo Alto

Phone:	650-328-8899	Lunch Fri – Sat
Web:	www.baumerestaurant.com	Dinner Wed – Sat
Prices:	$$$$	

A bold orange door in an otherwise nondescript single story building along Palo Alto's main thoroughfare marks the entrance to the lovely Baumé. Do yourself a favor and enter—for Chef Bruno Chemel's progressive fine dining is truly an otherworldly culinary experience.

Inside, you'll find an exquisite dining room with a pristine, modernist sensibility and that same beautiful orange hue accenting various walls and fabric room dividers. The kitchen may do only one dinner seating a night, but tables are refreshingly spaced widely for privacy and it's lovely not to be rushed. The service staff only adds to this luxurious and unhurried vibe with their warmth, knowledge, and clear enthusiasm for Chef Chemel's food.

Beginning with sublime and seasonal ingredients, the master creator takes his flavor profiles to truly profound levels. Dinner might include a gorgeous little plate of golden Osetra caviar spooned over a creamy panna cotta humming with fennel and tart kiwi; or a bright and perfectly poached Jidori egg paired with creamy polenta, frothy sabayon, smoky meringue and kale ragout. Conclude over a sensational goat cheese-and-parsley root mousse that is studded with pretty pink peppercorns and topped with tiny little crisps of caramel.

Bun Bo Hue An Nam

F3

2060 Tully Rd. (at Quimby Rd.), San Jose

Phone: 408-270-7100   Lunch & dinner Thu – Tue
Web: N/A
Prices:

Take a hint from the local Vietnamese families and head into this second San Jose outpost, a slightly more contemporary version of the original. Inside, walls hang with flat screens showing Vietnamese TV, and wooden tables and chairs sit atop tiled floors.

As the name suggests, *bun bo hue* soup is the specialty here, though it may be a pleasure limited to intrepid diners. This spicy beef noodle soup blazes with chili oil, lemongrass, scallions, and cilantro, yet remains slightly gamey and rich with ample portions of tripe, tendon, and congealed pork blood. An array of *pho* is also a popular choice. Folks can be found slurping down *pho dac biet*, a fragrant star anise and lemongrass broth overflowing with meat, served with lime, basil, and chilies.

Cascal

C2

400 Castro St. (at California St.), Mountain View

Phone: 650-940-9500   Lunch & dinner daily
Web: www.cascalrestaurant.com
Prices: $$

Pan-Latin Cascal in Mountain View is the go-to spot for local tech types, who gather after work to sip mojitos, sangria, and margaritas. They can be seen sharing small plates like flaky wild mushroom empanadas oozing with Manchego and truffle oil; *albondigas*, lamb meatballs in a savory roasted piquillo pepper sauce; or a Cuban wrap packed with adobo-marinated pork.

The food is always top-notch, but the vibe remains casual, with families enjoying dinner and couples with dogs in tow benefitting from the spacious patio. Efficient servers bustle between tables inside the colorful room, flooded with light thanks to walls of windows. Sharing is the ethos here, so there's no shame in saving room for a *tres leches* cake to split between friends.

Chez TJ ⁂

Contemporary **XXX**

C2

938 Villa St. (bet. Bryant & Franklin Sts.), Mountain View

Dinner Tue – Sat

Phone: 650-964-7466
Web: www.cheztj.com
Prices: $$$$

Set in a quaint Victorian, Chez TJ has launched the careers of innumerable culinary talents—and the latest chef at the helm, Jarad Gallagher, is more than worthy of its legacy. Though it may seem old-fashioned for its high-tech Mountain View zip code, this former home, stuffed with flowers and Tiffany lamps, has a throwback appeal that's perfect for escaping the demands of technology. Outstanding, gracious servers only add to the pleasure.

Two menus are offered in this dining room: an eight-course exploration into NorCal-centric seasonal fare, or a 17-course chef's tasting loaded with luxurious global ingredients. Both exhibit thoughtful technique, from supremely fresh abalone over creamy polenta and cured squab to golden-crusted halibut with parsnip purée, lobster, and chanterelle mushrooms. Even a simple cube of Crenshaw melon, strewn with *prosciutto di Parma*, dissolves magnificently in the mouth.

Intimacy is at a premium in the petite space, where an upscale crowd comes to celebrate special occasions. And when it comes to romantic, timeless settings, Chez TJ is unparalleled—especially for oenophiles, who will want to sample the small-production wines, several of which are made just for the restaurant.

279

Dio Deka

Greek ✗✗

D4

210 E. Main St. (near Fiesta Way), Los Gatos

Phone: 408-354-7700
Web: www.diodeka.com
Prices: $$$

Dinner nightly

Dio Deka may specialize in Greek food, but this is no typical taverna, as the stylish dining room (complete with a roaring fireplace) ably demonstrates. A wealthy, well-dressed Los Gatos crowd flocks to the front patio on warm evenings, dining and people-watching within the vine-covered walls of the Hotel Los Gatos. The bar also draws a brace of cheery regulars.

Skip the dull mesquite-grilled steaks and keep your order Greek: think stuffed grape leaves with tender braised beef cheek, or a bright pan-seared local salmon with roasted yellow peppers, potatoes, and artichokes. The adventurous shouldn't miss out on the fun offering of Greek wines and sweet buffs should allow space for the *crema me meli*, a fantastic burnt-honey mousse with almond and lemon.

DishDash

Middle Eastern ✗✗

C2

190 S. Murphy Ave. (bet. Evelyn & Washington Aves.), Sunnyvale

Phone: 408-774-1889
Web: www.dishdash.com
Prices: $$

Lunch & dinner Mon – Sat

Dining on the run is certainly possible at this Middle Eastern favorite on historic Murphy Avenue—just ask the tech types flooding the to-go counter to bring food back to their desks. Families and small groups congregate in the colorful dining room. But you might want to linger on the front sidewalk patio, all the better to people-watch while savoring a bright, tangy, and healthy tabbouleh salad, or indulging in the tender-crisp falafel, redolent of spices, topped with whipped tahini.

Served on griddled bread and topped with garlicky yogurt-parsley sauce, wraps like the incredibly tender, smoky, and juicy lamb shawarma are full-flavored and downright memorable. For dessert, try the *m'halabieh*, a floral rosewater and creamy pistachio pudding.

Evvia 🐕

Greek XX

A4

420 Emerson St. (bet. Lytton & University Aves.), Palo Alto

Phone: 650-326-0983
Web: www.evvia.net
Prices: $$

Lunch Mon – Fri
Dinner nightly

You'll feel like Adonis after ascending to the heights of this culinary Olympus, which serves some of the best Hellenic fare in the entire Bay Area. Inviting and cozy with its rustic wood beams, hanging copper pots, and roaring wood-burning fireplace, this Greek God's central Palo Alto location is a draw for local techies and VC's by day, and couples or families in the evening.

Much of the menu emerges from the wood-fired grill, including smoky, tender artichoke and eggplant skewers drizzled in olive oil and paired with garlicky Greek yogurt. The rustic, impossibly moist lamb souvlaki is nicely contrasted by a refreshing tomato, cucumber, and red onion salad. For dessert, pumpkin cheesecake is subtle, sweet, and accented with syrup-poached chunks of pumpkin.

Fratello

Italian XX

E3

1712 Meridian Ave. (at Lenn Dr.), San Jose

Phone: 408-269-3801
Web: www.fratello-ristorante.com
Prices: $$

Lunch Wed – Fri
Dinner Tue – Sun

Generous portions and a comfortable neighborhood vibe bring happy regulars to this casual Italian restaurant in San Jose's Willow Glen neighborhood. Its location at the edge of a shopping plaza is less than prepossessing, but the friendly staff and tasty dishes make up for any shortfalls. A live band sets up shop every Saturday, making it a particularly popular night for a visit.

Pastas—many of them homemade—star on the menu and include fettuccine in a ragù of grass-fed beef, Berkshire pork, and San Marzano tomatoes. Pizzas and hearty entrées like the pan-seared salmon with wild mushroom risotto and garlic spinach are also solid choices. For dessert, the tender, buttery apple tart is a tasty delight with sweet chunks of apple accented by cinnamon syrup.

Hachi Ju Hachi

C4

14480 Big Basin Way (bet. Saratoga Los Gatos Rd. & 3rd St.), Saratoga

Phone: 408-647-2258
Web: www.hachijuhachi88.com
Prices: $$

Dinner Tue – Sun

Through a refined small plates menu of traditional washoku cuisine, Chef Jin Suzuki shows true dedication to his craft. Dishes are subdued and delicate, celebrating just a few ingredients, like soft morsels of eggplant marinated in sweet miso-mirin. Crunchy salads may toss large pieces of cucumber and bamboo shoots in an earthy and tangy fermented barley-miso vinaigrette. Simple pleasures underscore the *gyu-niku* teriyaki, served as slices of tender marinated filet of beef with enticing salty-smoky flavors.

The restaurant itself is a serene space filled with blonde wood furnishings and a long counter facing the kitchen. After a kaiseki meal here, take the chef's invitation to sign the wall, or just peruse the names of those who went before you.

INDO

B2

3295 El Camino Real (at Lambert Ave.), Palo Alto

Phone: 650-494-7168
Web: www.indorestaurant.com
Prices: $$

Lunch Mon – Fri
Dinner nightly

The elite meet to eat at this smart, stylish Indonesian restaurant in the heart of Palo Alto, where deals are done over lunch and tech tycoons (including a big name or two) slip in unnoticed for a quiet, pretension-free family meal. At early-evening happy hours, single minglers hit the sizable bar and lounge for cocktails and industry gossip.

This kitchen's fare is best described as boldly flavored comfort food, whether that includes crunchy calamari with Makrut lime aïoli and galangal cocktail sauce, or sticky-sweet Indonesian-style ribs so tender, they're practically falling off the bone. Be sure to request a seat on the airy brick patio, where a trickling fountain, trellis, and heat lamps create a relaxing space to savor coconut fried rice or green vegetable curry.

Jang Su Jang

Korean ✗✗

D2

3561 El Camino Real, Ste.10 (bet. Flora Vista Ave. & Lawrence Expwy.), Santa Clara

Phone: 408-246-1212
Web: www.jangsujang.com
Prices: $$

Lunch & dinner daily

Smoky Korean barbecue, luscious soft tofu stews, and enormous seafood pancakes are among the standards at this Santa Clara classic and Koreatown star. Its strip-mall façade may not seem enticing, but the interior is classier than expected, thanks to granite tables equipped with grill tops and ventilation hoods, and a glass-enclosed exhibition kitchen located in the back.

This is fiery flavored cuisine for gourmands who can stand the heat. A heavy-handed dose of kimchi flavors soft beef and pork dumplings, while the fierce red chili paste that slicks garlicky slices of marinated pork may actually cook the meat in *daeji bulgogi*. Cool down with *mul naeng myun*, a cold beef broth with tender, nutty buckwheat noodles, and a pot of *bori cha*.

Kabab & Curry's

Indian ✗

D3

1498 Isabella St. (at Clay St.), Santa Clara

Phone: 408-247-0745
Web: www.kababandcurrys.com
Prices: 🌀🌀

Lunch & dinner Tue — Sun

The appeal is in the name at Kabab & Curry's, which has become a dining destination among Indian and Pakistani expats missing the comforts of home. On lunch breaks from the local tech giants, they pack the all-you-can-eat buffet, filling up their plates with fragrant chicken *boti kababs*, coupled with creamy *dal makhani* and slabs of charred naan for soaking up those savory sauces.

Set in a white house with simple tile floors and orange walls, Kabab & Curry's is more about food than service. But, that doesn't deter the crowd of local families from gushing in for dinner or to pick up take-out. With to-go bags laden with rich chicken *tikka masala* and pungent lamb *kadahi*, it's clear that everybody loves this *desi* diner's bold and authentic flavors.

Lau Hai San

E3

Vietnamese ✗

2597 Senter Rd. (bet. Feldspar Dr. & Umbarger Rd.), San Jose

Phone: 408-938-0650
Web: N/A
Prices: $$

Lunch & dinner Thu – Tue

Most Westerners don't think of hot pot when they're craving Vietnamese food, but it's actually a traditional favorite well worth sampling—and the proof is in this sunny spot. The overstuffed menu boasts 20 different variations on the theme, including a spicy seafood version with shrimp, mussels, squid, fish balls stuffed with salmon roe, and other aquatic delights. Dip them into the sour, tangy broth; twirl them with noodles; garnish with herbs—the choice is yours.

If hot pot isn't adventurous enough, bring a group to sample delicacies like chewy, flavorful curried coconut snails and crispy fried pork intestine. The diner-like space and strip-mall setting are nothing special, but the hot pot is so outstanding that lines are to be expected.

Liquid Bread

D3

Gastropub ✗

379 E. Campbell Ave. (bet. Central Ave. & Civic Center Dr.), Campbell

Phone: 408-370-3400
Web: www.liquidbreadcampbell.com
Prices: $$

Dinner Tue – Sun

Beer is serious business at this Campbell Avenue hot spot, which boasts a sizable menu of drafts and bottles. But the food is a step up from the typical brewpub, with dishes like an asparagus salad topped with shaved sunchokes, black garlic, and balsamic dressing; or roasted chicken breast over maple syrup-soaked waffles and garlicky escarole. Brews even show up on the food menu from time to time, as in the stout cream that crowns a fudgy chocolate brownie.

While it's far from a dive bar, Liquid Bread can get loud, making it better for sharing pints with friends than an intimate date-night. If the communal high-top tables, large front patio, and copious brews add up to a little too much fun, do as the regulars do and have Uber handle the drive home.

Manresa ✿✿✿

Contemporary ✗✗✗

D4

320 Village Ln. (bet. Santa Cruz & University Aves.), Los Gatos

Phone: 408-354-4330
Web: www.manresarestaurant.com
Prices: $$$$

Dinner Wed – Sun

Recovered, renewed, and fresh off its hiatus, Manresa has returned from its kitchen-fire ashes like a phoenix—and it just may be better than ever. The dining room appears unchanged; it is still elegant, celebratory, and distinctively stylish. Likewise, the service team remains synchronized and welcoming. Most importantly, Chef David Kinch's superb cooking is invigorated with focused brilliance.

The chef's one nightly menu is unknown until it arrives on the table as a parchment listing alphabetized ingredients. The food is at once cerebral and luxurious, yet grounded and thoroughly delicious. Each course is likely to represent a moment within a season, beginning with a selection of savory *petit fours* that are an illusory play on the palate. Sample red-pepper *pâtes de fruits*, black olive madeleines, or green-garlic panisse with Meyer lemon curd and tahini. Black cod is a surprising, clever, and cohesive dish featuring an exemplary fillet with crisped Brussels sprout leaves, tart vinegar reduction, and root purée served alongside a chestnut "truffle" rolled in truffle dust.

Memorable desserts feature pumpkin purée with chocolate crémeux as well as sherry vinegar. And finally, don't miss those excellent sea salt-caramels offered on your way out— you might even want to take a few for the ride home!

285

Naschmarkt

Austrian ✗✗

384 E. Campbell Ave. (bet. Central & Railway Aves.), Campbell

Phone: 408-378-0335   Dinner Tue – Sun
Web: www.naschmarkt-restaurant.com
Prices: $$

A slice of Vienna in downtown Campbell, Naschmarkt scores high marks for its authentic flavors, inviting space, and friendly service. The cozy, brick-walled dining room is a favorite among couples and solo diners will have a ball at the wraparound counter, which has a great view of the busy open kitchen.

Most of the menu is traditional: think bratwurst, krout roulade, and weiner schnitzel. The pan-roasted chicken breast, moist and juicy with a golden-brown seared crust, is served over a "napkin dumpling" made with compressed bread, tomato, and herbs. But, rest easy as there are a few items that have lighter Californian twists, like spätzle made with quark (a fresh white cheese) and tossed with smoked chicken, yellow corn, English peas, and wild mushrooms.

Nick's Next Door

American ✗✗✗

11 College Ave. (at Main St.), Los Gatos

Phone: 408-402-5053   Lunch & dinner Tue – Sat
Web: www.nicksnextdoor.com
Prices: $$

Though it originally opened as the sibling to Chef Difu's Nick's on Main, Nick's Next Door is now his sole restaurant—even more confusing given that it's actually across the street from his original spot. One fact is evident, though: the crowd here has ritzy tastes, often flocking in from the high-end cigar shop next door and Bentley dealership down the street.

Upscale American bistro cuisine is the focus with dishes like seared pepper-crusted ahi tuna, a veal rib chop with creamy Tuscan white beans, and meatloaf with potatoes and wild mushroom gravy. Whether you dine in the cozy yet elegant dining room with its black-and-gray motif or on the beautiful patio at the foot of a towering redwood, you'll receive a warm welcome, often from Nick himself.

Oak & Rye

Pizza ✗✗

D4

303 N. Santa Cruz Ave. (bet. Almendra & Bachman Aves.), Los Gatos

Phone: 408-395-4441
Web: www.oakandryepizza.com
Prices: $$

Lunch Tue – Sun
Dinner nightly

A longtime *pizzaiolo* from Brooklyn's acclaimed Roberta's is behind the pies at this South Bay jewel, where a coppery wood-fired oven produces chewy, blistered crusts. The pies' toppings are as quirky and delightful as their monikers, like the Scottie 2 Hottie (*soppressata*, *pepperoncini* oil, tomatoes, mozzarella, honey) and the Truffle Shuffle (Gruyère, green onion, truffle oil, cornichon).

The menu is rounded out by a handful of small plates like a shaved Brussels sprout, lemon, and pecorino salad, but the real focus is the pizza, for which Oak & Rye has quickly become Los Gatos' go-to. Friendly and casual, with gregarious servers, its only drawback is the need to arrive early—reservations for parties fewer than 10 aren't accepted, and waits can get long.

Orchard City Kitchen 🙂

International ✗✗

D3

1875 S Bascom Ave., Ste. 190 (off Campisi Way), Campbell

Phone: 408-340-5285
Web: www.orchardcitykitchen.com
Prices: $$

Lunch & dinner daily

Jeffrey Stout, who made his name at Alexander's Steakhouse, is at the helm of this international small-plates spot, which has already been getting a level of buzz that radiates far beyond its shopping-center environs. Polished yet casual with a big front bar and patio, it's best enjoyed with a group—so come prepared to max out the menu.

Kick things off with a cocktail; then get ready to savor a dizzying array of great dishes, including Sichuan dumplings stuffed with lobster and bathed in chili oil, crunchy nuggets of sweet-and-spicy Korean fried chicken, or Hawaiian-style hamachi crudo with pineapple and macadamia nuts. A rotating soft-serve special, like banana with candied walnuts and chocolate pearls, is a fun finish to this lively meal.

Orenchi

D3

✗

3540 Homestead Rd. (near Lawrence Expy.), Santa Clara

Phone: 408-246-2955　　　　　　　　　　　　Lunch & dinner Tue – Sun
Web: www.orenchi-ramen.com
Prices: 🥜

Whether at lunch or dinner, this ramen specialist is known for its lines of waiting diners that curl like noodles outside its door. Even those who arrive before they open may face a long wait, so don't come if you're in a rush. Once inside, you'll be seated at a simple wood table or at the bar, collaged with Polaroid portraits of guests savoring their ramen.

The reason for the wait becomes clear when you're presented with a rich and utterly delicious bowl of *tonkotsu* ramen full of chewy noodles, roasted pork, and scallions. *Shoyu* ramen is equally delish, but make a point to show up early for spicy miso *tsukemen* or miso ramen as they're limited to only 15 and 20 servings, respectively, at lunch and dinner.

Check out Iroriya next door for *robata* dining.

Oren's Hummus Shop

A4

✗

261 University Ave. (bet. Bryant & Ramona Sts.), Palo Alto

Phone: 650-752-6492　　　　　　　　　　　　Lunch & dinner daily
Web: www.orenshummus.com
Prices: 🥜

An authentic taste of the Holy Land in Silicon Valley, Oren's tiny space is as crowded as the Wailing Wall. At prime hours, expect to see diners spilling out onto the sidewalk and lining up for takeout at the back counter. The staff can seem overwhelmed at times, but it's an experience worth the wait, whether in Palo Alto or Mountain View.

You'll understand the lines after your first bite of the incredible hummus, drizzled with olive oil, and the crisp falafel with its moist, well-seasoned interior. Tender, spice-rubbed chicken breast in a fluffy pita, topped with a refreshing Israeli salad of chopped cucumber, tomato, onion, and parsley, as well as a spoonful of green harissa, is a satisfying lunch. Wash it all down with a dark Israeli beer.

Pampas

Brazilian ✗✗

A4

529 Alma St. (bet. Hamilton & University Aves.), Palo Alto

Phone: 650-327-1323
Web: www.pampaspaloalto.com
Prices: $$$

Lunch Mon – Fri
Dinner nightly

Pampas has a prime Palo Alto location across from the Caltrain, just steps from the shops on University Ave. The large brick façade is hard to miss, and judging by the half-off happy hour crowds, most yupsters don't. The voluminous, bi-level restaurant has the look of a sexy barn with dark masculine furnishings.

Pampas is a Brazilian *churrascaria* (carnivore heaven) where servers bring tender, well-seasoned, spit-roasted *rodizio* meat until you say "uncle." Standouts include the tenderloin filet seasoned with garlic and herbs; chicken legs marinated in garlic, chiles, and vinegar; and house-made chorizo with *harissa* and more chiles. In case this isn't enough, the sidebar buffet is unlimited. And, the slow-roasted pineapple makes an excellent finale.

Pastis

French ✗

B4

447 S. California Ave. (bet. Ash St. & El Camino Real), Palo Alto

Phone: 650-324-1355
Web: www.pastispaloalto.com
Prices: $$

Lunch Tue – Sun
Dinner Tue – Sat

Parisian charm flowers in the heart of Silicon Valley at Pastis, a delightful Palo Alto French bistro. Compact and cheery with yellow walls, a sprinkling of tables, and specials on the chalkboard, it's every inch the European experience (just don't bring along a big group). You'll hear a lot of French spoken by both the staff and guests as it's a favorite with the expats—always a good sign for American gastronomes.

The low-key, laid-back menu is heavy on Gallic classics like fluffy, buttery quiche Lorraine; a grilled merguez sandwich with roasted bell peppers and *harissa* mayonnaise; as well as a simple but perfect crème brûlée. *Le Benedict* and *les omelettes* are big draws for brunch, particularly when enjoyed on the lovely front patio.

Plumed Horse ✿

South Bay

14555 Big Basin Way (bet. 4th & 5th Sts.), Saratoga

Phone: 408-867-4711
Web: www.plumedhorse.com
Prices: $$$$

Dinner Mon – Sat

Set in what appears to be a cozy bungalow that opens into a surprisingly large space, Plumed Horse's small-town surroundings are belied by the McLarens and Lamborghinis regularly parked out front. Tech money infuses the well-to-do suburb, and this show pony is a fine-dining favorite among wealthy local retirees.

But even if you have to save your pennies, you will enjoy the creative and delectable dishes on offer here. These include a crunchy phyllo cannoli shell stuffed with smoked trout-mascarpone mousse and dusted with chives; or velvety sweet corn soup with a tangy chow-chow of pickled vegetables, smoked duck, and popped sorghum. Flaky butter-basted salmon rests in a bed of earthy porcini and fava beans, while tender chicken roulades are accented by chanterelles and sweet corn. A quenelle of blackberry sorbet served over honey-flavored tapioca pearls makes for a rich yet very refreshing finale.

Some technical touches, like an iPad wine list and fiber-optic chandeliers, are a nod to the clientele. But, the vibe generally tilts towards classic luxury—from the attentive and professional staff, to the contemporary space with its enormous glass wine cellar and arched barrel ceiling.

Rangoli

Indian

D4

3695 Union Ave. (at Woodard Rd.), San Jose

Phone: 408-377-2222   Lunch & dinner daily
Web: www.rangolica.com
Prices: $$

Set at the end of a strip mall, Rangoli is an opportune surprise with sophisticated Indian cooking. Named for the colorful folk art prevalent through the subcontinent, this upscale retreat features a vast dining room framed with vibrant accents and decorative demi-walls. Tables along cushioned banquettes on the fringes and several rounded booths provide ample real estate for assemblies of all size.

Businessmen love the lunch buffet for its assortment of popular dishes, but take a tip from the locals and come for dinner. *Bhindi masala*; vegetable *moile* starring a creamy coconut curry; and lamb Madras are all delicious, spicy, and served piping-hot. Couple these curries with warm, pliable, perfectly charred garlic naan for a contrast in flavor and texture.

Sakoon

Indian XX

C2

357 Castro St. (bet. California & Dana Sts.), Mountain View

Phone: 650-965-2000   Lunch & dinner daily
Web: www.sakoonrestaurant.com
Prices: $$

An Indian mainstay in Mountain View, Sakoon draws big techie crowds for its lunch buffet—and transforms into an upscale, contemporary dinnertime experience come sundown. Vibrant and cheerful, its oversized mirrors, modern furnishings, and brightly patterned banquettes delight the eye, as do the fiber-optic lights that pattern the ceiling with constantly shifting swirls of color.

The food and service are strikingly attentive and polished, with well-constructed dishes like *chaat ki parat* (fried shredded wheat topped with potatoes, chickpeas, red onion, and cilantro) and a flavor-packed Chettinad chicken curry. For an unusual and satisfying dessert-like bread, try the Kashmiri naan filled with rosewater-soaked shredded coconut and toasted chopped nuts.

Sawa Sushi

South Bay

Japanese ✗

D3

1042 E. El Camino Real (at Henderson Ave.), Sunnyvale

Phone: 408-241-7292   Dinner Mon – Sat
Web: www.sawasushi.net
Prices: $$$$

Strict rules and big rewards unite at this zany, unusual and randomly located (in a mall) dive, where Chef Steve Sawa rules the roost. After going through the rigmarole of landing a reservation for his omakase-only affair, throw all caution to the wind and just go with the flow. Yes, the décor is nothing special and downright weird; however, the food is anything but so-so and the ad hoc prices are usually quite high.

So what draws such a host of regulars? Their pristine and very sublime fish, of course—from creamy Hokkaido sea scallops to delicious toro ribbons. Sawa is also an expert on sauces: imagine the likes of *yuzu kosho* topping kanpachi, or a sweet-spicy tamarind glaze on ocean trout. Finish with a top sake or cold beer and feel the joy seep in.

The Sea

Seafood

B2

4269 El Camino Real (at Dinah's Ct.), Palo Alto

Phone: 650-213-1111   Dinner nightly
Web: www.theseausa.com
Prices: $$$$

Wealthy venture capitalists come ashore in waves to blow their expense accounts at this seafood-centric sister to Alexander's Steakhouse, where the central Palo Alto location is prime, the wine list is strewn with expensive bottles, and the menu brims with top-dollar delicacies. The white-tablecloth vibe is appropriately corporate and formal, so be sure to don your best.

The stratospherically priced selection ranges from Maine lobster to Hokkaido scallops to landlubber-friendly Australian Wagyu. But, for those seeking a closer shore, the Quinault River king salmon, served in a creamy, bacon-accented sauce over maitake mushrooms and haricots verts, is worthy. Don't skip dessert, either: the yuzu mousse with kumquats and avocado cream is quite simply fabulous.

Smoking Pig BBQ

Barbecue ✗

E2

1144 N. 4th St. (bet. Commercial St. & Younger Ave.), San Jose

Phone: 408-380-4784
Web: www.smokingpigbbq.net
Prices: 💷

Lunch & dinner daily

Identifiable by the aroma of wood smoke that surrounds it for a block in every direction, this barbecue-slinging dive is wildly popular. Read: plan on a wait in the smoker-ringed parking lot if you want to dine at prime meal times. Accommodations are beyond basic, with tattered booths and disposable servingware, but service is friendly, and something about the lack of ambience amplifies the gustatory pleasure.

Indeed, there is plenty of pleasure to be found on the combination plates, especially the signature pork ribs—smoky and well-seasoned, they fall off the bone. Order them in a combination plate of peppery brisket or juicy pulled pork, along with a cornbread muffin and tasty, smoky beans with burnt ends. This is pigging out at its finest.

South Legend

Chinese ✗

E1

1720 N. Milpitas Blvd. (bet. Dixon Landing Rd. & Sunnyhills Ct.), Milpitas

Phone: 408-934-3970
Web: www.southlegend.com
Prices: 💷

Lunch & dinner daily

In the Sunnyhills strip mall, packed with Chinese restaurants and Asian markets, South Legend stands out for its fiery and lip-numbing interpretations of classic Sichuan cooking. Though Chengdu-style dim sum provides a brief respite on weekend mornings, it's all about the heat for the rest of the week in dishes like fried Chongqing chicken topped with piles of dried chilies.

Large and no-frills, South Legend is usually crammed with locals looking for an authentic taste of their Chinese childhoods—grungy dining room and dated décor be damned. They're too busy sweating out spicy pickled vegetables and enormous braised whole fish covered in still more chilies, then cooling off with some blander *dan dan* noodles and a pot of hot black tea.

Sumika

Japanese

236 Plaza Central (bet. 2nd & 3rd Sts.), Los Altos

Phone: 650-917-1822
Web: www.sumikagrill.com
Prices: **$$**

Lunch Tue – Sat
Dinner Tue – Sun

Yak it up at this local hot spot for Japanese-style skewers, where every part of the chicken (from thighs to liver to skin) is grilled over charcoal to smoky deliciousness. Sumika's atmosphere may be no-frills, but the food is solid and its beloved sister ramen shop, Orenchi, gives it an enormous pedigree (which makes snagging a seat or two in the tiny space a real challenge).

If you're willing to sacrifice *yakitori*, crowds die down considerably during skewer-free lunches, when moist chicken *karaage* with a crisp, golden-brown exterior and the signature Sumika salad (featuring cabbage, chicken, and wonton strips) take center stage. Udon in an umami-rich dashi broth with fish cake, kombu, and a carrot-daikon *kakiage* fritter is always a solid bet.

Swaad

Indian

498 N. 13th St. (at Empire St.), San Jose

Phone: 408-947-2030
Web: www.swaadindiancuisine.com
Prices: **$$**

Lunch Mon – Sat
Dinner nightly

Indian transplants have quickly cottoned on to this ultra-authentic spot, whose dishes are jam-packed with flavor and liberally seasoned with herbs and spices that aren't toned down for Western palates. The space is simple and nondescript with yellow walls and stark furnishings, but no one seems to mind: they're just here for the food.

On that point, the kitchen delivers, with perfectly crispy vegetable samosas loaded with potatoes and green peas, creamy chicken korma full of tender vegetables and pungent spices, and massive rounds of naan stuffed with shredded cauliflower. Don't miss their flavorful, spicy *seekh* kebabs featuring ground lamb and presented on a smoking-hot iron skillet with tomatoes, peppers, and onion for terrific contrast in texture.

The Table

American 🍴

E3

1110 Willow St. (at Lincoln Ave.), San Jose

Phone: 408-638-7911
Web: www.thetablesj.com
Prices: $$

Lunch Fri – Sun
Dinner nightly

The casual, farm-to-table food that's standard fare in SF is harder to come by in San Jose, which explains why this ingredient-centric gathering place is always packed with diners. With long wood tables, large windows, a busy back bar, and lots of hard, modern surfaces—not to mention a bevy of craft cocktails fueling the crowds—it can get noisy. Read: don't plan an intimate evening here.

Instead, make The Table your spot to share bites and drinks with friends, like caramelized sourdough spaetzle with smoked butternut squash and pea tendrils, or sugar-dusted ricotta beignets with lemon curd. Brunch is so popular that it's offered on Fridays as well as weekends, but you should expect a wait to enjoy your omelette, hash browns, or more of those beignets.

Tamarine

Vietnamese 🍴🍴

A4

546 University Ave. (bet. Cowper & Webster Sts.), Palo Alto

Phone: 650-325-8500
Web: www.tamarinerestaurant.com
Prices: $$$

Lunch Mon – Fri
Dinner nightly

Tamarine has long been a Palo Alto standby for its refined take on Vietnamese food that doesn't sacrifice authentic flavor. There's nearly always a corporate lunch happening in the private dining room, and techies, families and couples alike fill the rest of its linen-topped tables.

Family-style sharing of dishes is encouraged, which is good because deciding on just one entrée is nearly impossible. To start, make like the regulars and order one of the "Tamarine Taste" appetizer platters with a round of tropical fruit-infused cocktails. Then move on to the fresh shrimp spring rolls, full of bean sprouts and mint; the springy ginger-chili seitan with steamed coconut rice; and curried long beans, sautéed with fragrant Makrut lime leaves and chili.

Tanto

D2

1063 E. El Camino Real (bet. Helen & Henderson Aves.), Sunnyvale

Phone: 408-244-7311
Web: N/A
Prices: $$

Lunch Tue – Fri
Dinner Tue – Sun

Lone rangers on tech-office lunch breaks pack this strip-mall Japanese spot, whose crowded parking lot belies its unimpressive façade. Waits are inevitable, but it's worth it to sit down to a steaming bowl of simple and flavorful udon. Indeed, all the standards are rendered beautifully here, from crisp vegetable tempura to tender, flaky grilled *unagi* set atop freshly steamed rice.

Tanto's menu expands a bit at dinner, bringing more grilled items and *izakaya*-style small plates. Pristine sushi and sashimi like albacore with ponzu are also a strong pick. You'll likely be seated at one of the closely-spaced dining room tables, but the occasional stroke of luck might land you in one of the curtained, semi-private alcoves popular with business diners.

Thiên Long

F3

3005 Silver Creek Rd., Ste.138 (bet. Aborn Rd. & Lexann Ave.), San Jose

Phone: 408-223-6188
Web: www.thienlongrestaurant.com
Prices:

Lunch & dinner daily

There are plenty of Vietnamese restaurants catering to the local expats in San Jose, but Thiên Long stands out for its pleasant dining room presenting delicious cooking—as the numerous families filling the large space will attest. Tile floors and rosewood-tinted chairs decorate the space, while walls hung with photos of Vietnamese dishes keep the focus on food.

Begin with sweet-salty barbecued prawns paired with smoky grilled pork and served atop rice noodles. But, it is really the *pho* with a broth of star anise, clove, and ginger, topped with perfectly rare beef that is a true gem—even the regular-sized portion is enormous. English is a challenge among the staff, but they are very friendly; plus the faithful flavors make up for any inadequacies.

Vung Tau

Vietnamese ✗✗

E3

535 E. Santa Clara St. (at 12th St.), San Jose

Phone: 408-288-9055   Lunch & dinner daily
Web: www.vungtaurestaurant.com
Prices: 💰

It's easy to see why Vung Tau is a longtime love and go-to favorite among South Bay locals: picture an elegant décor, hospitable service, massive menu, and tasty food. Inside, the large space combines several dining areas styled with soft beiges, wood accents, and pendant lights. Lunchtime draws in business crowds while dinner brings families, many of whom are of Vietnamese heritage.

Authenticity is paramount in such offerings as hearty *bun bo hue*—ask for Vietnamese not American style—which comes with sliced flank steak, beef tendons, and pork blood in a spicy, earthy broth, served with a side of fresh herbs, lime, onions, and bean sprouts. Delicately sweet and creamy pleasures abound in *bánh khot*, delightful coconut-prawn cups served with chili-fish sauce.

Walia

Ethiopian ✗

D3

2208 Business Cir. (at Bascom Ave.), San Jose

Phone: 408-645-5001   Lunch & dinner Wed – Mon
Web: www.waliaethiopian.com
Prices: 💰

Authentic Ethiopian flavors are delivered without pretense at this easygoing, affordable restaurant, housed in a strip mall just off Bascom Avenue. Though the space is basic, the service is friendly and it's casual enough for kids in tow.

Start things off with an order of *sambussas*, fried dough triangles filled with lentil, onion, and chilies. Then choose from an all-meat, all-veggie, or mixed selection of tasty Ethiopian stews, like *tibs firfir* featuring lamb in a garlicky berbere sauce) dolloped on spongy, flaky *injera*. Vegetarians will particularly love dining here, as all of the plant-based options including *alicha wot* or split peas in turmeric sauce, *shiro* (spiced chickpeas), and *gomen* (wilted collard greens with onion and spices), are big winners.

Zeni

D3

Ethiopian ✗

1320 Saratoga Ave. (at Payne Ave.), San Jose

Phone: 408-615-8282   Lunch & dinner Tue – Sun
Web: N/A
Prices: $$

Diners get to choose their own adventure at this Ethiopian standby located beside a shopping plaza. Zeni caters to expats as well as foodies of all stripes with traditional basket-like pedestals bounded by low stools. Regardless of your seat, you'll be served spongy, sour *injera* to scoop up delicious *yemisir wot* (red lentils with spicy *berbere*); *kik alicha* (yellow peas tinged with garlic and ginger); or beef *kitfo* (available raw or cooked), tossed with *mitmita* (an aromatic spice blend) and crowned with crumbled *ayib* cheese. Here, *injera* is your utensil so no need to ask for one; there's a sink in the back to clean up after.

Sip cool, sweet honey wine to balance the spicy food, or opt for an after-dinner Ethiopian coffee.

Zola

A4

French ✗✗

565 Bryant St. (bet. Hamilton & University Aves.), Palo Alto

Phone: 650-521-0651   Dinner Tue – Sat
Web: www.zolapaloalto.com
Prices: $$

A Palo Alto sparkler, Zola has already charmed its way into diners' hearts via a seductive French bistro menu with Californian flair. Whether you're spreading smoky salmon rillettes on toasted artisan levain, twirling pillowy caramelized ricotta gnocchi into the yolk of a soft-cooked egg in brown butter, or tucking into exquisite roasted pork loin and belly over Brussels sprouts and apple, you're sure to fall hard for the food.

The stylish space updates a few classics (wood tables, bistro chairs, pressed ceilings) with a dark teal color scheme and enticingly low lighting, and the well-chosen wine list is equal parts Gallic and Golden State. Crème caramel for dessert may be traditional, but it's also perfectly golden-brown and decadently creamy.

Zona Rosa

Mexican ✗

E3

1411 The Alameda (bet. Hester & Shasta Aves.), San Jose

Phone: 408-275-1411
Web: www.zonarosasj.com
Prices: $$

Lunch & dinner Tue – Sun

For food just like *abuela's* (but somehow even better), make a beeline to this soul-warming cantina, which makes its salsas, blue and white corn tortillas, and other timeless dishes by hand. Start with an *antojito* like *albondigas fundido,* then proceed to tacos filled with *guajillo*-braised pork ribs and tomatillo-avocado salsa or pan-seared skirt steak with vibrant and garlicky *chimichurri*. Another star: a roasted *chile relleno*, which is smoky, spicy, sweet, and earthy in equal measure.

What the space lacks in square footage, it more than makes up for in its down-home appeal. But, this isn't a great choice for those in a rush as the homespun service can get easily overwhelmed.

Check out the second location on Main Street in Los Gatos as well.

Sunday brunch plans?
Look for the 🖎 !

Wine Country

Picnicking on artisan-made cheeses and fresh crusty bread amid acres of gnarled grapevines; sipping wine on a terrace above a hillside of silvery olive trees; touring caves heady with the sweet smell of fermenting grapes—this is northern California's wine country. Lying within an hour's drive north and northeast of San Francisco, the hills and vales of gorgeous Sonoma County and Napa Valley thrive on the abundant sunshine and fertile soil that produce grapes for some of North America's finest wines.

FRUIT OF THE VINE

Cuttings of Criollas grapevines traveled north with Franciscan *padres* from the Baja Peninsula during the late 17th century. Wines made from these "mission" grapes were used primarily for trade and sacramental purposes. In the early 1830s, a French immigrant propitiously named Jean-Louis Vignes (*vigne* is French for "vine") established a large vineyard near Los Angeles using cuttings of European grapevines *(Vitis vinifera)*, and by the mid-19th century, winemaking had become one of southern California's principal industries. In 1857, Hungarian immigrant Agoston Haraszthy purchased a 400-acre estate in Sonoma County, named it Buena Vista, and cultivated Tokaji vine cuttings imported from his homeland. In 1861, bolstered by promises of state funding, Haraszthy went to Europe to gather assorted *vinifera* cuttings to plant them in California soil. Upon his return, however, the state legislature reneged on their commitment. Undeterred, Haraszthy forged ahead and continued to distribute (at his own expense) some 100,000 cuttings and testing varieties in different soil types. Successful application of his discoveries created a boom in the local wine industry in the late 19th century.

THE TIDE TURNS

As the 1800s drew to a close, northern California grapevines fell prey to phylloxera, a root louse that attacks susceptible *vinifera* plants, and entire vineyards were decimated. Eventually researchers discovered they could combat phylloxera by replanting vineyards with disease-resistant wild grape rootstocks, onto which *vinifera* cuttings could be grafted. The wine industry had achieved a modicum of recovery by the early 20th century, only to be slapped with the 18th Amendment to the Constitution, prohibiting the manufacture, sale, importation, and transportation of intoxicating liquors in the United States. California's winemaking industry remained at a near-standstill until 1933, when Prohibition was repealed. The Great Depression slowed the reclamation of vineyards and it wasn't until the early 1970s that California's wine industry was fully re-established. In 1976, California wines took top honors in a blind taste testing by French judges in Paris. The results helped open up a whole new world of respectability for Californian vineyards.

COMING OF AGE

As Napa Valley and Sonoma County wines have established their reputations, the importance of individual growing regions has increased. Many sub-regions have sought and acquired Federal regulation of place names as American Viticultural Areas, or AVAs, in order to set the boundaries of wine-growing areas that are distinctive for their soil, microclimate, and wine styles. Although this system is subject to debate, there is no doubt that an AVA like Russian River Valley, Carneros, or Spring Mountain can be very meaningful. The precise location of a vineyard relative to the Pacific Ocean or San Pablo Bay; the elevation and slope of a vineyard; the soil type and moisture content; and even the proximity to a mountain gap can make essential differences.

Together, Sonoma and Napa have almost 30 registered appellations, which vary in size and sometimes overlap. Specific place names are becoming increasingly important as growers learn what to plant where and how to care for vines in each unique circumstance. The fact that more and more wines go to market with a

specific AVA flies in the face of the worldwide trend to ever larger and less specific "branded" wines. Individual wineries and associations are working to promote the individuality of North Coast appellations and to preserve their integrity and viability as sustainable agriculture. In recent decades, Napa Valley and Sonoma County have experienced tremendous levels of development. Besides significant increases in vineyard acreage, the late 20th century witnessed an explosion of small-scale operations, some housed in old wineries updated with state-of-the-art equipment.

Meanwhile, the Russian River Valley remains less developed, retaining its rural feel with country roads winding past picturesque wineries, rolling hills of grapevines, and stands of solid redwood trees. With such easy access to world-class wines, organic produce and cheeses from local farms, residents of northern California's wine country enjoy an enviable quality of life. Happily for the scores of visitors, those same products supply the area's burgeoning number of restaurants, creating a culture of gourmet dining that stretches from the city of Napa all the way north to Healdsburg and beyond.

Note that if you elect to bring your own wine, most restaurants charge a corkage fee (which can vary from $10 to as much as $50 per bottle). Many restaurants waive this fee on a particular day, or if you purchase an additional bottle from their list.

Wine Country

Napa Valley

GRAPES GALORE

Revered as one of the most exalted wine growing regions in the world, Napa Valley is a 35 mile-long and luscious basin where wine is king. Given its grape-friendly climate and prime location (north from San Pablo Bay to Mount St. Helena, between the Mayacama and Vaca mountains), Napa ranks with California's most prestigious wineries. Here, powerfully hot summer days and cool nights provide the perfect environment for cabernet sauvignon grapes, a varietal for which the county is justifiably famous. But, it's not all about just *vino* here. Top chefs also have a buffet of exceptional ingredients to choose from, including locally grown and pressed extra virgin olive oils from the **Tasting Room**. **Butterscots**—an English-inspired bakery, deli, and culinary emporium housed within the Cairdean Estate compound—is primo for excursion essentials like shortbread, crumpets, game pies, and more. Moving on to more savory feats, foodies, cooks, and scientists make their annual expedition to the **Napa Truffle Festival**, a veritable shindig of all things lush and earthy. Also on offer here are cooking demos, seminars, and foraging. Among the region's many winemakers are names like **Robert Mondavi**, **Francis Ford Coppola**, and **Miljenko "Mike" Grgich**. Originally from Croatia, Grgich rose to fame as the winemaker at **Chateau Montelena** when his 1973 chardonnay took the top prize at the Judgment of Paris in 1976, outshining France's best white Burgundies. This triumph

turned the wine world on its ear, and put California on the map as a bona fide producer. Since then, Napa's indisputable success with premium wines has fostered endless pride, country-wide. American Viticultural Areas (AVAs) currently regulate the boundaries for districts such as Calistoga, Stags Leap, Rutherford, and Los Carneros.

SPECIALTY FINDS

The Valley's wine-rich culture coupled with its illustrious restaurants that are destinations in themselves, make this neighborhood one of the world's most popular tourist attractions. Reclaimed 19th century stone wineries and gorgeous Victorian homes punctuate this rolling landscape and serve as a constant reminder that there were some 140 wineries here prior to 1890. Up from a Prohibition-era low of perhaps a dozen, the region today boasts over 400 growers and producers. However, this is not to say that there aren't stellar alfresco dining spots and specialty stores situated along its

picturesque streets. Gourmands never fail to make the trek to **Rancho Gordo**, headquartered here, for heirloom beans of the highest quality. Serving as the main supplier to area chefs, it is also open to the public who seem smitten by their divine selection. Looking for some inspiration? They can also instruct you on how best to cook them! Picnic supplies are the main draw at **Oakville Grocery**, the oldest operating store in town on Route 29; while **Model Bakery** in St. Helena or **Bouchon Bakery** in Yountville are wildly popular for fresh-baked breads and finger-licking pastries.

Napa's continued growth in wine production has spawned a special kind of food and wine tourism in this county, and tasting rooms, tours, as well as farm-fresh cuisine are de rigueur here. **Olivier Napa Valley** is a quaint and historic retail shop in St. Helena that proffers oils, vinegars, and other local food products alongside beautiful handcrafted tableware and ceramics from Provence. Residents who aren't rejoicing over their wares may be found scouring the vendibles at **NapaStyle**, a lifestyle store from local celebrity chef Michael Chiarello, purveying everything from furniture and tabletop items, to kitchenware and pantry staples. Other megawatt personalities like Thomas Keller, Richard Reddington, Cindy Pawlsyn, and Philippe Jeanty also hail from around the way, and may be found rubbing elbows at the flagship location of gourmet grocer, **Dean & Deluca**.

SHOPPING TREATS

Visitors touring the Valley will spot fields of wild fennel, silvery olive trees, and rows of wild mustard that bloom between the grapevines in February and March. Mustard season kicks off each year with the **Napa Valley Mustard Festival** paying homage to the food, wine, art, and agricultural bounty of this region. Likewise, several towns host seasonal farmer's markets from May through October, including one in Napa (held near the **Oxbow Public Market** on Tuesdays and Saturdays); St. Helena (Fridays in Crane Park); and Calistoga (on Saturdays at Sharpsteen Museum plaza on Washington Street). Launched in early 2008, the **Oxbow Public Market** is a block-long, 40,000-square-foot facility that is meant to rival the

Ferry Building Marketplace that is housed across the Bay. Packed to the rafters with food artisans and wine vendors from within a 100-mile radius of the market, and cradled inside a barn-like building, Oxbow keeps fans returning for everything under the sun. Think cheese, charcuterie, and spices, or olive oils, organic ice cream, and specialty teas. Shoppers who work up an appetite while perusing these shelves can rest assured as there are numerous snacks available to take-away!

SIGHTS TO BEHOLD

Regional products such as **St. Helena Olive Oil** and **Woodhouse Chocolates** on Main Street, also in St. Helena, have similarly gained a large-scale nation-wide following. Three generations of one family run this charming chocolatier, also frequented for tasty, handmade toffees. Just north of downtown St. Helena, the massive stone building that was erected in 1889 as Greystone Cellars, now inhabits the West Coast campus of the renowned **Culinary Institute of America (CIA)**. Their intensive training and syllabus ensures a striking lineup of hot chefs in the making.

With all this going for the wine-rich valley, one thing is for certain—from the city of Napa (the county's largest population center) north to the town of Calistoga known for its mineral mud baths and clean, spa cuisine, this narrow yet noteworthy region is nothing short of nirvana for lovers of great food and fine wine.

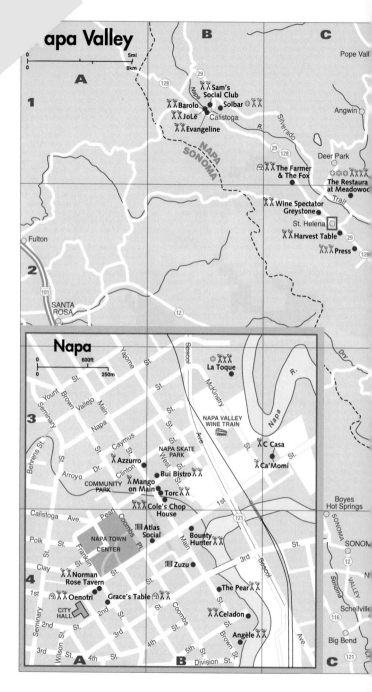

apa Valley

Pope Vall

Angwin

0 5mi
0 8km

A

1

XX Barolo
XX JoLe
XX Evangeline

XX Sam's
Social Club
Solbar ⊛ XX
Calistoga

128
29

NAPA
SONOMA

29 128

Deer Park

Silverado

XX The Farmer
& The Fox

⊛⊛⊛ XXXX
The Restaura
at Meadowoo

XX Wine Spectator
Greystone
St. Helena

Trail

XX Harvest Table
29

XXX Press
128

Fulton

101

2

SANTA
ROSA

12

Napa

0 600ft
0 250m

⊛ XXX
La Toque

Yajome

Soscol

McKinstry

Napa

R.

Yount

Brown

Vallejo

Main

St.

St.

St.

Seminary

3

Napa

St.

St.

Caymus

NAPA VALLEY
WINE TRAIN

Ave.

St.

Napa

Div

Behrens St.

St.

Clinton

Dr.

NAPA SKATE
PARK

West

St.

X C Casa

St.

X Azzurro

Arroyo

COMMUNITY
PARK

X Mango
on Main

Bui Bistro XX

Ca'Momi

Torc XX

1st

St.

XXX Cole's Chop
House

Boyes
Hot Springs

Calistoga Ave.

Pearl

Coombs

Franklin

Pl.

NAPA TOWN
CENTER

⊞ Atlas
Social

Bounty
Hunter XX

SONOMA

Polk

St.

Main

3rd

SONO

Clay

St.

⊞ Zuzu

St.

12

4

XX Norman
Rose Tavern

Sonoma

1st

⊛ XX Oenotri

Grace's Table ⊛ XX

St.

2nd

The Pear XX

VALLEY

Schellvill

Seminary

CITY
HALL

2nd

St.

Coombs

St.

XX Celadon

116

3rd

Wilson
St.

3rd

St.

4th

St.

4th St.

5th

Brown St.

Angèle XX

Division St.

Big Bend

121

A

B

C

308

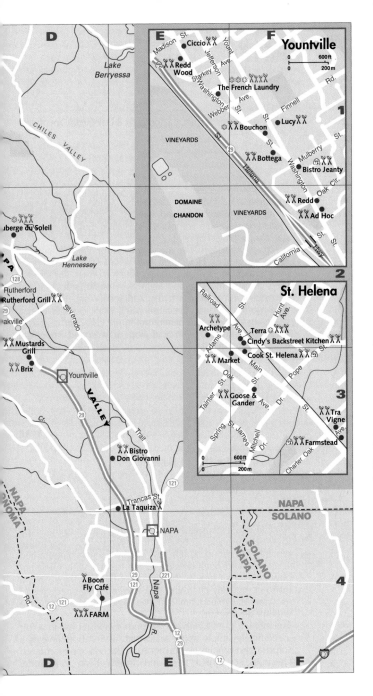

Yountville

Madison St.
Ciccio
Jefferson St.
Yount Ave.
Redd Wood
Starkey Ave.
St. Washington
The French Laundry
Webber Ave.
Finnell Rd.
Bouchon
Lucy
St.
VINEYARDS
Bottega
St. Helena
Mulberry
Washington
Bistro Jeanty
DOMAINE CHANDON
VINEYARDS
Oak St.
Redd
Ad Hoc
California Hwy.

0   600ft
0   200m

Lake Berryessa

CHILES VALLEY

Auberge du Soleil

Lake Hennessey

128

Rutherford
Rutherford Grill

29
Oakville

Silverado Trail

Mustards Grill

Brix

Yountville

NAPA VALLEY

29

Cr.

Bistro Don Giovanni

121

Trancas St.
La Taquiza

NAPA

NAPA SOLANO

SOLANO NAPA

Boon Fly Café

29
121

221

Napa R.

FARM

12
121

12

12
29

12

80

St. Helena

Railroad Ave.
Hunt Ave.
Archetype
Adams St.
Terra
Cindy's Backstreet Kitchen
Cook St. Helena
Market
Main St.
Pope St.
Oak Ave.
Tainter St.
Goose & Gander
Dr.
Tra Vigne Ave.
Spring St.
St. James
Mitchell Dr.
Farmstead
Charter Oak

0   600ft
0   200m

Ad Hoc

American ✗✗

F2

6476 Washington St. (bet. California Dr. & Oak Circle), Yountville

Phone: 707-944-2487   Lunch Sun
Web: www.adhocrestaurant.com   Dinner Thu – Mon
Prices: $$$

By far the most casual of Thomas Keller's three Yountville restaurants, Ad Hoc offers accessible American fare served family-style in a bright and inviting wood-paneled room. Waits are inevitable without a reservation, but the engaging staff keeps things hopping.

Ad Hoc's breezy prix-fixe menu boasts four delicious courses (three at brunch), kicking off with a salad like the luscious heirloom tomato, arugula, and pickled red onion. The famous fried chicken, now served nightly, is tender, spicy, deeply flavorful—and well worth the additional cost. Be sure to save room for dessert, because you'll want to linger over a wedge of the decadent peanut butter pie. Silky and custardy, it comes complete with a dollop of whipped chocolate Chantilly on top.

Angèle

French ✗✗

B4

540 Main St. (at 5th St.), Napa

Phone: 707-252-8115   Lunch & dinner daily
Web: www.angelerestaurant.com
Prices: $$

Nestled into a sun-splashed river bend adjacent to the Napa River Inn, Angèle is housed in a repurposed boathouse replete with wood panels and beams, French blue-framed windows, and linen-dressed tables topped with miniature olive trees. Not only is the setting of this downtown Napa bistro completely charming, but the impressive pedigree of its father-daughter team includes experience at key wine country destinations.

The menu is classic with a contemporary twist. Case in point: a seemingly simple apple salad that, at first bite, reveals a surprisingly complex composition of poached apples, roasted chestnuts, crumbled feta, and vanilla bean vinaigrette. Heartier items include a spot-on croque monsieur or roasted quail stuffed with bits of green chorizo.

Archetype

Californian ✕✕

E2

1429 Main St. (bet. Adams & Pine Sts.), St. Helena

Phone: 707-968-9200
Web: www.archetypenapa.com
Prices: $$

Lunch & dinner Wed – Sun

Simple, sophisticated, and stylish, Archetype—designed by legendary local architect Howard Backen—is "archetypally" wine country-chic. The former retail store still displays a few local goods, from pottery to small-batch spirits, but the array of regulars are really here to enjoy either lunch or dinner in its beautiful dining room, full of lush bamboo and rattan chairs. The team behind the Auberge Resorts runs the kitchen, riffing on American classics for a moneyed, stylish crowd. Wood-oven-grilled duck breast arrives over a delicate white miso and black tea jus, while thick buckwheat blinis are topped with creamy burrata and sweet huckleberry compote. And for a non-barbecue restaurant, the baby back ribs are surprisingly outstanding.

Atlas Social

International ✻

B4

1124 First St. (bet. Coombs & Main Sts.), Napa

Phone: 707-258-2583
Web: www.atlassocialnapa.com
Prices: $$

Lunch & dinner daily

The husband-and-wife duo behind Norman Rose Tavern and Azzurro have done it again with this Napa newbie, which traverses the globe to find influences from China (crab toast with ginger and scallion), Italy (shaved snap pea salad with pecorino and almonds), and even our neighbors across the pond (lamb chops with tart mint-lime marmalade). You'll also see Thai curry, masala chicken, and tempura in the mix of small, reasonably priced plates that encourage sharing.
Thanks to the owners' rosy reputation and a friendly staff, Atlas is already a hit with locals who come to kick back with a glass or two from a neighboring winery.
Sleek and industrial with chalkboard walls and modern plateware, it's a nice dose of urban cool in the countryside.

Auberge du Soleil

Californian 🍴🍴🍴

D2

180 Rutherford Hill Rd. (off the Silverado Trail), Rutherford

Phone: 707-963-1211
Web: www.aubergedusoleil.com
Prices: $$$$

Lunch & dinner daily

The approach to this wine country destination, tucked into a tiny hill among steep winding roads and famed wineries, is a treat in itself. Every corner of the building oozes warmth—even the terrace (kept toasty with space heaters) and its spectacular views overlooking that patchwork of vines and pine forests.

The classy and very cozy dining room boasts a wood-burning fire and a natural color scheme that flows from the rattan chairs and pumpkin-colored embroidered linens to the terra-cotta walls. Servers are equally warm, professional, and courteous. The sophisticated clientele (many of them guests of the hotel) seem to be relishing this as an escape from their busy and prosperous daily lives.

Still, the cooking trumps the setting with near-flawless preparations of seasonal, California-inspired cuisine. Begin with delicate gnocchi that promise to just melt in the mouth, swimming in a pungent, meaty parmesan and mushroom nage along with chopped pea shoots and sautéed wild mushrooms. Superlative entrées may feature succulent bay scallops, their sweetness offset by lemony roasted cauliflower, all surrounded by a pearly ribbon of prosciutto. Pumpkin mousse is the essence of fall on a plate.

Azzurro

Pizza ✗

A3

1260 Main St. (at Clinton St.), Napa

Phone: 707-255-5552
Web: www.azzurropizzeria.com
Prices: $$

Lunch & dinner daily

♿ This casual, well-executed Italian spot is the perfect place for a pizza and beer or glass of wine. The setting is semi-industrial with exposed ducts, polished concrete floors, and marble counters. Whether you dine with a group at the large wooden communal table or watch chefs toss arugula salads at the marble counter, you'll feel a brisk, friendly energy here. Ten kinds of thin, crisp pizzas are available, perhaps topped with slices of deliciously salty speck and creamy mozzarella, or the perennially popular *manciata*, a doughy crust topped with salad. (No health points for that one, sadly). Inventive and seasonal antipasti made with local produce and comforting desserts (think double-chocolate brownies) round out the top-notch offerings.

Barolo

Italian ✗✗

B1

1457 Lincoln Ave. (bet. Fair Way & Washington St.), Calistoga

Phone: 707-942-9900
Web: www.barolocalistoga.com
Prices: $$

Dinner nightly

♿
🛖 Set at the base of the Mount View Hotel & Spa in downtown Napa, this cheerful Italian restaurant is easily recognized—there's a Vespa scooter in the middle of the dining room. The pleasant space also combines red walls and white mosaic tiles with large, red-framed posters depicting pasta in all its glory. Local crowds flock to the small, close tables and expansive marble bar, which is perfect for solo dining.
The food spans all regions of Italy and unveils mozzarella- and pesto-stuffed fried risotto balls; rich spaghetti carbonara; and perfectly sautéed pork Milanese with mascarpone-parmesan risotto and *salsa rossa*. In keeping with the name, the wine list is stocked with sublime (if pricey) Barolos, while the bar holds plenty of premium spirits.

Bistro Don Giovanni

E3

Italian **XX**

4110 Howard Ln. (at Hwy. 29), Napa

Phone: 707-224-3300
Web: www.bistrodongiovanni.com
Prices: $$

Lunch & dinner daily

Located just off Highway 29, Bistro Don Giovanni can be easy to pass, but driving by would mean forgoing incredible Napa people-watching and superbly consistent Italian food. Park among the olive trees and grapevines, then take a seat in the airy, flower-decked dining room. If it's sunny, choose one of the rattan chairs on the peerless, postcard-perfect garden terrace.

A *pizzaiolo* mans the wood-burning oven in the front, firing up a selection of seasonal pies that are popular with families. Meanwhile, the adult set opts for fried olives with warm Marcona almonds, *garganelli* with duck ragù, and seared salmon with tomato-chive butter, all washed down with local wines. Already conquered a number of wineries? Switch to a cocktail at the busy front bar.

Bistro Jeanty 😊

F1

French **XX**

6510 Washington St. (at Mulberry St.), Yountville

Phone: 707-944-0103
Web: www.bistrojeanty.com
Prices: $$

Lunch & dinner daily

Napa transforms into the French countryside via a meal at Jeanty, which serves rib-sticking favorites like coq au vin, boeuf Bourguignon, and a sinfully rich milk-fed veal chop with chanterelle mushrooms and Camembert sauce. But California's lighter side is here, too: a salad of silken smoked trout and frisée is garden-fresh, and daily specials highlight the best in local produce.

The classic bistro accoutrements (yellow walls, wooden tables, framed retro posters) are present and accounted for, but there's an element of quirky fun here as well—from the flower-bedecked bicycle out front to the porcelain hens and hogs that dot the dining room. Like the flaky, caramelized, and unmissable tarte Tatin, this is a gorgeous update on a classic.

Boon Fly Café

Americ

D4

4048 Sonoma Hwy. (at Los Carneros Ave.), Napa

Lunch & dinner daily

Phone: 707-299-4870
Web: www.thecarnerosinn.com
Prices: $$

Set amid the verdant pastures of the chic Carneros Inn, this rustic red barn is a friendly and unpretentious modern roadhouse, complete with a gracious staff. Fresh and well-made American standards include a classic Caesar with toasted onion, shaved parmesan, and anchovy vinaigrette; or a generous Margherita flatbread pizza layered with mozzarella, tomatoes, and Italian sausage. Quesadillas and burritos are good, too. Be sure to check the blackboard for daily specials.

Though it's open from breakfast to dinner, Boon Fly Café's most popular meal is brunch, when parties wait on porch swings for eggs Benedict with jalapeño hollandaise. Whether they're locals in the know about its relaxed charm or travelers seeking a break, everybody leaves with a smile.

Bottega

Italian ✕✕

F1

6525 Washington St. (near Yount St.), Yountville

Lunch Tue – Sun
Dinner nightly

Phone: 707-945-1050
Web: www.botteganapavalley.com
Prices: $$

Michael Chiarello is one of the original celebrity chefs, and his higher-end Napa outpost draws fans from around the globe seeking a glimpse of the *NapaStyle* star. Hopefuls are indeed likely to see him in the kitchen, drizzling olive oil on plates of creamy, almost liquid fresh burrata and marinated mushrooms; or pouring persimmon purée across thick slices of yellowfin tuna crudo. Even the wine list features his house blends, which pair nicely with pastas like whole-wheat *tagliarini* tossed in a pitch-perfect Bolognese.

Large and boisterous, Bottega's autumn-hued dining room welcomes crowds with comfy banquettes; find lovely outdoor seating by the firepit. A well-made tiramisu and espresso offer a fine *Italiano* end to the festivities.

Bouchon ♛

French 🍴🍴

F1

6534 Washington St. (at Yount St.), Yountville

Phone: 707-944-8037
Web: www.bouchonbistro.com
Prices: $$$

Lunch & dinner daily

Timeless French food is recreated with great regard for quality and technique at Thomas Keller's exuberant brasserie, set down the street from his iconic French Laundry. Complete with lush potted palms, polished brass, and enormous mirrors, this chic dining room is the spitting image of a Parisian bistro. A theatrical crowd uplifts the space with conviviality, and every lavish banquette or stool at the bustling bar is full. Always.

You'll want to grab a hunk of the supremely fresh, crusty epi baguette to pair with perfectly executed bistro classics, including *pâté de campagne*, which arrives glistening with richly flavored fat and accompanied by crunchy, sour cornichons as well as that essential smack of fiery mustard. A link of boudin blanc is draped beside a mound of intensely buttery pommes purée and topped with dried French prunes to render a divine balance between flavor and texture.

Desserts are the very definition of decadence, like a fire engine-red cocotte filled with piping-hot slices of Braeburn apple soaked in a syrupy-sweet caramel sauce and capped by a crunchy baked pecan streusel. You're unlikely to find better execution—or, for that matter, a more intent and unobtrusive staff—in town.

Bounty Hunter

American XX

B4

975 First St. (at Main St.), Napa

Phone: 707-226-3976
Web: www.bountyhunterwinebar.com
Prices: $$

Lunch & dinner daily

California cowboys will want to post up at downtown Napa's fun fusion of a barbecue joint and wine bar. Large and well-lit, with taxidermy hung from the brick walls, country music on the playlist, and a striking saloon-like façade, this is a cool and unpretentious hangout.

If you're not all tasted out, Bounty Hunter's "wine slingers" will be happy to recommend something from the list of wines by the glass—there are forty!—available as two ounce pours, a flight, or for purchase. As for the food, wildly flavorful dry-rubbed St. Louis-style ribs practically fall off the bone, and three house-made sauces provide plenty of pep. Delicious shrimp and scallop ceviche tostadas are a fun south-of-the-border option with zippy acidity and creamy avocado.

Brix

Californian XX

D3

7377 St. Helena Hwy. (at Washington St.), Napa

Phone: 707-944-2749
Web: www.brix.com
Prices: $$$

Lunch & dinner daily

This roadside gem overlooking the Mayacamas Mountains is almost as well-known for its extensive, 16-acre produce garden, vineyard, and sheltered terrace, as it is for its ultra-seasonal French and Italian cuisine. Dishes are eclectic and often refined as in beautifully crafted ricotta gnocchi cooked to a gentle gold in rosemary-browned butter, with creamy squash, plump Medjool dates, and almonds. The saffron and orange salmon arrives firm and pink with quail eggs, dill aïoli, and potato salad. An extensive Sunday brunch buffet highlights offerings from the wood-fired oven and charcoal grill.

The interior feels like a mountain ranch with stone walls, fireplaces, exposed beams, and chandeliers cleverly crafted from cutlery. Service is exceptional.

Bui Bistro

 Vietnamese ✗✗

B3

976 Pearl St. (bet. Main & West Sts.), Napa

Phone: 707-255-5417
Web: www.buibistro.com
Prices: 💰

Lunch & dinner Mon – Sat

Large and airy, Bui looks and feels like an upscale French bistro, rife with an Asian pantry serving Vietnamese cuisine— and so the fun begins! Clean-lined but not stark, the space contrasts olive-green walls with bright red booths and tall paper lanterns. Solo diners hit the bar for a chardonnay and plate of fried rice with well-seasoned tofu. Dishes like earthy banana flower with strips of tender chicken and cubes of juicy Bosc pear aren't Hanoi-authentic, but are tasty all the same. Purists might prefer the mild yet fragrant chicken curry, studded with lemongrass and ginger.

Delicious sautéed pea sprouts with olive oil and garlic are a favorite among vegetarians. For dessert, a Kaffir lime crème brulée underscores the fusion of the menu.

Ca'Momi

Italian ✗

C3

610 1st St. (at McKinstry St.), Napa

Phone: 707-257-4992
Web: www.camomienoteca.com
Prices: $$

Lunch & dinner daily

As if the Oxbow Public Market wasn't already teeming with temptation, this *enoteca*-meets-*pasticceria* is sure to grab your attention even before you've wandered twenty paces. The seating inside is housed within a private corner of the sprawling emporium, donning wrought-iron furniture and yellow-stained cabinetry. However, the spacious terrace is the best seat in the house.

Authenticity is the Italian menu's strong suit. From the listing, enjoy specialties highlighted by their region of provenance, such as a bowl of tagliatelle twirled with crushed fava beans, fresh mint, and lots of finely grated Pecorino Romano as prepared in Marche. The house pizza is certified Verace Pizza Napoletana, while slow-cooked items like poached beef tongue with salsa verde are also praise-worthy.

C Casa

Mexican ✗

C3

610 1st St. (at McKinstry St.), Napa

Phone: 707-226-7700
Web: www.myccasa.com
Prices: 💰

Lunch & dinner daily

With a long line that marks it as one of the top destinations in the busy Oxbow Public Market, C Casa may look like a fast-food joint, but it's got serious sustainability credentials—all the more impressive given the reasonable prices.

Unique tacos are made to order and filled with the likes of mahi mahi or ground buffalo, then topped with plenty of fresh vegetables and garlic aïoli. If pork tacos with smashed white beans, cilantro, guacamole, and romaine don't appeal, then check out the daily specials on the small boards above the griddle and stoves. They might include rotisserie chicken with a pile of crisp Caesar salad or a rich duck *tostada*. Throw in a Mexican coffee, fresh juice, or glass of local wine, and you'll still have cash left over.

Celadon

International ✗✗

B4

500 Main St., Ste. G (at 5th St.), Napa

Phone: 707-254-9690
Web: www.celadonnapa.com
Prices: $$

Lunch Mon – Fri
Dinner nightly

Housed in the historic Napa Mill complex on the banks of the Napa River, Celadon is named for the comforting shade of gray-green that permeates its dining room. Inside, small tables, a quaint bar, and framed family photos lend charm, while a heated outdoor atrium with a corrugated aluminum roof lets in natural light by day and serene flickers from the brick fireplace at night. Oversized bottles of wine can be found throughout the dining room.

Chef Greg Cole is a Napa fixture and his signature global cuisine ranges from a nice rendition of classic Caesar salad, to plump and gently seared *togarashi*-crusted diver scallops set over creamy mashed potatoes. Friendly service adds to the appeal, as does the wide selection of local wines.

Ciccio

E1

Italian Italian

6770 Washington St. (bet. Madison & Pedroni Sts.), Yountville

Phone: 707-945-1000
Web: www.ciccionapavalley.com
Prices: $$

Dinner Wed – Sun

A pleasant contrast to the sleek new spots around town, Ciccio's country-style curtains and slatted front porch are a ticket to another era. Its location (a wood-framed 1916-era grocery) could pass as some John Wayne film set, but Ciccio is more of a spaghetti Western, thanks to the focused Italian-influenced menu featuring a mega-rich pasta accented with fresh uni, crisp breadcrumbs, and a generous dose of cream. Segue from carbs to the bone-in pork chop with fennel gratin, but don't miss the remarkable signature Ciccio sponge cake, soaked in citrus liqueur and topped with grapefruit and orange.

With turn-of-the-century square footage, tables are a hot ticket here. Expect a wait for even a lowly bar stool, happily passed with a glass of local pinot.

Cindy's Backstreet Kitchen

F2

American 🍴

1327 Railroad Ave. (bet. Adams St. & Hunt Ave.), St. Helena

Phone: 707-963-1200
Web: www.cindysbackstreetkitchen.com
Prices: $$

Lunch & dinner daily

Owner Cindy Pawlcyn may be a nationally renowned chef, but a meal at Backstreet feels like dining in a friend's home—albeit a well-appointed one with great food. From a blossoming garden retreat to the capacious dining area, this space is warm and comfortable. If there's a wait, be sure to perch at the bar, where genial regulars are happy to welcome new diners to the fold.

The cooking is eclectic and ingredient-driven, from the pristine tomatoes in a "Vietnamese vinaigrette" with fish paste, lemongrass, and Thai basil, to the radishes, crisp arugula, and tender chicken in a creamy curried salad. Enjoy it all with an excellent glass of local Chardonnay, and save room for the tart lemon buttermilk pudding cake with raspberries and crème fraîche.

Cole's Chop House

Steakhouse ✗✗✗

B3

1122 Main St. (bet. 1st & Pearl Sts.), Napa

Phone: 707-224-6328   Dinner nightly
Web: www.coleschophouse.com
Prices: $$$$

Prime meat at prime prices is the modus operandi at Cole's, which gives diners their pick of deeply flavorful cuts like dry-aged California rib-eye or 21-day Chicago dry-aged New York strip. Faithful accompaniments like baked potatoes, creamed spinach, and crisp asparagus with Hollandaise round out the menu. Traditional desserts like a comforting Bourbon bread pudding or perfect sugar-crusted crème brûlée are a satisfying end to the meal. A selection of gutsy red wines, bourbons, and single-malt Scotches stand up to the steak.

In place of the clubby atmosphere of traditional steakhouses, Cole's (which shares ownership with nearby Celadon) is more refined, with a barn-like stone interior and cozy selection of booths and mezzanine tables inside.

Cook St. Helena ☺

Italian ✗✗

F3

1310 Main St. (bet. Adams St. & Hunt Ave.), St. Helena

Phone: 707-963-7088   Lunch & dinner daily
Web: www.cooksthelena.com
Prices: $$

An artistically lit antelope head hangs in this Italian haven on St. Helena's main drag. Random? Not really, when one considers how rare solid cooking and sane prices can be in this tony burg. The cozy space has two seating options: a gleaming marble counter as well as tables that stretch from front to back (the ones up front are lighter, airier, and more preferable).

The food is thoughtful and refined with a daily rotating risotto, house-stretched mozzarella and burrata, and glorious pastas like ricotta *fazoletti* with a deeply flavored Bolognese. Grilled octopus salad with potatoes, olives, and tomato dressing is boosted by prime ingredients and careful seasoning. The wine list tempts at dinner, but bloody Mary's are all the rage at brunch, and are also served at Cook Tavern next door.

Evangeline

American 🍴🍴

B1

1226 Washington St. (bet. 1st St. & Lincoln Ave.), Calistoga

Phone:	707-341-3131
Web:	www.evangelinenapa.com
Prices:	$$

Lunch & dinner daily

Jazzy New Orleans flair infuses every inch of this Southern charmer, which adds just a hint of spice to the easy Californian charm of quaint Calistoga. A trellised garden patio (a must-visit on a warm day) blooms with fragrant jasmine, while the cozy indoor dining room provides an intimate retreat complete with midnight-blue banquettes.

A collection of French bistro- Californian- and Cajun-inspired dishes abound on the approachable menu. Rich, creamy duck rillettes arrive with toasted baguette and red pepper jelly; shrimp etouffee is spicy and complex, its thick, dark roux coating a heap of fluffy white rice; and melt-in-your-mouth tarte Tatin slathered with locally made Three Twins vanilla ice cream is as good as any beignet.

FARM

Californian 🍴🍴🍴

D4

4048 Sonoma Hwy. (at Old Sonoma Rd.), Napa

Phone:	707-299-4882
Web:	www.thecarnerosinn.com
Prices:	$$$

Dinner Wed – Sun

In the compound of the Carneros Inn, FARM welcomes diners with a spacious outdoor lounge area complete with glowing fire pits. Inside, canoodling couples fill the cavernous and dimly lit dining room, which features soaring farmhouse ceilings, cozy banquettes, and a soundtrack of sultry lounge beats.

The restaurant sources many ingredients from its own half-acre garden, which shine in dishes like a bean soup bursting with heirloom specimens from Rancho Gordo and accompanied by a DIY topping bar of fried garlic, spiced croutons, and smoked almonds. A flaky salmon fillet is crowned with crushed mustard seeds and set atop creamy parsnip purée. For dessert, delicate peanut butter panna cotta has a fun twist—a sprinkling of deep-fried jelly cubes.

Farmstead ⓐ

Californian XX

F3

738 Main St. (at Charter Oak Ave.), St. Helena

Phone: 707-963-9181   Lunch & dinner daily
Web: www.longmeadowranch.com
Prices: $$

For a down-home (but still Napa-chic) alternative to the Cal-Ital wine country grind, follow your nose to this Long Meadow Ranch-owned farmhouse, whose intoxicating smoker is parked right in the front yard. The cathedral ceiling, old-school country music, and boisterous locals give Farmstead a permanent buzz; for quieter dining, hit the front terrace.
Dishes are laden with ranch-grown products (from veggies to olive oil), utilized in outstanding preparations like a wood-grilled artichoke with sauce *gribiche*, meatballs with caramelized onions and tomato marmalade, or a smoked chicken sandwich with avocado, sweet onion rings, and a side of herb-fried potatoes. Try the ranch's own wine, or splurge on a fancy bottle at a shockingly reasonable markup.

Goose & Gander

American XX

F3

1245 Spring St. (at Oak Ave.), St. Helena

Phone: 707-967-8779   Lunch & dinner daily
Web: www.goosegander.com
Prices: $$

This Napa Valley gastropub has gotten an infusion of life with the arrival of Meadowood alum, Howard Ko, who's upped the ambition level without sacrificing the fun. The much-praised burger remains a juicy knockout (complete with duck-fat fries!), but other dishes like grilled asparagus with a *brandade* fritter, poached egg, and smoked trout roe are worthy of equal attention.
Housed in a cottage-like structure just off the St. Helena highway, the Goose has a dark, gentleman's club-like feel with leather chairs, tufted banquettes, and an intimate downstairs bar that serves the full menu. Drinks are a big deal here (the booze list is referred to as a "bible"), so be sure to peruse the wide selection of cocktails—or sip a local vintage.

The French Laundry  🌸 🌸 🌸

E1

Contemporary ✕✕✕✕

6640 Washington St. (at Creek St.), Yountville

Phone: 707-944-2380
Web: www.frenchlaundry.com
Prices: $$$$

Lunch Fri – Sun
Dinner nightly

After more than 20 years of gracing every foodie's bucket list from here to Hong Kong, Thomas Keller's legendary Napa Valley destination still doesn't miss a beat—irrespective of being in the midst of change. And, what's not to love? Chef Keller pairs incredibly technical cooking with wildly fresh and seasonal ingredients in a dreamy wine country setting. It's a perfect storm of restaurant greatness—and we should all be so lucky to score a reservation here in our lifetime.

Located in scenic Yountville, along a shady, bucolic, and winding road, the restaurant is the picture of countryside charm, with creeping ivy arching up its quaint stone exterior and a homey dining room set with elegant dishware.

There are two seasonal, nine-course tasting menus to choose from, including a vegetarian option. Dinner might kick off with the restaurant's signature oysters, paired with gleaming white sturgeon caviar pooled in a warm sabayon studded with tapioca pearls; before moving on to golden striped bass with deconstructed deviled eggs. Other treasures include unctuous pork belly set over creamy, spiced Rancho Gordo beans; or tender veal, paired with tomato-infused béarnaise sauce and a spectacular summer corn salad bursting with cherry tomato, chanterelle mushrooms, and a basil-scented cake.

Grace's Table

International ✗✗

A4

1400 2nd St. (at Franklin St.), Napa

Phone: 707-226-6200
Web: www.gracestable.net
Prices: **$$**

Lunch & dinner daily

Around the world in four courses without leaving wine country? It's possible at this bright, contemporary downtown Napa space that balances fun with excellence. Only here can a top-notch tamale filled with chipotle pulled pork, green chile, and black beans be followed by cassoulet that would do any Frenchman proud—thanks to its decadent mélange of butter beans, duck confit, and two kinds of sausage.

With Italian and American staples in the mix as well, it might sound too eclectic for one meal, but Grace's Table earns its name with charming service and a thoughtful, well-priced wine list to bridge any gaps between cuisines. Don't miss the satiny ganache-layered devil's food chocolate cake—a slice is big enough to split, and a winner in any tongue.

Harvest Table

Californian ✗✗

C2

1 Main St. (bet. Lewelling Ln. & Sulphur Springs Ave.), St. Helena

Phone: 707-967-4695
Web: www.harvesttablenapa.com
Prices: **$$$**

Lunch Wed – Sun
Dinner Tue – Sat

Charlie Palmer's Harvest Inn is now also a culinary destination with the arrival of Harvest Table. Its Californian menu relies on local purveyors and the Inn's own gardens for ingredients, and guests are encouraged to tour these grounds before or after meals. The space is simple and appealingly rustic thanks in part to the large brick fireplace. Two covered patios offer a comfy perch to enjoy the natural beauty of the inn.

Smooth dark wood tables can be seen groaning under the weight of such enjoyable items as crunchy pig's head fritters coupled with a light frisée salad and creamy *gribiche*. Batons of yellowfin are then crowned with shaved fennel for balance in texture as well as pickled Fresno chilies for that bit of heat. A sweet-salty peanut butter bar topped with a thin layer of chocolate should be saved (read savored) for the end.

JoLē

American ✕✕

B1

1457 Lincoln Ave. (bet. Fair Way & Washington St.), Calistoga

Phone: 707-942-5938   Dinner nightly
Web: www.jolerestaurant.com
Prices: $$

Calistoga's charming downtown brings you JoLē, which is located inside the Mount View Hotel and Spa, but can also be accessed via a separate entrance on Lincoln Avenue. The dining room offers several prix-fixe menus full of fresh, contemporary food. A meal might start with a bright salad of heirloom tomatoes, gypsy peppers, and blue cheese; before shifting to tender potato gnocchi with pesto, cherry tomatoes, and ricotta. Exquisite cheeses and desserts, like a frozen chocolate pistachio nougat with orange crème anglaise, are part of the package.

Done in calming, earthy colors, the dining room boasts a cheeky egg theme, with framed rows of ceramic egg cartons and a central eggshell painting. The newly expanded bar seating sets the scene, and the well-chosen wine selection aids enjoyment.

La Taquiza

Mexican ✕

E3

2007 Redwood Rd., Ste. 104 (at Solano Ave.), Napa

Phone: 707-224-2320   Lunch & dinner Mon – Sat
Web: www.lataquizanapa.com
Prices:

For sustainable *sabor* that doubles as a budget-saver in pricey Napa, La Taquiza's upscale take on Mexican fast food is well worth a visit. Whether you prefer your fish California-style (flame-grilled) or Baja-style (battered and fried), you'll find no end to spicy, tangy, and savory options, available in heat levels from mild to spicy and in configurations from tacos to burritos to rice bowls.

However, the adventurous shouldn't stop at crisp corn tortillas—there's also a fine selection of snappy ceviches, grilled octopus, beer-battered oysters, and other delights from the sea. Counter service is friendly and prompt, and massive, colorful paintings from a local artist give the room a vibe almost as bright as their delicious strawberry *agua fresca*.

La Toque ⌘

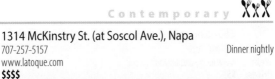

B3

1314 McKinstry St. (at Soscol Ave.), Napa

Phone:	707-257-5157	Dinner nightly
Web:	www.latoque.com	
Prices:	$$$$	

Wine Country ▶ Napa Valley

You'll want to tip your own toque in appreciation after a luxurious meal at this downtown Napa palace of fine dining, which blends a serious approach to cuisine and service with just enough cheeky touches to keep things lively.

Housed on the grounds of the Westin Verasa Napa, La Toque may boast an oversized inflatable chef's hat hanging above its walkway, but it's the soul of modern sophistication inside, with rich, leather-topped tables, a flickering fireplace, and an extensive wine list—proffered on an iPad. Service is particularly notable, and the well-trained, knowledgeable staff moves in perfect synchronicity amongst a dressed-up crowd of diners savoring special occasions.

Choose from a four- or five-course à la carte menu, with exquisite offerings like hand-rolled cavatelli in a deep green nettle pesto or luscious seafood congee packed with Dungeness crab and woodsy matsutake mushrooms. The trio of lamb is a real highlight, boasting slow-cooked collar, succulent merguez sausage, and moist, juicy loin. For dessert, a creamy semifreddo in apple broth is the perfect conclusion: like the restaurant itself, it's equal parts glamorous, homey, and exceptionally delicious.

Lucy

Californian ✗✗

F1

6526 Yount St. (bet. Finnell Rd. & Mulberry St.), Yountville

Phone: 707-204-6030   Lunch & dinner daily
Web: www.lucyrestaurantandbar.com
Prices: $$$

If you're not staying at the posh Bardessono hotel, come early for a glass of chardonnay and a stroll through the lovely gardens, which provide much of the food for this chic on-site restaurant. Savvy diners can keep the outdoorsy vibe going with a seat on the fountain-accented front terrace, where an afternoon can be happily spent exploring the wine list, heavy on local producers.

Lucy's food is refreshing and casual, with a few fun touches. First, a creamy chilled pea soup is amped up with the addition of yuzu crème fraîche and chunks of meaty lobster, while a spicy rhubarb-and-pineapple chutney electrifies the perfectly seared diver scallops, accompanied by peppery watercress and caramelized fennel. A rich, buttery, and delicious pound cake paired with grapefruit sorbet is a fresh finish worth savoring.

Mango on Main

Thai ✗

B3

1142 Main St. (bet. 1st & Pearl Sts.), Napa

Phone: 707-253-8880   Lunch Tue – Sat
Web: www.mangoonmain.com   Dinner Tue – Sun
Prices: ⊛⊛

Local Thai favorite Mango on Main has made a mega move to a surprisingly lovely, light-filled space in downtown Napa. (If you see the confusing "Bangkok Street" sign out front, you've come to the right place.) Inside, the gleaming kitchen, soft, clubby music, and paper parasols hanging from the ceiling add to the bright, airy feel.

Though this charming retreat's cuisine isn't wholly authentic, there's no denying its deliciousness. Highlights include deep-fried spring rolls stuffed with minced pork and shrimp and topped with a sticky plum sauce, and springy Siam egg noodles tossed with Dungeness crab, shiitake mushrooms, and peanut sauce. You'd be smart to keep space for dessert; the deep-fried Nutella-filled wontons are an outright sinful conclusion.

Market

American XX

F3

1347 Main St. (bet. Adams St. & Hunt Ave.), St. Helena

Phone:	707-963-3799
Web:	www.marketsthelena.com
Prices:	$$

Lunch & dinner daily

St. Helena's scenic main drag is a trip back to the '50s, complete with quaint shops and an old-school movie theater. But, the food at this legendary downtown fixture is happily modern. Lobster rolls forgo buttered buns for Vietnamese-inspired rice paper with avocado and mango (all dipped in a delicious cilantro-basil-lime sauce); while a seared steak sandwich, loaded with onion and jack cheese, gets a spark from pickled jalapeño. Childhood-inspired s'mores for dessert end the meal on a nostalgic and graceful note.

The massive mahogany bar (a magnificent eBay find) is the heart of the pleasant space, which boasts stone-covered walls and big, open windows for prime people-watching. Service is friendly and fuss-free, not unlike its picturesque surrounds.

Mustards Grill

American XX

D3

7399 St. Helena Hwy. (at Hwy. 29), Yountville

Phone:	707-944-2424
Web:	www.mustardsgrill.com
Prices:	$$

Lunch & dinner daily

At Cindy Pawlcyn's iconic roadhouse, it's a joy to eat your greens. Lettuces are freshly plucked from the restaurant's bountiful garden boxes and tossed with tasty dressings including a shallot- and Dijon mustard-spiked Banyuls vinaigrette. Fish of the day may unveil grilled halibut sauced with oxtail reduction and plated with silken leeks, fingerling potatoes, and baby carrots. But, save room as this is not the place to skip dessert, and the lemon-lime tart capped with brown sugar meringue that is fittingly described on the menu as "ridiculously tall," doesn't disappoint.

It should come as no surprise that there's usually a wait for a table here. But no matter; use the time to take a stroll on the grounds for a preview of what the kitchen has in store.

Norman Rose Tavern

A m e r i c a n ✗✗

A4

1401 1st St. (at Franklin St.), Napa

Phone: 707-258-1516
Web: www.normanrosenapa.com
Prices: $$

Lunch & dinner daily

Right in the heart of downtown Napa, this appealing gastropub offers something for everyone, from hearty bacon-wrapped meatloaf with a smoky coffee-barbecue glaze, to satisfying and soul-warming vegetable soup. Burgers, salads, and even a menu of dressed-up fries (from chili-cheese, truffle-parmesan and sausage gravy to cheddar "disco" fries) are both appealing and affordable.

The open, wood-beamed space with its rich leather banquettes and soft lighting, is ideal for both a beer-soaked game at the bar or group dinners in the bustling dining room. Solo diners will enjoy well-lit perches that peer into the kitchen, and charming servers are more than adept at keeping the party going until the last wedge of decadent, triple-layered carrot cake is devoured.

Oenotri

I t a l i a n ✗✗

A4

1425 1st St. (bet. Franklin & School Sts.), Napa

Phone: 707-252-1022
Web: www.oenotri.com
Prices: $$

Lunch Sat – Sun
Dinner nightly

There's no sweeter greeting than the aroma of wood smoke that beckons diners into this downtown standout. And with its Neapolitan pizza oven, sunny textiles, and exposed brick, Oenotri—from an ancient Italian word for "wine cultivator"—looks as good as it smells.

Chef/owner Tyler Rodde imbues the cooking of Southern Italy with a dash of Californian spirit and the resulting cuisine is nothing short of enticing. Options change with the season, but true fans know that pizza is a must. Mixed chicory salad with *mozzarella di bufala*, pickled red chilies, and house-cured *salametto* is also a crowd-pleaser. Not far behind the *torchio* or corkscrew pasta is presented with diced roasted winter squash, toasted pine nuts, fried sage, and a drizzle of brown butter.

Press

Steakhouse XXX

C2

587 St. Helena Hwy. (near Inglewood Ave.), St. Helena

Phone: 707-967-0550
Web: www.presssthelena.com
Prices: $$$$

Dinner Wed – Mon

It's hard to get more wine country-chic than this gorgeous farmhouse-inspired restaurant, perfectly situated along the St. Helena highway, for wrapping up a day of wine tasting. With a wood-burning fireplace, soaring ceilings, and rich leather chairs, it's a genuine looker, drawing an affluent crowd of tourists to relax and savor some great *vino*.

The casual yet chic vibe extends to the steakhouse menu, where gorgeous grass-fed bavettes and buttery filet mignons can be seen on nearly every table. You'll definitely want to order some of the generously portioned sides, like earthy brown butter mushrooms or caramelized Brussels sprouts with bacon, which can easily feed four. Velvety sunchoke soup with walnut yogurt is yet another exquisite addition.

Redd

Contemporary XX

F2

6480 Washington St. (at Oak Circle), Yountville

Phone: 707-944-2222
Web: www.reddnapavalley.com
Prices: $$$$

Lunch Wed – Mon
Dinner nightly

In this quaint hamlet, Redd stands out both for its modern look and contemporary approach to cuisine, with flavors from around the globe. A meal here might begin with Chinese-style lettuce cups filled with succulent chicken, stir-fried eggplant, and fresh herbs; then veer into India and Spain simultaneously via a Petrale sole fillet with coconut-jasmine rice, curry-saffron broth, and salty-spicy chorizo. And any Londoner would be proud of the buttery sticky toffee pudding, with tart crème fraîche ice cream and huckleberries. The sleek, modernist décor attracts a sedate crowd, attended to by professional servers. On nice days, be sure not to miss the serene outdoor patio, which begs to be savored with a glass of Joseph George sauvignon blanc from Yountville.

Redd Wood

Italian ✕✕

E1

6755 Washington St. (bet. Madison & Pedroni Sts.), Yountville

Phone: 707-299-5030   Lunch & dinner daily
Web: www.redd-wood.com
Prices: $$

Napa's answer to the hip Cal-Ital hot spots of San Francisco, Redd Wood boasts an edgy indie soundtrack and a parade of bearded, tattooed waiters. But unlike some cityside establishments, the staff here is personable and enthusiastic, and there's plenty of breathing room (including a private area that's popular for events).

Artisan pizzas are the main draw, like a sassy spin on "eggplant parm" with *coppa*, basil, crispy breadcrumbs, and fried garlic. But don't let that limit your choices, as the house-cured *salumi*, fresh pastas, and alluring antipasti (think chilled corn soup with house bacon and pickled chanterelles) are also winners. Just be sure to save some room for the outstanding toffee cannoli as they are some of the best you'll ever have.

Rutherford Grill

American ✕✕

D2

1180 Rutherford Rd. (at Hwy. 29), Rutherford

Phone: 707-963-1792   Lunch & dinner daily
Web: www.hillstone.com
Prices: $$

As the crowds filter out of neighboring Beaulieu Vineyards and other Highway 29 wineries, they head straight to this upscale chain, which boasts long lines at even the earliest hours. Kudos to the amiable host staff for handling them smoothly. The dark wood interior is clubby yet accommodating, and a large patio offers drinks for waiting diners.

Every portion here can easily serve two, beginning with a seasonal vegetable platter boasting buttery Brussels sprouts, a wild rice salad, and braised red cabbage. For those looking to stave off tasting-induced hangovers, the steak and enchilada platter is *the* ticket with plenty of juicy tri-tip, yellow and red *escabeche* sauce, and a poached egg. A wedge of classic banana cream pie delivers the knockout punch.

The Restaurant at Meadowood ✿ ✿ ✿

Contemporary ✗✗✗✗

C2

900 Meadowood Ln. (off Silverado Trail), St. Helena

Phone:	707-967-1205	Dinner Mon – Sat
Web:	www.therestaurantatmeadowood.com	
Prices:	$$$$	

Located in a sprawling verdant resort amid mountains and vineyards, Meadowood is the peak of wine country-chic. The bar and lounge resemble a plush mountain lodge, thanks to fireplaces, vintage books, and soft leather seating. Their extraordinary dining room boasts a lovely backlit vaulted ceiling over tables made from granite and columns of Canadian redwood. Every detail conveys American beauty and grace; service is usually faultless, anticipatory, and adept.

Chef Christopher Kostow's cuisine is not only stunning to behold but thoroughly delicious. Sample a ring of buttery Gwen avocado enhanced with Rancho Chimiles walnut oil and containing a perfectly chilled oyster as well as a few sea beans for exquisite crunch and flavor. Next, chunks of silky and translucent lobster are paired with crispy, sweet chestnuts and lemony purslane for a decadent study in texture, and work as a perfect foil to a simple yet sublime duck tea (a clear yet intense broth) with nothing but a few dill fronds for finish.

For dessert, silken chocolate custard with a potent dark chocolate sauce, fudgy dates, and sweet roasted chocolate panettone is a hauntingly complex pleasure on a plate.

Sam's Social Club

American **XX**

B1

1712 Lincoln Ave. (at Indian Springs Resort), Calistoga

Phone: 707-942-4913   Lunch & dinner daily
Web: www.samssocialclub.com
Prices: **$$**

Despite its historic Spanish colonial look, this easygoing restaurant at Calistoga's Indian Springs Resort is actually a newcomer. Named for resort founder Samuel Brannan, it boasts a sizable lounge full of comfortable couches and bright murals, a Mission Revival dining room with a stylish country-Western vibe, and a big patio, complete with a geyser-fed water feature.

The unpretentious atmosphere extends to the plates, from a lively gazpacho made from fresh local tomatoes and endowed with plenty of jalapeño bite to a delectable seared chicken paillard with rosemary Hollandaise as well as a potato-and-green bean salad. Napa tourists have already caught on: you'll find them happily sharing bottles of wine and digging into plates of strawberry-rhubarb crisp.

The Farmer & The Fox

Gastropub **XX**

C1

3111 St. Helena Hwy. N. (near Bea Ln.), St. Helena

Phone: 707-302-5101   Dinner nightly
Web: www.farmerandfox.com
Prices: **$$**

The sprawling Cairdean Estate encompasses a winery, tasting room, bakery, and this classed-up take on an English pub, featuring a fully loaded cocktail bar and wide selection of craft beers. With a black-and-white checkered floor, dark wood paneling, burgundy leather booths, and glass partitions between tables, it has an enticingly clubby vibe.

Expect creative versions of public-house favorites, from a nightly roast to a rich grass-fed burger on a golden brioche bun, accompanied by thick-cut "proper chips" dusted with vinegar powder. Dark, dense Scottish beer bread is laced with ribbons of silky house-cured salmon and wispy shavings of cucumber, while a buttery salted caramel-apple mille-feuille hits the dessert bull's-eye.

Solbar ⁂

Californian XX

B1

755 Silverado Trail (at Rosedale Rd.), Calistoga

Phone: 707-226-0850   Lunch & dinner daily
Web: www.solagecalistoga.com
Prices: $$$

It may take a few twists and turns around the palatial Solage Calistoga property to locate Solbar, but once inside, you'll find that a recent décor overhaul has it looking fresher and more sophisticated than ever. The dining room now features high-backed gray banquettes perfect for romance-seeking couples, and a contemporary fireplace still adds flickering warmth.

Well-heeled wine country tourists flock to the beautiful outdoor patio to dine under a canopy of palms and twinkling lights, while larger groups should consider another of Solbar's new additions: the glassed-in Chef's Atrium, which offers a private five-course chef's menu for parties of up to ten.

While its look is updated, Solbar's culinary focus hasn't changed: it still offers Californian cuisine at its finest, with ultra-local produce accented by globe-trotting influences, like an inspired Mexican appetizer of grilled gulf prawns, pickled nopales, fork-tender carnitas, and yellow *mole*. The lightly crusted red snapper comes bathed in a saffron soubise, with heavenly Yukon gold gnocchi and roasted red kale sprouts beneath. And the rum and butterscotch pudding, topped with amaretti cookies, is a buttery delight of a dessert.

335

Terra ⁂

Wine Country ▶ Napa Valley

F2

1345 Railroad Ave. (bet. Adams St. & Hunt Ave.), St. Helena

Phone: 707-963-8931
Dinner Thu – Mon
Web: www.terrarestaurant.com
Prices: $$$

Serious and mature yet understated, Terra is quaintly tucked away in a 19th century building known as The Hatchery (because it really was a hatchery). The décor embraces its rustic past with an eye on luxury, through floor-to-ceiling wine racks, exposed stone, and chunky wood beams. The resulting look is decidedly more old-world European than 21st century wine country.

The kitchen's distinct personality is evident in each seasonally driven menu, ranging from four to six courses of Japanese and Mediterranean-influenced cuisine. Begin with a daily crudo, perhaps featuring slices of tuna loin drizzled with soy and yuzu over thinly shaved cucumber, radish, hijiki, and yuzu tobiko. Follow this with short, chewy strands of fresh *umbricelli* lightly tossed with pork sugo and earthy black truffles, garnished with frills of pan-roasted maitake mushrooms. Highlights include salty-sweet sake marinated cod fillet presented alongside a single shrimp dumpling in a shallow bowl of dark, tart broth hinting of shiso and ginger.

For dessert, try the wedge of *gâteau mille crêpes* stacked with vanilla pastry cream, citrus segments, and fresh mint chiffonade beneath a crisp brûlée sugar crust.

The Pear

Southern ✗✗

B4

720 Main St. (at 3rd St.), Napa

Phone: 707-256-3900
Web: www.rodneyworth.com
Prices: $$

Lunch & dinner daily

The Pear is the brainchild of celebrated chef, Rodney Worth. He continues his love affair with Southern food at this Napa outpost, rife with stunning views of the promenade and river, a pristine exposed kitchen, and large dark wood tables. Speaking of *amour*, the Blues play in the background, further enhancing this sense of romance—look for the trumpet, violin, and saxophone, all hanging on pistachio-hued walls.

Generous portions of great food including a creamy crab dip crusted with parmesan and studded with baby artichokes plays into the Southern bent. Gumbo *ya-ya* is an intensely flavorful stock bobbing with chicken and seasoned with andouille, tomato, and garlic. Bourbon-glazed baby back ribs with crushed peanuts evoke Louisiana in all its glory.

Torc

American ✗✗

B3

1140 Main St. (bet. 1st & Pearl Sts.), Napa

Phone: 707-252-3293
Web: www.torcnapa.com
Prices: $$

Dinner nightly

Torc may be Gaelic for "boar," but the food from Chef Sean O'Toole (who boasts the aforementioned boar on his family crest) is definitely not Irish. The large menu offers dishes with globe-trotting influences: Italian-leaning gnocchi with peas and favas; swordfish with artichokes and calamari; as well as a free-range roast chicken for two are some of his signatures. Classic desserts include a highly refined milk-chocolate caramel bar, and the wines are great too—look to the warm and genuine staff to recommend a well-priced bottle from the moderately-sized list.

As for the ambience, the former Ubuntu space remains quite the looker with its exposed brick walls, highly coveted banquettes (complete with views of the open kitchen), and industrial-barn vibe.

Tra Vigne

Italian ✗✗

F3

1050 Charter Oak Ave. (off Hwy. 29), St. Helena

Phone:	707-963-4444	Lunch & dinner daily
Web:	www.travignerestaurant.com	
Prices:	$$$	

Cal-Italian cuisine got its start with Chef/owner Michael Chiarello and this Napa grand-dame remains a tourist favorite. The vine-covered stone exterior could have been plucked out of Umbria, were it not for the surprisingly timeless, airy, light-filled dining room it contains. Service is less appealing, heavy on suggestions and smiles that wow the tour-bus crowds but may disappoint others.

The cadre of servers will push the mozzarella *al minuto*, memorable and famous in its own right, but find more modern offerings like enticingly chewy, palate-awakening kale and farro salad. Pasta courses may feature black tagliatelle with Meyer lemon, *bottarga*, and poached tuna. Worthy entrées include pan-seared wild cod over tender artichoke hearts.

Wine Spectator Greystone

Californian ✗✗

C2

2555 Main St. (at Deer Park Rd.), St. Helena

Phone:	707-967-1010	Lunch & dinner Tue – Sat
Web:	www.ciarestaurants.com	
Prices:	$$$	

The kitchen is the classroom at the Culinary Institute of America's West Coast training restaurant, housed (along with the school) in the former Christian Brothers château. The big, visually impressive room—with stone walls, copper lighting, and display of oversized spoons and whisks—is a comfortable perch in which to watch students at work in the open kitchen.

Dishes are conceived and prepared using local and seasonal ingredients with global influences. Though the menu may change daily, expect the likes of roast quail, moist with lightly crisped skin, served with carrot-parsnip purée and squash ribbons. Swordfish arrives fresh and meaty, accompanied by lemon risotto and a bisque-like sea urchin broth packed with flavor.

Zuzu

829 Main St. (bet. 2nd & 3rd Sts.), Napa

Phone: 707-224-8555	Lunch Mon – Fri
Web: www.zuzunapa.com	Dinner nightly
Prices: $$	

B4

This Mediterranean-inspired cutie was dishing out small plates long before it was cool, and its rustic bi-level space still draws a steady crowd of local regulars. Spanish-style tile floors, a pressed-tin ceiling, and honey-colored walls give Zuzu an enchanting old-world vibe, setting the scene for sharing the more than two dozen tapas, both *frio* (cold) and *caliente* (hot).

They include the popular *boquerónes*, grilled bread heaped with aïoli, hard-boiled eggs, and cured anchovies, as well as the outstanding pork cheek—its rich, caramelized flavor balanced by a tart sherry gastrique. In the evening, killer wood-fired paellas are worth saving a slot for.

For similar cuisine in a more modern atmosphere, sister restaurant La Taberna is also worth a visit.

Wine Country ▶ Napa Valley

Your opinions are important to us. Please write to us directly at: michelin.guides@ us.michelin.com

WINE & DINE

Bordering the North Bay, Sonoma County boasts around 76 miles of Pacific coastline and over 250 wineries. Eclipsed as a wine region by neighboring Napa Valley, this area's wineries know how to take full advantage of some of California's best grape-growing conditions. Today, thirteen distinct wine appellations (AVAs) have been assigned in this area, which is slightly larger than the state of Rhode Island itself, and produce a groundbreaking range of fine wines. But, this county is also cherished for its culinary destinations starting with **The Naked Pig**, an amazing pit-stop for brunch or lunch. Reinforcing the wine country's ethos of farm-to-table dining, the items on offer here ooze with all things local and sustainable—maybe savory leek waffles with SCMC bacon and Point Reyes blue cheese? But, there are plenty of big and bold bites to be had in town. **Bar-B-Que Smokehouse** in Sebastopol is quite literally award-winning, when their 'cue took home the crown at the **Sonoma County Harvest Fair** in 2010. Other premium pleasures include **Screamin' Mimi's**, a local but nationally known ice cream shop that has been preparing its 300-plus recipes since 1995, as well as **Moustache Baked Goods**, a boutique operation churning out exceptional, all-American baked goods with quirky names. In fact, cupcakes

(like The Outlaw or The Vitner?) have been known to cultivate a sizable following. The North American headquarters of the South American energy-boosting beverage line, **Guayaki Yerba Mate Cafe**, is also settled here as a café-cum-community center, while **The National Heirloom Exposition**, is commended among epicureans for its sustainable farming and healthy food practices.

Along Highway 12 heading north, byroads lead to isolated wineries, each of which puts its own unique stamp on the business of winemaking. Named after the river that enabled Russian trading outposts along the coast, **The Russian River Valley** is one of the coolest growing regions in Sonoma, largely due to the river basin that acts as a conduit for coastal climates. At the upper end of the Russian River, **Dry Creek Valley** yields excellent sauvignon blanc, chardonnay, and pinot noir. This region is also justifiably famous for zinfandel, a grape that does especially well in the valley's rock-strewn soil. And for snacks to go with these notable sips, the town's eight-acre plaza is occupied by restaurants, shops, and more. Of epicurean note is building contractor Chuck Williams who bought a hardware store here in 1956. He gradually converted its stock to unique French cookware and kitchen tools, and today, **Williams-Sonoma** has over 200 stores nationwide. Following in his footsteps, **Bram** is beloved for sleek and handmade earthenware inspired by the Egyptian clay pots of yore. Located on the same square, **Sign of the Bear** is another specialty shop and essential stop for all types of table- and kitchen-ware.

BEST IN LIFE

Throughout scenic and bucolic Sonoma County (also known locally as SoCo), vineyards rub shoulders with orchards and farms. The words "sustainable" and "organic" headline these local farmer's markets, where one may find every item imaginable—from just-picked heirloom vegetables to uni so fresh that it still appears to be moving. Communal bliss is the name of the game at **Epicurean Connection**, a specialty shop-cum-café featuring evening music events for the community. In business since 2010, **Petaluma Pie Co.** keeps picky palates sated and happy with both sweet and savory pies crafted from organic ingredients. And over on Petaluma Blvd., find a cult of carb fans collect at **Della Fattoria** for an amazing selection of just-baked bread.

This very fertile territory also has flaunts than a just fair share of fresh seafood. In fact, some of the best oysters can be found off of the Sonoma coast and enthusiasts drive along Highway 1 to sample as many as varieties as possible—from **Tomales Bay Oyster Company** and **The Marshall Store**, to **Hog Island Oyster Company**. Of course, there is more than just mollusks to be relished here. Start your day right with a serious

breakfast at **The Fremont Diner** where the Bellwether Farms ricotta pancakes are light, fluffy, and of course, regionally sourced. Quench these hearty eats at local sensation **Bear Republic Brewing Company Pub & Restaurant**—a family-owned Healdsburg hot spot favored for unique, award-winning brews and tours (by appointment only); or over a top-notch IPA, which are all the rage at **Lagunitas Brewing Co.**, a taproom for the Petaluma-based brewery. And what goes best with beer? Small bites of course, with an enticing lineup of authentically prepared, globally inspired fare at roadside stall extraordinaire— **The Secret Kitchen**. Meals here are composed of fresh herbs, spices, succulent grilled meats, and locally sourced fruits and vegetables. They're usually ready to go at a moment's notice, so peruse the menu beforehand and enjoy its benevolence later.

Numerous ethnic food stands bring global cuisines to this wine-centric community, with offerings that have their roots as close as Mexico and far off as India or Afghanistan. Thanks to Sonoma County's natural bounty, farm-to-table cuisine takes on new heights in many of its surrounding restaurants and some chefs need go no farther than their own on-site gardens for fresh fruits, vegetables, and herbs. With such easy access to local products like Dungeness crab from Bodega Bay, poultry from Petaluma, and cheeses from the **Sonoma Cheese Factory**, it's no wonder that the Californian cuisine here has attracted such high-levels of national attention. Serious home gardeners should make sure to scour the shelves of **Petaluma Seed Bank**, located in the historic Sonoma County Bank Building, as it happily counts motivated farmers among its clientele. Find them along with a host of other visitors rejoicing at the Bank's selection of over 1500 heirloom seeds, after which a scoop or slice from stylish **Noble Folk Ice Cream & Pie Bar** seems perfectly in order. Finally, both area residents as well as tourists in town can't seem to get enough of the local, hand-crafted bounty found inside the original **Powell's Sweet Shoppe** in Windsor. This old-fashioned candy store carries an impressive spectrum of old-world classics, modern (gluten-free) items, and "sweet gift boxes" that are big during the holidays. Walk in, pick up a pail, and start filling up! If that doesn't result in a sugar rush, there's no going wrong with a scoop of creamy gelato.

SHED

HealdsburgShed.com

OPEN WED-MON: 8AM-7PM CL

= COFFEE BAR =
Ban Tan
Breakfast Pastries
Cookies and Ice Cream

= CAFE =
~Breakfas
8-11AM

~Lunch-
11:30AM-3
changing M

= FERMENTATION BAR =
Local Wines, Beers,
Kombuchas and other
Fermented Beverages,
Afternoon Savories,
Flatbreads Charcuterie
and Cheese Plates

~Brunch
Saturday-S
8AM-3

= LARDER & PANTRY =
Farmhouse Cheeses, Charcuterie,
Vinegars, Freshly Milled Flours, Arti
Breads, Local Produce, Prepared Food

HOUSEWARES
Traditional Wares Focusing on S
Cooking and Food Preservatio

= FARM & GARDEN =
Quality Tools, Supplies and

= COMMUNITY & PRIVATE =
Workshops, Classes, Sunday
Private Events & Tasting

= 25 NORTH ST. 707-4

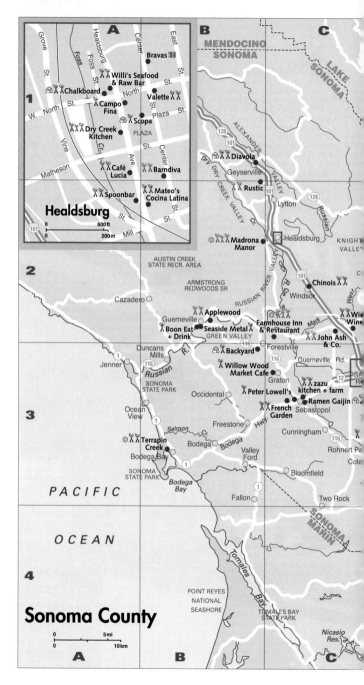

Healdsburg

A
- Bravas
- Willi's Seafood & Raw Bar
- Chalkboard
- Campo Fina
- Valette
- Scopa
- Dry Creek Kitchen
- Café Lucia
- Barndiva
- Spoonbar
- Mateo's Cocina Latina

Sonoma County

MENDOCINO
SONOMA

LAKE
SONOMA

ALEXANDER VALLEY

Diavola

Geyserville

Rustic

Lytton

DRY CREEK VALLEY

Madrona Manor

Healdsburg

KNIGHTS VALLEY

AUSTIN CREEK STATE RECR. AREA

ARMSTRONG REDWOODS SR

Cazadero

Chinois

Windsor

RUSSIAN RIVER VALLEY

Applewood

Guerneville

Boon Eat + Drink

Seaside Metal

GREEN VALLEY

Farmhouse Inn & Restaurant

Wine

John Ash & Co.

Duncans Mills

Backyard

Forestville

Jenner

Russian

SONOMA STATE PARK

Willow Wood Market Cafe

Guerneville Rd.

Graton

Ocean View

Occidental

Peter Lowell's

zazu kitchen + farm

Ramen Gaijin

French Garden

Sebastopol

Freestone

Cunningham

Terrapin Creek

Bodega

Bodega

Valley Ford

Bodega Bay

Bloomfield

SONOMA STATE PARK

Bodega Bay

Fallon

Two Rock

PACIFIC

SONOMA
MARIN

OCEAN

POINT REYES NATIONAL SEASHORE

TOMALES BAY STATE PARK

Rohnert Park

Cotati

Nicasio Res.

Sonoma County

0   5mi
0   10km

344

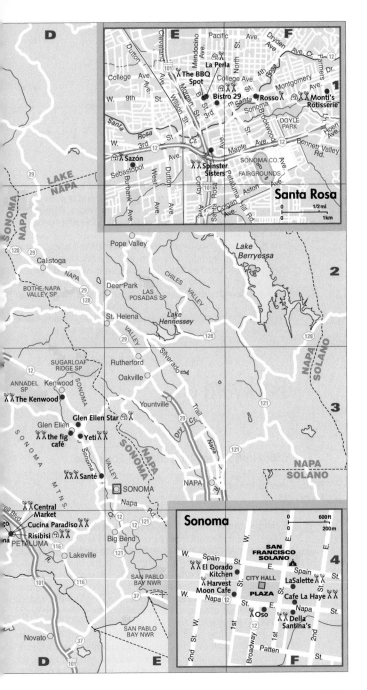

Santa Rosa

D · E · F

Cleveland · Pacific · Ave. · Dryden · Ave. Cr. · 12 · Parmers · Dr.

Dutton · E · Mendocino · Ave. · North · St. · 4th · St. · Montgomery · Santa · Rosa

101 · College · Ave. · ✗✗ La Perla · College Ave.

W. · 9th · St. · Wilson St. · B St. · 3rd St. · Madgen St. · ✗✗ The BBQ Spot · ● Bistro 29 · m · Santa · ● Rosso ✗ · ✗✗ ● Monti's Rotisserie

Santa · Rosa · St. · Sonoma · Brookwood · St. · DOYLE PARK

W. · Rosa · St. · Cr. · 12 · Maple · Ave. · 12 · Bennett Valley Rd.

3rd · Ave. · SONOMA CO. · Hoen Ave.

Sebastopol · Dutton · West · ✗ Sazón · Corby · Ave. · Petaluma · Hill · Rd. · Aston · Ave. · FAIRGROUNDS

Burbank · Ave. · Ave. · 101 · ✗✗ ● Spinster Sisters · Santa Rosa · Colgan · Ave.

Santa Rosa

0 _____ 1/2mi
0 _____ 1km

29 · NAPA · LAKE

SONOMA · NAPA

128 · 29 · ○ Calistoga

NAPA · ○ Pope Valley · Lake Berryessa · 2

BOTHE-NAPA VALLEY SP · 29 · 128 · ○ Deer Park · CHILES VALLEY

St. Helena · LAS POSADAS SP · Lake Hennessey · 128

SUGARLOAF RIDGE SP · ○ Rutherford · Silverado · NAPA · SOLANO

12 · ANNADEL SP · ○ Kenwood · SONOMA · ○ Oakville · 3

✗✗ The Kenwood · Glen Ellen Star ✗ · ○ Yountville · 29 · 121

Glen Ellen · ✗✗ the fig café · ● Yeti ✗✗ · SONOMA · Dry · NAPA · SOLANO

SONOMA · MTNS. · Sonoma · VALLEY · ✗✗✗ Santé · NAPA · 121

○ SONOMA · NAPA · 121

✗✗ Central Market · Napa · 12 · 121

Cucina Paradiso ✗✗ · 12

Risibisi ✗✗ · ○ Big Bend · 121 · **Sonoma**

PETALUMA · 116 · ○ Lakeville · 0 ___ 600ft · 0 ___ 200m

101 · 116 · SAN PABLO BAY NWR · W. · Spain · St. · SAN FRANCISCO SOLANO · E. · 4

37 · ✗✗ El Dorado Kitchen · CITY HALL · Spain · St.

37 · ✗ Harvest Moon Cafe · W. · Napa · 12 · PLAZA · LaSalette ✗✗ · St.

○ Novato · 37 · D · E · SAN PABLO BAY NWR · St. · Oso ✗ · St. · Cafe La Haye ✗✗ · Napa · St.

2nd · St. W. · 1st · St. W. · Broadway · 1st · St. E. · Patten · St. · ✗✗ Della Santina's · 2nd · St. E. · F

345

Applewood

Californian 🍴🍴

B2

13555 Hwy. 116, Guerneville

Phone: 707-869-9093   Dinner Wed – Sun
Web: www.applewoodinn.com
Prices: $$$

With a sweeping view over well-manicured grounds, a top-notch spa, and 19 romantic rooms, Applewood is as much an appealing getaway as it is a destination restaurant. The lodge-like dining room is rustic and cozy, with flickering fireplaces that add to the relaxed vibe.

The diners here have their choice of à la carte or tasting menus teeming with ingredients grown in the inn's own gardens. Standouts include heirloom tomatoes with whipped burrata, black sesame soil, and tangy lime curd; thick chunks of moist, juicy roast lamb served atop nutty farro "risotto" with maitake mushrooms; and decadent mocha mousse cake for dessert. To make the most of the Russian River Valley-centric wine list, you may even want to consider staying the night.

Backyard 😊

Californian 🍴

B3

6566 Front St. (bet. 1st & 2nd Sts.), Forestville

Phone: 707-820-8445   Lunch & dinner Thu – Mon
Web: www.backyardforestville.com
Prices: $$

Centered in the sleepy main drag of serene Forestville, this hyper-local restaurant from a husband-and-wife team aims to make the most of Sonoma's seasonal and sustainable foods. Even some of the serving dishes are made from salvaged hazelnut and redwood. With credits for purveyors taking up more than half its length, the menu prominently features house-made pasta, sausage, and *salumi*. Begin with starters like deliciously creamy chicken liver mousse with sourdough points.

The butter-yellow walls of the open dining room display old window frames and hanging succulents. The red-brick courtyard offers seating under a giant oak and live music on weekends. Family-style fried chicken Thursdays are popular, as is the succinct list of local wines.

Barndiva

B1

231 Center St. (bet. Matheson & Mills Sts.), Healdsburg

Phone: 707-431-0100
Web: www.barndiva.com
Prices: $$

Lunch & dinner Wed – Sun

Pristine ingredients are the real stars at this decidedly un-diva-like restaurant, which thoughtfully showcases California's bounty. Beautifully composed salads, like a combo of romaine, apples, avocado, blue cheese, and bacon, shine bright; while creative takes on croquettes (with goat cheese and tomato jam) and lobster rolls (a "club" with bacon, tomato, and arugula) don't sacrifice balance or technique.

With a thoughtfully constructed cocktail menu boasting an array of spirits, herbs, and infusions, Barndiva offers lots to explore off the plate. Witty decorative touches like two-story green velvet curtains and a wall-hanging made of wood shoe stretchers only add to the fun. And for post-meal perusing, there's even an art gallery located right next door.

The BBQ Spot

Barbecue $\times$

E1

458 B St. (at 7th St.), Santa Rosa

Phone: 707-585-2616
Web: www.thebbqspot.net
Prices: ☜☜

Lunch daily
Dinner Mon – Sat

Already a local favorite, this laid-back, no-frills 'cue joint has gotten a shot in the arm with a recent move to bigger and better digs in downtown Santa Rosa. It's not fine dining (the menu's plastered on the wall, ordering happens cafeteria style, and games rule the TV screen), but the numerous photos of barbecue mecca Memphis, Tennessee, hint that the kitchen definitely knows what it's doing.

Pay at the counter, then wait for a server to deliver your hulking two-way combo, featuring thick slices of fork-tender brisket and savory-salty dry-rubbed ribs that fall off the bone, all coated in sweet and smoky house barbecue sauce. Delicately crumbly cornbread, crunchy cabbage coleslaw with a kick of onion, and creamy macaroni salad are worthy sidekicks.

Bistro 29 🐶

French 🍴🍴

E1

620 5th St. (bet. D St. & Mendocino Ave.), Santa Rosa

Phone: 707-546-2929
Web: www.bistro29.com
Prices: $$

Dinner Tue — Sat

French pride oozes from every pore of this vibrant Breton charmer, where tiny French flags, a replica Eiffel Tower, and signs reading "I Love Paris" decorate *le petit* dining room. With its white tile floors and parchment-topped tables, it's every inch the classic bistro—and Santa Rosa locals wouldn't have it any other way.

Savory and sweet galettes (buckwheat crêpes) appear on the menu, their bubbly exteriors concealing a rich filling of tender duck confit, spinach, mushrooms, and Gruyère. The exquisite seafood cassoulet is satisfying yet light, nestling prawns, mussels, calamari, and crab around buttery flageolet beans in a bright tomato broth. For dessert, a moist sticky toffee pudding, accented with fresh figs and whipped cream, is sheer delight.

Boon Eat + Drink

Californian 🍴

B2

16248 Main St. (bet. Armstrong Woods Rd. & Church St.), Guerneville

Phone: 707-869-0780
Web: www.eatatboon.com
Prices: $$

Lunch & dinner Thu — Tue

Its setting on cheerful Main Street may suggest small-town Americana, but Boon's fare is globally inflected. This is clear from the cool and refreshing toasted cumin yogurt that enlivens a tender Moroccan lamb stew, to the tang of buttermilk in an enticingly sour panna cotta with blueberry-thyme compote and plenty of vanilla. A large chalkboard offers numerous specials, tempting the crowds that flock here each evening.

The petite space is lovingly pitched between old-fashioned and modern, with extraordinary tables cut straight from large trees and aluminum bistro chairs. With lots of demand, even the outdoor seats are a hot ticket. French-press pots of locally roasted coffee and glasses of cabernet adorn each tabletop throughout the day.

Bravas

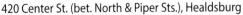

Spanish

B1

420 Center St. (bet. North & Piper Sts.), Healdsburg

Phone: 707-433-7700

Web: www.starkrestaurants.com

Prices: $$

Lunch & dinner daily

This spot from Willi's Wine Bar legends Mark and Terri Stark is named for the classic Spanish potato dish. Given their longstanding expertise with small plates, a truly Spanish tapas spot is right in their wheelhouse. Located in a small, quaint cottage two blocks north of Healdsburg's central plaza, the orange-walled dining room draws lines for first-come first-serve seats at the metal bar. Psychedelic posters and a beaded curtain evoke the '70s.

Bites are traditional yet flaunt California flair, perhaps beginning with a refreshing yet bold tuna belly salad with squid-ink vinaigrette, or a rich *jamón Serrano* and Manchego *bocadillo*. Spanish wines and sherries figure prominently, and soft-serve ice cream provides a fun end to the lively meal.

Cafe La Haye

Californian

F4

140 E. Napa St. (bet. 1st & 2nd Sts.), Sonoma

Phone: 707-935-5994

Web: www.cafelahaye.com

Prices: $$

Dinner Tue – Sat

For years, Cafe La Haye has been a standby off the square in downtown Sonoma. One bite of its luscious burrata, surrounded with Early Girl tomatoes and crispy squash blossoms in the summer, or vinaigrette-dressed pea shoots in spring, proves it hasn't aged a day. The small, modern space is still charming, with large windows and lots of mirrors. Stunning local artwork for sale decorates the walls.

The food spans cultural influences, including a delicate risotto with pine nuts in a cauliflower broth, or soy-sesame glazed halibut atop whipped potatoes and braised kale. A postage stamp-sized bar pours glasses of Sonoma chardonnay and cabernet, perfect with rich *strozzapreti* tossed with braised pork ragù, Grana Padano, and toasted breadcrumbs.

Café Lucia

Portuguese ✕✕

235 Healdsburg Ave., Ste. 105 (bet. Matheson & Mill Sts.), Healdsburg

Phone: 707-431-1113
Web: www.cafelucia.net
Prices: $$

Lunch & dinner daily

Tucked just outside of Healdsburg's main plaza, this sibling to LaSalette shares its emphasis on authentic Portuguese ingredients, like seafood, stewed meats, tomatoes, garlic, and olive oil. Day boat scallops seared with a thin crust of *chouriço* sausage set over mashed Japanese sweet potatoes, and tender wood-oven roasted sea bass are among the delicious options.

A serene, plant-lined interior courtyard leads to an airy dining room with a dark red horseshoe bar and prints of the owners' hometown, São Jorge, in the Azores. Settle into one of the espresso leather banquettes and be rewarded with cumin- and cinnamon-tinged dinner rolls, just like the chef's mother used to make—perfect for savoring over generous flights of Portuguese or Sonoma wine.

Campo Fina

Italian ✕

330 Healdsburg Ave. (bet. North & Plaza Sts.), Healdsburg

Phone: 707-395-4640
Web: www.campo-fina.com
Prices: ⊖⊘

Lunch & dinner daily

Just as card games inspire Scopa, this sister restaurant features a highly coveted patio for backyard bocce during the sunny months (expect a wait). The long, narrow dining room combines brick walls, Edison bulbs, and a wood-burning pizza oven, then gives way to the patio's arched twig roof for a lovely balance of sun and shade.

An antipasto like roasted and chilled spicy-sweet cherry peppers stuffed with tuna salad or burrata with grilled bread are great for savoring with a Negroni or black-walnut Manhattan. Sandwiches like *il nonno* with house-made *soppressata*, rapini, fried egg, salsa verde, and Calabrian chilies make for a hearty lunch. At dinner, the Neapolitan pies take center stage, while a rich *shakerato* iced coffee is perfect anytime.

Central Market

Mediterranean ✗✗

D4

42 Petaluma Blvd. N. (at Western Ave.), Petaluma

Phone:	707-778-9900	Dinner nightly
Web:	www.centralmarketpetaluma.com	
Prices:	$$	

Petaluma locals go gaga for this outstanding Mediterranean restaurant, which produces its own meats and vegetables, bakes delicious baguettes in-house, and serves as a community gathering place. The décor is equal parts French country farmhouse and art gallery, with colorful paintings on the walls, fresh flowers on the tables, and a wood-burning oven in the open kitchen.

The nightly prix-fixe offers a tour of the menu, from cabbage rolls stuffed with ground lamb and plump rice to perfectly seared diver scallops atop a silken potato purée, accented by chopped black olives and sweet roasted cherry tomatoes. The buttery, flaky strawberry galette, full of deep red candied berries and topped with excellent vanilla ice cream, is a draw in and of itself.

Chalkboard 😊

Contemporary ✗✗

A1

29 North St. (bet. Foss St. & Healdsburg Ave.), Healdsburg

Phone:	707-473-8030	Lunch Sat – Sun
Web:	www.chalkboardhealdsburg.com	Dinner nightly
Prices:	$$	

The space that long housed Cyrus now presents Chalkboard—enter Hotel Les Mars, pass by a gracious hostess, and head straight to this contemporary bistro adorned with vaulted ceilings, hardwood floors, casual banquettes, and very snug tables. The open kitchen may be ubiquitous but fits in beautifully with California's sensibility.

This small plates venue underlines an organic, seasonal menu capped off by local ingredients. The result is an excellent marriage of technique and flair as seen in hamachi crudo accented with fruity olive oil, sea salt, and ruby red grapefruit; or well-executed *strozzapretti* twirled with spicy sausage and leafy *broccolini*. A warm vanilla bean cake crested with Cointreau-and-crème fraîche sherbet makes for a perky finish.

Chinois

C2

Asian ✗✗

186 Windsor River Rd. (at Bell Rd.), Windsor

Phone: 707-838-4667
Web: www.chinoisbistro.com
Prices: $$

Lunch Mon – Fri
Dinner Mon – Sat

Pan-Asian fare is given the fresh, seasonal California treatment at this Windsor bistro. The menu offers everything: plump, flavorful Filipino *lumpia*; Chinese dim sum; calamari and prawns in a peppy Cambodian garlic sauce. Thai curries, Taiwanese honey prawns, and even Indian *roti prata* are also represented, but the dance between cuisines is elegant and streamlined, not muddled.

The entry features a small wine bar that's great for solo dining, while the modern dining room is marked by red and white barrel light fixtures. The wine list is respectable (thanks to the surroundings); beer and sake or *sochu* cocktails are also strong. Happy hour, with $5 dishes and drinks, packs in crowds until 6:00 P.M. on the dot—get there early to savor it all.

Cucina Paradiso

D4

Italian ✗✗

114 Petaluma Blvd. N. (bet. Washington St. & Western Ave.), Petaluma

Phone: 707-782-1130
Web: www.cucinaparadisopetaluma.com
Prices: $$

Lunch & dinner Mon – Sat

Set adjacent to the art galleries, boutiques, and theaters of Petaluma's delightful downtown, a meal at this farmhouse-style restaurant is like a jaunt to the Italian countryside. Deep yellow walls lined with wine bottles, embedded arches, and dark wood trestles set the rustic scene, while a large windowed façade gives diners a showcase view of the pedestrians strolling by.

Dinner always commences with fluffy house-made focaccia, a favorite among regulars. From there, choose from other delectable offerings like deliciously briny spaghetti with clams and mussels or tender, lightly crisped veal cutlets Saltimbocca, oozy with *Prosciutto di Parma* and provolone. Pair your meal with a bottle of great Italian wine, which the warm servers will happily recommend.

Della Santina's

Italian ✗✗

F4

133 E. Napa St. (bet. 1st & 2nd Sts.), Sonoma

Phone:	707-935-0576
Web:	www.dellasantinas.com
Prices:	$$

Lunch & dinner daily

Diners at this homey trattoria off Sonoma's town square are treated like members of the Della Santina family, whose vintage photographs fill the walls and whose treasured family recipes pour out of the kitchen regularly. From the first welcome to the final goodbye, the namesake tribe is here to look after you, with warm smiles and friendly pats on the back.

The rustic food has its roots in Tuscany, with favorite dishes like pappardelle in a rich, hearty duck sugo with chunks of tender garlic and sweet tomato. A spatchcocked roast quail has juicy flesh and a beautifully browned, spice-coated exterior, alongside a heaping helping of nutty wild rice and meaty mushrooms. On the way out, grab a bottle of Italian wine from the *enoteca* next door.

Diavola 😁

Italian ✗✗

B1

21021 Geyserville Ave. (at Hwy. 128), Geyserville

Phone:	707-814-0111
Web:	www.diavolapizzeria.com
Prices:	$$

Lunch & dinner daily

Its home in downtown Geyserville may look like the Wild West, but this devilishly good Italian restaurant can hold its own with any city slicker. Festooned with statues of saints, boar tusks, and stacks of cookbooks, it has a playful yet smart vibe.

Excellent pizzas, like the signature combo of spicy meatballs, red peppers, provolone, pine nuts, and raisins, are the reason why crowds pack this spot. And top-notch house ingredients like *salumi*, *lardo*, and cured olives elevate each and every dish. But, that's not to count out their exquisite pastas, including linguine tossed with baby octopus, bone marrow, zucchini, and *bottarga*. Desserts, like the chocolate pistachio semifreddo paired with a perfectly pulled Blue Bottle espresso, are yet another delight.

Dry Creek Kitchen

Californian XXX

A1

317 Healdsburg Ave. (bet. Matheson & Plaza Sts.), Healdsburg

Phone: 707-431-0330
Web: www.drycreekkitchen.com
Prices: $$$

Dinner nightly

With its white tablecloths, plush cushioned banquettes, and formally attired waiters, this Charlie Palmer-owned restaurant is dressy enough for a special occasion. Yes, it's pricey, but the food is unpretentious, the servers are friendly, and there's more than enough wine-country charm to go around.

A cast-iron pan of fluffy focaccia precedes the no-fuss Californian food, like crisp Delta asparagus and salty *boquerones* with a tangy buttermilk-lemon vinaigrette. The pan-seared local halibut arrives atop a summery succotash of fava beans, sweet corn, and cherry tomatoes, and desserts include a quirky take on s'mores complete with Pop Rocks. To ease the sting on your wallet, come at lunchtime as the prix-fixe is a particularly good deal.

El Dorado Kitchen

Californian XX

F4

405 1st St. W. (at Spain St.), Sonoma

Phone: 707-996-3030
Web: www.eldoradosonoma.com
Prices: $$

Lunch & dinner daily

Bigger than the hotel of the same name that houses it, El Dorado Kitchen proves that dining is a big deal in Sonoma. With its long wood communal table, decorative succulents, and palette of warm earth tones, it's a comfy and minimalist space. When the weather is right, grab one of the outdoor tables, nestled poolside beneath fig trees.

The Cal-French menu gets some pop from Latin accents, like a fresh and flavorful pizza topped with *carne seca* (Brazilian salted dried beef), tomato salsa, cilantro, and jalapeños. A selection of charcuterie, from tart wine-cured salami to spicy chorizo, is made in house, as is the excellent country bread. Finally, it would be a sin to miss the rich and flaky fried fig pie, accented by tangy balsamic ice cream, for dessert.

Farmhouse Inn & Restaurant ❀

Californian ✗✗✗

C2

7871 River Rd. (at Wohler Rd.), Forestville

Phone: 707-887-3300   Dinner Thu – Mon
Web: www.farmhouseinn.com
Prices: **$$$**

Urbanites seeking an escape from the fray head to this charming inn, nestled in a quiet, woodsy corner of Sonoma, for fine cooking, upscale accommodations, or both. Dinner guests will find themselves charmed by the dining room's soothing colors, rustic-elegant décor, crackling fireplace, and numerous intimate nooks—including an enclosed patio.

The protein-centric menu reads like an ode to California's purveyors, and a focus on seasonality is in keeping with the area's ethos. Not surprisingly, the results are often rewarding: succulent, perfectly balanced heirloom tomatoes are twirled with crunchy seaweed, briny clams, and mirin dressing, while flaky halibut arrives atop a richly flavored fennel-tomato beurre blanc, dotted with corn and *huitlacoche* pudding. The signature "rabbit, rabbit, rabbit" showcases the kitchen's creativity, bringing together a confit rabbit leg, an applewood-smoked bacon-wrapped loin, and a minuscule rack of chops rounded out with Yukon potatoes and whole grain mustard-cream sauce.

Pair your meal with a bottle from the impressive list of local and European wines, and complete the seduction with an airy soufflé concealing a treasure of Blenheim apricot preserves.

French Garden

International ✕✕

C3

8050 Bodega Ave. (at Pleasant Hill Ave.), Sebastopol

Phone: 707-824-2030
Web: www.frenchgardenrestaurant.com
Prices: $$

Lunch & dinner Wed – Sun

With "garden" in the name, it's no surprise that this local fixture is surrounded by manicured plants and a trickling fountain. Pull yourself away to enter an equally attractive dining room filled with white linen-topped tables. Its Southern France vibe is heightened by large windows that provide views back to their lovely garden.

Eclectic touches define the food here, like the creamy tomato sauce that enlivens a wild mushroom mac and cheese; or the hint of saffron that perks up a dish of fresh Prince Edward Island mussels in fennel-leek broth. The restaurant boasts its own 30-acre farm, from which it gets nearly all of its produce. You'll be able to taste the difference this makes in the pecorino-accented shortcake with fresh berries and lavender cream.

Glen Ellen Star

Californian ✕

D3

13648 Arnold Dr. (at Warm Springs Rd.), Glen Ellen

Phone: 707-343-1384
Web: www.glenellenstar.com
Prices: $$

Dinner nightly

The country charm of this quaint cottage belies the level of culinary chops that will impress even a hardened city slicker. With knotty pine tables, well-worn plank floors, and a wood-burning oven, the space is delightful. A perch at the chef's counter affords a great view of the selections.

Seasonal dishes can include large and plump wood-roasted asparagus with thin shards of *lavash* crackers and shaved radish over a tangy hen egg emulsion; or chicken cooked under a brick with creamy coconut curry and sticky rice. The daily pizzas like the tomato-cream pie with Turkish chilies are also a must. Save room for the excellent, freshly churned, house-made ice cream in flavors like vanilla maple Bourbon, salted peanut butter, and peach verbena.

Hana

Japanese 🍴

C3

101 Golf Course Dr. (at Roberts Lake Rd.), Rohnert Park

Phone: 707-586-0270
Web: www.hanajapanese.com
Prices: $$

Lunch Mon – Sat
Dinner nightly

Rohnert Park denizens continue their love affair with this little gem of a spot, tucked in a hotel plaza next to the 101, and run by affable owner, Chef Ken Tominaga, who sees to his guests' every satisfaction. For the full experience, park it at the sushi bar where the obliging chefs can steer you through the best offerings of the day.

Traditional, fresh sushi and Japanese small plates are the secret to Hana's success, though simply exquisite items like pan-seared pork loin with ginger-soy jus, and pots of steaming udon also hit the spot. The chef's omakase is a fine way to go—six pieces of nigiri which could include toro, hamachi belly, kampachi, *tai*, halibut with ponzu sauce, or sardine tangy from lemon juice and sprinkled with Hawaiian lava salt.

Harvest Moon Cafe

Californian 🍴

F4

487 1st St. W. (bet. Napa & Spain Sts.), Sonoma

Phone: 707-933-8160
Web: www.harvestmooncafesonoma.com
Prices: $$

Dinner nightly

Local sourcing and sustainability are top-of-mind and top-of-menu at this small, unassuming restaurant from a husband-and-wife duo of CIA grads. The simple dining room and heated, covered outdoor patio are favorites among the Sonoma locals. They flood this café for the freshest ingredients from area producers, served at moderate prices by a welcoming, genuine waitstaff.

The menu keeps pace with the seasons, but might include a roasted pear topped with potent black truffle-goat cheese and crispy prosciutto, or juicy, perfectly cooked duck breast over crunchy green romanesco and golden-crusted sweet potatoes. For dessert, house-made peppermint ice cream—spiked with tiny bits of chewy candy—arrives atop a fudgy wedge of brownie.

John Ash & Co.

Californian ✗✗

C2

4330 Barnes Rd. (off River Rd.), Santa Rosa

Phone: 707-527-7687   Dinner nightly
Web: www.vintnersinn.com
Prices: $$$

The Vintner's Inn's restaurant—where the terra-cotta walls, wrought-iron chandeliers, and a flickering fireplace lead to acres of vineyards—exudes the romance of a Tuscan farmhouse. Yet even solo diners can enjoy a taste of John Ash thanks to the clubby Front Room, where the hunting-lodge vibe meets a chic bar menu of sweet-and-sour meatballs or avocado fries.

The food here emphasizes seasonal ingredients, and on-site gardens provide much of the produce. Expect the likes of zippy tuna tartare with *sriracha* aïoli and house-pickled ginger, or chorizo-crusted sea bass over beans and roasted cauliflower. Noted Sonoma winery Ferrari-Carano may own the inn and dominate the wine list, but other fine local and international selections are also available.

The Kenwood

Californian ✗✗

D3

9900 Sonoma Hwy. (near Libby Ave.), Kenwood

Phone: 707-833-6326   Lunch & dinner Wed – Sun
Web: www.kenwoodrestaurant.com
Prices: $$

Meals at The Kenwood are long and leisurely, with appropriately paced service to match. Nestled amid the sprawling vineyards along the Sonoma Highway, it's the kind of place made for lingering, either on the covered patio with its gurgling water fountain, or in the casual dining room or front bar.

The menu is simple but packed with pristine ingredients, like the juicy cherry tomatoes and perfectly ripe avocado that top slices of thick grilled toast. Moist, flaky king salmon boasting a nicely blackened skin and peppery seasoning is another winner, and its accompanying summer squash, white bean and corn succotash is full of flavor. Skip the forgettable desserts in favor of another glass of wine, perhaps from one of the neighboring vintners.

La Perla 🏵️

Peruvian ✗

E1

522 7th St. (bet. B St. & Mendocino Ave.), Santa Rosa

Phone:	707-324-9548	Lunch & dinner Mon – Sat
Web:	www.laperlasr.com	
Prices:	$$	

CIA-educated Chef/owner Edwin Martinez Jimenez expertly prepares the foods of his native Peru at this affordable strip-mall spot, where everything—from their classic *aji* to the fermented corn *chicha*—is made from scratch. The spare surrounds boast only a few colorful woven prints on the walls, but the welcome here is warm while tables are well-spaced and comfortable.

You'll get your first taste of Lima with the delicious *causas*, fluffy mashed potato cakes topped with fresh fish ceviche, creamy cheese sauce, and a sprinkle of chili pepper. The *aji de gallina*, tender-stewed chicken bathed in a silky yellow *aji* sauce and topped with boiled egg and botija olives, is pure comfort. For dessert, try the vibrant orange *lucuma* ice cream, made by Jimenez's own uncle.

LaSalette

Portuguese ✗✗

F4

452 1st St. E., Ste. H (bet. Napa & Spain Sts.), Sonoma

Phone:	707-938-1927	Lunch & dinner daily
Web:	www.lasalette-restaurant.com	
Prices:	$$	

Portuguese fare with wine country-flair is the name of the game at this stalwart off downtown Sonoma's central square, where gleaming azulejo tiles point the way into the dark wood dining room, adorned with hanging copper pots and pans.

Most diners begin with *tascas*, customizable appetizer tasting plates packed with delicacies like garlic-brined lupini beans, pig's feet terrine, and sardine pâté. Heirloom tomato salad arrives with chickpea purée, creamy fresh cheese, and toasted almonds, while chipotle-port barbecue pork and melted onions are stuffed into a traditional Portuguese roll and accompanied by crispy *piri piri* fries. For a sweet finish, try the creamy, cinnamon-infused rice pudding topped with Madeira-braised figs.

Luma

D4

C a l i f o r n i a n   🍴

500 1st St. (at G St.), Petaluma

Phone: 707-658-1940
Web: www.lumapetaluma.com
Prices: $$

Lunch & dinner Tue – Sun

A glowing presence in its industrial neighborhood, Luma's attractive red-and-yellow neon sign (the handiwork of owner Tim Tatum) is immediately recognizable. The artsy atmosphere meshes well with sunny orange walls and deep chocolate booths, though it can get a bit noisy. For a quieter meal, request a table in the front corner nook. This is a friendly, crowd-pleasing, neighborhood destination drawing local families to dine on crispy build-your-own pizzas and other comforting delights.

Consider your pizza options while indulging in guilt-ridden starters like "friends of the devil," a duo of prosciutto-wrapped figs and bacon-wrapped dates filled with goat cheese. Follow your pizza with chocolate-raspberry crêpes and excellent French-press coffee.

Mateo's Cocina Latina

B2

M e x i c a n   🍴🍴

214 Healdsburg Ave. (bet. Matheson & Mill Sts.), Healdsburg

Phone: 707-433-1520
Web: www.mateoscocinalatina.com
Prices: $$

Lunch & dinner Wed – Mon

On a warm Sonoma day, it's hard to beat the patio at Mateo's, unquestionably one of the area's most captivating. Surrounded by planter beds and protected by Sunbrellas, guests have a full view into the kitchen. And if the weather takes a turn, the interior, full of rustic wood furnishings and soft lighting, is just as beautiful as the outdoors.

Flavors of the Yucatán abound here, from a heap of succulent *cochinita pibil*, to *panucho* pockets filled with a delicious black bean purée and topped with chicken and avocado. For extra heat, add a drop or two of the house-made habanero sauces. If you love them, you can buy bottles to take home—and if you can't handle the heat, a tall glass of hibiscus-raspberry *agua fresca* will cool things down.

Madrona Manor ✿

Contemporary ✗✗✗

B2

1001 Westside Rd. (at W. Dry Creek Rd.), Healdsburg

		Dinner Wed – Sun
Phone:	707-433-4231	
Web:	www.madronamanor.com	
Prices:	$$$$	

This romantic Victorian mansion, the unexpected home of a very forward-looking kitchen, is the kind of place that makes one want to dress up—at least a little bit—to fully engage in the art of dining. Arrive early to enjoy a drink on the terrace at sunset, then settle into one of several posh dining rooms.

The showmanship here extends to the artistic, often theatrical plates, which range from scallop carpaccio, topped with flowers and herbs and flavored with lemon, a hint of wasabi and fleur de sel, to carbonated kohlrabi with pickled mustard seeds that snaps in the mouth like Pop Rocks. But some dishes need no embellishment, particularly an outstanding seared Wagyu beef, accompanied by nothing more than some buttery fava beans and a dusting of pine salt.

The final courses bring another burst of flourish, with a tableside cheese cart leading into a flash-frozen take on rocky road ice cream, churned before your eyes with liquid nitrogen. Even a classic cheesecake gets new life, arriving as streusel layered with vanilla cream and tiny beads of sour cream "dip'n dots" that will make anyone's inner child smile. Not ready to leave? Stroll through the manor's stunning gardens before you depart.

Monti's Rotisserie 😊

American ✕✕

F1

714 Village Court (at Sonoma Ave.), Santa Rosa

Phone: 707-568-4404
Web: www.starkrestaurants.com
Prices: $$

Lunch & dinner daily

With the scent of wood smoke hanging in the air, it seems impossible to resist ordering the day's offering hot off the rotisserie. Those smoked prime ribs or pomegranate-glazed pork ribs do not disappoint. But the oak-roasted chicken is a perennial favorite and deserves a visit all its own. Succulent auburn skin, lusciously seasoned flesh, heirloom carrots, smashed fingerling potatoes, and crisped pancetta render this dish a thing of beauty. End your meal with baby lettuces with Point Reyes blue cheese, candied walnuts, and shallot vinaigrette; and butterscotch pudding for lip-smacking comfort food, Monti's-style.

Set within Santa Rosa's Montgomery Village, this spot is dressed up with wrought-iron accents and a quirky collection of decorative roosters.

Oso

International ✕

F4

9 E. Napa St. (at Hwy. 12), Sonoma

Phone: 707-931-6926
Web: www.ososonoma.com
Prices: $$

Lunch Thu – Sun
Dinner nightly

Though Oso means "bear" in Spanish, Sonoma locals are actually quite bullish about this good-natured little restaurant, where the "small" plates are generously portioned and the welcome is warm. The globe-trotting menu is ever-changing, and might include an ultra-fresh ahi tuna poke with cucumber, avocado, and sesame oil; charred asparagus in a Caesar dressing with buttery croutons; and flaky sea bass over light and tangy romesco sauce, with a hint of piquant olive tapenade.

The décor inside features an appealing mix of '80s rock and California rustic barnyard, with baseball-capped cooks—including owner David Bush—working furiously at the open kitchen counter. Night owls, rejoice: it's also open late, at least by the area's standards.

Peter Lowell's

Californian 🍴

C3

7385 Healdsburg Ave. (at Florence Ave.), Sebastopol

Lunch & dinner daily

Phone: 707-829-1077
Web: www.peterlowells.com
Prices: $$

With a devoted following in an artsy neighborhood, Peter Lowell's finely tuned design, staff, food, and philosophy are entirely in sync. The lofty, minimalistic space has a modern pantry-like vibe, with comfortable nooks for relishing the Italian-inspired Californian food.

Hyper-local, largely organic produce arrives in starters like caramelized acorn squash tossed with spiced chickpeas and chard from the restaurant's own farm. Then, move on to smoked-trout ravioli with apples, fennel, and whole-grain mustard. Or, feast on a carefully grilled swordfish steak basted with herb-infused olive oil over red quinoa, matsutake, and shiitake mushrooms.

Bring home some muffins with house Meyer lemon marmalade from the adjacent café for the morning after.

Ramen Gaijin 😊😊

Japanese 🍴

C3

6948 Sebastopol Ave. (bet. Main St. & Petaluma Ave.), Sebastopol

Lunch & dinner Wed – Sat

Phone: 707-827-3609
Web: www.ramengaijin.com
Prices: $$

"Gaijin" is the none-too-polite Japanese term for a foreigner, but the American chefs of this clandestine noodle joint clearly take pride in their outsider status, fusing local ingredients with traditional technique. Finding Gaijin is a journey in itself (it's actually in the back of another restaurant), but the friendly and casual vibe rewards the effort.

The best seats are at the counter, where you can chat with the chef as he assembles bowls of light, fresh *shoyu* ramen filled with thick house-made rye noodles and caramelized pork belly *chashu*. Appetizers are also notable, like a surprisingly elegant salad of smoked cod and baby gem lettuces. And, don't leave without dessert: the black-sesame ice cream with miso caramel is creative and delicious.

Risibisi

D4   Italian ✕✕

154 Petaluma Blvd. N. (bet. Washington St. & Western Ave.), Petaluma

Phone: 707-766-7600   Lunch & dinner daily
Web: www.risibisirestaurant.com
Prices: $$

Though it's named for a comforting dish of rice and peas, Risibisi's seafood-heavy take on Italian cuisine is a bit more sophisticated. A meal at this Petaluma treasure might begin with tissue-thin morsels of fresh salmon carpaccio mingled with julienned celery; or blanched potato salad tossed with an orange-herb vinaigrette and zesty horseradish cream. Gnocchi with chunky wild boar ragù are so light and tender that it somehow seems easy to finish the generous portion. End with their house-made tiramisu or cannoli, and feel like you were transported to Italy.

A makeshift picture gallery constructed out of salvaged Tuscan chestnut window frames, wine barrels, and wagon wheels bring character to this inviting brick-walled dining room.

Rosso

F1   Pizza ✕

53 Montgomery Dr. (at 3rd St.), Santa Rosa

Phone: 707-544-3221   Lunch & dinner daily
Web: www.rossopizzeria.com
Prices: $$

Red wine, red sauce, and red meat are only the beginning at this pizzeria and wine bar. In fact, you're just as likely to go on to enjoy a fresh crab Louie, tender fried calamari and green beans with a green chili aïoli, or a Caesar salad with Gorgonzola Dolce. Crunchy, uniquely-topped pizzas fly out of the wood oven and may feature a braised short rib number topped with gooey cheddar and tomato marmalade.

Set in a small shopping mall, Rosso is identifiable by the locals dining on its terrace, many of whom sign on for the restaurant's regular schedule of cooking classes. Rely on the upbeat staff for friendly advice on the Californian/Italian wine selection, all of which is also available to-go—an ideal alternative given their strong takeout business.

Rustic

Italian XX

B2

300 Via Archimedes (off Independence Ln.), Geyserville

Lunch & dinner daily

Phone: 707-857-1485
Web: www.franciscoppolawinery.com
Prices: $$

Those Godfather Oscars certainly could have funded a posh restaurant for Francis Ford Coppola, but the director has kept it relatively simple at his enormous Geyserville eatery, offering Italian classics from his childhood. Savory *pettole* doughnuts in a paper bag kick off the meal, followed by crispy chicken *al mattone* sautéed in olive oil with strips of red pepper.

Coppola's personality is a big part of Rustic's appeal, and these walls are covered with his film memorabilia as well as his own wines. Although the real reason for the crowds is the Italian-American music, games, and nostalgia that define the past of Coppola and his many customers. Tuesdays are known not only for the special prix-fixe, but when the sociable staff don vintage garb.

Santé

Californian XXX

D3

100 Boyes Blvd. (at Hwy. 12), Sonoma

Dinner nightly

Phone: 707-939-2415
Web: www.santediningroom.com
Prices: $$$

This classic spot in the Fairmont Sonoma Mission Inn seems to get just better and better. Decorated with exposed log rafters, thick stone walls, and a dramatic view of a lit pool outside, it's a dark and sultry space perfect for the diverse wine country clientele. Service is attentive, right down to the complimentary valet parking for diners.

Start your meal with a palate-pleasing cauliflower custard topped with briny caviar and served in a warm eggshell, then indulge in a plate of Carnaroli risotto with forest mushrooms that boasts both chopped black truffles and white truffle foam. Dessert delivers a thick and vanilla-rich Bavarian cream, accented by Riesling-poached pears, crumbled chocolate crêpe, and a touch of Roquefort ice cream.

Sazón 😃

E1

1129 Sebastopol Rd. (at Roseland Ave.), Santa Rosa

Phone: 707-523-4346
Web: sazonsr.com
Prices: 🍜

Lunch & dinner daily

A menu full of appealing choices makes for difficult decision-making at this cute Peruvian spot. Whether you select the tilapia ceviche with an acidic and spicy *leche de tigre* leavened by sharp red onion and cubes of sweet potato, or a meatier dish like marinated free-range chicken followed by wok-fried tenderloin, you're sure to enjoy the signature sweet and spicy flavors. At lunch, the selection of sandwiches and highly popular sweet potato fries are big hits.

Sazón's teeny space has just a handful of tables, but framed photos of Machu Picchu and Peruvian landscapes set the scene, and the friendly staff (it's family-run) make it homey. A pisco sour or passion fruit-infused sangria nicely complement the meal. Finish with a fresh-brewed Peruvian coffee.

Scopa 😃

B1

109A Plaza St. (bet. Center St. & Healdsburg Ave.), Healdsburg

Phone: 707-433-5282
Web: www.scopahealdsburg.com
Prices: $$

Dinner nightly

The house always wins at Scopa, which is named for a bluff-centric Italian card game. Patrons will happily concede victory after their first bite of the heady *spaghettini* with a deeply flavored, spicy Calabrese beef and pork rib sugo. Fans of rarely seen Italian treats like thick-skinned, munchable *lupini* beans or *ciambella*, a cornmeal cake studded with citrus and cranberries, have definitely met their match.

Loud and dimly lit, Scopa's cool, railroad-narrow space quickly fills with bar-goers looking to achieve the other sense of its name ("scoring"—and, ahem, we don't mean points in a card game). Glasses of local cabernet sauvignon fuel the meeting and eating, though perfectly pulled espressos are always available for a little sobering up.

Seaside Metal

Seafood   ✗

B2

16222 Main St. (bet. Armstrong Woods Rd. & Church St.), Guerneville

Phone: 707-604-7250   Dinner Wed – Sun
Web: www.seasidemetal.com
Prices: $$

Quaint Guerneville has gotten an infusion of cityside-chic thanks to this younger sibling of SF favorite, Bar Crudo. Located in the heart of town, its relaxed vibe and kind service draw both tourists and locals. They perch at the white marble counter, where an extensive raw bar is displayed alongside jars of house-pickled vegetables and a sizable cookbook collection.

You'll definitely want at least one raw item to start, whether it's fresh, briny Walker Creek oysters from nearby Point Reyes, or a vibrant yellowtail crudo with lemon curd, crispy shallots, and basil. Move on to the outstanding smoked shellfish platter of Dungeness crab, shrimp, and scallops that arrives on a wood board with crostini, coarse mustard, and those tangy pickled veggies.

Spinster Sisters

American   ✗✗

E1

401 S. A St. (at Sebastopol Ave.), Santa Rosa

Phone: 707-528-7100   Lunch daily
Web: www.thespinstersisters.com   Dinner Tue – Sun
Prices: $$

This terra cotta-tinged bungalow is housed on a residential block off the city center, and flaunts a very hip and modern vibe as evidenced in concrete walls and a large circular wood counter. The urban respite also reeks of good taste—not only in design but also in their delicious range of food crafted from local Californian produce.

Open from breakfast to dinner, Sonoma County crowds come swarming in for Spinster Sisters' enticing cocktails impeccably paired with updated but serious American cuisine. A substantial wilted kale salad tosses creamy goat cheese, smoky bacon, pickled onion, and moist slices of chicken. The well-priced wine selection is as luring as a flaky quiche with gooey fontina, spicy sausage, and lemon vinaigrette.

Spoonbar

A2

Contemporary XX

219 Healdsburg Ave. (bet. Matheson & Mill Sts.), Healdsburg

Phone: 707-433-7222
Dinner nightly
Web: www.spoonbar.com
Prices: $$

For a hipper, more modern take on ingredient-driven cuisine, locals head to this ambitious restaurant in the eco-chic h2hotel, where Chef Louis Maldonado whips up inventive and colorful compositions. The space boasts a serene and natural vibe thanks to ambient lounge music, a fully stocked cocktail bar, and retracting windowed walls made purely for enjoying warm days.

The menu changes regularly, but diners can expect Instagram-worthy plates like tempura-fried soft-shell crab with kohlrabi slaw, pickled mango, and grilled chorizo; or addictively charred *plancha*-grilled broccolini with chickpea fritters, pickled shallots, and cauliflower. Finish with a buttery tart, nicely sweet and sour thanks to plum-peach jam and a frozen yuzu glacé.

Sugo

D4

Italian X

5 Petaluma Blvd. S. (at B St.), Petaluma

Phone: 707-782-9298
Lunch & dinner daily
Web: www.sugotrattoria.com
Prices: $$

A family-friendly, farm-to-table ethos is embodied in this cute Italian-American trattoria, brought to you by a husband-and-wife team. Housed in a petite, blink-and-you'll-miss-it strip mall, Sugo is decorated with vibrant photos including those of roosters (a tribute to Petaluma's agricultural past). The walls may be plain brick, but they are adorned with chalkboards that offer insight into the colorful display of wine bottles.

Straightforward dishes here include panzanella with chunks of grilled ciabatta, tomato, and fresh mozzarella; as well as a creamy fettuccine Alfredo intertwined with poached salmon, sweet cherry tomatoes, and wilted spinach. Finish with a lovely *affogato* (vanilla ice cream drowned with espresso), which hits the spot at all times.

Terrapin Creek ❀

Californian ✗✗

B3

1580 Eastshore Rd. (off Hwy. 1), Bodega Bay

Dinner Thu – Mon

Phone: 707-875-2700
Web: www.terrapincreekcafe.com
Prices: $$

Terrapin Creek isn't easy to find, but those who persevere will be rewarded with a delightful little hideaway bearing delicious cuisine. Dramatically situated high above picturesque Bodega Bay, this lovely restaurant is just steps from the water. (During the January-March whale-watching season, you might even catch a glimpse of these gentle giants bobbing in the Pacific.)

The upbeat, sun-filled dining room, done in bright orange and yellow and filled with big, bold paintings, is clean and unfussy. The small-town staff are every bit as warm as the space, and treat everyone like a regular. A meal might begin with a mixed-green salad topped with creamy goat cheese, sweet persimmon, bits of prosciutto, and a tart cherry vinaigrette; then segue into a nest of al dente linguine twirled with crumbled merguez and minty feta in a spicy tomato broth. A tender local ribeye is accented by creamy bordelaise and buttery potatoes, then strewn with sautéed *broccolini* and mushrooms; paired with a Napa red blend, it's equal parts modern and classic.

Be sure not to miss the fluffy, velvety German chocolate cake, full of crunchy-chewy pecans and coconut that give it a powerful, but never heavy, flavor.

the fig café

D3

Californian ✗✗

13690 Arnold Dr. (at O'Donnell Ln.), Glen Ellen

Phone: 707-938-2130
Web: www.thefigcafe.com
Prices: $$

Lunch Sat – Sun
Dinner nightly

Sondra Bernstein's Cal-Med café got a big refresh this year, taking on a more modern look with communal tables, orange bar stools, and geometric lighting. But pilgrims to this sleepy address shouldn't fret: Rhone-style wines (a house specialty) remain on the shelves, and inviting horseshoe-shaped booths are still the best seats in the house. The nightly prix-fixe—displayed on butcher paper—is as great a deal as ever, and approachable faves like fried olives and a burger are out in force. Start with a salad like grill-charred romaine Caesar with anchovy-spiked dressing; then segue to a seasonal entrée like trout with wild rice, caramelized onions, and green beans.

For like-minded cuisine, visit the girl & the fig in Sonoma's main square.

Valette

B1

Californian ✗✗

344 Center St. (at North St.), Healdsburg

Phone: 707-473-0946
Web: www.valettehealdsburg.com
Prices: $$$

Lunch Fri – Sun
Dinner nightly

Housed in the former Zin space, this contemporary darling is actually a full-circle comeback for Chef Dustin Valette and his brother/General Manager Aaron Garzini, whose grandfather owned the building in the 1940s. Its current look, however, is as cutting-edge as ever thanks to dandelion-like light fixtures, industrial concrete walls, and horseshoe-shaped banquettes. The bill of fare is modern American with a few French twists. Scallops arrive beneath squid ink puff pastry, into which a server pours caviar-flecked champagne-beurre blanc. Then, tart and salty pickled cauliflower is taken to the next level with a gentle deep-fry.

For a happy ending, dig into the smooth, creamy block of chocolate mousse with a luscious salted caramel center.

Willi's Seafood & Raw Bar

Seafood 🍴🍴

A1

403 Healdsburg Ave. (at North St.), Healdsburg

Lunch & dinner daily

Phone: 707-433-9191
Web: www.starkrestaurants.com
Prices: $$

"Eat oysters, love longer," reads a cheeky neon sign above the raw bar at Willi's, and seafood fans certainly feel affection for local restaurant mavens Mark & Terri Stark's love boat. The eclectic seafood offerings are designed for smiles, as in the crisp-fried oyster over jicama kimchi and Key lime aïoli, or bamboo skewers of plump bacon-wrapped scallops with tamarind-barbecue glaze.

The quirky space is a fun blend of tropical and New England accents. This is a favorite for groups, trading sips of cocktails and tasty bites of grilled fish tacos topped with plenty of salsa and avocado. The diet-conscious and landlubbers will find enticing options, as will the environmentalists: all the fish and shellfish served here are Safe Harbor certified.

Willi's Wine Bar

International 🍴🍴

C2

4404 Old Redwood Hwy. (at Ursuline Rd.), Santa Rosa

Lunch Tue – Sat
Dinner nightly

Phone: 707-526-3096
Web: www.starkrestaurants.com
Prices: $$

Don't be fooled by the roadhouse vibe at Mark and Terri Stark's flagship spot, which actually boasts an extremely well-traveled menu. The eclectic dishes are meant to be shared—and paired with local wine, naturally—and the clean, comfortable environs, rich with dark wood, create an ideal setting for a fun evening out with friends.

Willi's wide-ranging menu isn't afraid to take inspiration from wherever it comes—whether adding pancetta and sherry vinegar butter to scallop dumplings; or piling Dungeness crab, baby artichokes, and crescenza cheese on a puffy flatbread. To really indulge, opt for the warm spinach salad with goat cheese and dates, before digging into the Meyer lemon pudding cake, with its airy top and delightful lemon curd.

Wine Country ▶ Sonoma County

371

Willow Wood Market Cafe

C3

Californian ✗

9020 Graton Rd. (at Edison St.), Graton

Phone: 707-823-0233
Web: www.willowwoodgraton.com
Prices: **$$**

Lunch daily
Dinner Mon – Sat

Whether they're fueling up for work or for wine tasting, a down-to-earth crowd can always be found at this friendly, casual neighborhood diner, full of quirky local art, shelves stocked with gag food gifts and local sundries. Then there's also that big wall of wines (this is Sonoma, after all). Waitresses shout orders, coffee comes from serve-yourself thermoses, and guests couldn't be happier.

Get your veggies with the generously portioned farmer's scramble, full of soft and spicy peppers and onions, not to mention plenty of creamy white cheddar and springy, meaty New Mexican chicken-turkey sausage. For a sweet tooth, the challah French toast, golden-brown and topped with a generous scoop of cinnamon butter and chopped pecans, is where it's at.

Yeti

D3

Nepali ✗✗

14301 Arnold Dr., Ste. 19 (in Jack London Village), Glen Ellen

Phone: 707-996-9930
Web: www.yetirestaurant.com
Prices: **$$**

Lunch & dinner daily

Its sleepy location may be unusual, but with a creekside view and friendly service, Yeti makes for a pleasant getaway from the wine country grind. Inside the sunken dining room, soft folk music, Tibetan artwork, and a blisteringly hot tandoor set an authentic scene.

Though the fare is described as Nepalese-cum-Indian, most dishes are from both the north (think grilled meats and biryanis) as well as the coastal regions of the sub-continent (fish curries and coconut sauces). Try the lamb chops coated in *garam masala* and served over a bed of charred onion and bell pepper. Vegetable *momos* (steamed dumplings stuffed with cabbage, carrots, beans, and green onion) served with spicy *sambal*, cilantro, and sweet tamarind dipping sauces, are a party in your mouth.

zazu kitchen + farm

C3

6770 McKinley St., Ste. 150 (bet. Brown & Morris Sts.), Sebastopol

Phone: 707-523-4814
Web: www.zazukitchen.com
Prices: $$

Lunch Wed – Sun
Dinner Wed – Mon

A fun change from the rustic décor seen in much of wine country, this big and bright industrial space is practically translucent, thanks in large part to its garage-like doors and glossy cement floors. Natural wood tables and huge wild flower arrangements keep it from feeling chilly, as do surprisingly great acoustics—you won't struggle to be heard, even if the massive 20-seat family table is full.

Pork is the priority here, as evidenced by the sharp, spicy, and addictive Cuban sandwich with house-made mortadella. Vegetarians will delight in the tart tomato soup with an oozing Carmody grilled cheese, or the black beans with baked eggs. But the real key for carnivores is to bring home the bacon; it's a little bit pricey, but worth every penny.

Look for our symbol 🍇,
spotlighting restaurants
with a notable wine list.

Wine Country ▶ Sonoma County

Where to **Eat**

Alphabetical List of Restaurants

Restaurants by Cuisine

Austrian

Leopold's	✕✕	108
Naschmarkt	✕✕	286

Barbecue

BBQ Spot (The)	✕	347
4505 Burgers & BBQ	✕	31
Smoking Pig BBQ	✕	293

Basque

Piperade	✕✕	126

Belgian

Belga	✕✕	59

Brazilian

Pampas	✕✕	289

Burmese

Burma Superstar	✕	135
Burmatown	✕	221

Californian

Al's Place	✿	✕✕	76
Alta CA		✕✕	28
Applewood		✕✕	346
Archetype		✕✕	311
Aster	✿	✕✕	77
Auberge du Soleil	✿	✕✕✕	312
Backyard	✪	✕	346
Bar Agricole		✕✕	151

Barndiva		✕✕	347
Barrel House Tavern		✕✕	219
Boon Eat + Drink		✕	348
Boulevard		✕✕	153
Brix		✕✕	317
Cafe La Haye		✕✕	349
Camino		✕	180
Central Kitchen		✕✕	81
Chez Panisse		✕✕	181
Commissary (The)		✕✕	62
Dry Creek Kitchen		✕✕✕	354
El Dorado Kitchen		✕✕	354
FARM		✕✕✕	322
Farmhouse Inn & Restaurant	✿	✕✕✕	355
Farmstead	✪	✕✕	323
Flea St. Café		✕✕	245
Frances		✕✕	19
Gather	✪	✕✕	188
Glen Ellen Star	✪	✕	356
Harvest Moon Cafe		✕	357
Harvest Table		✕✕	325
Heirloom Café		✕✕	85
Jardinière		✕✕✕	32
John Ash & Co.		✕✕	358
Kenwood (The)		✕✕	358
Lord Stanley	✿	✕✕	110
Lucy		✕✕	328
Luma		✕	360
Metro Lafayette		✕	198
Molina		✕✕	226
Nopa		✕✕	33
Octavia	✿	✕✕	68
One Market		✕✕	159
Parallel 37		✕✕✕	112

Mexican

Middle Eastern

Moroccan

Nepali

Persian

Peruvian

Pizza

Piccino		✕✕	92
Pizzaiolo		✕	203
Pizzetta 211		✕	140
Rosso		✕	364
Tony's Pizza Napoletana		✕	128
Una Pizza Napoletana		✕	166
Vesta	⊛	✕✕	263
Zero Zero	⊛	✕✕	167

Portuguese

Café Lucia		✕✕	350
LaSalette		✕✕	359

Scandinavian

Pläj		✕✕	34

Seafood

alaMar		✕	174
Anchor Oyster Bar	⊛	✕	18
Bar Crudo		🍴	29
Farallon		✕✕✕	47
Fish		✕	223
New England Lobster Company		✕	253
Sea (The)		✕✕✕	292
Seaside Metal		✕	367
Waterbar		✕✕	166
Willi's Seafood & Raw Bar		✕✕	371

Southern

Boxing Room		✕✕	29
Brenda's		✕	30
Rusty's Southern		✕	36
The Pear		✕✕	337

Spanish

Aatxe		✕	18
Bravas		🍴	349

Contigo	⊛	✕✕	19
Coqueta	⊛	✕✕	47
Duende		✕✕	186
Zuzu		🍴	339

Sri Lankan

1601 Bar & Kitchen	⊛	✕✕	164

Steakhouse

Alexander's Steakhouse		✕✕✕	276
Bourbon Steak		✕✕✕	45
Cole's Chop House		✕✕✕	321
El Paseo		✕✕	222
Epic Steak		✕✕	154
Press		✕✕✕	331

Thai

Arun		✕	217
Baan		✕	218
Bangkok Jam		✕✕	176
Farmhouse Kitchen Thai	⊛	✕	83
Grand Avenue Thai		✕✕	189
Imm Thai Street Food		✕	193
Infinite Thai Eatery		✕✕	194
Khan Toke Thai House		✕	137
Kin Khao	✿	✕	49
Mango on Main		✕	328
Manora's Thai Cuisine		✕	156
Modern Thai		✕	111
R'Noh Thai		✕✕	229
Sweet Basil		✕	261
Thai Aroi-Dee		✕	231
Thai House	⊛	✕✕	208
Thep Phanom		✕	38
Tycoon		✕	38

Turkish

Kitchen Istanbul		✕	137
Tuba		✕✕	96

Cuisines by Neighborhood

SAN FRANCISCO

Castro

Californian

Frances		XX	19
Starbelly	☺	XX	23

Chinese

Mama Ji's		X	21

French

L'Ardoise		XX	21

Italian

Pesce		XX	22

Japanese

Saru		X	23

Korean

Janchi		X	20

Mexican

La Corneta		X	20
Padrecito		XX	22

Seafood

Anchor Oyster Bar	☺	X	18

Spanish

Aatxe		X	18
Contigo	☺	XX	19

Civic Center

American

State Bird Provisions	✿	XX	37

Barbecue

4505 Burgers & BBQ		X	31

Californian

Alta CA		XX	28

Indexes ▲ Cuisines by Neighborhood

Mama Papa Lithuania *(Alameda)*   X   197

Ethiopian
Café Colucci *(Oakland)*   X   179
Café Romanat *(Oakland)*   X   179

French
Artisan Bistro *(Lafayette)*   XX   175
Bistro Liaison *(Berkeley)*   XX   177
Chevalier *(Lafayette)*   ☺ XX   180
Michel Bistro *(Oakland)*   ☺ X   198

Fusion
Va de Vi *(Walnut Creek)*   XX   210

Gastropub
Longbranch Saloon *(Berkeley)*   X   196
Sidebar *(Oakland)*   X   207
Tribune Tavern *(Oakland)*   XX   210

Greek
Pathos *(Berkeley)*   XX   202

Indian
High Peaks Kitchen *(Oakland)*   X   191
Royal Indian Grill *(Danville)*   X   206

International
The Peasant & The Pear *(Danville)*   XX   209

Italian
Bellanico *(Oakland)*   XX   177
Corso *(Berkeley)*   ☺ X   183
Desco *(Oakland)*   XX   185
Oliveto *(Oakland)*   XX   201
Prima *(Walnut Creek)*   XX   204
Riva Cucina *(Berkeley)*   X   205
Trabocco *(Alameda)*   XX   209

Japanese
Ippuku *(Berkeley)*   ☺ X   194
Iyasare *(Berkeley)*   XX   195
Ramen Shop *(Oakland)*   X   204

Korean
Ohgane *(Oakland)*   X   201
Sahn Maru *(Oakland)*   X   206

MARIN

American
Brick & Bottle *(Corte Madera)*	⊛	XX	219
Buckeye Roadhouse *(Mill Valley)*		XX	220
Bungalow 44 *(Mill Valley)*		XX	220
Nick's Cove *(Marshall)*		XX	227
Sir and Star *(Olema)*	⊛	XX	230

Burmese
Burmatown *(Corte Madera)*		X	221

Californian
Barrel House Tavern *(Sausalito)*	XX	219
Molina *(Mill Valley)*	XX	226

French
Left Bank *(Larkspur)*		XX	224
Le Garage *(Sausalito)*	⊛	X	225

Indian
Arti *(Lagunitas)*	X	217
Prabh *(Mill Valley)*	XX	229

Italian
Frantoio *(Mill Valley)*		XX	223
Osteria Stellina *(Point Reyes Station)*		XX	227
Picco *(Larkspur)*		XX	228
Poggio *(Sausalito)*	⊛	XX	228
Valenti & Co. *(San Anselmo)*		XX	231

Japanese
Sushi Ran *(Sausalito)*	⊛	XX	230

Latin American
Marinitas *(San Anselmo)*	⊛	XX	226

Mediterranean
Insalata's *(San Anselmo)*	⊛	XX	224
Marché aux Fleurs *(Ross)*		XX	225

Mexican
Copita *(Sausalito)*	XX	221
El Huarache Loco *(Larkspur)*	X	222

Pizza
Bar Bocce *(Sausalito)*	X	218

Gastropub

Indian

International

Italian

Japanese

Latin American

Mediterranean

Mexican

Indexes ▲ Cuisines by Neighborhood

Sonoma County

American

Asian

Barbecue

Californian

Contemporary

French

International

Starred Restaurants

Within the selection we offer you, some restaurants deserve to be highlighted for their particularly good cuisine. When giving one, two, or three Michelin stars, there are a number of elements that we consider including the quality of the ingredients, the technical skill and flair that goes into their preparation, the blend and clarity of flavours, and the balance of the menu. Just as important is the ability to produce excellent cooking time and again. We make as many visits as we need, so that our readers may be assured of quality and consistency.

A two or three-star restaurant has to offer something very special in its cuisine; a real element of creativity, originality, or "personality" that sets it apart from the rest. Three stars – our highest award – are given to the choicest restaurants, where the whole dining experience is superb.

Cuisine in any style, modern or traditional, may be eligible for a star. Due to the fact we apply the same independent standards everywhere, the awards have become benchmarks of reliability and excellence in over 20 countries in Europe and Asia, particularly in France, where we have awarded stars for 100 years, and where the phrase "Now that's real three-star quality!" has entered into the language.

The awarding of a star is based solely on the quality of the cuisine.

✿✿✿

Exceptional cuisine, worth a special journey
One always eats here extremely well, sometimes superbly. Distinctive dishes are precisely executed, using superlative ingredients.

Benu	XxX	152
French Laundry (The)	XxxX	324
Manresa	XxX	285
Restaurant at Meadowood (The)	XxxX	333
Saison	XxX	163

✿✿

Excellent cuisine, worth a detour
Skillfully and carefully crafted dishes of outstanding quality.

Acquerello	XxX	102
Atelier Crenn	XX	60
Baumé	XxX	277
Campton Place	XxX	46
Coi	XxX	121
Commis	XX	184
Quince	XxxX	127

✿

A very good restaurant in its category
A place offering cuisine prepared to a consistently high standard.

All Spice	XxX	104
Al's Place	XX	76
Ame	XxX	150
Aster	XX	77
Auberge du Soleil	XxX	312
Aziza	XX	134
Bouchon	XX	316
Californios	XX	80

Chez TJ	XxX	279
Commonwealth	XX	82
Farmhouse Inn & Restaurant	XxX	355
Gary Danko	XxX	124
Keiko à Nob Hill	XxX	107
Kin Khao	X	49
Kusakabe	XX	50
La Toque	XxX	327
Lazy Bear	XX	87
Lord Stanley	XX	110
Luce	XxX	157
Madrona Manor	XxX	361
Michael Mina	XxX	51
Mourad	XxX	158
Nico	XX	67
Octavia	XX	68
Omakase	XX	160
Plumed Horse	XxX	290
Rasa	XX	257
Solbar	XX	335
Sons & Daughters	XX	114
SPQR	XX	69
Spruce	XX	70
State Bird Provisions	XX	37
Sushi Yoshizumi	X	260
Terra	XxX	336
Terrapin Creek	XX	369
Village Pub (The)	XxX	264
Wako	X	142
Wakuriya	X	266

Bib Gourmand

This symbol indicates our inspectors' favorites for good value.
For $40 or less, you can enjoy two courses and a glass of wine or a dessert
(not including tax or gratuity).

Anchor Oyster Bar	X	18
A16	XX	59
Backyard	X	346
Bar Tartine	XX	78
Bistro Aix	XX	61
Bistro Jeanty	XX	314
Bistro 29	XX	348
Brick & Bottle	XX	219
Chalkboard	XX	351
Chapeau!	XX	135
Chevalier	XX	180
China Village	XX	182
Chino	X	81
Comal	XX	183
Contigo	XX	19
Cook St. Helena	XX	321
Coqueta	XX	47
Corso	X	183
Cotogna	XX	122
Delfina	XX	83
Diavola	XX	353
Dosa	XX	63
Evvia	XX	281
Farmhouse Kitchen Thai	X	83
Farmstead	XX	323
FIVE	XX	188
Fringale	XX	156
Gather	XX	188
Glen Ellen Star	X	356
Grace's Table	XX	325
Great China	XX	189
Hong Kong Lounge II	XX	65
Insalata's	XX	224
Ippuku	X	194
Izakaya Rintaro	XX	86

Indexes ▲ Bib Gourmand

Brunch

Credits

Michelin is committed to improving the mobility of travellers

ON EVERY ROAD AND BY EVERY MEANS

Since the company came into being – over a century ago – Michelin has had a single objective: to offer people a better way forward. A technological challenge first, to create increasingly efficient tires, but also an ongoing commitment to travelers, to help them travel in the best way. This is why Michelin is developing a whole collection of products and services: from maps, atlases, travel guides and auto accessories, to mobile apps, route planners and online assistance: Michelin is doing everything it can to make traveling more pleasurable!

→ Michelin Apps

Because the notions of comfort and security are essential, both for you and for us, Michelin has created a package of six free mobile applications—a comprehensive collection to make driving a pleasure!

→ *Michelin MyCar* • *To get the best from your tires; services and information for carefree travel preparation.*

→ *Michelin Navigation* • *A new approach to navigation: traffic in real time with a new connected guidance feature.*

→ *ViaMichelin* • *Calculates routes and map data: a must for traveling in the most efficient way.*

→ *Michelin Restaurants* • *Because driving should be enjoyable: find a wide choice of restaurants, in France and Germany, including the MICHELIN Guide's complete listings.*

→ *Michelin Hotels* • *To book hotel rooms at the best rates, all over the world!*

→ *Michelin Voyage* • *85 countries and 30,000 tourist sites selected by the Michelin Green Guide, plus a tool for creating your own travel book.*

A tire...
→ what is it?

Round, black, supple yet solid, the tire is to the wheel what the shoe is to the foot. But what is it made of? First and foremost, rubber, but also various textile and/or metallic materials... and then it's filled with air! It is the skilful assembly of all these components that ensures tires have the qualities they should: grip to the road, shock absorption, in two words: 'comfort' and 'safety.'

1 TREAD
The tread ensures the tire performs correctly, by dispersing water, providing grip and increasing longevity.

2 CROWN PLIES
This reinforced double or triple belt combines vertical suppleness with transversal rigidity, enabling the tire to remain flat to the road.

3 SIDEWALLS
These link all the component parts and provide symmetry. They enable the tire to absorb shock, thus giving a smooth ride.

4 BEADS
The bead wires ensure that the tire is fixed securely to the wheel to ensure safety.

5 INNER LINER
The inner liner creates an airtight seal between the wheel rim and the tire.

Michelin
→ *innovation in movement*

Created and patented by Michelin in 1946, the belted radial-ply tire revolutionized the world of tires. But Michelin did not stop there: over the years other new and original solutions came out, confirming Michelin's position as a leader in research and innovation.

→ *the right pressure!*

One of Michelin's priorities is safer mobility. In short, innovating for a better way forward. This is the challenge for researchers, who are working to perfect tires capable of shorter braking distances and offering the best possible traction to the road. To support motorists, Michelin organizes road safety awareness campaigns all over the world: "Fill up with air" initiatives remind everyone that the right tire pressure is a crucial factor in safety and fuel economy.

The Michelin strategy:
→ *multi-performance tires*

Michelin is synonymous with safety, fuel saving and the capacity to cover thousands of miles. A MICHELIN tire is the embodiment of all these things – thanks to our engineers, who work with the very latest technology.

Their challenge: to equip every tire – whatever the vehicle (car, truck, tractor, bulldozer, plane, motorbike, bicycle or train!) – with the best possible combination of qualities, for optimal overall performance.

Slowing down wear, reducing energy expenditure (and therefore CO_2 emissions), improving safety through enhanced road handling and braking: there are so many qualities in just one tire – that's Michelin Total Performance.

MICHELIN
Total Performance

Every day, **Michelin** is
working towards
sustainable
mobility

OVER TIME,
WHILE
RESPECTING
THE PLANET

Sustainable mobility
→ *is clean mobility... and mobility for everyone*

Sustainable mobility means enabling people to get around in a way that is cleaner, safer, more economical and more accessible to everyone, wherever they might live. Every day, Michelin's 113,000 employees worldwide are innovating:

• by creating tires and services that meet society's new needs.

• by raising young people's awareness of road safety.

• by inventing new transport solutions that consume less energy and emit less CO_2.

→ *Michelin Challenge Bibendum*

Sustainable mobility means allowing the transport of goods and people to continue, while promoting responsible economic, social and societal development. Faced with the increasing scarcity of raw materials and global warming, Michelin is standing up for the environment and public health. Michelin regularly organizes 'Michelin Challenge Bibendum', the only event in the world which focuses on sustainable road travel.

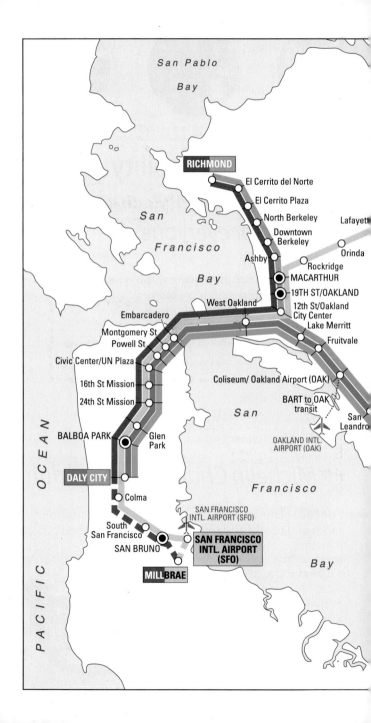

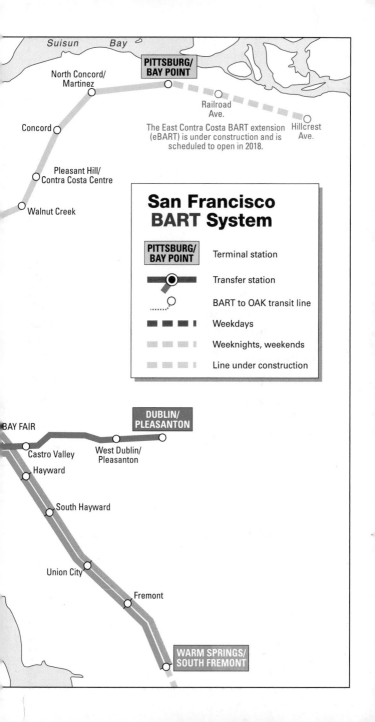

Suisun Bay

North Concord/
Martinez

**PITTSBURG/
BAY POINT**

Railroad
Ave.

Hillcrest
Ave.

Concord

The East Contra Costa BART extension
(eBART) is under construction and is
scheduled to open in 2018.

Pleasant Hill/
Contra Costa Centre

Walnut Creek

San Francisco
BART System

PITTSBURG/ BAY POINT	Terminal station
◉	Transfer station
○	BART to OAK transit line
▬ ▬ ▬	Weekdays
▬ ▬ ▬	Weeknights, weekends
▬ ▬ ▬	Line under construction

BAY FAIR

**DUBLIN/
PLEASANTON**

Castro Valley

West Dublin/
Pleasanton

Hayward

South Hayward

Union City

Fremont

**WARM SPRINGS/
SOUTH FREMONT**

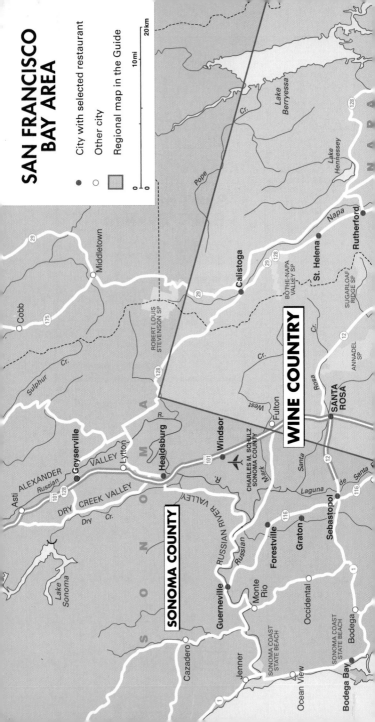